Mobilizing Adults for
Positive Youth Development

The Search Institute Series on Developmentally Attentive Community and Society

Series Editor
Peter L. Benson, *Search Institute, Minneapolis, Minnesota*

Series Mission
To advance interdisciplinary inquiry into the individual, system, community, and societal dynamics that promote developmental strengths; and the processes for mobilizing these dynamics on behalf of children and adolescents.

A Continuation Order Plan is available for this series. A continuation order will bring delivery of each new volume immediately upon publication. Volumes are billed only upon actual shipment. For further information please contact the publisher.

Mobilizing Adults for Positive Youth Development

Strategies for Closing the Gap between Beliefs and Behaviors

Edited by

E. Gil Clary
College of St. Catherine, St. Paul, Minnesota, USA

Jean E. Rhodes
University of Massachusetts, Boston, Massachusetts, USA

 Springer

Library of Congress Cataloging-in-Publication Data: 2005933717

ISBN 0-387-29173-3   e-ISBN 0-387-29340-X   Printed on acid-free paper.
ISBN-13: 978-0387-29173-4

Printed in the United States of America.   (TB/IBT)

9 8 7 6 5 4 3 2 1

springer.com

Preface

Perhaps no other challenge is more pressing in creating "developmentally attentive community and society" (the theme of this book series) than mobilizing adults to play active, constructive roles in the lives of children and adolescents. In a society that too easily defaults to designing programs as cure-alls for meeting young people's needs, particular attention must be paid to understanding and mobilizing the kind of positive, relational energy that prepares each successive generation to assume its place in society. Although programs and institutions certainly play important roles, the key lies in the personal commitment, involvement, and investment of adults in young people's lives.

In *Mobilizing Adults for Positive Youth Development: Strategies for Closing the Gap between Beliefs and Behaviors,* E. Gil Clary and Jean E. Rhodes have assembled the insights of leading scholars from multiple disciplines and contexts for engaging a broad cadre of adults as allies for youth development. As the editors write, the question guiding the book is, "How can we most effectively encourage adults, both individually and collectively, to begin to behave differently with respect to the young people of a community, to do so consistently, and to do so in a variety of ways?" What is being proposed, then, is nothing less than a social movement that engages individuals, small groups, neighborhoods, workplaces, schools, faith communities, and broader social institutions in attending to the well-being and healthy development of young people.

A growing number of books and reports already explore the *why* of adult engagement, and those foundational questions are appropriately addressed in this volume. What makes *Mobilizing Adults for Positive Youth Development* unique and compelling, however, is its focus on the *how*—the strategies that can lead to real change, transformation, and engagement at the individual, organizational, and societal levels. This focus on change strategies requires understanding not only the needs of young people but also the realities, motivations, and priorities of adults. In addition, it demands careful attention to the processes of change at the individual, organizational, and societal levels.

Since the field of positive youth development is only now beginning to examine these complex dynamics, this volume invites experts in these issues to use their knowledge in responding to the specific question of engaging adults in the lives of young people. Hence, the contributors introduce and apply to youth development a broad range of theories and approaches, from volunteer management and mentoring (which focus on engaging individual adults) to civic engagement and social marketing (which focus on mobilizing adults at a community or societal level). When drawn together, these chapters offer a multifaceted, multidisciplinary blueprint for the kind of social change needed to ensure that all young people experience the kinds of positive relationships, supports, and opportunities they need to grow up healthy, caring, and responsible.

At its core, the Search Institute Series on Developmentally Attentive Community and Society is intended to advance interdisciplinary inquiry into the processes for mobilizing all aspects of society to build developmental strengths for and with young people. This book exemplifies the goal of the series, making a vital and unique contribution to the field—and to the adults who invest in the lives of children and youth.

Peter L. Benson, Ph.D.

Search Institute
Series Editor

Acknowledgments

Why do people with good intentions often fail to translate those intentions into action, and how might the gap between intentions and action be closed? These two questions arise in many areas of human life, and students of human behavior have devoted a great deal of conceptual and empirical attention to these questions. The chapters in this volume focus on these and related questions as they arise in connection with adults' intentions to contribute to the positive development of the youth of our communities. Specifically, why do adults, who believe in the importance of adults in a community assisting with the development of young people, and not just their own but also other people's children, often fail to engage in activities that assist in that development? And how might a community or society effectively encourage and mobilize its adults to participate in positive youth development?

As with any work of this sort, many people have made important contributions to the preparation of this volume. To begin, let us recognize the efforts of the contributors to this volume, who were willing to consider the above questions from the perspective of their programs of research. Several of the authors have been wrestling with questions about positive youth development, while others have been focusing on these kinds of questions as they concern mobilizing adults. In all cases, the authors were asked to contribute their best thinking to the fundamental question of how a community can encourage large numbers of adults to practice positive youth development.

We also wish to recognize the contributions of several members of Search Institute. The volume emerged from conversations among the editors, Peter Benson, and Gene Roehlkepartain, and was further shaped through discussions with Patricia Seppanen, Peter C. Scales, and Arturo Sesma Jr. We also wish to recognize the guidance that Gene has provided throughout the process of organizing this volume. Finally, Mary Byers did exceptional work in copyediting the volume, and Lynn Marasco provided valuable assistance.

Our colleagues from other institutions generously contributed to the volume. Mark Snyder and Arthur A. Stukas offered important and useful feedback as we were planning this volume, as well as contributed chapters to the volume. The Summit on Youth Mentoring, which was sponsored by the National Mentoring Partnership, provided a rich context for exploring these issues in depth. Along with valuable conversations with many participants at the summit, Kenneth Maton, Andrea S. Taylor, and Abraham Wandersman contributed chapters to the volume.

Last, we wish to acknowledge the support provided by the Lilly Endowment for the Search Institute Series on Developmentally Attentive Community and Society. We also acknowledge the contributions of the acquiring editor at Springer, Judy Jones, and assistant editor Angela Quilici-Burke, who shepherded the volume through production.

Contents

1 Introduction and Conceptual Foundations

E. Gil Clary

College of St. Catherine

Jean E. Rhodes

University of Massachusetts, Boston

"It takes a village to raise a child." This principle and the idea behind it have been repeated often in the past several years. It has been the subject of numerous articles and several books, including volume 1 in the Search Institute Series on Developmentally Attentive Community and Society. In effect, that book, *Developmental Assets and Asset-Building Communities: Implications for Research, Policy, and Practice*, edited by Richard M. Lerner and Peter L. Benson (2003), was devoted to the science and practice of the hypothesis implied by this phrase: that the healthy development of children and adolescents is tied to the community or communities in which young people live. Several of the authors in volume 1 documented the empirical basis for the importance of developmental supports or assets coming from a wide variety of sources in the communities (e.g., families, schools, peers, neighbors, religious congregations, and other segments of society) for the acquisition of valued characteristics and skills. And other authors described attempts by communities or some segment of the community to translate the concepts of developmental supports and assets into practice.

The second volume in this series, Peter C. Scales's (2003) *Other People's Kids: Social Expectations and American Adults' Involvement with Children and Adolescents*, reports the findings of a national survey showing widespread agreement that it is important for the adults in a community to provide developmental supports and assets to nonfamilial children and adolescents. The survey reveals that, although many adults recognize the importance of close, one-to-one relationships with youth, far fewer are willing to act to develop such relationships. To illustrate, the poll reveals that 75% of adults reported that it is "very important" to have meaningful conversations with children and youth, whereas fewer than 35% reported actually having such conversations. Scales delves into the reasons for this disconnection between values and action, illuminating the psychological basis for the relative neglect of our nation's youth and mapping out a means for redressing it. As Scales suggests, the diminishing availability of caring adults is caused not only by changing communities, schools, and families but also by a deep cultural ambivalence that has emerged regarding what it means to connect with other people's children. In Western societies, parents have come to be considered solely responsible for their children, so the involvement of other adults is often met with suspicion and discomfort. Scales finds considerable evidence for a significant gap between adults' beliefs about providing supports and assets for nonfamilial young people and their behaviors that represent supports and assets.

The present volume, the fourth in this series, is devoted to strategies and tactics that are designed to close gaps between beliefs and actions, or put another way, strategies that seek to mobilize adults to contribute to the positive development of young people. To be more specific, this volume focuses on conceptual and empirical work related to social influence strategies, broadly defined, that might assist individuals and communities in moving from the current state of affairs, as documented by Scales's *Other People's Kids*, to a society in which individuals and communities provide young people with the supports and assets they need for positive development, as documented by Lerner and Benson's *Developmental Assets and Asset-Building Communities*. In the following discussion, we first explore what is meant by mobilizing adults—who is to be mobilized and how that is best accomplished; second, we consider the meaning of positive youth development—what young people need. In short, what are the goals of positive development, and what can adults do that will help bring about positive development?

Mobilizing Adults for Action

The central question to be explored in this volume is how best to encourage adults to act—specifically, to translate good intentions into behaviors that promote positive youth development. Moreover, this question is applied to the actions of individuals, small groups, neighborhoods, municipalities, workplaces, school districts, and religious communities, as well as to large groups of adults as represented by society. Although each chapter of this volume may focus on only one or two of these targets of influence, we contend that to create developmentally attentive community and society, action must occur at all levels.

Gaps between intentions and actions occur in many areas of life. At the individual level, people intend to adopt a healthy diet, engage in physical exercise, quit smoking, put into practice their moral beliefs, and the like, but they frequently fail to achieve these goals. Organized collections of individuals often struggle to encourage and even pressure their members to act in ways that help achieve group goals, including attendance at meetings, participation in committee work, generating funds, and recruiting members. Questions about influencing actions, and particularly about closing the gap between people's beliefs and actions, have long occupied behavioral scientists attempting to understand the conditions under which a person's attitudes or beliefs will or will not serve as the basis for action (Olson & Zanna, 1993).

On its face, the problem of mobilizing adults for positive youth development seems a simple matter, given that the beliefs of individual adults (1) are already highly favorable to the cause of the positive development of youth and (2) are shared by a large number of adults, with the result that these beliefs also stand as social norms (Scales, 2003). At the same time, some force or set of forces seems to be preventing the behavioral expression of these beliefs. Broadly speaking, these forces may be of two types: an absence of one or more critical factors (e.g., motivation, time, appropriate venues) that are necessary for action to occur; and the presence of factors that serve as barriers or obstacles to action, or otherwise suppress the behavioral tendency to contribute to youth development. These considerations, of course, raise questions about what exactly these missing ingredients and barriers to action might be.

A possible answer to the obstacle posed by missing ingredients comes from research that has asked what motivation is necessary for a person to put a belief into practice. One conceptual approach to this issue, the functional approach to attitudes and behavior (e.g., Katz, 1960; Smith, Bruner, & White, 1956), suggests that both attitudes and behaviors serve important personal and social functions, and that different individuals may hold similar attitudes or engage in similar behaviors for very different reasons. This means that simply holding a belief (without practicing its corresponding action) may fulfill the individual's purpose. Thus, motivations appear to play a key role in translating beliefs into action, a process that several contributors to this volume consider in greater detail.

Another possible answer to questions about missing ingredients comes from an older line of research on truisms and their vulnerability to challenge (McGuire, 1964) and the more recent efforts to apply these ideas and findings to values (Bernard, Maio, & Olson, 2003; Maio & Olson, 1998). Maio and Olson's research provided support for the "values as truisms hypothesis," especially the idea that values such as altruism, equality, and helpfulness sometimes lack cognitive support or rather arguments supporting their value. Furthermore, Bernard et al. provided evidence that such values are vulnerable to attack, although resistance to challenges can be developed by generating supportive arguments or by refuting weaker forms of the attack prior to the primary attack on the values (an inoculation process).

It may well be the case that these kinds of concerns apply to values such as "it takes a village to raise a child," values that clearly enjoy widespread agreement (Scales, 2003). As with the factors in the Maio and Olson (1998) investigations, values with respect to positive youth development may not have an elaborate set of cognitive supports, may not have received extensive thought, and may rarely have been questioned. The foundation for this kind of belief, in other words, may be thin and shallow, and many of us may not know the precise meanings of these statements. That is, in our highly individualistic society, what are the responsibilities of the "village" to the child, and what, exactly, constitutes a "village"? Moreover, what are the responsibilities of any individual member of the village, and how should the responsibilities of the individual be expressed in terms of behaviors? The upshot of these beliefs is that to the extent they pertain here, they lack supports that make them resistant to countervailing forces.

Along with these missing supports that may be necessary for beliefs and values to be translated into action, there may be actual barriers or obstacles to participation. This possibility, of course, is suggested by the research discussed earlier indicating that truistic values may have opposing values; in fact, Maio and Olson's (1998) research used such antivalue reasons as one might be taken advantage of if one acts on a value and a value is an unattainable ideal. These counterarguments would seem to apply here, along with such values as a child's development is the responsibility of the parent and the importance of "minding one's own business."

In addition to these more abstract, value-based counterarguments, there are concrete barriers to acting on beliefs and values. The first set of obstacles to consider is a general one facing those who currently have habits of inaction and the forces that maintain inaction and discourage action. Habits of exercise, as well as those of acting on behalf of young people, start with a kind of behavioral inertia that must be overcome. In many cases, especially today, the obstacle involves lack of time for a new activity. According to Schor (1991), Americans in the late 1980s worked an average of 160 more hours each year than they had in the late 1960s—the equivalent of nearly an extra month of full-time work. As a greater share of married-couple families consist of two working parents, these individuals certainly feel additional pressure to balance the demands of work and home. Indeed, the entry of more and more women into the workforce over the past 30 years has changed the landscape of American families, making it increasingly difficult for adults to act on behalf of unrelated youth (see Tiehen, 2000). Finally, we should at least recognize the difficulties that almost always arise as the actions of individuals occur in the context of a group or community, including problems of coordination of efforts and determining whose action plan for meeting the group's goals will be adopted.

Youth Development: Adults Assisting Young People

We have, to this point, considered the general issue of encouraging adults to act on behalf of children and adolescents, but what specifically is being called for here? What does it mean when we ask adults to act on behalf of young people to whom they are not related? In other words, for what are adults being mobilized? In effect, these kinds of activities performed by adults for the benefit of young people represent a form of helping behavior, community service, contributing to the common good, or, as it is known in the behavioral sciences literature, prosocial activity. As these terms imply, the efforts being considered here involve adults directly or indirectly sharing with young people their time, energy, knowledge, skills, and/or money, to name several resources, and doing so to benefit the young people who are the recipients of the shared resources.

An important framework for viewing positive youth development, one that identifies both the goals of positive youth development and the means of achieving those goals, is Search Institute's 40 developmental assets (Scales & Leffert, 2004). This perspective emphasizes a host of positive qualities or strengths in the lives of young people that are associated with socially valued outcomes (Benson, Leffert, Scales, & Blyth, 1998; Leffert et al., 1998; Scales, Benson, Leffert, & Blyth, 2000). Moreover, as can be seen in Table 1, the 40 developmental assets are classified into 20 external and 20 internal assets, depending on whether the strengths or supports are viewed as coming from the young person's environment or are qualities that the young person has internalized. As we discuss, this framework and the language it supplies serve as a starting point for considerations of the goals or purpose of positive youth development (the internal assets) and the activities of parental and nonparental adults that can facilitate the acquisition of those assets.

The Needs of Youth

The 20 internal assets represent one conceptualization of positive youth development and, as such, serve as a possible target of adults' activities on behalf of young people. Clearly, several of the goals center on education; others revolve around a positive self-concept; and still others concern ways of regarding and interacting with other people. A somewhat expanded and slightly repackaged version of these components can be found in the identification of the "'five Cs' of positive youth development: competence, confidence, connection (to family, peers, and community), character, and caring/compassion" (Lerner, 2003, p. 8).

There are, of course, other conceptualizations that emphasize different features and/or offer different labels but that, in fundamental ways, are highly similar. Some, for example, focus on the qualities a young person will need for productive adulthood, including education and preparation for work, beneficial health practices, and preparation for parenting and citizenship (Scales, 2003; Takanishi, Mortimer, & McGourthy, 1997). Others concentrate more on the process of youth development and the kinds of experiences that schools might provide, as reflected in the work of the Child Development Project, an applied research investigation that is creating and evaluating a type of school environment more likely to result in positive youth development by meeting students' most fundamental needs (Solomon, Battistich, Watson, Schaps, & Lewis, 2000). From the standpoint of this project, "an effective school environment supports students' basic psychological needs to: (a) belong to a social group whose members are mutually supportive and concerned, (b) have age-appropriate opportunities to be autonomous, self-directing and influential, and (c) feel competent and effective in valued activities" (Solomon et al., 2000, p. 4).

Table 1. Search Institute's Framework of 40 Developmental Assets

External Assets

Support

1. *Family support*—Family life provides high levels of love and support.
2. *Positive family communication*—Young person and her or his parent(s) communicate positively, and young person is willing to seek advice and counsel from parent(s).
3. *Other adult relationships*—Young person receives support from three or more nonparent adults.
4. *Caring neighborhood*—Young person experiences caring neighbors.
5. *Caring school climate*—School provides a caring, encouraging environment.
6. *Parent involvement in schooling*—Parent(s) are actively involved in helping young person succeed in school.

Empowerment

7. *Community values youth*—Young person perceives that adults in the community value youth.
8. *Youth as resources*—Young people are given useful roles in the community.
9. *Service to others*—Young person serves in the community one hour or more per week.
10. *Safety*—Young person feels safe at home, at school, and in the neighborhood.

Boundaries and Expectations

11. *Family boundaries*—Family has clear rules and consequences and monitors the young person's whereabouts.
12. *School boundaries*—School provides clear rules and consequences.
13. *Neighborhood boundaries*—Neighbors take responsibility for monitoring young people's behavior.
14. *Adult role models*—Parent(s) and other adults model positive, responsible behavior.
15. *Positive peer influence*—Young person's best friends model responsible behavior.
16. *High expectations*—Both parent(s) and teachers encourage the young person to do well.

Constructive Use of Time

17. *Creative activities*—Young person spends three or more hours per week in lessons or practice in music, theater, or other arts.
18. *Youth programs*—Young person spends three or more hours per week in sports, clubs, or organizations at school and/or in the community.
19. *Religious community*—Young person spends one or more hours per week in activities in a religious institution.
20. *Time at home*—Young person is out with friends "with nothing special to do" two or fewer nights per week.

Internal Assets

Commitment to Learning

21. *Achievement motivation*—Young person is motivated to do well in school.
22. *School engagement*—Young person is actively engaged in learning.
23. *Homework*—Young person reports doing at least one hour of homework every school day.
24. *Bonding to school*—Young person cares about her or his school.
25. *Reading for pleasure*—Young person reads for pleasure three or more hours per week.

Positive Values

26. *Caring*—Young person places high value on helping other people.
27. *Equality and social justice*—Young person places high value on promoting equality and reducing hunger and poverty.
28. *Integrity*—Young person acts on convictions and stands up for her or his beliefs.

Table 1. (Cont.)

29. *Honesty*—Young person "tells the truth even when it is not easy."
30. *Responsibility*—Young person accepts and takes personal responsibility.
31. *Restraint*—Young person believes it is important not to be sexually active or to use alcohol or other drugs.

Social Competencies

32. *Planning and decision making*—Young person knows how to plan ahead and make choices.
33. *Interpersonal competence*—Young person has empathy, sensitivity, and friendship skills.
34. *Cultural competence*—Young person has knowledge of and comfort with people of different cultural/racial/ethnic backgrounds.
35. *Resistance skills*—Young person can resist negative peer pressure and dangerous situations.
36. *Peaceful conflict resolution*—Young person seeks to resolve conflict nonviolently.

Positive Identity

37. *Personal power*—Young person feels he or she has control over "things that happen to me."
38. *Self-esteem*—Young person reports having a high self-esteem.
39. *Sense of purpose*—Young person reports that "my life has a purpose."
40. *Positive view of personal future*—Young person is optimistic about her or his personal future.

Finally, in an attempt to identify the most essential goal of positive youth development, Larson (2000) points to the acquisition of initiative as the essential objective of positive adolescent development and the quality that is critically important for being able to function as an adult in Western societies. Moreover, his conceptualization of initiative identifies three features: intrinsic motivation, using this motivation in active encounters with the environment, and experiencing these encounters over time. According to Larson, "To be an agentic adult, one needs to be able to mobilize one's attention, one's mental powers, on a deliberate course of action, without being deterred by the first obstacle one encounters. Initiative is the devotion of cumulative effort over time to achieve a goal" (p. 172).

We find a great deal of agreement among these conceptualizations with respect to the needs of young people. First, all of these perspectives highlight the importance of the development of competence, the ability to function in the adult world, or efficacy. Second, all of the perspectives seem to refer to some aspect of the positive self-concept, although they emphasize different features (e.g., agency, healthy habits, character, self-esteem). Finally, most of these perspectives also underscore positive connections to other people, in some cases belonging to a social network and in others connecting with the community.

The Activities of Adults

The external assets identified by Search Institute serve as a starting point for considerations of the kinds of activities that volunteers might be asked to engage in with unrelated children and adolescents. As can be seen in Table 1, many of these external assets concern actions that parents are expected to perform, although several others involve the participation of nonparent adults. Several of the assets center on supportive relationships that adults could have with the children and adolescents of their neighborhood and/or social network (i.e., caring neighborhood, other adult relationships, high expectations) and with the parents of young people (i.e., neighborhood boundaries). Other assets involve contributions an adult could make to her or his community, for example, modeling responsible behavior, providing ways for youth to contribute to the community, valuing young people, helping to create a safe environment, and creating and staffing opportunities for youth to participate in youth programs in the community (e.g., scouting, 4-H clubs, and athletic clubs), in religious institutions, and at school.

At the same time, positive youth development involves not only volunteering formally with a youth-serving organization but also engaging in a much broader range of activities. To provide an overview of these activities, perhaps it would be useful to think about adults' actions with respect to positive youth development as varying on two dimensions: first, whether the actions take place in a formal versus an informal context; and second, whether the actions involve a direct or indirect relationship with a young person. With this scheme, presented in Table 2, we can begin to sort some of Search Institute's developmental assets into the following categories, as well as suggest some additional activities.

The clearest type of positive youth development activity is one that involves a direct relationship between an individual adult and an individual young person, a relationship that can emerge in either a formal or an informal setting. Many young people are in a mentoring relationship with an adult from their neighborhood, religious community, or extended family, and some research suggests that these natural mentoring relationships can have an important protective influence on young people (Collins, 1987). In addition, more than 2.5 million American youth are involved in school- or community-based volunteer mentoring

Table 2. A Taxonomy of Adults' Positive Youth Development Activities

Relationship	Context of Adult Activity	
	Informal	Formal Program
Adult to young person	Adult talks with, advises, encourages young person	Mentoring, coaching, providing youth leadership
Adult to parents	Adult talks with, advises, encourages parents	Mentoring parents, teaching parenting classes, staffing crisis nursery, etc.
Adult to community	Adult models responsible behavior	Creating programs for youth, supporting public policies that promote positive youth development, etc.

programs each year, and the number is rising at an unprecedented rate. Still more children develop informal mentoring bonds with caring adults in their schools, congregations, and communities. At the same time, there is some concern that these latter kinds of relationships are less prevalent than in the past. The expansion of professional human services over the past 30 years has also stifled the growth of informal mentoring relationships. In particular, increased professionalization in these fields has led many adults to doubt their "common capacity to care" and to withhold guidance and support because of a mistaken belief that the social services sector will provide intervention programs to take up the slack (McKnight, 1995, ix–x). Shifting family, marital, and employment patterns, overcrowded schools, and less cohesive communities have dramatically reduced the presence of caring adults in the lives of youth (Eccles & Grootman, 2002; Putnam, 2000). The social fabric is stretched thin in urban centers, which are largely bereft of the middle-class adults who once served as respected authority figures in the community (Anderson, 1999).

Mentoring programs are being increasingly advocated as a means of redressing the decreased availability of adult support and guidance in the lives of youth (Grossman & Tierney, 1998; Rhodes, 2002). Although the structure and aims vary considerably—the focus may be on companionship in some cases; on academic skills or career development in others; on character development in still other cases—almost all formal mentoring programs are characterized by regular meetings between the mentor and mentee and the establishment of a relationship. A growing number of evaluations suggest that volunteer mentoring relationships can positively influence a range of outcomes, including improved peer and parental relationships, academic achievement, self-concept, and behavior (Aseltine, Dupre, & Lamlein, 2000; DuBois, Holloway, Valentine, & Cooper, 2002; Grossman & Tierney, 1998). Like other relationships, however, youth-mentoring relationships can vary in closeness and duration, in ways that have implications for their effectiveness. Whereas some mentoring relationships can be extraordinarily influential, others are only marginally helpful or even dissatisfying and hurtful.

One step removed from providing an asset or support directly to an individual young person is providing the support or asset to the young person's parent or guardian. Here again, this might be done informally or formally. Similar to the case in which a young person is mentored by an extended family member or neighbor, we might expect that many parents of young people will receive guidance, advice, and support for child rearing from a member of their extended family or neighborhood. In fact, many communities have so-called natural helpers, people who are known for their ability to solve problems (Patterson, 1977; Patterson & Brennan, 1983), and it would not be surprising if some of the problems a neighbor might have concern parenting and child rearing.

On a formal basis, there are individuals and organizations that provide these and other kinds of services to parents on a more professional basis. Many communities provide parent education classes, self-help groups, and family enrichment experiences; moreover, some communities provide child care, either on an emergency basis or as a regular resource for families (see Roehlkepartain, Scales, Roehlkepartain, & Rude, 2002). Finally, in a study by Cowan and Cowan (2002), professional therapists provided couples with training that focused either on parenting skills or on marriage; relative to a no-training control group, the training was found to have positively affected children's academic performance and social skills.

Finally, there are activities adults can perform that involve no direct contact with a young person but that can contribute to the positive development of the youth of a community. These activities largely involve actions that affect the community as a community, beginning with an adult behaving in socially appropriate or socially desirable ways. The importance of this sort of effort has been shown recently in a series of studies by Cialdini and his colleagues on social norms, particularly on injunctive norms that indicate which actions are socially approved and which are disapproved. In several investigations with the injunctive norm of antilittering, these investigators found that making a norm salient (e.g., a model picking up a piece of litter) had an important impact on an observer's own littering (Kallgren, Reno, & Cialdini, 2000). Thus, an adult behaving in a socially responsible way that is consistent with community norms can serve as a powerful reminder to young people to do likewise.

More formally, an individual adult or groups of adults might create a program or organization for the youth of a community, actively support public policies that benefit the youth of the community, or simply vote for candidates or policies that are youth friendly. For example, the National 4-H Council offers programs and assistance to youth workers who assist youth in finding solutions to the challenges they face. It creates partnerships with corporations, foundations, the Cooperative Extension System, and other organizations to bring together resources (e.g., training, curricula, technical assistance, youth forums) and employs a variety of methods (community service activities, clubs, enrichment programs) with the objective of developing youth as individuals and as responsible and productive citizens (Lerner, 2002).

To summarize, the activities in which adults might engage that would serve the young people of a community and stand as positive youth development are many and diverse. Adults' actions might involve direct or indirect contact with a young person, and they might be performed formally or informally. In addition, along with the range of activities, it is also important that the actions be sustained over time; this is generally the case in formal, direct, positive youth development activities, in which there is the expectation that a mentor or volunteer youth leader will be serving over time, and it is very likely important for the other categories of activities. More important, perhaps, than a specific context is that positive youth development is more likely if all of these activities take place in a community and to a great degree. Analyses with the framework of 40 developmental assets find that desired outcomes (e.g., lower levels of risky behaviors and higher levels of thriving behaviors) are positively associated with the number of assets in young people's lives (Leffert et al., 1998; Scales et al., 2000). This kind of community focus underlies the concept of a youth charter, which is "a consensus of clear expectations shared among the important people in a young person's life and communicated to the young person in multiple ways" (Damon & Gregory, 2003, p. 55). A youth charter, which emerges from discussions taking place within the community, locates the moral education of young people in the community.

The Present Volume

We have, to this point, presented a broad-brush view of the goals of positive youth development and the kinds of activities that adults might engage in to achieve those goals. Moreover, we have seen that there are indications that fewer adults are engaging in these activities than are needed: It appears that many more young people could benefit from a mentoring relationship than are currently involved in such a relationship; fewer adults are available in a community to serve as informal mentors; and there is a gap between beliefs and actions with respect to other people's children. The question to be examined in this volume, then, is, how can we most effectively encourage adults, both individually and collectively, to begin to behave differently with respect to the young people of a community, to do so consistently, and to do so in a variety of ways?

Taken together, the chapters in this volume contemplate the means of creating a kind of social movement for positive youth development. This aspect of mobilizing adults for positive youth development can be seen in the concept of youth charters mentioned earlier, whereby, in fact, each community would create partnerships among various segments of the community in order to develop a framework of healthy development (Damon, 1997). And as a social movement, the kinds of changes that are being considered would occur at virtually all levels and arenas of society: in individual adults and neighborhoods; among other local groups of adults, including the workplace, religious institutions, and educational institutions; and in local communities, society as a whole, and the global community.

Accordingly, the authors in this volume all have experience with change at one or more of these levels of society, and they have been asked to apply that understanding to the issue of mobilizing adults for positive youth development. At the same time, it should be recognized that many of these authors do not conduct research on youth development but are included here because of their knowledge of some aspect of encouraging adults to be involved in service to the community. In fact, the guiding image for this volume is that of a worker in the field of youth development on an airplane flight finding her- or himself seated next to a person with expertise in some area of mobilizing adults. After the youth development worker describes her or his concerns—the current state of youth development, the future desired state, and moving from the present to the future—the worker asks the expert for her or his thoughts about getting to this desired future. In other words, with this volume we are attempting to capture some of the best thinking on the topic of mobilizing or changing adults and then applying this thinking to the specific issue of mobilizing adults to make an active contribution to the healthy development of children and adolescents.

Fundamentally, then, this volume is concerned with applying understandings of social influence to the objective of narrowing the gap between *beliefs* that support youth development and *behaviors* that intentionally promote youth development. In some way, all of the chapters in this volume contribute to this narrowing of the gap, either by discussing key principles and strategies of influence or mobilization, by analyzing some of the personal and social forces that may be leveraged for adult involvement and/or tackling some of the obstacles to involvement, by looking at opportunities and barriers that may be present in the young people who are the ultimate goal of all of these efforts, or by considering practical efforts to encourage greater involvement among adults in the lives of young people.

Put another way, we believe that efforts to mobilize adults for youth development could benefit from greater understanding of:

- Social influence strategies and strategies that might be applied to different levels of society;
- The adult targets of this social influence;
- The nature of the work that adults are being asked to perform (i.e., what it is that adults are supposed to do with young people); and
- Previous efforts to mobilize adults.

Although individual chapters may tackle only one or two of these facets of mobilizing adults for youth development, we hope that collectively this volume addresses all of these concerns. Ideally, this volume will serve as a blueprint for those who are attempting to create a society that is attentive to the developmental needs of children and adolescents. Given this goal, we are assuming that a multipronged and multidisciplinary approach will be needed, so that the promotion of action on behalf of young people can occur at the level of individual adults, communities of adults, and a society of adults.

The Structure of This Book

This volume is organized into four parts. The first provides the context for efforts to mobilize adults for youth development by reviewing the present state of youth development work, the world in which adolescents live, and the world that adults face. In Chapter 2, Richard M. Lerner, Amy E. Alberts, Helena Jelicic, and Lisa M. Smith focus on the world of adolescents, juxtaposing the frequently encountered viewpoint that adolescents are problems to be managed with the emerging perspective that young people are resources to be developed. Within this emerging perspective, Lerner and his colleagues discuss the goals of positive youth development, including the five Cs of positive youth development, and the key components of programs that are attempting to achieve those goals. In Chapter 3, Peter C. Scales provides a look at the realities of the lives of adults, along with the possibilities. Here we take a closer look at the goals the adult world has for young people today, as well as the pressures adults experience to remain uninvolved with other people's children.

Each of the next three parts looks at one general route to promoting adult involvement. The chapters in Part II focus on mobilizing individual adults, in theory attempting to persuade one individual at a time to contribute to positive youth development. Arthur A. Stukas, Maree Daly, and E. Gil Clary, in Chapter 4, discuss the applications of research on volunteers' motivations and encouraging individuals' involvement in volunteerism by targeting motivations to the promotion of involvement in positive youth development. In Chapter 5, Andrea S. Taylor provides an overview of generativity—and how an understanding of this phase of adulthood might be leveraged for positive youth development. Alexander J. Rothman and Katherine C. Haydon (Chapter 6) consider the applications and implications for youth development of work on encouraging individuals to engage in healthy behavior. Their discussion underscores the importance of quality and commitment in relationships between adults and young people.

Each of the chapters in Part III focuses on work that has examined the contributions of specific types of organizations or groups of individuals to positive youth development goals. The areas examined here are for-profit organizations (Susan Elaine Murphy and Ellen A. Ensher, Chapter 7), community groups (Pamela S. Imm, Renie Kehres, Abraham Wandersman, and Matthew Chinman, Chapter 8), religious institutions (Kenneth I. Maton and Mariano R. Sto. Domingo, Chapter 9), and higher education (Linda Camino and Shepherd Zeldin, Chapter 10). For each type of organization, the authors describe specific activities and programs that adults are providing, research that speaks to the effectiveness of these efforts, and some of the theoretical and practical issues that arise.

Part IV addresses the question of mobilizing a society of adults, or rather the ways in which a society can become more attentive to the developmental needs of adolescents. In Chapter 11, Constance A. Flanagan, Nicole S. Webster, and Daniel F. Perkins describe the contributions of civil society and the public sector to mobilizing adults for positive youth development, looking in particular at public policies that encourage adult involvement. In Chapter 12, Sameer Deshpande and Michael Basil discuss social marketing, which targets society at large and markets social change. Tina M. Durand and M. Brinton Lykes (Chapter 13) provide an international perspective on youth development work and emphasize efforts outside the United States where youth development is more youth-driven and is marked by youth in partnership with adults. The volume concludes with Mark Snyder's reflections on some of the key themes and key concerns facing attempts to mobilize adults for positive youth development.

Concluding Thoughts

Throughout this volume, we find indications that young people need many adults in their lives if they are to experience positive development but that far too many young people do not have significant attachments to nonparental adults. We also find that most adults do not need to be convinced that positive youth development is an important goal and worthy of their time and effort. Many adults, however, apparently need help translating favorable beliefs and even good intentions into action. Put another way, many adults need help ending their noninvolvement and becoming involved in the lives of other people's children.

Taking these chapters together, we see that adult involvement in the lives of young people can assume many forms and that the diversity of forms—where individual adults in both large and small ways contribute to young people's development—is an especially powerful attribute of a positive youth development movement. Moreover, it would seem that a society that is serious about positive youth development would encourage youth development activities in a variety of venues and, in fact, in all sectors of society. Using adult mentoring as the prototypical positive youth development approach, we find this type of activity in formal programs in nonprofit organizations, schools, workplaces, and religious institutions, and informally in these same environments, as well as in neighborhoods and communities; and where the goals may be highly specific (e.g., academic or career based) or quite general (e.g., acting as an older friend).

As a final thought about this volume, we note that all of the chapters speak to the fact that positive youth development fundamentally centers on relationships. Most obviously, all of the chapters touch on, to a degree, the relationship that an adult who is engaged in positive youth development has with a young person. Some of the chapters also consider the other relationships that adults involved in youth development work will have, including a relationship with the parent or parents of the young person, relationships with fellow workers, and relationships with key representatives of the organization where one works (e.g., leaders, paid staff, committees, and so on).

We hasten to add, however, that relationships present both opportunities and challenges. Among other opportunities, the key one may well be that significant progress, at a societal level, will be possible only when many adults and groups of adults combine their efforts to provide positive developmental experiences for all young people. And herein lies the central challenge: mobilizing the efforts of individuals and groups in many different locations, and then coordinating and combining them to create a different way of advancing the positive development of all young people.

References

Anderson, E. (1999). *Code of the street: Decency, violence, and the moral life of the inner city.* New York: Norton.

Aseltine, R. H., Dupre, M., & Lamlein, P. (2000). Mentoring as a drug prevention strategy: An evaluation of Across Ages. *Adolescent and Family Health, 1,* 11–20.

Benson, P. L., Leffert, N., Scales, P. C., & Blyth, D. A. (1998). Beyond the "village" rhetoric: Creating healthy communities for children and adolescents. *Applied Developmental Science, 2,* 138–159.

Bernard, M. M., Maio, G. R., & Olson, J. M. (2003). The vulnerability of values to attack: Inoculation of values and value-relevant attitudes. *Personality and Social Psychology Bulletin, 29,* 63–75.

Cialdini, R. B., Reno, R. R., & Kallgren, C. A. (1990). A focus theory of normative conduct: Recycling the concept of norms to reduce littering in public places. *Journal of Personality and Social Psychology, 58*, 1015–1026.

Collins, P. H. (1987). The meaning of motherhood in black culture and black mother/daughter relationships. *Sage: A Scholarly Journal of Black Women, 4*, 3–10.

Cowan, P. A., & Cowan, C. P. (2002). What an intervention design reveals about how parents affect their children's academic achievement and behavior problems. In J. Borkowski, S. L. Ramey, & M. Bristol-Power (Eds.), *Parenting and the child's world: Influences on academic, intellectual, and social-emotional development* (pp. 75–98). Mahwah, NJ: Erlbaum.

Damon, W. (1997). *The youth charter: How communities can work together to raise standards for all of our children.* New York: Free Press.

Damon, W., & Gregory, A. (2003). Bringing in a new era in the field of youth development. In R. M. Lerner & P. L. Benson (Eds.), *Developmental assets and asset-building communities: Implications for research, policy, and practice* (pp. 47–64). New York: Kluwer Academic/Plenum.

DuBois, D. L., Holloway, B. E., Valentine, J. C., & Cooper, H. (2002). Effectiveness of mentoring programs for youth: A meta-analytic review. *American Journal of Community Psychology, 30*, 157–197.

Eccles, J., & Grootman, J. (2002). *Community programs to promote youth development.* Washington, DC: National Academy Press.

Grossman, J. B., & Tierney, J. P. (1998). Does mentoring work? An impact study of the Big Brothers Big Sisters program. *Evaluation Review, 22*, 403–426.

Independent Sector. (1999). *Giving and volunteering in the United States: Findings from a national survey.* Washington, DC: Author.

Kallgren, C. A., Reno, R. R., & Cialdini, R. B. (2000). A focus theory of normative conduct: When norms do and do not affect behavior. *Personality and Social Psychology Bulletin, 26*, 1002–1012.

Katz, D. (1960). The functional approach to the study of attitudes. *Public Opinion Quarterly, 24*, 163–204.

Larson, R. W. (2000). Toward a psychology of positive youth development. *American Psychologist, 55*, 170–183.

Lerner, R. M. (2002). *Adolescence: Development, diversity, context, and application.* Upper Saddle River, NJ: Prentice Hall.

Lerner, R. M. (2003). Developmental assets and asset-building communities: A view of the issues. In R. M. Lerner & P. L. Benson (Eds.), *Developmental assets and asset-building communities: Implications for research, policy, and practice* (pp. 3–18). New York: Kluwer Academic/Plenum.

Lerner, R. M., & Benson, P. L. (2003). *Developmental assets and asset-building communities: Implications for research, policy, and practice.* New York: Kluwer Academic/Plenum.

Leffert, N., Benson, P. L., Scales, P. C., Sharma, A. R., Drake, D. R., & Blyth, D. A. (1998). Developmental assets: Measure and prediction of risk behaviors among adolescents. *Applied Developmental Science, 2*, 209–230.

Maio, G. R., & Olson, J. M. (1998). Values as truisms: Evidence and implications. *Journal of Personality and Social Psychology, 74*, 294–311.

McGuire, W. J. (1964). Inducing resistance to persuasion: Some contemporary approaches. In L. Berkowitz (Ed.), *Advances in experimental social psychology* (Vol. 1, pp. 191–229). San Diego: Academic Press.

McKnight, J. (1995). *The careless society: Community and its counterfeits.* New York: Basic Books.

Olson, J. M., & Zanna, M. P. (1993). Attitudes and attitude change. *Annual Review of Psychology, 44*, 117–154.

Patterson, S. L. (1977). Toward a conceptualization of natural helping. *Aretê, 4*, 161–173.

Patterson, S. L., & Brennan, E. M. (1983). Matching helping roles with the characteristics of older natural helpers. *Journal of Gerontological Social Work, 5*, 55–66.

Putnam, R. D. (2000). *Bowling alone: The collapse and revival of American community.* New York: Simon & Schuster.

Rhodes, J. E. (2002). *Stand by me: The risks and rewards of mentoring today's youth.* Cambridge, MA: Harvard University Press.

Roehlkepartain, E. C., Scales, P. C., Roehlkepartain, J. L., & Rude, S. P. (2002). *Building strong families: An in-depth report on a preliminary survey of what parents need to succeed.* Minneapolis, MN: Search Institute.

Scales, P. C. (with Benson, P. L., Mannes, M., Hintz, N. R., Roehlkepartain, E. C., & Sullivan, T. K.). (2003). *Other people's kids: Social expectations and American adults' involvement with children and adolescents.* New York: Kluwer Academic/Plenum.

Scales, P. C., Benson, P. L., Leffert, N., & Blyth, D. A. (2000). Contribution of developmental assets to the prediction of thriving among adolescents. *Applied Developmental Science, 4,* 27–46.

Scales, P. C., & Leffert, N. (2004). *Developmental assets: A synthesis of the scientific research on adolescent development* (2nd ed.). Minneapolis, MN: Search Institute.

Schor, J. B. (1991). *The overworked American: The unexpected decline of leisure.* New York: Basic Books.

Smith, M., Bruner, J., & White, R. (1956). *Opinions and personality.* New York: Wiley.

Solomon, D., Battistich, V., Watson, M., Schaps, E., & Lewis, C. (2000). A six-district study of educational change: Direct and mediated effects of the child development project. *Social Psychology of Education, 4,* 3–51.

Takanishi, R., Mortimer, A. M., & McGourthy, T. J. (1997). Positive indicators of adolescent development: Redressing the negative image of American adolescents. In R. M. Hauser, B. V. Brown, & W. R. Prosser (Eds.), *Indicators of children's well-being* (pp. 428–441). New York: Russell Sage Foundation.

Tiehen, L. (2000). Has working more caused married women to volunteer less? Evidence from time diary data, 1965 to 1993. *Nonprofit and Voluntary Sector Quarterly, 29,* 505–529.

I The Context of Adults Helping Youth Develop

2 Young People Are Resources to Be Developed: Promoting Positive Youth Development through Adult–Youth Relations and Community Assets

Richard M. Lerner, Amy E. Alberts, Helena Jelicic, and Lisa M. Smith

Tufts University

How do we know if American children and adolescents are doing well in life? What vocabulary do American parents, teachers, policy makers, and often young people themselves use to describe a young person—a person in the first two or so decades of life—who is showing successful development?

All too often in the United States we discuss positive development in regard to the absence of negative or undesirable behaviors. Typically, such descriptions are founded on the assumption that children are "broken" or in danger of becoming "broken" (Benson, 2003), and thus we regard young people as "problems to be managed" (Roth, Brooks-Gunn, Murray, & Foster, 1998). As such, when we describe a successful young person we speak about a youth whose problems have been managed or are, at best, absent. We might say, then, that a youth who is manifesting behavior indicative of positive development is someone who is *not* taking drugs or using alcohol, is *not* engaging in unsafe sex, and is *not* participating in crime or violence.

Benson (2003) explains that the focus in Americans' discussions of youth on their problems and the use by Americans of a vocabulary that stresses the risks and dangers of young people occur because we have

> a culture dominated by deficit and risk thinking, by pathology and its symptoms. This shapes our research, our policy, our practice. It fuels the creation of elaborate and expensive service and program delivery infrastructures, creates a dependence on professional experts, encourages an ethos of fear, and by consequence, derogates, ignores and interferes with the natural and inherent capacity of communities to be community. (p. 25)

The deficit model of youth that shapes our vocabulary about the behaviors prototypic of young people results, then, in an orientation in the United States to discuss positive youth development as the absence of negative behaviors. Unfortunately, even as recently as 1999, and even in programs purportedly focused on positive youth development, a predominant emphasis in the youth development field continued to be a reliance on this deficit model of youth and, as such, on defining positive youth development as the absence of adolescent problem behaviors. For instance, Catalano, Berglund, Ryan, Lonczak, and Hawkins (1999) noted that "currently, problem behaviors are tracked more often than positive ones and, while an increasing number of positive youth development interventions are choosing to measure both, this is still far from being the standard in the field" (p. vi).

The absence of an accepted vocabulary for the discussion of positive youth development is, then, a key obstacle to evaluating the effectiveness of programs or policies aimed at promoting such change. People do not measure what they cannot name, and they often do not name what they cannot measure (T. Gore, personal communication, December 13, 2002).

In short, characterizations of young people as problems to be managed or as primarily in need of fixing reflect both a deficit approach to human development and a belief that there is some shortcoming of character or personality that leads youth to become involved in risky or negative behaviors. Given the presence of such a deficit, the appropriate and humane actions to take in regard to young people are to prevent the actualization of the inevitable problems they will encounter. Indeed, policy makers and practitioners are pleased when their actions are associated with the reduction of such problem behaviors as teenage pregnancy and parenting, substance use and abuse, school failure and dropout, and delinquency and violence.

Everyone should, of course, be pleased when such behaviors diminish. However, it is very dispiriting for a young person to learn that he or she is regarded by adults as someone who is likely to be a problem for others as well as for him- or herself. It is very discouraging for a young person to try to make a positive life when he or she is confronted by the suspicion of substance abuse, sexual promiscuity, and a lack of commitment to supporting the laws of society. What sort of message are we sending our children when we speak of them as inevitably destined for trouble unless we take preventive steps? How do such messages affect the self-esteem of young people, and what is the impact of such messages on their spirit and motivation?

Some words for describing positive behaviors about youth exist, for example, pertaining to academic achievement and activities relating to current or potentially successful entrepreneurship. Nevertheless, the vocabulary for depicting youth as "resources to be developed" (Roth et al., 1998) is not as rich or nuanced as the one available for depicting the problematic propensities of young people.

As a society, we must do a better job of talking about the positive attributes of young people. We must talk to our youth about what they should and can become, and not only about what they must avoid being. We should then act on our statements, and work with young people to promote their positive development. In the context of nurturing and healthy adult–youth relationships, we need to offer young people the opportunities to learn and use the skills involved in participating actively in their communities and in making productive and positive contributions to themselves and their families and society.

These "oughts" for social change for youth represent a formidable challenge involving nothing short of thorough systems change in the United States. The challenge is to provide for Americans a new vision and vocabulary about youth. This challenge is being met by a historically unique and significant convergence of efforts by scholars, practitioners, policy makers, and youth and families.

Toward a New Vision and Vocabulary for Youth

In these early years of the 21st century, a new, positive, and strength-based vision and vocabulary for discussing America's young people are beginning to emerge. Propelled by the increasingly more collaborative contributions of scholars (e.g., Benson, 2003; Benson, Mannes, Pittman, & Ferber, 2004; Damon & Gregory, 2003; Lerner, 2004; Roth et al., 1998; Villarruel, Perkins, Borden, & Keith, 2003), practitioners (e.g., Pittman, Irby, & Ferber, 2001; Wheeler, 2000, 2003), and policy makers (e.g., Cummings, 2003; Engler & Binsfeld, 1998; Gore, 2003), youth are increasingly seen within numerous sectors of U.S. society as resources to be developed (Roth & Brooks-Gunn, 2003a, 2003b). The new vocabulary about positive youth development emphasizes the strengths present within all young people and involves concepts such as developmental assets (Benson, 2003), moral development (Damon, 1988), noble purpose (Damon, Menon, & Bronk, 2003), civic engagement (e.g., Sherrod, Flanagan, & Youniss, 2002a, 2002b), community youth development (e.g., Villarruel et al., 2003), well-being (Bornstein, Davidson, Keys, Moore, & the Center for Child Well-being, 2003), and thriving (Dowling, Gestsdottir, Anderson, von Eye, & Lerner, 2003; Dowling et al., 2004; Scales, Benson, Leffert, & Blyth, 2000). All concepts are predicated on the ideas that *every* young person has the potential for successful, healthy development and that *all* youth possess the capacity for positive development.

This vision for and vocabulary about positive youth development have evolved over the course of a scientifically arduous path, given the historical precedence and continued wide subscription to the deficit model of youth. Complicating the acceptance of the new, positive conceptualization of the character of youth as resources for the healthy development of self, families, and communities, is that the antithetical deficit approach conceptualizes youth behaviors as deviations from normative development (see Hall, 1904). In this history of the study of youth development, understanding such deviations was not seen as being of direct relevance to scholarship aimed at discovering the principles of basic developmental processes. Accordingly, the characteristics of youth were regarded as issues of "only" applied concern—and thus of secondary scientific interest. Not only did this model separate basic science from application, it also disembedded the adolescent from the study of normal or healthy development.

In short, the deficit view of youth as problems to be managed split the study of young people from the study of healthy and positive development (Lerner, 2004; Lerner, Brentano, Dowling, & Anderson, 2002; Overton, 1998; Roth & Brooks-Gunn, 2003a).

Scholars studying human development in general, and youth development in particular, used a theoretical model that was not useful in understanding the relational nature of development (Overton, 1998), the synthesis between basic and applied science, or how young people developed in normative, healthy, or positive ways. However, the integration of person and context, of basic and applied scholarship, and of young people with the potential for positive development was legitimated by the relational, developmental systems models that emerged as cutting-edge scholarship by the end of the 20th century (Damon, 1988; Lerner, 1998a, 1998b, 2002a).

Developmental systems theory eschews the reduction of individual and social behavior to fixed genetic influences and, in fact, contends that such a hereditarian conception is counterfactual (Gottlieb, 1997, 1998). Instead, developmental systems theory stresses the *relative plasticity* of human development. This concept means that there is always at least some potential for systematic change in behavior.

This potential exists as a consequence of mutually influential relationships between the developing person and his or her biology, psychological characteristics, family, community, culture, physical and designed ecology, and historical niche. The plasticity of development means that one may expect that ways may be found to improve human life.

Plasticity, then, legitimizes an optimistic view of the potential for promoting positive changes in humans. The presence of plasticity is an asset in attempts to enhance the human condition and, as such, plasticity directs interest to the strengths for positive development that are present within all people. It also directs both science and applications of science—for example, involving public policies and the programs of community-based organizations—to find ways to create optimal matches between individuals and their social worlds. Such fits may capitalize on the potential for positive change in people and for promoting such development.

The social policy implications of developmental systems theory counter negative formulations about human capacity, potential, and freedom. Developmental systems theory affords a means to pursue human development as it might ideally be (Benson, 2003; Bronfenbrenner, 1974): Developmental systems theory provides also a framework for developing a model of positive youth development. As explained by Lerner (2004), there are five sets of interrelated ideas in this theory of positive youth development. First, there is a universal structure for adaptive developmental regulations between people and their contexts. This structure involves mutually beneficial relations between people and their social worlds, and may be represented as individual $\leftarrow \rightarrow$ social context.

Second, these mutually beneficial, individual $\leftarrow \rightarrow$ social context relations have their historical roots in humans' integrated biological and cultural evolutionary heritage. Third, when instantiated in ideal ways, adaptive developmental regulations involve reciprocally supportive relations between thriving individuals and social institutions supporting the freedom of individuals. Fourth, thriving youth have noble purposes; they have an integrated moral and civic sense of self that impels them to transcend their own interests and contribute to others and to society in ways that extend beyond them in time and place.

Finally, this idealized relation between individuals and society may be realized within diverse cultural systems. However, when universal structures of mutually beneficial person–context relations are coupled with behavioral and social characteristics consistent with the idea of America, then youth are maximally likely to thrive and, reciprocally, free society is most likely to flourish.

Promoting Positive Youth Development within the Developmental System

The plasticity of human development emphasized in developmental systems models means that we may always remain optimistic about finding some intervention to reduce problem behaviors. However, plasticity within the developmental system can be directed to the promotion of desired outcomes of change, and not only to the prevention of undesirable behaviors. Pittman (1996; Pittman et al., 2001) has emphasized that prevention is not the same as *provision*: Preventing a problem from occurring does not, in turn, guarantee that we are providing youth with the assets they need for developing in a positive manner.

Simply, problem free is not prepared (Pittman, 1996). Not having behavioral problems (e.g., not using drugs and alcohol, not engaging in crime or unsafe sex) is not equivalent to possessing the skills requisite to productively engage in a valued job or other role in society. Preventing negative behaviors is, then, not the same as promoting in youth the attributes of positive, healthy development. Accordingly, as noted by several scholars working within a developmental systems framework (e.g., Lerner, 2004; Lerner, Sparks, & McCubbin, 1999; Roth et al., 1998), to ensure the development of prepared and productive youth, communities need proactively to provide resources to young people so that they develop in positive ways, for example, in regard to what have been termed the "five Cs" of positive youth development (Lerner, Fisher, & Weinberg, 2000).

That is, as have others (e.g., Eccles & Gootman, 2002; Lerner, 2004; Lerner et al., 2000; Roth & Brooks-Gunn, 2003a, 2003b), we suggest that "five Cs" may be used to represent the key features of positive youth development: competence, character, confidence, connection, and compassion. Together, these five characteristics enable an adolescent to make an optimal, or idealized, transition to the adult world. When these five characteristics place the young person on a life path toward a hopeful future, the youth is manifesting exemplary positive development: He or she may be said to be thriving (Lerner, 2004). Such a youth will become a generative adult, a person who makes simultaneously productive contributions to him- or herself, to family and community, and to civic life. The individual will develop, then, a "sixth C," contribution.

The theory of positive youth development that we propose specifies that if young people are engaged in adaptive regulations with their context, if mutually beneficial individual ← → context relations exist, then young people will be on the way to a hopeful future marked by positive contributions to self, family, community, and civil society. Young people will be thriving. As a result of such relations, youth will manifest several functionally valued behaviors, which in American society can be summarized by the five Cs (competence, confidence, connection, character, and caring). A thriving youth will be on a developmental trajectory toward an ideal adulthood status; that is, the person will develop behaviors that are valued by society because they act to structurally maintain it. Such behaviors reflect, then, contribution and, consistent with the mutually beneficial individual ← → context relations that comprise adaptive developmental regulations, such contributions should support the health and positive development of self, others, and the institutions of civil society.

The Contributions of William Damon

What is required for the promotion of exemplary positive development—or thriving—among young people interacting with the institutions of civil society in mutually beneficial ways? Damon (1997; Damon & Gregory, 2003) has envisioned the creation of a "youth charter" in each community in our nation and world. The charter consists of a set of rules, guidelines, and plans of action that each community can adopt to provide its youth with a framework for development in a healthy manner. Damon (1997) describes how youth and significant adults in their community (for example, parents, teachers, clergy, coaches, police, and government and business leaders) can create partnerships to pursue a common ideal of positive moral development and intellectual achievement.

To illustrate, Damon (1997) explains how a youth charter can be developed to maximize the positive experiences and long-term desired developmental outcomes of youth in community sports activities. Damon points out that there may be important benefits of such participation. Young people enhance their physical fitness, learn athletic and physical skills, and, through sports, experience lessons pertinent to the development of their character (for example, they learn about the importance of diligence, motivation, teamwork, balancing cooperation and competition, balancing winning and losing, and the importance of fair play). Moreover, sports can be a context for positive parent–child relations, and such interactions can further the adolescent's successful involvement in sports. For instance, parental support of their male and female adolescents' participation in tennis is associated with the enjoyment of the sport by the youth and with an objective measure of performance (Hoyle & Leff, 1997).

As illustrated by the youth charter in regard to sports participation, embedding youth in a caring and developmentally facilitative community can promote their ability to develop morally and to contribute to civil society. In a study of about 130 African American parochial high school juniors, working at a soup kitchen for the homeless as part of a school-based community service program was associated with identity development and with the ability to reflect on society's political organization and moral order (Yates & Youniss, 1996).

In a study of more than 3,100 high school seniors (Youniss, Yates, & Su, 1997), the activities youth engaged in were categorized into (a) school-based, adult-endorsed norms; or (b) peer fun activities that excluded adults. Youth were then placed into groups that reflected orientations to (1) school–adult norms, but not peer fun (the "School" group); (2) peer fun but not school–adult norms (the "Party" group); or (3) both "1" and "2" (the "All-around" group). The School and the All-around seniors were both high in community service, religious orientation, and political awareness. In turn, the Party group seniors were more likely to use marijuana than were the School group (but not the All-around group) seniors (Youniss et al., 1997).

Furthermore, African American and Latino adolescents who were nominated by community leaders for having shown unusual commitments to caring for others or for contributions to the community were labeled "care exemplars" and compared to a matched group of youth not committed to the community (Hart & Fegley, 1995). The care exemplars were more likely than the comparison youth to describe themselves in terms reflective of moral characteristics, to show commitment to both their heritage and to the future of their community, to see themselves as reflecting the ideals of both themselves and their parents, and to stress the importance of personal philosophies and beliefs for their self-definitions (Hart & Fegley, 1995).

In sum, then, Damon (1997) envisions that by embedding youth in a community where service and responsible leadership are possible, the creation of community-specific youth charters can enable adolescents and adults to, together, systematically promote positive youth development. Youth charters can create opportunities to actualize both individual and community goals to eliminate risk behaviors among adolescents and promote in them the ability to contribute to high-quality individual and community life. Through community youth charters, youth and adults may work together to create a system wherein civil society is maintained and perpetuated (Damon, 1997; Damon & Gregory, 2003).

The Contributions of Search Institute

What, precisely, must be brought together by communities to ensure the promotion of positive youth development? Researchers at Search Institute in Minneapolis, Minnesota, believe that what is needed is the application of "assets" (Benson, 1997; Benson, Leffert, Scales, & Blyth, 1998; Leffert et al., 1998; Scales & Leffert, 1999). That is, they stress that positive youth development is furthered when actions are taken to enhance the strengths of a person (e.g., a commitment to learning, a healthy sense of identity), a family (e.g., caring attitudes toward children, rearing styles that both empower youth and set boundaries and provide expectations for positive growth), and a community (e.g., social support, programs that provide access to the resources for education, safety, and mentorship available in a community) (Benson, 1997).

Accordingly, researchers at Search Institute, led by its president, Peter L. Benson, believe there are both internal and external attributes that comprise the developmental assets needed by youth. Through their research they have identified 40 such assets, 20 internal ones and 20 external ones. Benson and his colleagues have found that the more developmental assets possessed by an adolescent, the greater is his or her likelihood of positive, healthy development.

For instance, in a study of 99,462 youth in grades 6 through 12 in public and/or alternative schools from 213 U.S. cities and towns who were assessed during the 1996–1997 academic year for their possession of the 40 assets, Leffert et al. (1998) found that the more assets present among youth, the lower the likelihood of alcohol use, depression/suicide risk, and violence. Consistent with Benson's (1997) view of the salience of developmental assets for promoting healthy behavior among young people, Leffert et al. (1998) illustrate the importance of the asset approach in work aimed at promoting positive development in our nation's children and adolescents. This congruence strengthens the argument for the critical significance of a focus on developmental assets in the promotion of positive youth development and, as such, in the enhancement of the capacity and commitment of young people to contribute to civil society.

Other data gathered by Benson and his colleagues provide direct support for this argument. Scales et al. (2000) measured thriving among 6,000 youth in grades 6 to 12, evenly divided across six ethnic groups (American Indian, African American, Asian American, Latino, European American, and Multiracial). Thriving was defined as involving seven attributes: school success, leadership, valuing diversity, physical health, helping others, delay of gratification, and overcoming adversity. Most, if not all, of these attributes are linked to the presence of prosocial behavior (e.g., helping others, delay of gratification) and to the behaviors requisite for competently contributing to civil society (e.g., valuing diversity, leadership, overcoming adversity). The greater the number of developmental assets possessed by youth, the more likely they were to possess the attributes of thriving.

Other data support the importance of focusing on developmental assets in both understanding the bases of positive youth development and in using that knowledge to further civil society. Luster and McAdoo (1994) sought to identify the factors that contribute to individual differences in the cognitive competence of African American children in early elementary grades. Consistent with an asset-based approach to promoting the positive development of youth (Benson, 1997; Scales & Leffert, 1999), they found that favorable outcomes in cognitive and socioemotional development were associated with high scores on an advantage index. This index was formed by scoring children on the basis of the absence of risk factors (e.g., pertaining to poverty or problems in the quality of the home environment) and the presence of more favorable circumstances in their lives.

Luster and McAdoo (1994) reported that, whereas only 4% of the children in their sample who scored low on the advantage index had high scores on a measure of vocabulary, 44% of the children who had high scores on the advantage index had high vocabulary scores. Similar contrasts between low and high scorers on the advantage index were found in regard to measures of math achievement (14% versus 37%, respectively), word recognition (0% versus 35%, respectively), and word meaning (7% versus 46%, respectively).

Luster and McAdoo (1996) extended the findings of their 1994 research. Seeking to identify the factors that contribute to individual differences in the educational attainment of African American young adults of low socioeconomic status, Luster and McAdoo (1996) found that assets linked with the individual (cognitive competence, academic motivation, and personal adjustment in kindergarten) and the context (parental involvement in school) were associated longitudinally with academic achievement and educational attainment.

Research reported by Search Institute, as well as data provided by other scholars (e.g., Furrow, Wagener, Leffert, & Benson, 2003), indicate clearly that individual and contextual assets of youth are linked to their positive development. These data legitimate the idea that the enhancement of such assets—the provision of such developmental "nutrients" (Benson, 2003)—will be associated with the promotion of positive youth development. Importantly, Benson and his colleagues (e.g., Scales et al., 2000) link these assets for positive youth development to effective, community-based programs:

> Time spent in youth programs [was the developmental asset that] appeared to have the most pervasive positive influence in [being a]...predictor of...thriving outcomes...Good youth programs...provide young people with access to caring adults and responsible peers, as well as skill-building activities than can reinforce the values and skills that are associated with doing well in school and maintaining good physical skills. (Scales et al., 2000, p. 43)

Accordingly, policies must be directed to designing, bringing to scale, evaluating, and sustaining programs effective in the provision of developmental assets and in using those assets to promote positive development and, ideally, thriving (Lerner, 2002a, 2002b). As such, it is important to understand the principles behind, and characteristics of, such programs.

Designing Programs That Promote Positive Youth Development

Programs promote positive youth development when they instill in youth attributes of competence, such as self-efficacy, resilience, or social, cognitive, behavioral, and moral competence; attributes of confidence, such as self-determination and a clear and positive identity; attributes of social connection, such as bonding; and attributes of character, such as spirituality and a belief in the future (Catalano et al., 1999). In addition, programs promote positive youth development when they promote ecological assets related to empowerment, such as recognition for a young person's positive behaviors, provision of opportunities for prosocial involvement, and support of prosocial norms or standards for healthy behavior (Catalano et al., 1999). In this regard, Roth and Brooks-Gunn (2003a) compare programs that seek to promote the five Cs—that is, programs that are aimed at youth *development*—with programs that just have a youth focus but are not developmental in orientation and, in particular, are not aimed at the promotion of positive development. Roth and Brooks-Gunn (2003a) note that the former, youth development programs, are "more successful in improving participants' competence, confidence, and connections" (p. 217).

The "Big Three" Components of Effective Youth Development Programs

What are the specific actions taken by youth development programs that make them effective in promoting the five Cs? Catalano et al. (1999) found that the preponderant majority (about 75%) of effective positive youth development programs focus on the "Big Three" design features of effective positive youth development programs (Eccles & Gootman, 2002; Roth & Brooks-Gunn, 2003a, 2003b). That is, the program provides (1) opportunities for youth participation in and leadership of activities; that (2) emphasize the development of life skills; within the context of (3) a sustained and caring adult–youth relationship.

For instance, Catalano et al. (1999) note that effective positive youth development programs "targeted healthy bonds between youth and adults, increased opportunities for youth participation in positive social activities, . . . [involved] recognition and reinforcement for that participation" (p. vi), and often used skills training as a youth competency strategy. These characteristics of effective positive youth development programs are similar to those identified by Roth and Brooks-Gunn (2003b), who noted that such programs transcend an exclusive focus on the prevention of health-compromising behaviors to include attempts to inculcate behaviors that stress youth competencies and abilities through "increasing participants' exposure to supportive and empowering environments where activities create multiple opportunities for a range of skill-building and horizon-broadening experiences" (p. 94). In addition, Roth and Brooks-Gunn (2003a) indicate that the activities found in these programs offer both "formal and informal opportunities for youth to nurture their interests and talents, practice new skills, and gain a sense of personal and group recognition. Regardless of the specific activity, the emphasis lies in providing real challenges and active participation" (p. 204).

In this regard, Roth and Brooks-Gunn (2003a) note that when these activities are coupled with an environment that creates an atmosphere of hope for a positive future among youth, when the program "conveys the adults' beliefs in youth as resources to be developed rather than as problems to be managed" (p. 204), then the goals of promoting positive youth development are likely to be reached. In other words, when activities that integrate skill-building opportunities and active participation occur in the presence of positive and supportive adult ← → youth relations, positive development will occur.

Blum (2003) agrees. He notes that effective youth programs offer to youth activities through which to form relationships with caring adults, relations that elicit hope in young people. When these programs provide as well the opportunity for youth to participate in community development activities, positive youth development occurs (Blum, 2003).

The role of positive adult ← → youth relationships has been underscored as well by Rhodes (2002; Rhodes & Roffman, 2003). Focusing on volunteer mentoring relationships, for instance, Rhodes and Roffman (2003) note that these nonparental "relationships can positively influence a range of outcomes, including improvements in peer and parental relationships, academic achievement, and self-concept; lower recidivism rates among juvenile delinquents; and reductions in substance abuse" (p. 227).

However, Rhodes and Roffman (2003) also note that there is a developmental course to these effects of volunteer mentoring on youth. When young people are in relationships that last a year or longer, they are most likely to experience improvements in academic, psychological, social, and behavioral characteristics. On the other hand, when youth are in relationships that last only between 6 and 12 months, fewer positive outcomes of mentoring are evident. When young people are in mentoring relationships that end relatively quickly, it appears that mentoring may actually be detrimental. Decrements in positive functioning have been reported in such circumstances (Rhodes, 2002; Rhodes & Roffman, 2003).

Of course, parents may also serve as the adults in positive adult ← → youth relations. Bornstein (2003) notes that the positive influences of parents on their children's healthy development may be enhanced when parents have several "tools" to facilitate their effective parenting behaviors. These tools include possessing accurate knowledge about child and adolescent development, being skilled at observing their children, possessing strategies for discipline and for problem prevention, and being able to provide to their children effective supports for their emotional, social, cognitive, and language development. Another resource for positive parenting is for adults to have their own sources of social support (Bornstein, 2003).

In addition to the "Big Three" components of programs that effectively support positive youth development, there are, of course, other important characteristics of programs that are effective in promoting such development. Among these are the presence of clear goals; attention to the diversity of youth and of their family, community, and culture; assurance that the program represents a safe space for youth and that it is accessible to them; integration of the developmental assets within the community into the program; a collaborative approach to other youth-serving organizations and programs; contributing to the provision of a "seamless" social support across the community; engagement in program evaluation; and advocacy for youth (Dryfoos, 1990, 1998; Eccles & Gootman, 2002; Lerner, 1995; Little, 1993; Roth & Brooks-Gunn, 2003a; Schorr, 1988, 1997).

However, youth participation, adult mentorship, and skill building are the bedrocks upon which effective programs must be built. As we noted earlier,

Scales et al. (2000), in their survey of thriving—of exemplary positive youth development—among 6,000 youth participating in the 1999–2000 Search Institute survey of developmental assets, found that spending time in youth programs was the key developmental asset that promoted thriving.

In sum, the promotion of positive youth development has at its core the enhancement—through the civic engagement of young people—of the active contribution of the young person to both self and context, of the individual as an active producer of his or her own positive development (Lerner, 1982; Lerner & Busch-Rossnagel, 1981; Lerner, Theokas, & Jelicic, 2005; Lerner & Walls, 1999). As such, among the "Big Three" characteristics of effective youth programs, youth participation and leadership would seem to be most critical for fostering such active contributions. When such participation engages the young person in taking actions that serve both self and context (i.e., when the young person behaves to both enhance his or own life and to be positively civically engaged), positive youth development (thriving) in the direction of an ideal adulthood should be seen. This linkage between youth participation and civic engagement is becoming a prominent part of the youth development field. For instance, as noted by Wheeler (2003):

> The rediscovery of youth leadership development as a core component of positive youth development (PYD) strategies and programs, however, has an even more significant impact: It validates a growing recognition within the philanthropic community and among leadership theorists that personal development and social development are essential conditions for strengthening a community's capacity to respond to its problems and build its future. (p. 491)

She goes on to indicate that "a complementary strategy is civic activism, which has reemerged as a viable means for young people to develop and exercise leadership while effecting concrete changes in their communities" (p. 492).

Consistent with the vision of Wheeler (2003), Kirshner, O'Donoghue, and McLaughlin (2002) define youth participation as "a constellation of activities that empower adolescents to take part in and influence decision making that affects their lives and to take action on issues they care about" (p. 5). However, when youth participation occurs in and is enabled by either community-based organizations or the institutions of civil society, it should involve actions pertinent to both self and context. In other words, when youth participation reflects the adaptive individual ← → context relations indicative of thriving and predicated on the synthesis of moral and civic identity within a young person, it may be characterized as civic engagement.

As such, we may extend Kirschner et al.'s (2002) definition of youth participation by linking it to the conception of youth participation presented more than a quarter century earlier by the National Commission on Resources for Youth (1975), wherein youth participation was seen as "involving youth in responsible, challenging action, that meets genuine needs, with opportunity for planning and/or decision making affecting others, in an activity whose impact or consequences extend to others, i.e., outside or beyond the youth themselves" (p. 25). In the context of this conception, youth participation is a core component of civil society (Camino & Zeldin, 2002). As Wheeler (2003) stresses, "Participating as civic activists often becomes the path or gateway to a lifetime of public service" (p. 495).

Skelton, Boyte, and Leonard (2002) agree. They point out that beginning in the mid 1990s there has been a growing awareness "of the need to stress more public and political dimensions of youth civic engagement" (p. 9). Skelton et al. (2002) note that there are four indicators of this emerging stress on the civic contributions made through youth participation. These dimensions of youth civic engagement include (1) the recognition that youth are not future citizens but are citizens in the here and now; (2) the idea that young people do not just engage in individual volunteering but, instead, are collaborators within a diverse community of engaged citizens; (3) youth engagement in the actual work of contributing to the enhancement of society; and (4) the development within a young person not only of civic values but also of skills and capacities pertinent to contributing to civil society.

Skelton et al. (2002) indicate that these skills and capacities include "taking responsibility for decisions and choices; learning to speak publicly; the capacity to thoughtfully listen; and working as a team with a diverse group" (p. 9). Skelton and colleagues also contend that when a young person develops such skills, he or she will "discover how he or she fits into and shapes a flourishing demo-cratic society" (p. 9). Camino and Zeldin (2002) explain that the effectiveness for positive youth development of the pathways that exist for becoming civically engaged may be enhanced in several ways. These enhancements occur (1) when youth take "ownership" of their participation (that is, when—consistent with the developmental systems theory notion that individuals are producers of their own development—the young person shapes his or her role, instead of having it "given to" or imposed on him or her; Lerner, 1982; Lerner et al., 2005); (2) when civic engagement occurs within the context of healthy and sustained youth–adult partnerships (i.e., when, as in the 4-H model of youth programming, this instance of the "Big Three" design features of effective youth programs occurs); and (3) when youth civic engagement is facilitated by supportive social and institutional polices.

From Programs to Policies Promoting Positive Youth Development

If programs are to be successful in addressing the combined individual and contextual influences on youth, and, in turn, if they are to be associated with positive youth development, it is reasonable to believe that they must engage all levels within the developmental system (Benson, 1997, 2003; Benson et al., 2004; Lerner, 1995; Pittman, 1996; Pittman & Irby, 1995; Pittman, Irby, & Cahill, 1995; Trickett, Barone, & Buchanan, 1996). In other words, effective programs engage the system of individual and contextual variables affecting youth development.

By involving multiple characteristics of the young person—for instance, his or her developmental level, knowledge of risk taking, intrapersonal re-sources (e.g., self-esteem, self-competence, beliefs, and values), interpersonal management skills (e.g., being able to engage useful social support and prosocial behaviors from peers)—successful risk prevention programs may be developed (Levitt, Selman, & Richmond, 1991). However, as emphasized by the positive youth development perspectives, programs must do more than diminish risk. They must emphasize the strengths and assets of young people, that is, their capacities for positive development, their possession of attributes—*strengths*—that keep them moving forward in a positive developmental path.

Such strengths involve individual attributes, such as self-esteem, spirituality, religiosity, knowledge, skills, and motivation to do well (e.g., Benson, 1997, 2003). In addition, these strengths are constituted by contextual characteristics such as relations with parents, with other adults, with friends, and with community organizations that are marked by providing models for positive values, providing boundaries and expectations, promoting health and encouraging positive growth, instilling a climate of love and caring and providing youth with a sense of hope for the future, offering positive links to the community, providing opportunities for the constructive use of time, and providing a safe environment that is free of prejudice and discrimination. These individual and contextual strengths are, in essence, the assets for healthy development that are described by Search Institute (e.g., Benson, 1997, 2003; Scales & Leffert, 1999) and others (e.g., Blum, 2003; Bornstein, 2003; Catalano et al., 1999; Damon, 1997; Damon et al., 2003; Damon & Gregory, 2003; King & Furrow, 2004; Lerner et al., 2000; Roth & Brooks-Gunn, 2003a). Focus on these assets provides a means to envision the key features of successful youth programs, ones associated with healthy adolescent development.

How might this knowledge of program components be more effectively used to devise social policy changes that would maximize the fit between the idealized developmental pathways depicted in the theory of exemplary positive youth development—thriving—and the actual life courses of young people? Policies reflect what a people value, what they believe is right; policies tell people where resources will be invested and what actions will be taken in support of beliefs and values. What is the action agenda that may be derived legitimately from the positive youth development theory we present, of the ideas and research evidence linking moral and civic identity and thriving?

A useful developmental theory is not just a means for integrating data about what "is" in human life. As suggested by Bronfenbrenner (1974), the idealization of the course of life represented in a useful developmental theory provides a means for the scientist to generate data about what "might be" in human life. Such an approach also has import for social action and public policy. The key to ensuring the positive development of youth—development marked by the emergence of an integrated moral and civic identity that results in contributions to self, family, community, and ultimately civil society—rests on developing policies that strengthen in diverse communities the capacities of families to raise healthy, thriving children. We will describe a set of policy principles and policy recommendations that support such family-centered community building for youth (Gore, 2003; Gore & Gore, 2002).

There are three key principles within the theory of positive youth development we suggest (Lerner, 2004). The first two principles are that any policy pertinent to young people must be based on the presence of strengths among *all* young people and the potential to enhance these strengths through supporting their healthy development. In other words, policies must be developmental and positive in their orientation to young people. Accordingly, deficits and their prevention should be placed on the back burner of the policy-making agenda, and focus should be given to how we can, at each point in the young person's life, find age-appropriate ways to support positive development by building on his or her specific set of strengths.

Benson et al. (2004) agree with this perspective, noting that public policies for youth need to be sensitive to the development status and pathways of youth, and that policies must reflect the tenets of theory and practice defining the positive youth development perspective. For example, policies that are useful for building skills in elementary school age children (e.g., regarding basic literacy abilities in language, science, civics, mathematics, and health) may not be appropriate for youth in the midst of adolescence (who may need to possess advanced skills in the above-named domains and, as well, who may be actively using these skills in interpersonal, for instance, dating, situations, in part-time employment positions, and in service in their communities) or for older youth who are contemplating the transition from high school to work or military service (e.g., see Hamilton & Hamilton, 2004).

Accordingly, Benson et al. (2004) indicate that if policies for youth are to be both developmentally appropriate and embrace the cutting edge of science and practice of the field of positive youth development, then first, policies must move beyond negative outcomes and academic success; they must encompass both positive and nonacademic outcomes. Second, public policies should involve both children and adolescents, and view more integratively the development of young people across the first two decades of life. Third, policies must provide a broad range of services, supports, and opportunities to young people. Fourth, Benson et al. note that young people must be regarded as agents of positive change: Their voices and actions should contribute centrally to developmental policy.

A third principle of policy design associated with the theory of positive youth development under discussion here is to focus policy on the dynamic relation between the developing youth and his or her context, on the individual ← → context relation, and not on person or context per se. If adaptive human development involves reciprocal links between the engaged and active individual and his or her supportive and changing context, then policies should be focused on strengthening these relations. Put simply, to produce and further the thriving youth ← → civil society relations upon which liberty is predicated, policies must be directed to these relations.

Focusing just on the young person without attending to development within a specific family, community, and cultural context will fail to improve development; such focus will not be sensitive to the specific individual ← → context relations elicited by the person's and the setting's characteristics of individuality. Focusing on just the context without attention to the developmental attributes of the growing individual also will fail to improve his or her development; such focus is not likely to have a better than random chance of attaining a goodness of fit with the individual's characteristics of individuality and developmental status.

While it is of course the case that a particular policy may seem to be situated logically at the level of either individual or context, this third principle indicates that this focus may be more apparent than real. The education of children and adolescents may serve as an example. Enhancing the knowledge or literacy skills of youth per se is not really the goal of education, especially education financed by public dollars. Rather, the goal of education is to enhance the probability that our young people will become more competent and confident individuals, that they will use their knowledge to become people able to make valued contributions to their lives and to the lives of others. Education serves active citizenship, and, in turn, education for active citizenship should become a core ubiquitous feature of all of American education. In other words, the goal of education is *not* to make a child competent for the sake of possessing a competency; rather, it is to enable the child to be engaged with society in the exercise of his or her competency. Through education we should seek to increase the probability that individuals will become contributing members of society, productive agents within the thriving youth $\leftarrow \rightarrow$ civil society relation.

In sum, there are at least three essential principles for policy design legitimated by the present theory of positive development: Policies must take a strength-based approach to youth; policies should be developmental in nature; and policies should focus on (have as their target or unit of analysis) the individual $\leftarrow \rightarrow$ context relation.

When these three principles are translated into ideas for specific policies, they result in the formulation of a set of ideas that engage the breadth of the developmental system involved in promoting positive youth development. They integrate the developing young person, his or her family, the community, and all facets of civil society in the active promotion of positive youth development and, ideally, in producing the thriving youth $\leftarrow \rightarrow$ civil society relation.

Conclusions

The present theory of dynamic, person $\leftarrow \rightarrow$ context relations provides a model for the general structure of policies that would promote both positive youth development and civil society, that is, the thriving youth $\leftarrow \rightarrow$ civil society relation. The model is founded on the idea that the plasticity of youth development constitutes a basic strength in all young people; plasticity constitutes a potential for systematic change, and by appropriately supporting the strengths of young people, they may develop in positive directions. The model suggests as well that appropriate support for youth involves providing the developmental assets needed for furthering their healthy—indeed, exemplary—development. Developmental assets, in short, are the nutrients for positive development, and providing them to young people fosters youth thriving. As previously stated, these assets may be developed through three "big" actions associated with programs that are effective in promoting positive youth development: providing youth with positive and supportive relationships with adults; affording youth opportunities to build the skills needed to make productive contributions to self, family, community, and civil society; and supplying youth with opportunities to be civically engaged and to take leadership roles in enacting skills and in making contributions to their communities. Moreover, when youth develop within families and communities that ensure these important assets for their positive development, they will thrive during their adolescence: They will be on a developmental path toward an ideal adult status, a status marked by making productive contributions to self and others and to the institutions of civil society.

The five Cs of positive youth development may be best thought of as clusters of individual attributes, for example, intellectual ability and social and behavioral skills (competence); positive bonds with people and institutions (connection); integrity, moral centeredness, and spirituality (character); positive self-regard, a sense of self-efficacy, and courage (confidence); and humane values, empathy, and a sense of social justice (caring/compassion) (Roth & Brooks-Gunn, 2003a). When these five sets of outcomes are developed, civil society is enhanced as a consequence of young people becoming adults morally and civically committed to providing the assets they received to succeeding generations.

How does one develop and implement a youth policy? At least four interrelated sets of actions need to be taken:

- First, we need to articulate the principles that should guide our specification of the particular policies that will be derived from our vision of positive youth development and, more concretely, from our theoretical model;
- Second, we need to develop a set or sets of specific policies that may be derived from our model;
- Third, we need to devise strategies for translating our vision and specific policy ideas into effective actions; and
- Finally, we need to take action; we need to become active participants in the political process within our democracy.

Authors' Note

The preparation of this paper was supported in part by grants from the National 4-H Council and by the William T. Grant Foundation.

References

Benson, P. (1997). *All kids are our kids: What communities must do to raise caring and responsible children and adolescents.* San Francisco: Jossey-Bass.

Benson, P. L. (2003). Developmental assets and asset-building community: Conceptual and empirical foundations. In R. M. Lerner & P. L. Benson (Eds.), *Developmental assets and asset-building communities: Implications for research, policy, and practice* (pp. 19–43). New York: Kluwer Academic/Plenum.

Benson, P. L., Leffert, N., Scales, P. C., & Blyth, D. A. (1998). Beyond the "village" rhetoric: Creating healthy communities for children and adolescents. *Applied Developmental Science, 2*(3), 138–159.

Benson, P. L., Mannes, M., Pittman, K., & Ferber, T. (2004). Youth development, developmental assets, and public policy. In R. M. Lerner & L. Steinberg (Eds.), *Handbook of adolescent psychology* (2nd ed., pp. 781–814). New York: Wiley.

Blum, R. W. (2003). Positive youth development: A strategy for improving health. In F. Jacobs, D. Wertlieb, & R. M. Lerner (Eds.), *Handbook of applied developmental science: Promoting positive child, adolescent, and family development through research, policies, and programs: Vol. 2. Enhancing the life chances of youth and families: Public service systems and public policy perspectives* (pp. 237–252). Thousand Oaks, CA: Sage.

Bornstein, M. H. (2003). Positive parenting and positive development in children. In R. M. Lerner, F. Jacobs, & D. Wertlieb (Eds.), *Handbook of applied developmental science: Promoting positive child, adolescent, and family development through research, policies, and programs: Vol. 1. Applying developmental science for youth and families: Historical and theoretical foundations* (pp. 187–209). Thousand Oaks, CA: Sage.

Bornstein, H. H., Davidson, L., Keyes, C. M., Moore, K., & the Center for Child Well-being (Eds.). (2003). *Well-being: Positive development across the life course.* Mahwah, NJ: Erlbaum.

Bronfenbrenner, U. (1974). Developmental research, public policy, and the ecology of childhood. *Child Development, 45,* 1–5.

Camino, L., & Zeldin, S. (2002). From periphery to center: Pathways for youth civic engagement in the day-to-day life of communities. *Applied Developmental Science, 6,* 213–220.

Catalano, R. F., Berglund, M. L., Ryan, J. A. M., Lonczak, H. S., & Hawkins, J. D. (1999). *Positive youth development in the United States: Research findings on evaluations of youth development programs.* Washington, DC: U.S. Department of Health and Human Services.

Cummings, E. (2003) Foreword. In D. Wertlieb, F. Jacobs, & R. M. Lerner (Eds.), *Handbook of applied developmental science: Promoting positive child, adolescent, and family development through research, policies, and programs: Vol. 3. Promoting positive youth and family development: Community systems, citizenship, and civil society* (pp. ix–xi). Thousand Oaks, CA: Sage.

Damon, W. (1988). *The moral child.* New York: Free Press.

Damon, W. (1997). *The youth charter: How communities can work together to raise standards for all our children.* New York: Free Press.

Damon, W., & Gregory, A. (2003). Bringing in a new era in the field of youth development. In R. M. Lerner, F. Jacobs, & D. Wertlieb (Eds.), *Handbook of applied developmental science: Promoting positive child, adolescent, and family development through research, policies, and programs: Vol. 1. Applying developmental science for youth and families: Historical and theoretical foundations* (pp. 407–420). Thousand Oaks, CA: Sage.

Damon, W., Menon, J., & Bronk, K. C. (2003). The development of purpose during adolescence. *Applied Developmental Science, 7,* 119–128.

Dowling, E., Gestsdottir, S., Anderson, P., von Eye, A., Almerigi, J., & Lerner, R. M. (2004). Structural relations among spirituality, religiosity, and thriving in adolescence. *Applied Developmental Science, 8*(1), 7–16.

Dowling, E., Gestsdottir, S., Anderson, P., von Eye, A., & Lerner, R. M. (2003). Spirituality, religiosity, and thriving among adolescents: Identification and confirmation of factor structures. *Applied Developmental Science, 7*(4), 253–260.

Dryfoos, J. G. (1990). *Adolescents at risk: Prevalence and prevention.* New York: Oxford University Press.

Dryfoos, J. G. (1998). *Safe passage: Making it through adolescence in a risky society.* New York: Oxford University Press.

Eccles, J., & Gootman, J. A. (Eds.). (2002). *Community programs to promote youth development.* Washington, DC: National Academy Press.

Engler, J., & Binsfeld, C. (1998). Partnership in action: The governor's clergy summit in the city of Detroit. In R. M. Lerner & L. A. K. Simon (Eds.), *University-community collaborations for the twenty-first century: Outreach scholarship for youth and families* (pp. 451–459). New York: Garland.

Furrow, J., Wagener, L. M., Leffert, N., & Benson, P. L. (2003). *The measurement of developmental assets in youth and the structure of a self-report survey: Search Institute Profiles of Student Life.* Unpublished manuscript. Pasadena, CA: Fuller Theological Seminary.

Gore, A. (2003). Foreword. In R. M. Lerner & P. L. Benson (Eds.), *Developmental assets and asset-building communities: Implications for research, policy, and practice* (pp. vii–ix). New York: Kluwer Academic/Plenum.

Gore, A., & Gore, T. (2002). *Joined at the heart: The transformation of the American family.* New York: Henry Holt.

Gottlieb, G. (1997). *Synthesizing nature-nurture: Prenatal roots of instinctive behavior.* Mahwah, NJ: Erlbaum.

Gottlieb, G. (1998). Normally occurring environmental and behavioral influences on gene activity: From central dogma to probabilistic epigenesis. *Psychological Review, 105,* 792–802.

Hall, G. (1904). *Adolescence.* New York: Appleton.

Hamilton, S. F., & Hamilton, M. A. (2004). Contexts for mentoring: Adolescent–adult relationships in workplaces and communities. In R. M. Lerner & L. Steinberg (Eds.), *Handbook of adolescent psychology* (2nd ed., pp. 395–428). New York: Wiley.

Hart, D., & Fegley, S. (1995). Prosocial behavior and caring in adolescence: Relations to self-understanding and social judgement. *Child Development, 66,* 1346–1359.

Hoyle, R. H., & Leff, S. S. (1997). The role of parental involvement in youth sport participation and performance. *Adolescence, 32*(125), 233–243.

King, P. E., & Furrow, J. L. (2004). Religion as a resource for positive youth development: Religion, social capital, and moral outcomes. *Developmental Psychology, 40*(5), 703–713.

Kirshner, B., O'Donoghue, J. L., & McLaughlin, M. (Eds.). (2002). *New directions for youth development: Vol. 96. Youth participation: Improving institutions and communities.* Editor in chief: G. G. Noam. San Francisco: Jossey-Bass.

Leffert, N., Benson, P. L., Scales, P. C., Sharma, A. R., Drake, D. R., & Blyth, D. A. (1998). Developmental assets: Measurement and prediction of risk behaviors among adolescents. *Applied Developmental Science, 2,* 209–230.

Lerner, R. M. (1982). Children and adolescents as producers of their own development. *Developmental Review, 2,* 342–370.

Lerner, R. M. (1995). *America's youth in crisis: Challenges and options for programs and policies.* Thousand Oaks, CA: Sage.

Lerner, R. M. (Ed). (1998a). *Handbook of child psychology: Vol. 1. Theoretical models of human development* (5th ed.). Editor in chief: W. Damon. New York: Wiley.

Lerner, R. M. (1998b). Theories of human development: Contemporary perspectives. In R. M. Lerner (Ed.), *Handbook of child psychology: Vol. 1. Theoretical models of human development* (5th ed., pp. 1–24). Editor in chief: W. Damon. New York: Wiley.

Lerner, R. M. (2002a). *Concepts and theories of human development* (3rd ed.). Mahwah, NJ: Erlbaum.

Lerner, R. M. (2002b). *Adolescence: Development, diversity, context, and application.* Upper Saddle River, NJ: Prentice-Hall.

Lerner, R. M. (2004). *Liberty: Thriving and civic engagement among America's youth.* Thousand Oaks, CA: Sage.

Lerner, R. M., Brentano, C., Dowling, E. M., & Anderson, P. M. (2002). Positive youth development: Thriving as a basis of personhood and civil society. In R. M. Lerner, C. S. Taylor, & A. von Eye (Eds.), *New directions for youth development: Vol. 95. Theory, practice and research: Pathways to positive development among diverse youth* (pp. 11–34). Editor in chief: G. Noam. San Francisco: Jossey-Bass.

Lerner, R. M., & Busch-Rossnagel, N. A. (Eds.). (1981). *Individuals as producers of their development: A life-span perspective.* New York: Academic Press.

Lerner, R. M., Fisher, C. B., & Weinberg, R. A. (2000). Toward a science for and of the people: Promoting civil society through the application of developmental science. *Child Development, 71,* 11–20.

Lerner, R. M., Sparks, E., & McCubbin, L. (1999). *Family diversity and family policy: Strengthening families for America's children.* Norwell, MA: Kluwer Academic.

Lerner, R. M., Theokas, C., & Jelicic, H. (2005). Youth as active agents in their own positive development: A developmental systems perspective. In W. Greve, K. Rothermund, & D. Wentura (Eds.), *The adaptive self: Personal continuity and intentional self-development* (pp. 31–47). Göttingen, Germany: Hogrefe/Huber.

Lerner, R. M., & Walls, T. (1999). Revisiting individuals as producers of their development: From dynamic interactionism to developmental systems. In J. Brandtstädter & R. M. Lerner (Eds.), *Action and self-development: Theory and research through the life span* (pp. 3–36). Thousand Oaks, CA: Sage.

Levitt, M. Z., Selman, R. L., & Richmond, J. B. (1991). The psychosocial foundations of early adolescents' high-risk behavior: Implications for research and practice. *Journal of Research on Adolescence, 1*(4), 349–378.

Little, R. R. (1993, March). *What's working for today's youth: The issues, the programs, and the learnings.* Paper presented at the ICYF Fellows Colloquium, Michigan State University, East Lansing.

Luster, T., & McAdoo, H. P. (1994). Factors related to the achievement and adjustment of young African American children. *Child Development, 65,* 1080–1094.

Luster, T., & McAdoo, H. (1996). Family and child influences on educational attainment: A secondary analysis of the High/Scope Perry Preschool data. *Developmental Psychology, 32*(1), 26–39.

National Commission on Resources for Youth. (1975). *Youth participation: A concept paper* (RFY Reports). New York: Author.

Overton, W. F. (1998). Developmental psychology: Philosophy, concepts, and methodology. In R. M. Lerner (Ed.), *Handbook of child psychology: Vol. 1. Theoretical models of human development* (5th ed., pp. 107–187). Editor in chief: W. Damon. New York: Wiley.

Pittman, K. (1996). Community, youth, development: Three goals in search of connection. *New Designs for Youth Development,* Winter, 4–8.

Pittman, K., & Irby, M. (1995, December). *Promoting investment in life skills for youth: Beyond indicators for survival and problem prevention.* Paper presented at Monitoring and Measuring the State of Children: Beyond Survival, an Interactional Workshop. Jerusalem, Israel.

Pittman, K., Irby, M., & Cahill, M. (1995). *Mixing it up: Participatory evaluation as a tool for generating parent and community empowerment.* Cambridge, MA: Harvard Family Research Project.

Pittman, K., Irby, M., & Ferber, T. (2001). Unfinished business: Further reflections on a decade of promoting youth development. In P. L. Benson & K. J. Pittman (Eds.), *Trends in youth development: Visions, realities and challenges* (pp. 4–50). Norwell, MA: Kluwer Academic.

Rhodes, J. E. (2002). *Stand by me: The risks and rewards of mentoring today's youth.* Cambridge, MA: Harvard University Press.

Rhodes, J. E., & Roffman, J. G. (2003). Relationship-based interventions: The impact of mentoring and apprenticeship on youth development. In F. Jacobs, D. Wertlieb, & R. M. Lerner (Eds.), *Handbook of applied developmental science: Promoting positive child, adolescent, and family development through research, policies, and programs: Vol. 2. Enhancing the life chances of youth and families: Public service systems and public policy perspectives* (pp. 225–236). Thousand Oaks, CA: Sage.

Roth, J. L., & Brooks-Gunn, J. (2003a). What is a youth development program? Identification and defining principles. In F. Jacobs, D. Wertlieb, & R. M. Lerner (Eds.), *Handbook of applied developmental science: Promoting positive child, adolescent, and family development through research, policies, and programs: Vol. 2. Enhancing the life chances of youth and families: Public service systems and public policy perspectives* (pp. 197–223). Thousand Oaks, CA: Sage.

Roth, J. L., & Brooks-Gunn, J. (2003b). What exactly is a youth development program? Answers from research and practice. *Applied Developmental Science, 7,* 94–111.

Roth, J., Brooks-Gunn, J., Murray, L., & Foster, W. (1998). Promoting healthy adolescents: Synthesis of youth development program evaluations. *Journal of Research on Adolescence, 8,* 423–459.

Scales, P. C., Benson, P. L., Leffert, N., & Blyth, D. A. (2000). The contribution of developmental assets to the prediction of thriving among adolescents. *Applied Developmental Science, 4,* 27–46.

Scales, P. C., & Leffert, N. (1999). *Developmental assets: A synthesis of the scientific research on adolescent development.* Minneapolis, MN: Search Institute.

Schorr, L. B. (1988). *Within our reach: Breaking the cycle of disadvantage.* New York: Doubleday.

Schorr, L. B. (1997). *Common purpose: Strengthening families and neighborhoods to rebuild America.* New York: Doubleday.

Sherrod, L., Flanagan, C., & Youniss, J. (Eds.). (2002a). Growing into citizenship: Multiple pathways and diverse influences [Special issue]. *Applied Developmental Science, 6*(4).

Sherrod, L., Flanagan, C., & Youniss, J. (2002b). Dimensions of citizenship and opportunities for youth development: The *what, why, when, where,* and *who* of citizenship development. *Applied Developmental Science, 6*(4), 264–272.

Skelton, N., Boyte, H., & Leonard, L. S. (2002). *Youth civic engagement: Reflections on an emerging public idea.* Minneapolis: University of Minnesota, Center for Democracy and Citizenship.

Trickett, E. J., Barone, C., & Buchanan, R. M. (1996). Elaborating developmental contextualism in adolescent research and intervention: Paradigm contributions from community psychology. *Journal of Research on Adolescence, 6,* 245–269.

Villarruel, F. A., Perkins, D. F., Borden, L. M., & Keith, J. G. (Eds.). (2003). *Community youth development: Programs, policies, and practices.* Thousand Oak, CA: Sage.

Wheeler, W. (2000). Emerging organizational theory and the youth development organization. *Applied Developmental Science, 4*(Suppl. 1), 47–54.

Wheeler, W. (2003). Youth leadership for development: Civic activism as a component of youth development programming and a strategy for strengthening civil society. In R. M. Lerner, F. Jacobs, & D. Wertlieb (Eds.), *Handbook of applied developmental science: Promoting positive child, adolescent, and family development through research, policies, and programs: Vol. 2. Enhancing the life chances of youth and families: Public service systems and public policy perspectives* (pp. 491–505). Thousand Oaks, CA: Sage.

Yates, M., & Youniss, J. (1996). Community service and political-moral identity in adolescents. *Journal of Research on Adolescence, 6*(3), 271–284.

Youniss, J., Yates, M., & Su, Y. (1997). Social integration: Community service and marijuana use in high school seniors. *Journal of Adolescent Research, 12*(2), 245–262.

3 The World of Adults Today: Implications for Positive Youth Development

Peter C. Scales

Search Institute

Most American adults are not playing the roles they could in promoting positive youth development. The focus of this chapter is not so much on the roles parents play, nor on the roles played by adults who have some occupational or legally defined relationship with young people, such as child care providers or teachers. We will allude to the roles parents and teachers, for example, can play in affecting the climate for greater engagement by other adults, but the focus of this chapter is largely on those other adults who complete young people's developmental ecology: the adults who are unrelated to them and not bound by law or contract to relate to them at all. What roles are the rest of these adults playing in promoting young people's positive development, what issues and trends affect the level of their engagement with other people's kids, and what can be done to maximize the contribution those adults can make to young people's well-being?

The Limited Involvement of Adults with Young People

> [A]lthough not everyone can offer youth a well-designed experience that builds their planning and decision-making skills, everyone can talk with adolescents, keep an eye on them when their parents are not around, protect them, and give them help when they need it. Everyone can help make youth feel valued and supported.
> —Scales & Leffert, 2004 (p. 14)

Research shows that children and adolescents benefit from having caring relationships with adults outside their own families (Rhodes & Roffman, 2003; Scales & Leffert, 2004). Previous research has shown, however, that only a minority of young people say they enjoy such extrafamilial relationships with adults. For example, in an aggregate sample of more than 217,000 6th- to 12th-grade students, only 40% said they had caring neighbors, and just 30% said they had adults in their lives who modeled positive, responsible behaviors (Search Institute, 2001). The figures were better in a sample of 4th to 6th graders, but even so, nearly half (45%) said they did not have caring neighbors or positive adult role models (Scales, Sesma, & Bolstrom, 2004).

Both positive and more troubling findings come from studies Search Institute has done with nationally representative samples of U.S. adults in 2000 and 2002. In the 2002 study, for example, 48% of adults said they had a good talk or did something with a child outside their own family at least once a week; but one-third said they only did this every few months or hardly ever. Moreover, only 23% said they very often have conversations with kids outside their family that allow both to really get to know each other. Just 29% of kids agree that most of the adults they know do this (Scales, Benson, & Mannes, 2002a, 2002b). The relative agreement between adults and adolescents leads to the dispiriting conclusion that no more than 30% of adults and unrelated youth, and quite probably less than that, are connecting at a meaningful level.

In the 2000 study, we asked adults how many young people they played, talked, or worked with on a regular basis, and only 42% said they did so with three or more. Another 34% reported never even seeing kids or seeing them but rarely talking, playing, or working with them. These figures include children or youth an adult worked with, making for a generous estimate inflated by those such as teachers or child care providers whose jobs put them in touch with numerous children every day. So only a minority of adults have *informal but regular* contact with at least three young people. Scales (2003) argued that regular contact with at least three kids is theoretically important because it suggests involvement is not just highly individualistic, idiosyncratic, or due to special circumstances. Rather, such levels of involvement may suggest that connecting with young people has become part of adults' routines, suggesting perhaps a "broader sense of responsibility for all young people, and feeling more capacity to act on that sense" (pp. 190–191). Certainly, the prevalence of social norms discouraging such relationships, as discussed below, arguably makes it impressive for an adult to form a connection with just one nonfamilial child. Nevertheless, the ability to establish *multiple* relationships with children outside one's family may reflect a greater commitment on that adult's part to the *principle* of sharing responsibility for raising the next generation.

The Weakness of Social Norms for Engagement with Young People

Several national studies Search Institute has conducted over the past few years of U.S. adults and adolescents ages 12 to 17 provide a sobering perspective on adults' engagement with unrelated young people (Scales, 2003; Scales et al., 2002a, 2002b). In brief, most adults think it is very important for them to engage positively with unrelated young people, but only a small minority of adults do so consistently in ways that can promote young people's well-being. For example, most adults say they encourage young people outside their families to take school seriously and do well, and teach young people widely shared values such as equality, honesty, and responsibility. But far fewer say they help unrelated young people with making decisions, or have meaningful conversations with them. Still fewer say they tell parents when their children do something wrong or good, or discuss their personal values with unrelated young people.

The disjunction between what adults believe it is important to do, and what they actually do in relating to young people, owes its existence to an absence of a strong social norm that promotes adult–youth engagement, as well as to the presence of strong norms that discourage such relationships. The responsibility for children's development is held by most adults, understandably, to lie primarily with parents. But that appropriate attribution to parents of the primary responsibility for children's well-being contributes to a cultural norm of disengagement with other people's kids so solid that the majority of adults are reluctant to get involved even in cases of clear parental maltreatment of children (Child Welfare League of America, 1999).

There seems to be little social support for getting positively involved with young people outside one's family, but quite a lot of perceived negative social consequences for getting involved where one perceives one is not welcome. Social science studies notwithstanding, high-profile popular culture influences such as the coverage given widespread sexual abuses by Catholic priests, or allegations of abuse by celebrities such as Michael Jackson, clearly do little to weaken the fears of most adults that the best policy with kids outside one's own family is distance. Given that social equation, only a minority of adults other than those in formal roles with children (e.g., child care providers, teachers) risk more than fairly superficial engagement.

The relative weakness of the social expectations for engagement with young people is important. Anthropologists have concluded that social norms help "stabilize" behavior by establishing "commitments to particular ways of acting in common situations" (Ensminger & Knight, 1997, p. 2). Social psychologists note, too, the role that abiding by perceived social norms has in helping individuals maintain a coherent and favorable self-image (Wood, 2001). This occurs in part because correctly perceiving and then doing what others expect them to do allows people to maintain or establish a sense of belonging to valued groups (Forsyth, 1999). Cialdini and Goldstein (2004) refer to these three motivations for explaining compliance and conformity as the need to perceive reality accurately, to affiliate, and to maintain a positive self-concept.

Perceived norms about a behavior, along with one's attitudes toward that behavior and the sense of perceived control one has over doing the behavior, generally have been found to predict *intentions* to do that behavior, and behavioral intentions are highly related to actual behavior (Azjen, 2001). Thus, even if one's attitudes are favorable, perceiving a strong restrictive norm about a behavior, especially if one's sense of perceived control is uncertain, can be sufficient to suppress that behavior in the maintenance of personal and group identity.

These elements appear to be operating to influence how adults relate with children and adolescents outside their own families. There is little obvious reward for getting engaged with other people's children, little if any sanction (as simple as social disapproval) for failing to do so, and a considerable amount of possible socially negative consequences an adult can imagine for getting involved. A prime example is one's interest in a child being considered, not noble and positive, but inappropriate and harmful. A focus group participant in our study of adult–youth engagement in several Kansas communities described this as occurring even among staff of a child care center. Those adults presumably have implicit permission to know all the children, not just the ones they immediately care for: "We were just talking ... the other day on how many of us have gotten that 'You Child Molester' stare ... " for greeting a child outside the center when the parents did not really know the child care worker (Mannes & Foster, 2004). The result of repeatedly experiencing or hearing about such interactions is another layer of cultural distance of adults from young people. In the process, countless meaningful opportunities are missed every day in neighborhoods and communities for adults to positively influence the development of all children and adolescents.

The Role of Developmental Assets in Positive Youth Development

The nature of those positive influences adults can provide and promote is explicated by Search Institute's framework of developmental assets (Benson, 1997; Benson, Scales, Hamilton, & Sesma, 2004; Benson, Scales, Leffert, & Roehlkepartain, 1999). The framework is a theoretical and applied approach to positive youth development that describes the building blocks of success that young people need for healthy development, and the dynamic person–context relations that define positive developmental trajectories (Benson, Leffert, Scales, & Blyth, 1998; Lerner, 2003). Forty assets have been identified (see Table 1) and grouped for communication purposes into eight broad categories, which are further delineated into "external" and "internal" assets: The former describe the relationships and opportunities that adults (and peers) provide for young people; the latter outline the values, skills, and self-perceptions young people develop over time to guide and regulate themselves.

An explicit tenet of the developmental assets framework is that the sources of core developmental processes—support, engagement, empowerment, belonging, affirmation, boundary setting, structure, and connectedness—are the broad socialization systems inherent in communities and the relational capacities of their residents. *Thus, asset building and social and community change are inextricably linked to maximize the contribution of socializing systems and residents to positive child and youth development* (Benson, Scales, & Mannes, 2003).

One implication of asset-oriented approaches to development is that much of the source of developmental assets is adults outside young people's own families. This includes adults with whom they have a formal relationship, such as teachers, but also those with whom they have informal relationships, such as neighbors; the adults they encounter in stores or parks; and the adults they interact with as a by-product of their involvement with youth organizations and

Table 1. Search Institute's Framework of 40 Developmental Assets

External Assets	Internal Assets

Support
1. **Family support**—Family life provides high levels of love and support.
2. **Positive family communication**— Young person and her or his parent(s) communicate positively, and young person is willing to seek advice and counsel from parent(s).
3. **Other adult relationships**—Young person receives support from three or more nonparent adults.
4. **Caring neighborhood**—Young person experiences caring neighbors.
5. **Caring school climate**—School provides a caring, encouraging environment.
6. **Parent involvement in schooling**—Parent(s) are actively involved in helping young person succeed in school.

Empowerment
7. **Community values youth**—Young person perceives that adults in the community value youth.
8. **Youth as resources**—Young people are given useful roles in the community.
9. **Service to others**—Young person serves in the community one hour or more per week.
10. **Safety**—Young person feels safe at home, at school, and in the neighborhood.

Boundaries and Expectations
11. **Family boundaries**—Family has clear rules and consequences, and monitors the young person's whereabouts.
12. **School boundaries**—School provides clear rules and consequences.
13. **Neighborhood boundaries**—Neighbors take responsibility for monitoring young people's behavior.
14. **Adult role models**—Parent(s) and other adults model positive, responsible behavior.
15. **Positive peer influence**—Young person's best friends model responsible behavior.
16. **High expectations**—Both parent(s) and teachers encourage the young person to do well.

Constructive Use of Time
17. **Creative activities**—Young person spends three or more hours per week in lessons or practice in music, theater, or other arts.

18. **Youth programs**—Young person spends three or more hours per week in sports, clubs, or organizations at school and/or in community organizations.
19. **Religious community**—Young person spends one or more hours per week in activities in a religious institution.
20. **Time at home**—Young person is out with friends "with nothing special to do," two or fewer nights per week.

Commitment to Learning
21. **Achievement motivation**—Young person is motivated to do well in school.
22. **School engagement**—Young person is actively engaged in learning.
23. **Homework**—Young person reports doing at least one hour of homework every school day.
24. **Bonding to school**—Young person cares about her or his school.
25. **Reading for pleasure**—Young person reads for pleasure three or more hours per week.

Positive Values
26. **Caring**—Young person places high value on helping other people.
27. **Equality and social justice**—Young person places high value on promoting equality and reducing hunger and poverty.
28. **Integrity**—Young person acts on convictions and stands up for her or his beliefs.
29. **Honesty**—Young person "tells the truth even when it is not easy."
30. **Responsibility**—Young person accepts and takes personal responsibility.
31. **Restraint**—Young person believes it is important not to be sexually active or to use alcohol or other drugs.

Social Competencies
32. **Planning and decision making**—Young person knows how to plan ahead and make choices.
33. **Interpersonal competence**—Young person has empathy, sensitivity, and friendship skills.
34. **Cultural competence**—Young person has knowledge of and comfort with people of different cultural/racial/ethnic backgrounds.

(cont.)

Table 1. (Continued)

External Assets	Internal Assets
35. **Resistance skills**—Young person can resist negative peer pressure and dangerous situations.	38. **Self-esteem**—Young person reports having a high self-esteem.
36. **Peaceful conflict resolution**—Young person seeks to resolve conflict nonviolently.	39. **Sense of purpose**—Young person reports that "my life has a purpose."
Positive Identity	40. **Positive view of personal future**—Young person is optimistic about her or his personal future.
37. **Personal power**—Young person feels he or she has control over "things that happen to me."	

congregations. Although research over the past decade has clearly documented the value of formal mentoring relationships for young people (see Rhodes & Roffman, 2003), the more global influence of these "other adult assets" that can occur quite naturally in young people's lives is potentially more far-reaching but has been less well studied. The limited data suggest a lack of such developmental attentiveness in the lives of most young people.

Young people derive even greater benefit when they experience assets *across* different life contexts, but such redundancy appears to be uncommon. For example, in Search Institute's study of a diverse sample of Colorado Springs, Colorado, youth, only 35% said they *consistently* experienced 11 behavioral expectations from "most" of their parents, teachers, neighbors, and other adults they knew (Scales et al., 2003). The expectations included such unexceptional admonitions as expecting youth to avoid the use of alcohol, help others, and try their best at school. Civic engagement is often named as a key value and behavior to promote in young people, but the adolescents in this study reported that helping others and contributing to the community were the expectations adults were *least* likely on a consistent basis to tell them are important.

Similarly, Scales (2003) found that only 15% of the more than 217,000 young people surveyed in the 1999–2000 school year were rich in "other adult" relationships (having 9–12 of 12 assets that adults other than parents can provide). This is important because for every increase in the quartile level of "other adult" assets (i.e., from 0–2 assets to 3–5, 6–8, and 9–12), young people were significantly less likely to engage in risky behavior patterns and significantly more likely to report thriving indicators. For example, 81% of those with 9–12 other adult assets said they valued diversity, versus 70% for those with 6–8 other adult assets, 59% of those with 3–5 of those assets, and just 47% of those with 0–2 other adult assets. Similarly, only 8% of those with 9–12 other adult assets reported problem alcohol use, compared with 16% for those with 6–8 of those assets, 25% of those with 3–5 of those assets, and 38% of those with just 0–2 of the other adult assets.

The Role of Social Trends in Affecting Patterns of Engagement with Young People

If adults' connection to young people outside their families is distressingly limited, we must ask how it has come to be so. Was there a time in recent U.S. history when things were different, when it was quite common for adults to have a clear sense of their reasonable responsibility for the well-being of unrelated children and youth, and when they acted commensurately on that sense of social expectation? It is quite difficult to answer such questions simply, because there are no earlier national data strictly comparable to the two Search Institute studies of adults conducted in 2000 and 2002. And yet a circumstantial case can be developed that suggests that there is less consensus today than in previous eras about the role unrelated adults can and should play in young people's development. For example, the chances that an adult will even casually encounter a young person today would appear to be less than in prior decades, simply due to demographic shifts. Children under 18 make up just 26% of the U.S. population today, versus 36% in 1960 (U.S. Department of Health and Human Services, 1998), and the proportion of households with children under 18 has declined even more, from 57% in 1960 to just 36% in 2000 (U.S. Bureau of the Census, 2001).

Time pressures have also increased among many adults. For example, the average commute time to and from work has increased 10% since 1990, to 50 minutes round-trip; and 10 million Americans commute 2 hours or more a day round-trip to work (McGuiken & Srinivasan, 2003). Such increases obviously affect how much discretionary time one has. In addition, although the hours worked by the average employee over the past 30 years have not increased overall (some groups have increased and some declined), the patterns for specific groups may well have had an impact on adults' involvement with unrelated young people. For example, women's labor force participation has of course changed dramatically. The average weekly hours worked by women rose 42% between 1976 and 1998, and the percentage of women with children 6–17 who worked *full-time* jumped from 26% in 1969 to 40% in 1998. The increases have come largely among the more educated and affluent mothers, who formerly would have been a core group providing volunteers for activities and programs for children and youth (Kundu, 1999).

Patterns of overall community involvement have changed as well, further distancing adults from the young. For example, religious congregations are arguably one of the few settings in which most adults can get to know unrelated young people under circumstances in which core values and beliefs are shared with others, an environment that invites rather than discourages interpersonal connection among adults and the young. And yet, among both adults and youth, attendance at religious services has declined over the past 30 years. Among 12th graders, for example, weekly attendance declined from 41% in 1976 to just 33% in 2001 (U.S. Department of Health and Human Services, 2003).

Putnam (2000) reported on a variety of data sources that suggest what he called a "striking diminution" of ordinary contact among friends and neighbors having meals, talking, or doing leisure activities together, as well as a decline in participation in organized leagues, clubs, and other kinds of civic connection. And there may be differences, too, in such connective patterns, depending on one's relationship status. For many of the not inconsiderable number of adults who are neither married nor in a satisfying relationship, the pursuit of meeting those personal needs likely takes precedence over connecting with other people's kids, and may get reflected in a retreat from traditional ways of meeting other adults in face-to-face settings, another form of decline of community.

For example, Hollander (2003) reported on a journalistic study of Internet dating services. He notes that 16.6 million people visited matchmaking Web sites in September 2002; describes the users as "apparently successful, attractive, and well educated"; and remarks that the abandonment of conventional ways of creating serious romantic relationships for so many people is just one more reflection of the "characteristics and problems of modernity, including the decline of community, the growth of social isolation (especially in major urban settings) and the tension between the demands of professional work and those of emotionally gratifying intimate personal relationships" (p. 69). He concludes by noting the "problem of heightened expectations" in modern society. Our society, says Hollander, produces a "way of life that provides an abundance of 'options' and is free of pressing material concerns but is weighted down by the imbalance between material need easily gratified and emotional ones largely unmet" (p. 77). Of course, not all people are free of "pressing material concerns," but Hollander's point about the relative lack of connective nourishment in the United States seems more generalizable.

Sustained and deep contact is needed for adults to contribute a meaningful positive influence to youth development. But the decline in civic involvements, from the purely personal (as in seeking romantic partners) to the more broadly social (as in participation in organized leagues or clubs) makes sustained and deep connection among adults and unrelated young people less likely. Arguably, this occurs in part because that decline has a deleterious impact both on the frequency of adult–youth contact and on the degree of trust adults share among themselves.

For example, the Knight Foundation's national Community Indicators study found that nearly two in three Americans (63%) said they knew none or only some of the names of the neighbors who live closest to them (Knight Foundation, 1999). If neighbors are lacking such basic information as each other's names, how likely are they to communicate about anything meaningful or personal? And without such communication, how likely is it that unrelated adults will feel a sense of permission to get involved with neighborhood kids?

Indeed, the degree to which adults communicate among themselves has long been shown to be a key part of the connective tissue that strengthens the developmental attentiveness of young people's overall environments (Bronfenbrenner, 1979; Price, Cioci, Penner, & Trautlein, 1993). In the absence of more naturally occurring communications, such as when we hardly know our closest neighbors' names, planned communication may be critical. This is why we suggested in *Other People's Kids* (Scales, 2003) that adults in neighborhoods and communities may benefit from intentionally talking about and defining their collective and personal "reasonable responsibility" for nurturing other people's kids, and what the social expectations should be that guide those relationships.

Volunteer activities are, of course, another possible way in which adults and youth can connect informally (and adults with other adults), in structured and/or supervised settings with at least implied permission that those relationships are acceptable. In our national studies, we have found that frequent volunteers are more likely to be highly engaged with unrelated young people than people who rarely or never volunteer. For example, in our 2002 study, we found that 46% of those who volunteer at least monthly report high personal engagement with unrelated young people, versus 14% for those who never volunteer (Scales et al., 2002b). Because this was a cross-sectional study, we cannot conclude that volunteering causes engagement with young people. It may be that those who volunteer and those who engage with other people's kids share common characteristics that cause the covariation, such as being female, or feeling a duty to contribute to society. On the other hand, the settings in which people choose to volunteer, from religious congregations to after-school programs and sports leagues, may structurally increase access to young people and therefore promote engagement.

Independent Sector surveys going back to 1987 suggest that about 50% of adults volunteer each year, a figure that has been roughly stable (i.e., between about 45% and 55%) over time (Independent Sector, 1999). And the percentage of adolescents who say they volunteer at least once a month increased between 1991 and 2001 for 8th, 10th, and 12th graders, significantly so for 12th graders, from 27% to 35% (Child Trends Data Bank, 2003). So, on the face of it, opportunities for adult–youth engagement through volunteering may not have lessened, and may even have increased some.

Although volunteering may not have declined over the past two decades, or at least not as much as other indicators of civic engagement, that is not the whole story. For one thing, the above figures show that volunteering is *not* characteristic of the great majority of either adults or young people.

In addition, *regular* volunteering by the nation's adults is only about half as common as volunteering just once during a year (Child Trends Data Bank, 2003), and the same seems to be true of adolescents (Clary & Roehlkepartain, 2004). For example, just 20% of the 370 adolescents in our St. Louis Park longitudinal study volunteered an average of 1 hour a week or more during *each* sampling time when they were in the 6th–8th, 7th–9th, and 10th–12th grades (Clary & Roehlkepartain, 2004). While any volunteering may make a contribution to a cause, one-time or occasional volunteering is hardly the foundation on which meaningful relationships are likely to be built between adults and unrelated children and youth.

Moreover, the settings in which adults volunteer certainly affect the likelihood of their being engaged with young people. The September 2003 Current Population Survey, a monthly survey of 60,000 American families, reported that it is parents with children under 18 who are the most likely group to volunteer in education or youth-related organizations, or to coach, mentor, or tutor young people (U.S. Bureau of Labor Statistics, 2003). In contrast, adults without children under 18 are more likely to volunteer in social service or religious settings. Those settings *can* provide plenty of contact with young people, but it appears that adults without children under 18 choose the volunteer opportunities that do not give them as much chance to have direct contact with young people.

We have also found in both of our national studies of adults' engagement with young people that adults who often participate in neighborhood or community meetings are significantly more likely to be highly engaged with young people than are adults who report rarely or never participating. For example, among those who often participate in neighborhood meetings, 53% are highly engaged with unrelated young people, versus about 25% for those who either rarely or never attend such meetings (Scales et al., 2002b). But, as for regular volunteering, it is a relative minority of people who are social activists at such levels. For example, only 20% of a neighborhood's residents are likely to participate in *any* neighborhood meetings over the course of a year (Saguaro Seminar, 2001).

Parents are more connected to other people's kids, but variations in parents' lives can affect that pattern as well. For example, in a recent national survey of African American and Latino/Latina parents, Search Institute and the YMCA of the USA found, not surprisingly, that the more economic stress parents experience, the more challenging they find being a parent. In addition, the better their relationship with their spouse/partner, the less challenging they find parenting (Roehlkepartain, Mannes, Scales, Lewis, & Bolstrom, 2004). Differences among parents in their poverty status or the quality of their partner relationship are likely to have complicated and nontrivial influences on how much those parents engage with children outside their own families.

Finally, the intersection of some of these trends arguably has also affected patterns of adult–child interaction. Although annual reports of volunteering among all adults at all times during the year have stayed roughly stable, there has been a decline since 1985 in the proportion of volunteers who are women with children 18 and under (Tiehen, 2000). Since parents are more likely to volunteer in settings where there are children, and women are more likely overall to engage with children (Scales, 2003), that combined social trend would appear to have depressed the volunteer pool that is more disposed to and finds it more socially acceptable to engage with unrelated children and youth.

Nevertheless, frequent volunteers—those who do so at least monthly—are more likely to connect with young people. So are women, African Americans and Hispanics, parents, longtime neighborhood residents (10 or more years), and those highly connected to community through the frequency of their attendance at religious services, and participation in neighborhood meetings (Scales, 2003). All of these groups give a higher degree of importance to engagement with the young, are surrounded more by adults who are engaged with young people, and report being personally more engaged with unrelated young people (Scales et al., 2001; Scales et al., 2002b). Some of those variables cannot be changed, at least not easily. But some can be modified. Clearly, one consistent and significant implication from our studies is that efforts to increase adults' broader civic

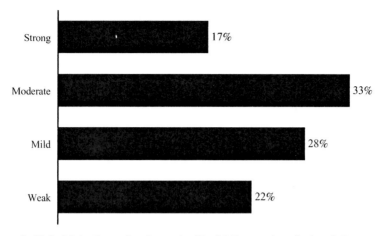

Figure 1. U.S. Adults Reporting Strength of Social Expectations for Youth Engagement

engagement are likely to positively affect patterns of adult engagement with young people as well. The linkage of positive civic development and positive youth development is apparent.

The Influence of Social Expectations on Engagement with Young People

Search Institute's national studies of U.S. adults and adolescents have increased understanding of the role the social environment plays in encouraging or discouraging adults' positive involvement with unrelated children and youth. For example, in our 2002 study of a national sample of U.S. adults, we asked respondents how strong the expectations were from the adults closest to them that they would be positively involved with other people's children and adolescents. We then investigated the relation of these social expectations for engagement to three measures of self-reported adult involvement: (a) adults' views on the importance of engaging with children and youth outside their own families; (b) how much they perceived the adults around them to be engaged; and (c) how much they said they personally were engaged with other people's children and adolescents.

As Figure 1 shows, we found that fewer than one in five U.S. adults report feeling a strong social expectation to get involved with "other people's kids" (Scales, 2003).

We concluded that the missing ingredient in this social calculus was a societal consensus on what the *reasonable responsibility* is for most adults to assume in helping young people develop. Somewhere between the primary role of parents, and the absent role most adults play today, lies an articulable territory for a supportive role most unrelated adults could play in promoting the healthy development of the young. If adults could more clearly define that territory, then more would feel a social permission and, perhaps ultimately, an expectation, to

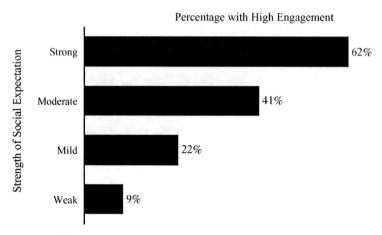

Figure 2. Relation of Strength of Social Expectation to Reported Personal Engagement with Other People's Kids

get involved with other people's kids, to the betterment of young people, adults, and their communities.

We confirmed the relationship between social expectations and engagement in our 2002 national study. Those adults experiencing strong social expectations were consistently more likely than those with weaker social expectations to say engagement with unrelated young people was important, that the majority of adults they knew were highly engaged with young people, and that they personally were highly engaged (see Figure 2).

Since 2002, we have supplemented that national quantitative data with learnings gleaned from local qualitative case studies of adult–youth engagement conducted in three Kansas communities (Mannes & Foster, 2004). Confirming much of what the national data led us to speculate, the local qualitative data suggested that the biggest barrier to adults being positively involved with other people's kids is their concern over what other adults will think. Repeatedly, focus group participants in that study noted two things that can facilitate adult engagement: (1) getting to know a child's parents, even minimally, as a prerequisite for connecting with that child, and (2) having explicit guidelines about when and how adults should get engaged, that is, some codification, however informal it might be, of social expectations for engagement, so that most adults will not choose to keep their distance from unrelated kids. These two themes substantially reflect our findings and suggestions derived from the national quantitative studies.

The combination of national quantitative data and local qualitative data provides a powerful two-tiered perspective on how adults define their reasonable responsibility for involvement and what promotes that engagement. For example, both sources of data show that concern for how other adults, especially parents, will react, is a principal barrier to engagement for most adults. But the two quantitative national studies also showed that parents are even more in favor of unrelated adults engaging with children and youth than are nonparents. This is an implicit "permission" for engagement that too often stays hidden.

In our 2000 national study, for example (and largely replicated in our 2002 study), parents rated it significantly more important than nonparents did for all adults to do a dozen things with unrelated children and youth that can promote their positive development. Those actions included encouraging young people to take school seriously, helping them with decisions, having meaningful conversations with them, and telling parents when their children do something wrong (Scales et al., 2004).

If parents are generally favorable to unrelated adults' engagement with their children, but most adults think they are not, then "pluralistic ignorance" (Miller, Monin, & Prentice, 2000) is driving social behavior. That pluralistic ignorance reinforces the norm of disengagement. The result is that, despite parental approval of adult engagement, only a minority of adults say they actually engage with young people in those ways.

For example, 79% of parents in our 2000 study approved of all adults helping kids with decision making (Scales et al., 2004), but in our 2002 study, when adults were asked how much they and the adults they knew actually engaged with young people, only 41% said they very often helped unrelated young people with decisions (Scales et al., 2002a). Similarly, 64% of parents said it was very important for all adults to tell them when their child misbehaves, but only 45% of adults said they and the adults they know actually do this. Finally, 77% of parents give high importance to all adults having meaningful conversations with unrelated young people, but just 39% of adults say they and the other adults they know do so. Similar disparities between belief and action occurred on most of the 20 engagement actions we studied in 2000 and the 16 studied in 2002, despite the significantly higher importance parents gave in each study to adults actually engaging in these ways.

Thus, for at least some and perhaps a sizable percentage of adults, simply knowing that parents tend to be open to their involvement—and knowing how supportive parents were found to be of some very specific ways adults can engage—might facilitate those relationships among adults and unrelated young people. Obviously, parents do not mean they are open to just any adult being involved with their children, but, as the Kansas qualitative study suggested, they are open to those adults whom they know and trust. Such a relationship requires communication among parents and those other adults, communication that, in effect, makes explicit the permission many parents essentially want to be able to give for positive engagement by other adults with their children. As Scales et al. (2004) described it, "Parents and the adults in the lives of their children need to take more initiative to build that modicum of perceived value similarity and social trust that allows for the kind of engagement parents appear to want" (p. 754).

Figure 3 (from Scales et al., 2002b) shows that when such communication occurs, it has a powerful positive effect on adults' engagement with kids: People who "very often" ask for such parental guidance are 2.5 times more likely to be highly engaged with other people's kids. But only 12% of U.S. adults say they *very often* ask parents, and 13% say they *often* do, as compared with 49% who say they *rarely or never* do.

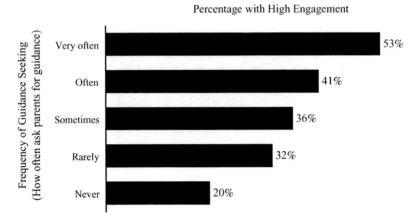

Figure 3. Proportion of Adults Highly Engaged with Other People's Kids Based on Asking for Parental Guidance

Parents can, of course, take the initiative and make clear to selected other adults the kinds of involvement with their children that are acceptable. But that communication too is generally lacking. For example, in a national study of parents, Search Institute and the YMCA of the USA found that half of all parents say trusted adults spending more time with their kids would help them "a lot" as parents. Whites and Hispanics were especially favorable to other adult involvement with their children (59% among Hispanics, 55% among Whites, and 48% among African Americans) (Roehlkepartain et al., 2004). But, out of 11 actions studied that parents can do to build their children's developmental assets, the one parents most often say they do not do "nearly enough" is encourage other adults to spend time with their child. Seventeen percent of Hispanics and 16% of African Americans say they do not ask other adults "nearly enough," and another 32% and 30%, respectively, say "not quite enough" (White parents were not asked this question in the survey).

Similarly, in our 2002 national study of U.S. adults' engagement with young people (Scales et al., 2002a, 2002b), only 22% of parents with children under 18 said they often (11%) or very often (11%) advised neighbors or other adults on engagement with their children, and 29% said they rarely or never did. So despite parents themselves saying it is highly important for other trusted adults to be more involved in their children's lives, only a minority of parents take proactive steps to give the guidance and permission that would promote the potentially positive engagement they want for their children.

Young People as Shapers of Adult Engagement with Them

Young people's civic development has an impact of its own on patterns of adult–youth engagement. Ecological and developmental systems theories of positive youth development hold that young people themselves do not simply interact with their environments; they actively shape them as well through their temperaments, personalities, and behaviors (Benson et al., 2004; Lerner, 2003). For example, we have seen that adults who are connected to their community through volunteering, and through attendance at religious services and neighborhood meetings, are more likely to be positively engaged with unrelated children and youth. Likewise, it makes sense that young people who are similarly connected will report greater adult engagement. But we hypothesized that young people who were more connected to community in terms of their frequency of volunteering, participation in youth programs, and attendance at religious services, would report not only *more* engagement with unrelated adults but also a *greater breadth* of engagement (Scales, Benson, Mannes, & Sesma, in press).

In other words, experiencing a greater amount of positive engagement with unrelated adults may not be the only developmental benefit of young people's community involvements. The ways in which adults interact with them may also qualitatively be different. Most young people appear to experience unrelated adults reinforcing expectations to do well in school, for example. But with young people who appear more conventional and connected to social institutions and approved adult values, adults might relate in ways they less commonly do, such as helping young people with decisions, or talking about personal values or religious beliefs with them (Scales, 2003). Such actions could have even deeper developmental impact than more common ways adults relate to young people, in part because their rarity makes them more salient experiences, and in part because they may more profoundly facilitate young people's introspection, reflection, and identity formation. *Thus, connected young people may experience both more adult engagement and more developmentally powerful kinds of engagement.*

To test the hypothesis that young people with more community involvement also experience a broader range of adult engagement, we asked a national sample of 614 12- to 17-year-olds to identify the frequency with which they experienced each of 16 asset-building actions from unrelated adults. As reported by Scales et al. (2002a, 2002b), five actions were experienced by a majority of young people: Adults' encouraging school success; teaching young people respect for cultural differences; teaching them widely shared values such as equality, honesty, and responsibility; feeling responsible to ensure the well-being of neighborhood kids; and knowing the names of young people in their neighborhood. These five actions were defined as relatively common kinds of adult engagement.

We then conducted analyses to determine whether young people with more contextual involvements in volunteering, youth programs, and religious community experienced more of the relatively *unusual* kinds of engagement. The less common kinds of adult engagement included reporting either positive behavior or misbehavior to parents; guiding young people's decision making; providing them opportunities to serve or help others; seeking young people's opinions; giving them financial guidance; passing down cultural traditions to them; having meaningful conversations with them; playing sports or doing art activities with young people; and discussing religious beliefs and personal values with them.

Table 2 shows that, as hypothesized, young people with greater community connectedness reported not just more adult engagement, but a different kind of engagement. Specifically, they were significantly more likely to report more of

Table 2. Breadth of Adult–Youth Engagement by Level of Youth
Community Connections

Level of Community Connectedness**	Uncommon Adult Engagement Score*	
	Mean	SE
High	3.12	.04
Medium	2.89	.04
Low	2.69	.04

*$F(2, 1240) = 28.74$, $p \leq .0001$. Tukey post hoc comparisons show that youth in each higher level of community connection report a significantly broader range of adult engagement.
** Community connectedness scores were derived by summing responses for time spent volunteering, in youth programs, and in religious community. The top third of those summed scores were considered high in community connectedness; the next third, medium; and the bottom third, low.

the less common kinds of adult engagement. We simply divided the sample into thirds based on the sum of connectedness scores for volunteering, time in youth programs, and time in religious community. At each successive level of increase in connectedness, from low to medium to high, young people reported a developmentally *broader* range of adult engagement than young people who are less connected to community ($F[2,1240] = 28.74$, $p \leq .0001$). Females and middle school students also reported more of this greater breadth of engagement ($F[1,1240] = 7.14$, $p \leq .005$).

Thus, expanding young people's community involvements should be related to increases in both the amount and breadth of the developmental attentiveness young people experience from unrelated adults. Strategies to promote that involvement, for example, include promoting service-learning in school and community settings, funding a variety of school- and community-sponsored after-school youth programs, and strengthening congregations' integration of youth throughout the life of their religious community, not just in the "youth program."

Differences in young people's community involvement translate to substantial differences in the odds young people experience this broader kind of engagement from unrelated adults. We conducted a logistic regression that showed that young people who were above the mean on involvement with youth programs, religious community, and volunteering were 47% more likely also to be above average in uncommon kinds of adult engagement than those who had average or below levels of community connectedness ($B = .39$, $Se\beta = .11$, $e^B = 1.47$).

A different analysis of the same data set showed a rather significant average decline from 6th through 12th grades in these kinds of community involvements. But individual trajectories mattered. For example, young people who consistently volunteered, or whose volunteering emerged later, had higher levels of developmental assets and more indicators of thriving than either one-time volunteers who no longer did or those who consistently did not volunteer (Clary & Roehlkepartain, 2004).

However, despite the key role that young people's prosocial behavior and community involvement take in promoting access to positive engagement with unrelated adults, our data suggest that the majority of adults are not explicitly encouraging, modeling, and promoting such participation. For example, just 22% of U.S. adults say they very often show young people the importance of volunteering or giving money to help others. And, as noted earlier, helping others and working to improve their communities are two of the least commonly experienced expectations young people hear from their parents, teachers, neighbors, and other adults (Scales et al., 2003).

Conclusion: What Facilitates Engagement?

Our national quantitative and community-level qualitative studies together suggest that there are a number of factors that facilitate adults' engagement with young people (see sidebar). Some of these are not possible to change (e.g., one's cultural background) or necessarily easy to change, such as the neighborhood in which one lives (i.e., living in a neighborhood with children obviously facilitates engaging with children) or personality factors. Parents may more readily meet unrelated children than nonparents because of their own children's relationships with other kids. Parents and nonparents alike might serve as coaches or camp counselors, etc., but those involvements are not possible for many. Our studies suggest that there is a large store of potential informal ways in which most adults can be engaged positively with children and youth in their neighborhoods, places where they shop, and the religious and other organizations to which they might belong but in which they might not specifically *volunteer*.

Factors That Facilitate Adults' Engagement with Unrelated Children and Youth

- Physical proximity to neighborhood children and youth
- Access to youth through employment or own children's friends/playmates
- Access through involvement in sports teams and community organizations
- Getting to know parents
- Common interests of adult and child/youth
- Connection through small-town life (i.e., greater cohesion, sense of shared roots); adults knowing each other
- Favorable adult personality or temperamental factors (e.g., outspoken, comfort with youth)
- Belief systems and values that ascribe high importance to engagement
- Sense of obligation to pay back for own experience with an unrelated adult as a kid
- Experiencing explicit guidelines for engagement
- Recognition of "selfish" rewards for engagement

Most of the factors that can be changed belie the possible explanation that adults do not get more involved with young people because they do not have time. Although time certainly may be an issue for some adults working long hours or more than one job, for many adults greater engagement with young people is possible by taking advantage of opportunities that already exist in one's world. As one adult in a Kansas community noted, "Take a look around and just open yourselves to the youth that are near you. You don't have to go out searching for them. Just open yourselves to the ones that are around" (Mannes & Foster, 2004).

Some opportunities for engagement exist because of one's daily schedule, such as being able to be outside doing something when the neighborhood kids come home on the school bus. But almost any adult can simply smile and wave more to young people, and greet them by name. Sometimes an adult can have a profound impact on development without even talking to the young person. Kimball-Baker (2003) advises adults to "look out your window" (p. 20) in the way an elderly Kansas woman did. For years, she simply stood at her window and watched as a youth got on the school bus in front of her house. She waved and smiled once in a while but that was it. The youth and the woman never met, but years later the now-grown man cannot help but remember her when he passes that spot, recalling her "powerful, quiet presence" watching over him and making him feel safe and cared for.

But even such simple informal activities may need a push from stronger social expectations. In our 2002 national study, 46% of adults said it was highly important for adults to play sports or do art activities with kids, a relatively easy way of being involved with them and a frequent recommendation from the focus group participants in our study of several Kansas communities. But only 20% of U.S. adults said they very often did this (and only 28% of kids agreed that most adults they know did this with them; Scales et al., 2002a).

Public communications that focus on the "selfish" rewards of engagement more than on fulfilling a sense of responsibility to help nurture the next generation may also help motivate some adults to greater engagement. Scales (2003) described several possible selfish rewards, including feelings of goodness and happiness; feelings of self-satisfaction and accomplishment; the intrinsic reward of helping those in need; improved relations among adults and young people through teaching kids responsibility; giving young people ideas to think about; helping young people make the right choices; showing young people that others care about them; playing games that most adults cannot; staying young, enhancing the joy of living, experiencing fresh ways of seeing the world; and enjoying additional opportunities to give and receive affection. Engaged adults also can strengthen social norms by sharing with other adults about how much they are engaged with young people (everyone's doing it—why not you?), why they do so, and the positive personal feelings and other benefits they derive from such relationships.

In the end, this approach to facilitating adult engagement utilizes for its energy the meeting of adults' own developmental needs to feel connected and worthwhile, engaged with zest for life. The personal developmental impact of such relationships for adults may ultimately stimulate more engagement than exhortations about what adults "should" be doing in the name of their duty to help nurture the coming generations. In the overscheduled, duty-filled world so many adults in developed societies live in today, the most powerful stimulus for adults to engage more with other people's kids may be one of the most simple—those relationships can be a source of great pleasure.

References

Azjen, I. (2001). Nature and operation of attitudes. *Annual Review of Psychology, 52,* 27–58.

Benson, P. L. (1997). *All kids are our kids: What communities must do to raise responsible and caring children and adolescents.* San Francisco: Jossey-Bass.

Benson, P. L., Leffert, N., Scales, P. C., & Blyth, D. A. (1998). Beyond the "village" rhetoric: Creating healthy communities for children and adolescents. *Applied Developmental Science, 2,* 138–159.

Benson, P. L., Scales, P. C., Hamilton, S., & Sesma, A. (2004). Positive youth development: Theory, research, and applications. In W. Damon and R. M. Lerner (Eds.), *Handbook of child psychology: Vol 1. Theoretical models of human development.* New York: Wiley.

Benson, P. L., Scales, P. C., Leffert, N., & Roehlkepartain, E. C. (1999). *A fragile foundation: The state of developmental assets among American youth.* Minneapolis, MN: Search Institute.

Benson, P. L., Scales, P. C., & Mannes, M. (2003). Developmental strengths and their sources: Implications for the study and practice of community-building. In R. M. Lerner, F. Jacobs, & D. Wertlieb (Eds.), *Handbook of applied developmental science: Vol. 1. Applying developmental science for youth and families: Historical and theoretical foundations* (pp. 369–406). Thousand Oaks, CA: Sage.

Bronfenbrenner, U. (1979). *The ecology of human development: Experiments by nature and design.* Cambridge, MA: Harvard University Press.

Child Trends. (2003). *Child Trends Data Book.* Washington, DC: Author.

Child Welfare League of America. (1999). *Assessing public opinion and perceptions regarding child abuse in America.* Washington, DC: Author. (Final report available from Liberman Research Worldwide, Los Angeles, at www.lrw.com.)

Cialdini, R. B., & Goldstein, N. J. (2004). Social influence: Compliance and conformity. *Annual Review of Psychology, 55,* 591–621.

Clary, E. G., & Roehlkepartain, E. C. (2004). *Adding it up: Youth engagement.* Manuscript in preparation.

Search Institute. (2001). *Developmental assets: A portrait of your youth.* [Unpublished 1999–2000 school year aggregate database.] Minneapolis, MN: Search Institute

Ensminger, J., & Knight, J. (1997). Changing social norms: Common property, bridewealth, and clan exogamy. *Current Anthropology, 38,* 1–14.

Forsyth, D. R. (1999). Norms: Coercive sources of influence? Course materials, Virginia Commonwealth University. Retrieved from www.vcu.edu/hasweb/psy/psy341/norms.html

Hollander, P. (2003). The counterculture of the heart. *Society, 41*(2), 69–77.

Independent Sector. (1999). *Giving and volunteering in the United States: Findings from a national survey.* Washington, DC: Author.

Kimball-Baker, K. (2003). *Tag, you're it! 50 easy ways to connect with young people.* Minneapolis, MN: Search Institute.

Knight Foundation. (1999). *Community Indicators Survey—National.* Miami, FL: Author.

Kundu, K. (1999). Hours of work: A matter of choice for most Americans. *Fact & Fallacy: Contemporary Issues in Employment and Workplace Policy, 5* (8), 1–4.

Lerner, R. M. (2003). Developmental assets and asset-building communities: A view of the issues. In R. M. Lerner & P. L. Benson (Eds.), *Developmental assets and asset-building communities: Implications for research, policy, and practice* (pp. 3–18). New York: Kluwer Academic/Plenum.

Mannes, M., & Foster, K. (2004). *Cultivating human development for young Kansans: How people, places, and permission are making it happen.* Minneapolis, MN: Search Institute.

McGuiken, N., & Srinivasan, N. (2003). *Journey to work trends in the United States and its major metropolitan areas, 1960–2000.* Washington, DC: U.S. Department of Transportation.

Miller, D. T., Monin, B., & Prentice, D. A. (2000). Pluralistic ignorance and inconsistency between private attitudes and public behaviors. In M. A. Hogg & D. J. Terry (Eds.), *Attitudes, behavior, and social context: The role of norms and group membership* (pp. 95–113). Mahwah, NJ: Erlbaum.

Price, R. H., Cioci, M., Penner, W., & Trautlein, B. (1993). Webs of influence: School and community programs that enhance adolescent health and education. *Teachers College Record, 94,* 487–521.

Putnam, R. (2000). *Bowling alone: The collapse and revival of American community.* New York: Simon & Schuster.

Rhodes, J. E., & Roffman, J. G. (2003). Nonparental adults as asset builders in the lives of youth. In R. M. Lerner & P. L. Benson (Eds.), *Developmental assets and asset-building communities: Implications for research, policy, and practice* (pp. 195–212). New York: Kluwer Academic/Plenum.

Roehlkepartain, E. C., Mannes, M., Scales, P. C., Lewis, S., & Bolstrom, B. (2004). *Building strong families 2004: A study of African American and Latino/Latina parents.* Preliminary Report to the YMCA of the USA. Minneapolis, MN: Search Institute.

Saguaro Seminar. (2001). *Social Capital Community Benchmark Survey.* Cambridge, MA: Harvard University, John F. Kennedy School of Government. Retrieved April 4, 2001, from www.cfsv.org./communitysurvey/results/html

Scales, P. C. (with Benson, P. L., Mannes, M., Hintz, N. R., Roehlkepartain, E. C., & Sullivan, T. K.). (2003). *Other people's kids: Social expectations and American adults' involvement with children and adolescents.* New York: Kluwer Academic/Plenum.

Scales, P. C., Benson, P. L., & Mannes, M. (2002a). *Grading grown-ups 2002: How do American kids and adults relate? Key findings from a national study.* Minneapolis, MN: Search Institute.

Scales, P. C., Benson, P. L., & Mannes, M. (2002b). *Grading grown-ups 2002: How do American kids and adults relate? A national study* (expanded report downloadable from www.search-institute.org). Minneapolis, MN: Search Institute.

Scales, P. C., Benson, P. L., Mannes, M., & Sesma, A. (in press). The contribution to adolescent well-being made by nonfamily adults: An examination of developmental assets as contexts and processes. *Journal of Community Psychology.*

Scales, P. C., Benson, P. L., Roehlkepartain, E. C., Hintz, N. R., Sullivan, T. K., & Mannes, M. (2001). The role of neighborhood and community in building developmental assets for children and youth: A national study of social norms among American adults. *Journal of Community Psychology, 29,* 703–727.

Scales, P. C., Benson, P. L., Roehlkepartain, E. C., Hintz, N. R., Sullivan, T. K., & Mannes, M. (2004). The role of parental status and child age in the engagement of children and youth with adults outside their families. *Journal of Family Issues, 25,* 735–760.

Scales, P. C., & Leffert, N. (2004). *Developmental assets: A synthesis of the scientific research on adolescent development* (2nd ed.). Minneapolis, MN: Search Institute.

Scales, P. C., Leffert, N., & Vraa, R. (2003). The relation of community developmental attentiveness to adolescent health. *American Journal of Health Behavior, 27* (Suppl. 1), S22–S34.

Scales, P. C., Sesma, A., & Bolstrom, B. (2004). *Coming into their own: How developmental assets help promote positive growth in middle childhood.* Minneapolis, MN: Search Institute.

Tiehen, L. (2000). Has working more caused married women to volunteer less? Evidence from time diary data, 1965 to 1993. *Nonprofit and Voluntary Sector Quarterly, 29,* 505–529.

U.S. Bureau of the Census. (2001). *Profiles of general demographic characteristics, 2000: 2000 census of population and housing.* Washington, DC: U.S. Department of Commerce.

U.S. Bureau of Labor Statistics. (2003). *Volunteering in the United States, 2003.* Retrieved December 30, 2003, from ftp://ftp.bls.gov/pub/news.release/volun.txt

U.S. Department of Health and Human Services. (1998). *Trends in the well-being of America's children and adolescents, 1998.* Washington, DC: Author.

U.S. Department of Health and Human Services. (2003). *Trends in the well-being of America's children and youth, 2002.* Washington, DC: Author.

Wood, W. (2001). Attitude change: Persuasion and social influence. *Annual Review of Psychology, 52,* 539–570.

II Mobilizing Individual Adults

4 Lessons from Research on Volunteering for Mobilizing Adults to Volunteer for Positive Youth Development

Arthur A. Stukas and Maree Daly

La Trobe University

E. Gil Clary

College of St. Catherine

Children and youth, growing up in the United States and around the world, face many challenges. The guidance and support of parents and other adults are crucial for positive youth development. Recently, Search Institute developed an empirically sound framework of 40 developmental assets that children and adolescents need to become mature and productive adults (see Clary & Rhodes, Chapter 1, this volume). Unfortunately, research suggests that some youth do not have access to these assets (e.g., Scales & Leffert, 1999). But to whom can they turn? Certainly, our governments have not been able to address the needs of young people (e.g., Children's Defense Fund, 2002), leaving some children behind, through lack of developmental opportunities and assets and positive adult role models to provide them, or through inadequate educational systems and neglect. So, in the context of diminishing top–down solutions from states or nations, communities must look inward for bottom–up solutions to the problems of young people.

In the second volume in this series, Scales (2003) convincingly makes the case that a key strategy to avert the disenfranchisement of today's youth may be to change social norms about adults' interactions with youth. He suggests that, although young people clearly benefit from active connections with adults other than their parents, getting involved with "other people's kids" is perceived to be risky or an intrusion on parents' rights or wishes. Nevertheless, most respondents to Scales's survey of American adults rated the types of behaviors that provide developmental assets to youth (such as talking about values or encouraging school success) as very important, even as they saw that the adults in their community failed to engage in them. Scales hopes that widely publicizing the finding that parents are open to having their kids interact informally with other adults in the community might dispel "pluralistic ignorance" (p. 126) and therefore increase positive action. In other words, once community members learn that parents are okay with, and even approve of, other adults interacting with their kids, then we should all feel free to develop connections with neighborhood youth.

But perhaps removing the barrier of perceived parental opposition will not be enough to encourage widespread action. Scales (2003) noted that norms that encourage desirable behavior are often weaker than norms that discourage undesirable behavior. White (1984) also found that whereas social norms for prosocial behavior were consensually agreed upon, they lacked regulatory power. Indeed, there are no sanctions against adults who fail to connect with other people's kids, and adults who do not occupy roles that specifically prescribe involvement with youth (such as teacher or religious leader) often avoid such involvement. The most common youth development workers are still likely to be parents who get involved, as Scout leaders, coaches, classroom volunteers, or mentors, initially in the interests of helping their own children, and then, perhaps, by broadening their activities to help others' children (Jones, 2001). Scales discussed a number of potentially successful methods for encouraging *other* adults to engage informally with the youth in their communities, including talking up the benefits of engagement, challenging negative statements about involvement, and reinforcing self-perceptions related to prosocial behaviors. These strategies may move some adults to help youth in some communities. An additional strategy that communities can adopt to facilitate the involvement of adults is to turn to volunteers who engage with youth through programs sponsored by formal volunteer organizations.

Although youths' more informal engagement with adults from their own communities may offer unique and invaluable benefits, a case can be made that structured formal activities linking young people and adults, arranged by volunteer organizations like the Scouts, Big Brothers Big Sisters of America, or 4-H, may be a stable and reliable solution to the problems of disengagement (see Rhodes, 2002). Formal volunteer programs, with their orientation sessions, training, safeguards, and evaluation or review (e.g., Sipe & Roder, 1999), may also reduce worries on the part of adults that they may be intervening inappropriately, ineffectively, or intrusively with other people's kids. It may be easier to encourage adults to volunteer for organizations that provide services to youth (such as Big Brothers Big Sisters of America) than it is to encourage them to learn the names of their neighbors' children and to engage those children in discussions about values.

Volunteerism has been defined as "any activity in which time is given freely to benefit another person, group, or organization" (Wilson, 2000, p. 215). Clary and Snyder (1999) added several criteria: (a) The helper typically seeks out the opportunity to help (or at least carefully considers any requests); (b) the helper deliberates about how and whether to help, weighing his or her own needs and goals, as well as those of others; (c) the helper provides assistance over an extended period of time; and (d) the helper receives no financial incentives for his or her service. These definitions might well encompass the informal, as well as formal, guidance and mentoring activities that involved adults engage in with youth in their communities (e.g., Scales, 2003). Thus, research on volunteerism, while often focusing on promoting activities in formal organizations (see Penner, 2002), has great relevance for this volume's concern with mobilizing adults for positive youth development.

The range of activities undertaken by volunteers who work with youth in formal programs is broad, but through varied means their service is directed toward improving the psychological or physical health and welfare of children and adolescents. Roughly 10% of American volunteers serve with organizations that work with youth (Independent Sector, 1999; see also Clary, Snyder, & Worth, 2003). A prototypical example of volunteer work aimed at encouraging positive youth development is mentoring (see Rhodes, 2002; Stukas & Tanti, 2005). Mentors act as role models, friends, and advisers to youth who have been robbed of suitable adult figures by circumstance (Rhodes, 2002). Results from recent investigations of the effects of youth mentoring on psychosocial and academic outcomes are somewhat promising (see DuBois, Holloway, Valentine, & Cooper, 2002, for a meta-analysis).

Formal volunteer programs rely on adults who freely give of their time, and therefore such programs inevitably suffer from what Snyder (1993) has called the "problem of inaction": Although a large number of people are willing to say that volunteerism is worthwhile, fewer actually engage in service. In the most recent Independent Sector survey to assess the issue, Americans agreed by a 3 to 1 margin that volunteerism is important, but only 38.5% had volunteered in the previous month (Independent Sector, 1988). More recent data indicate that currently only 28% of Americans over the age of 21 volunteer monthly or more frequently (a somewhat different statistic; Independent Sector, 2001). Youth mentoring programs also face the problem of inaction. A recent AOL Time Warner survey (O'Connor, 2002) found that whereas 11% of adults surveyed were mentoring through a formal program, such as Big Brothers Big Sisters of America, and another 23% claimed to be mentoring youth informally, a further 42% of adults were not mentoring but said that they would be interested in doing so. Such numbers represent both an untapped future resource and a frustrating current disappointment. Organizations who match volunteer mentors with youth in need often have trouble recruiting sufficient numbers of mentors and sustaining mentoring relationships over time (e.g., Roaf, Tierney, & Hunte, 1994). The trick for organizations seeking volunteers, then, is to turn good intentions into good behavior, to overcome the "problem of inaction." In this chapter, we review the evidence for a number of theoretically based methods for recruiting and retaining volunteers to work for positive youth development. In conjunction with efforts to change norms about informal interactions with youth (e.g., Scales, 2003), we hope that these methods also prove fruitful for the provision of developmental assets to children and young people.

Persuading Adults to Volunteer

One of the most common strategies for recruiting volunteers is through carefully targeted advertising and persuasive messages. Within social psychology, persuading individuals to change their attitudes and behaviors for the greater good has been the target of a long history of research (see Eagly & Chaiken, 1993, for a thorough review). For example, early post–World War II research at Yale University (Hovland, Janis, & Kelley, 1953) began a trend toward identifying the elements of successful persuasive communication attempts: source factors, message factors, audience factors, and channel factors (i.e., "who says what in which channel to whom"; Lasswell, 1948). Later research on dual process models identified how different factors (such as attractive or expert sources and relevant or strong messages) could enhance persuasion, depending upon whether the audience had the ability and/or motivation to pay attention (Petty & Cacioppo, 1986). This research has demonstrated that it should be possible to craft persuasive communications containing strong arguments that elicit positive thoughts about volunteering from most people (for example, by reporting how youth mentoring directly improves the outcomes of youth; Grossman & Tierney, 1998). Other research, however, suggests that targeting messages to the specific interests, needs, or goals of potential volunteers might work best.

Understanding Adults' Needs and Goals

Functional approaches to attitudes and persuasion (e.g., Katz, 1960; Smith, Bruner, & White, 1956) offer a theoretically based and practically applicable framework for designing recruitment messages that take individual differences among potential volunteers into account. These approaches started with the assumption that the same attitude may serve different needs for different individuals. According to Katz (1960), attitudes may allow individuals variously to express their values, to fit into their social environments, to organize their knowledge about the world, or to defend their egos from threat. A key postulate of functional theories is that any attempts to change attitudes or encourage action consistent with the attitude will best succeed if they target the underlying purpose, or function, that the attitude or behavior serves for the target individual. This "matching hypothesis" therefore provides a key to crafting recruitment messages that might appeal to a variety of potential volunteers from different walks of life. Messages that highlight an individual's important reasons and purposes, goals and needs, for behavior should be more attractive and persuasive than messages pitched at a more generic level (see Snyder & Cantor,

1998, for a theoretical review of functional approaches). A recent program of research by Clary and Snyder and their colleagues (e.g., Clary et al., 1998; Snyder, Clary, & Stukas, 2000) has applied a functional approach to the study of volunteerism.

The functional approach to volunteerism proposes that different people may have different reasons (or even multiple reasons) for engaging in volunteer work and that different aspects of volunteer work might attract them to a particular task (Clary & Snyder, 1993; Clary, Snyder, Ridge, Miene, & Haugen, 1994). To better craft persuasive messages, Clary and Snyder began by identifying the primary functions that volunteerism may serve for individuals, eventually developing the Volunteer Functions Inventory (VFI; Clary et al., 1998). This survey asks potential or current volunteers to rate the importance of 30 reasons for volunteering, organized into six functions or goals (see Table 1 for examples):

- Values—to express humanitarian and prosocial values through action;
- Career—to explore career options and increase the likelihood that a particular career path can be pursued;
- Understanding—to gain greater understanding of the world, the diverse people in it, and ultimately oneself;
- Enhancement—to boost self-esteem, to feel important and needed by others, and to form new friendships;
- Protective—to distract oneself from personal problems or to work through problems in the context of service; and
- Social—to satisfy the expectations of friends and close others.

Omoto and Snyder (1995) have also designed an inventory to assess why people volunteer to be "buddies" for people with AIDS. Their scale contains similar, though more specifically focused, scales to the VFI, but notably adds:

- Community concern—to demonstrate one's interest in, and commitment to, one's community.

In general, then, volunteer work can allow individuals to fulfill a number of important goals and needs. Volunteer activities focused on working with young people may offer opportunities to fulfill some or all of these motives for volunteering. Two recent surveys offer some suggestive data about how youth development volunteers may differ from other types of volunteers. First, in secondary analyses of a 1992 national U.S. survey by Gallup, which included data on a subset of VFI items from more than 2,500 Americans interviewed in their homes, Clary, Snyder, and Stukas (1996) found that volunteering to work in the broad area of youth development involved higher understanding, and somewhat lower enhancement, motives than other types of volunteerism. More recently, Clary et al. (2003) surveyed 1,388 volunteers from 83 affiliates of the Volunteer Resource Center, a regional volunteer placement agency in Minneapolis–St. Paul, Minnesota. From the total sample, 82 volunteers reported working in the area of youth development; these volunteers

Table 1. Motivations for Volunteerism, with Sample Items from the Volunteer Functions Inventory (VFI)

Function	Sample VFI Item	Motivation for Positive Youth Development
Values	"I am genuinely concerned about the particular group I am serving."	To show one's concern for youth and belief that adults must be engaged with youth
Career	"Volunteering allows me to explore different career options."	To explore the roles of formal youth worker, teacher, or even parent prior to, or during, formal education for these roles
Understanding	"Volunteering allows me to gain a new perspective on things."	To learn more about youth culture; to reflect on and pass along the lessons one has learned in life; to understand those who grow up in different circumstances
Enhancement	"Volunteering makes me feel needed."	To feel as though one is making a difference in another person's development; to experience across-age relationships; to be looked up to
Protective	"Doing volunteer work relieves me of some of the guilt over being more fortunate than others."	To feel less selfish and disconnected; to resolve intergenerational conflict or guilt
Social	"Others with whom I am close place a high value on community service."	To live up to the types of norms that Scales (2003) espouses; to be seen as living up to one's responsibilities in the community
Community concern	"I volunteer because of my sense of obligation to the community."	To show that one cares for the youth of the community; to make connections with youth as a way of directing them away from problem areas and into positive action in the community

Sources: Clary et al. (1998); "Community concern": Omoto and Snyder (1995).

were involved with a variety of organizations: Boy and Girl Scouts, Camp Fire Groups, 4-H Clubs, youth groups with religious affiliations, and Little Leagues and other athletic groups. Compared to volunteers working for other types of organizations, youth development volunteers were generally higher in VFI-assessed values, career, and understanding motivation. A general rank ordering of motives for these volunteers shows, however, that values, understanding, and enhancement motives were most important, followed by social, protective, and career motives. Youth development volunteers also reported having more opportunities to act on and to express their values than other volunteers and fewer opportunities to meet the social expectations of their friends and family.

Recruitment Messages

Such findings could be helpful to organizations seeking to recruit volunteers. Recruitment messages could be targeted toward the values, understanding, and enhancement motives potentially held by prospective youth development volunteers. The "matching hypothesis" of the functional approach (e.g., Clary & Snyder, 1993; Snyder et al., 2000) suggests that such a strategy is likely to be successful when recruitment messages are seen to match the underlying motivations that volunteers seek to fulfill. In a test of this hypothesis, Clary et al. (1994) first assessed participants' motives with the VFI and later asked them to evaluate a videotaped recruitment advertisement for volunteerism (in general) that focused on a motive they had previously rated as high in importance (functionally matched) or low in importance (functionally mismatched). Participants who saw matched ads reported finding them more persuasive (and felt more motivated to volunteer as a result) than participants who saw mismatched ads. Clary et al. (1998) later replicated these findings by showing six brochures (focused again separately on each of the six motives from the VFI) to participants who had previously taken the VFI. Each participant's ratings of the persuasiveness of the respective brochures correlated highly with his or her respective VFI function scores (and, in general, average brochure ratings correlated with average VFI scores in the whole sample).

Advertising opportunities to volunteer for positive youth development with direct reference to the benefits available for volunteers may help overcome the problem of inaction for many volunteers; being able to fulfill primary motives or serve important functions in one's life is undoubtedly attractive. Recruitment efforts may be enhanced still further, however, by taking the social context surrounding potential volunteers into account. For example, the theory of planned behavior (Ajzen, 1991) proposes that attitudes (e.g., "Volunteerism is a good thing to do") may have an impact on behavior (e.g., actual volunteerism) through their influence on behavioral intentions (e.g., "I intend to volunteer"). Attitudes are not the only predictor of behavioral intentions, however. Ajzen and Fishbein (1980) demonstrated that perceived "subjective" norms of significant others also influence intentions. This point is represented in the VFI (Clary et al., 1998) by the social function (for which "People I'm close to want me to volunteer" is a prototypical item). Research by Piliavin and Callero (1991) has shown that the perceived expectations of significant others can influence both self-concept and blood donation behavior over a sustained period of time. Recently, Omoto and Snyder (2002) have focused on the similar construct of psychological sense of community, suggesting that it sets the stage for many types of volunteerism. Thus, Scales's (2003) suggestion that social norms need to be changed and to be made more salient in order to encourage more adults to volunteer for positive youth development finds solid theoretical support.

The theory of planned behavior (Ajzen, 1991) also suggests that physical context may play a role in intentions to act on one's attitudes. "Perceived behavioral control," one's perception that one can successfully enact the behavior in question, may significantly influence intentions (Ajzen, 1991). Indeed, Okun

(2002) found that perceived behavioral control was the strongest predictor of intentions to enroll in a college volunteer program, although attitudes and subjective norms were also significant predictors. Physical constraints that keep people from volunteering may result in a lack of perceived behavioral control. For example, a recent survey of Canadians (Hall, McKeown, & Roberts, 2001) found that, of those not currently volunteering, 69% said they didn't have the time, 25% said they had no interest in volunteering, 24% said that health problems kept them away, and 20% couldn't figure out exactly how to get involved; others indicated that they usually gave money instead of volunteering (38%) (Hall et al., 2001). Psychological constraints may also affect rates of volunteering. For example, Bandura's (1997) program of research on self-efficacy indicates that confidence that an action can be successfully completed to reach a desired goal is a good predictor of actual action. Recent longitudinal research on youth mentoring by Parra, DuBois, Neville, Pugh-Lilly, and Povinelli (2002) has found that mentors' self-efficacy beliefs (measured prior to service) predicted greater amounts of mentor and youth contact and closeness as well as significant benefits to youth. Thus, making sure that adults know how, when, and where to volunteer, are aware of the potential benefits for themselves, for youth, and for the community, and feel confident that they can both find the time and energy to volunteer and reach these goals will help mobilize them for youth development.

Retaining the Recruited

Once an organization has successfully recruited volunteers, an additional and separate challenge is the retention of this volunteer workforce. The operation of many organizations may be dependent upon retaining long-term, committed, and active volunteers. Experienced volunteers can provide a meaningful service to recipients on behalf of the organization (e.g., Gidron, 1985); they can be persuasive recruiters of new volunteers to the agency (e.g., McLearn, Colasanto, & Schoen, 1998; Omoto & Snyder, 2002); and they can provide leadership and training to new volunteers (e.g., Jenner, 1984).

Consequently, volunteer turnover can have significant detrimental effects on the volunteer organization and on those who rely on its services. This is perhaps especially the case for organizations that work in areas where relationships form the basis of the service provided. For example, Grossman and Rhodes (2002) have found that the premature termination of youth mentoring relationships not only prevents the achievement of psychosocial and academic gains but may actually result in negative effects for youth, such as deterioration in self-worth and perceived scholastic competence. Turnover not only may disrupt program delivery and have adverse effects on the recipients of programs (Gidron, 1985; Miller, Powell, & Seltzer, 1990), it also has the potential to undermine community confidence in the organization. Recruiting and training new volunteers is expensive and can result in a severe financial drain on community organizations that typically are already underfunded (Gidron, 1985; Miller et al.,

1990). Retaining volunteers and minimizing turnover is therefore one way for agencies to maximize service delivery and keep costs down.

The Volunteer Process

Recent theories of volunteer behavior have sought to predict volunteer longevity, or retention. For example, Omoto and Snyder's (1995, 2002) Volunteer Process Model reviewed potential antecedents, experiences, and consequences of volunteerism, suggesting that antecedents (e.g., personality attributes and motivations) and experiences (e.g., satisfaction with volunteer work and integration within the organization) may influence later consequences such as volunteer retention. Thus, positive or negative experiences, leading to volunteer satisfaction or dissatisfaction, may affect volunteers' decisions to stay or to leave. In Omoto and Snyder's (1995) study of volunteers serving as buddies to people with AIDS, satisfaction was a direct predictor of sustained volunteerism. To date, researchers have identified a number of antecedents and subsequent experiences of the volunteer process that may have an impact on sustained volunteerism. These antecedents include motivations (Omoto & Snyder, 1995; Penner & Finkelstein, 1998), personality traits or types (e.g., empathy, Davis, Hall & Meyer, 2003; prosocial personality, Penner & Finkelstein, 1998), and features of organizational environments (Clary et al., 2003; Gagné, 2003). Subsequent volunteer experiences that may predict continued volunteer activity include satisfaction (Omoto & Snyder, 1995; Penner & Finkelstein, 1998), motive fulfillment or functional benefits received (Clary et al., 1998; Davis et al., 2003; Tschirhart, Mesch, Perry, Miller, & Lee, 2001), and emotional responses to volunteer work (Clary et al., 2003; Davis et al., 2003).

Omoto and Snyder's (1995) Volunteer Process Model allows for antecedents and experiences of volunteerism to interact to predict later consequences. That is, certain experiences may be appealing or less appealing for volunteers with certain personalities or motives. Conceptualizing the volunteer process within an interactionist framework has advantages in theoretical, empirical, and applied domains. Theoretically, it can provide a more comprehensive account of the volunteer process than earlier "main effects" models, which looked only at the features of individuals. Empirically, it generates a whole range of testable hypotheses, especially those that seek to identify person–environment fit. Finally, in an applied setting, it provides opportunities for volunteer agencies to intervene in the process in order to obtain more favorable outcomes (e.g., by tailoring environments and tasks to the qualities of individuals). Although some features of persons (gender, age, personality, motives) may be fixed, many features of the situation or environment (volunteer tasks, organizational characteristics) are malleable, and therein lies the possibility of effecting change and facilitating higher levels of retention of volunteers.

Clary and Miller (1986) provided a good example of the way in which organizational variables can influence the effects of preexisting, person-centered factors. Volunteer telephone counselors were categorized as either internally or externally motivated, based on their responses to a range of questionnaire items prior to commencing as volunteers. As predicted, those who were primarily motivated by internal factors, as opposed to external factors, were more likely to complete their volunteer assignment. However, a subsequent situational variable, participation in a cohesive training group, negated the effects of initial motivation. Those externally motivated volunteers who underwent training in a cohesive group were just as likely as internally motivated volunteers to remain volunteers for the period of the assignment. Thus, careful attention to environmental factors (e.g., the quality of training) may override individual differences that might otherwise undermine sustained volunteerism. Recent research on youth mentoring has similarly found that more extensive orientation programs may lead to greater satisfaction with the mentoring relationship (DuBois et al., 2002; Herrera, Sipe, & McClanahan, 2000), and more hours of training and meetings with other mentors (perhaps in support groups) have been shown to lead to longer mentoring relationships (McClanahan, 1998).

However, using situational variables to overwhelm individual differences, although likely to be successful at times, is not as subtle an approach as those that seek to adjust (or select) the environment according to the skills, goals, or needs of individual volunteers. The functional approach to volunteerism (Clary et al., 1998; Snyder et al., 2000) offers a systematic, clearly interactionist, and strategic means of addressing problems with volunteer retention, by focusing explicitly on the motivations individuals expect can be served by volunteer work. As detailed earlier, Clary et al. (1998) posited that individuals are attracted to volunteer work as a means of meeting their needs, goals, and motives. Furthermore, the functional approach predicts that they will be satisfied with their work and will continue volunteering, as long as their needs, goals, or motives are adequately addressed within the volunteer environment (Snyder et al., 2000). Different volunteer tasks or environments may offer opportunities—or "affordances"—to meet different motivational goals. The benefits that may be afforded by volunteering for positive youth development are numerous; however, organizations may need to ensure that those benefits are indeed available and salient to volunteers. Of course, it may be possible to frame the same task (if an organization's offerings are limited) in terms of an array of potential goals and benefits; the key may be to remind volunteers of the ways in which service can meet their particular goals, although actual goal satisfaction is undoubtedly necessary to sustain volunteers over the long term. That is, levels of volunteer satisfaction and future intentions to volunteer should be positively influenced by the extent to which volunteer motives are "matched" by the environment.

Several recent studies have examined both initial volunteer motivations and later "functionally relevant" benefits to properly assess the interaction of person and environment predicted by the functional approach. Using the VFI to measure initial volunteer motivations, Clary et al. (1998, Studies 5 and 6) found that both elderly and college student volunteers who subsequently received benefits relevant to their important motives were more satisfied than those who did not receive functionally matched benefits (including those who received other benefits). Furthermore, in addition to experiencing greater satisfaction in their volunteer roles, volunteers who received "matched" benefits also indicated greater intentions to continue as volunteers in both the short- and long-term future, compared to other volunteers (Clary et al., 1998, Study 6). Tschirhart et al. (2001) also found that the matching of the initial goals of stipended AmeriCorps volunteers with functionally relevant outcomes reported 1 year later, analyzed as a whole set (with matching of five goals better than matching of only four goals, and so on), strongly predicted both satisfaction and future intentions to volunteer after the contracted work was completed.

Interactionism and Volunteering for Youth Development

To date, however, research on motivational differences focused on youth mentoring has taken a "main effect" approach rather than an interactionist approach, often contrasting altruistic goals with egoistic goals, seeking to show that one type of motive leads to more beneficial outcomes than the other. For example, Karcher, Nakkula, and Harris (2005) found that mentors were less likely to perceive their relationships positively if they were motivated by self-interested reasons. Similarly, Rubin and Thorelli (1984) found that the number of egoistic motives indicated by volunteers was related inversely to their longevity of participation. In contrast, Starke and DuBois (1997) found that initial ratings of egoistic motivation, but not altruistic motivation, predicted later ratings of positive impact on youth (but not longevity) at a 6-month follow-up assessment. Given the lack of data on situational affordances in any of these studies, it is possible that altruistic and egoistic motives may both lead to better consequences from volunteerism—but only to the extent that actual opportunities allow these motives to be fulfilled (see Snyder et al., 2000), a factor that may have varied across these studies.

Fortunately, research that takes an interactionist approach, assessing both features of individuals and features of the volunteer environment (e.g., Clary et al., 2003), is on the rise. For example, Davis et al. (2003) assessed motives and their fulfillment in actual volunteer activities as predictors of satisfaction in a sample of community volunteers recruited from a range of volunteer agencies. "Altruistic" and "self-fulfillment" motivations were measured at the commencement of service. The extent to which volunteers saw each motive fulfilled was also assessed, along with satisfaction with service, on four occasions over the subsequent 12 months. Results suggested a significant relationship between motive fulfillment and volunteer satisfaction, but only across the first two time points. Given the length of time between the initial assessment of motivations, and the measures of motive fulfillment, it is possible that the motivations of volunteers changed over this time, such that fulfillment of the original motivations was no longer relevant to feelings of satisfaction with the overall volunteer experience (Davis et al., 2003).

Indeed, volunteer organizations may need to pay attention to, and carefully assess, potential changes in volunteers' motivations over time; this might occur informally in meetings between supervisors and volunteers or as part of a formal performance review process. Although Clary et al. (1998) demonstrated stability in VFI-assessed motives across a 4-week period, Snyder et al. (2000) suggested that the importance of these motives may change across the life span of long-term volunteers. Cross-sectional findings of volunteers in different age groups suggest that older volunteers have lower career and understanding motives and higher social motives than younger volunteers (Okun & Schultz, 2003). Such differences may represent historical or cohort-related factors, but it seems likely that career needs will eventually be reduced for individuals who have firmly established themselves at work (or who have retired). Individuals also may cease to be motivated to learn new things from a particular volunteer activity over time—or more likely, they may find that a familiar activity no longer offers understanding benefits. Tschirhart et al. (2001) found that altruistic, instrumental, and social goals (modeled on VFI functions but not using the scale) declined over a 1-year period for stipended AmeriCorps volunteers, while self-esteem and avoidance goals remained stable. These findings suggest that it may be useful for volunteer organizations to shift volunteers to new activities if a point of diminishing returns is reached (e.g., Snyder et al., 2000). Otherwise, failures in motive fulfillment may lead to attrition.

In addition to investigations of service duration, a small body of research has focused on volunteer attrition. Although retention and attrition may seem like two sides of the same coin, the distinction is important, as there is evidence to suggest that the factors that influence one are not simply the reverse of the factors influencing the other (Gidron, 1985). Investigations into volunteer turnover have tended to draw from the literature on turnover in paid employment to identify variables of potential relevance. Gidron (1985) collected data from volunteers on two occasions separated by a 6-month interval. On the second occasion, he identified those volunteers who had remained with the agency ("stayers") and those who had left by choice ("leavers"), and then compared their earlier responses. Gidron found that stayers could best be distinguished from leavers on variables related to task achievement, relationships with other volunteers, the extent of preparation involved in the work, and the nature of the work itself (e.g., level of challenge and interest). The predictive ability of this combination of factors was substantially higher, however, for stayers (81% correctly identified) than for leavers (43% correctly identified). Such a finding supports the idea that reasons for staying are not the reverse of reasons for leaving. It also suggests that there are further predictors of leaver status, beyond those examined in Gidron's work.

Although attitudinal and experiential variables have been seen to predict retention and turnover (e.g., Gidron, 1985; Omoto & Snyder, 1995; Penner & Finkelstein, 1998), additional external factors may also need to be considered when attempting to understand the reasons volunteers decide to leave. In their qualitative research on volunteers in a hospice organization in the United Kingdom, Field and Johnson (1993) reported that the main reasons given by volunteers for leaving related to external demands placed on them by employment and family commitments, along with personal problems, such as illness. Similarly,

Davis et al. (2003) noted that the vast majority of volunteers who left did so for reasons unrelated to dissatisfaction, such as time conflicts, emergencies, holidays, and moving house. These reasons echo the findings of the Canadian national survey that lack of time and other personal concerns were the primary reasons for not volunteering (Hall et al., 2001). Thus, it would behoove youth development organizations to pay careful attention to the additional needs of their volunteers, with an aim toward maintaining a flexible approach to volunteer management that would allow volunteers to meet all of their competing commitments (e.g., Grossman & Rhodes, 2002). In line with this, the recent AOL Time Warner survey on mentoring (O'Connor, 2002) also found that potential mentors varied in the types of activities they preferred, suggesting that a choice among mentoring options, depending on schedule and interests, was desirable.

Making it easy for volunteers to schedule tasks that also allow them to meet their goals and interests may go a long way toward establishing them as committed and long-term volunteers. Continued experience may encourage the development of a "role identity" in which the role of volunteer becomes a central or important feature of the person (e.g., Grube & Piliavin, 2000). Piliavin and Callero (1991) provided data to show that the more often someone donates blood, the more likely he or she is to donate blood in the future. Role identity as a volunteer has been shown to be a significant predictor of future intentions (Lee, Piliavin, & Call, 1999) and actual prosocial behavior (Piliavin & Callero, 1991). Grube and Piliavin (2000) extended the theory to examine both general role identity (as a volunteer) and specific role identity (as an American Red Cross volunteer), finding that specific role identity predicts service for a specific organization, whereas general role identity predicts overall commitment to service (across organizations). In either case, the development of a role identity may go hand in hand with the development of a social network that holds expectations for the individual about sustained volunteerism (e.g., Piliavin & Callero, 1991). Organizations that facilitate connections among volunteers or that encourage volunteers to internalize the importance of the role may do better at retaining their volunteer workforce. Attending youth mentor support groups, which may help volunteers develop a role identity and internalize these expectations, has been related to longer mentoring relationships and greater amounts of career mentoring and social activities (McClanahan, 1998).

No doubt there is even more that volunteer organizations can do to increase retention of volunteers. Clary et al. (2003) focused on the differential ability of volunteer organizations and environments to offer facilitators and remove barriers for motive fulfillment. Gagné (2003) discussed how organizations might offer support for the autonomy, competence, and relatedness needs of volunteers (e.g., Ryan & Deci, 2000). Penner (2002) suggested that an organization's reputation and practices, which have an impact on how a volunteer is treated and how a volunteer feels about the organization, may play a role in both recruitment and retention. Despite these inroads, it seems clear that, to date, the social psychological literature has focused heavily on person-centered variables that might predict sustained volunteerism, leaving our understanding of equally important situational and environmental predictors relatively impoverished.

The Big Picture

Having reviewed theories and research relevant to the recruitment and retention of volunteers who can build developmental assets for and with youth through formal organizations, we turn now to a societal level of analysis. We have briefly touched on the ways in which adults may become involved with young people to encourage their positive social development, ranging from informal activities (such as talking about values or supporting school achievement) to more formal activities (e.g., working for a volunteer organization). Despite the fact that many adults do volunteer, we agree with those who see room for improvement (Scales, 2003; Snyder, 1993). Our approach thus far has been to detail relevant theoretical and empirical approaches from the psychology of volunteerism that may be applicable to the problem of mobilizing adults for positive youth development. As so often happens, however, policy makers and practitioners have worked hard to develop ways to increase volunteerism in society (often without heed of the research literature).

Policies

Many of these new policies offer *incentives* to new volunteers (such as AmeriCorps, the National Civilian Community Corps, or Volunteers in Service to America), but some policies *require* students to engage in the types of community service usually engaged in by volunteers (e.g., Maryland requires 75 hours for high school students to graduate; Sobus, 1995). Other policies treat community service as a way to repay "debts" to society (Australia's Work for the Dole program; community service orders for criminal offenders). All of these policies can increase the amount of community service that is performed in society, and this potentially includes activities that build developmental assets. Indeed, 7% of all Canadian volunteers in 2000 (484,000 people) indicated that they were required to perform community service by their school, employer, or the government (Hall et al., 2001).

Any increase in volunteer labor due to incentives and requirements may come at a cost, however (e.g., Sobus, 1995). Social psychologists have often pointed out that incentives and requirements may undermine earlier intrinsic interest in an activity, thus diminishing future intentions to continue (e.g., Deci & Ryan, 1987; Lepper, Greene, & Nisbett, 1973). Such an undermining effect has already been demonstrated for helping behavior more generally (e.g., Batson, Coke, Jasnoski, & Hanson, 1978; Kunda & Schwartz, 1983; Piliavin & Callero, 1991) and has recently been demonstrated as a result of required community service as part of an educational course and in a laboratory analogue, particularly for individuals who found the requirement especially controlling (Stukas,

Snyder, & Clary, 1999). Nevertheless, when attention is paid to appropriate factors, community service organized through university academic courses (elective or required) can have benefits for volunteers and communities (see Stukas, Clary, & Snyder, 1999, for a review). Such service-learning courses may achieve benefits, beyond merely providing volunteer labor, by ensuring that those who are required or encouraged to volunteer (a) are given autonomy to determine the details of their service activities; (b) are able to develop respectful, collegial, and mutually fulfilling relationships with supervisors, instructors, and the recipients of their help; (c) are able to fulfill their own goals and needs through their service activity; and (d) are encouraged to reflect on the links between their service and their academic course, or the larger context of the world and their lives (Stukas, Clary, et al., 1999). These moderating factors bear a strong resemblance to the core human needs of autonomy, competence, and relatedness identified by Ryan and Deci (2000). Recent empirical work by Gagné (2003) suggests that perceived autonomy support from supervisors may predict the number of hours provided by, and the longevity of, volunteers.

Civil Society

So, it may be possible socially to engineer a new volunteer labor force—and potentially one whose members learn the benefits of volunteering and continue to volunteer throughout their life span. Such increased prosocial activity, and particularly activity directed toward positive youth development, has the potential to achieve much practical good (see Scales, 2003). But the new connections between individuals that are established through volunteerism may themselves offer benefits to society that reduce alienation, crime, and other social problems for adults as well as for young people. This is the essence of social capital theory, with social capital being defined as the sum total of social connections in a society, where these connections establish generalized norms of reciprocity and generalized interpersonal trust (e.g., Putnam, 2000; Yamagishi & Yamagishi, 1994). Putnam believes that trust can build through active participation in society and plays a role in the amelioration of social ills.

A society-wide increase in prosocial behavior, generalized trust, and social capital could have run-on effects in building developmental assets for and with young people. A larger proportion of the Search Institute framework of 40 assets (see Clary & Rhodes, Chapter 1, this volume; Scales & Leffert, 1999) would be accessible to more young people were communities to become more connected and rates of volunteerism to increase. Increased social capital then might feed back to maintain an increased level of prosocial activity, dedication to positive youth development, generalized trust, and a positive sense of community (see Omoto & Snyder, 2002). Current volunteers could be used to recruit new volunteers by singing the praises of the activities (e.g., Omoto & Snyder, 2002; Roaf et al., 1994), parents might model prosocial activities for their children to later take up (e.g., Clary & Miller, 1986; Stukas, Switzer, Dew, Goycoolea, & Simmons, 1999), and unrelated adults will perceive social norms and social expectations that guide them more to get involved in the lives of today's youth (e.g., Piliavin & Callero, 1991; Scales, 2003).

References

Ajzen, I. (1991). The theory of planned behavior. *Organizational Behavior & Human Decision Processes*, 50(2), 179–211.

Ajzen, I., & Fishbein, M. (1980). *Understanding attitudes and predicting social behavior*. Englewood Cliffs, NJ: Prentice-Hall.

Bandura, A. (1997). *Self-efficacy: The exercise of control*. New York: Freeman.

Batson, C. D., Coke, J. S., Jasnoski, M. L., & Hanson, M. (1978). Buying kindness: Effect of an extrinsic incentive for helping on perceived altruism. *Personality and Social Psychology Bulletin, 4*, 86–91.

Children's Defense Fund. (2002). *The state of children in America's union: A 2002 action guide to Leave No Child Behind*. Retrieved on July 12, 2004, from http://www. childrensdefense.org/data/default.asp

Clary, E. G., & Miller, J. (1986). Socialization and situational influences on sustained altruism. *Child Development, 57*, 1358–1369.

Clary, E. G., & Snyder, M. (1993). Persuasive communications strategies for recruiting volunteers. In D. R. Young, R. M. Hollister, & V. A. Hodgkinson (Eds.), *Governing, leading and managing nonprofit organizations* (pp. 121–137). San Francisco: Jossey-Bass.

Clary, E. G., & Snyder, M. (1999). The motivations to volunteer: Theoretical and practical considerations. *Current Directions in Psychological Science, 8*(5), 156–159.

Clary, E. G., Snyder, M., Ridge, R. D., Copeland, J., Stukas, A. A., Haugen, J., et al. (1998). Understanding and assessing the motivations of volunteers: A functional approach. *Journal of Personality and Social Psychology, 74*(6), 1516–1530.

Clary, E. G., Snyder, M., Ridge, R. D., Miene, P., & Haugen, J. (1994). Matching messages to motives in persuasion: A functional approach to promoting volunteerism. *Journal of Applied Social Psychology, 24*, 1129–1149.

Clary, E. G., Snyder, M., & Stukas, A. A. (1996). Volunteers' motivations: Findings from a national survey. *Nonprofit and Voluntary Sector Quarterly, 25*, 485–505.

Clary, E. G., Snyder, M., & Worth, K. (2003). *The volunteer organization environment: Key dimensions and distinctions*. Report to the Aspen Institute Nonprofit Sector Research Fund.

Davis, M. H., Hall, J. A., & Meyer, M. (2003). The first year: Influences on the satisfaction, involvement, and persistence of new community volunteers. *Personality and Social Psychology Bulletin, 29*(2), 248–260.

Deci, E. L., & Ryan, R. M. (1987). The support of autonomy and the control of behavior. *Journal of Personality and Social Psychology, 53*, 1024–1037.

DuBois, D. L., Holloway, B. E., Valentine, J. C., & Cooper, H. (2002). Effectiveness of mentoring programs for youth: A meta-analytic review. *American Journal of Community Psychology, 30*, 157–197.

Eagly, A. H., & Chaiken, S. (1993). *The psychology of attitudes*. Fort Worth, TX: Harcourt Brace Jovanovich.

Field, D., & Johnson, I. (1993). Satisfaction and change: A survey of volunteers in a hospice organisation. *Social Science & Medicine, 36*(12), 1625–1633.

Gagné, M. (2003). The role of autonomy support and autonomy orientation in prosocial behavior engagement. *Motivation and Emotion, 27*(3), 199–223.

Gidron, B. (1985). Predictors of retention and turnover among service volunteer workers. *Journal of Social Service Research, 8*(1), 1–16.

Grossman, J. B., & Rhodes, J. E. (2002). The test of time: Predictors and effects of duration in youth mentoring relationships. *American Journal of Community Psychology, 30*, 199–219.

Grossman, J. B., & Tierney, J. P. (1998). Does mentoring work? An impact study of the Big Brothers/Big Sisters. *Evaluation Review, 22*, 403–426.

Grube, J. A., & Piliavin, J. A. (2000). Role identity, organizational experiences, and volunteer performance. *Personality and Social Psychology Bulletin, 26*, 1108–1120.

Hall, M., McKeown, L., & Roberts, K. (2001). *Caring Canadians, involved Canadians: Highlights from the 2000 national survey of giving, volunteering, and participating.* Retrieved on July 12, 2004, from http://www.givingandvolunteering.ca/reports/2000_NSGVP_highlights.asp

Herrera, C., Sipe, C. L., & McClanahan, W. S. (2000). *Mentoring school-age children: Relationship development in community-based and school-based programs.* Philadelphia: Public/Private Ventures.

Hovland, C. I., Janis, I. L., & Kelley, H. H. (1953). *Communication and persuasion: Psychological studies of opinion change.* New Haven, CT: Yale University Press.

Independent Sector. (1988). *Giving and volunteering in the United States.* Washington, DC: Author.

Independent Sector. (1999). *Giving and volunteering in the United States.* Washington, DC: Author.

Independent Sector. (2001). *Giving and volunteering in the United States.* Washington, DC: Author.

Jenner, J. R. (1984). Organizational commitment among women volunteers. *Psychological Reports, 54*, 991–996.

Jones, F. (2001). Volunteering parents: Who volunteers and how are their lives affected? *Izuma: Canadian Journal of Policy Research, 2*(2), 69–74.

Karcher, M. J., Nakkula, M. J., & Harris, J. (2005). Developmental mentoring match characteristics: Correspondence between mentors' and mentees' assessments of relationship quality. *Journal of Primary Prevention, 26*, 93–110.

Katz, D. (1960). The functional approach to the study of attitudes. *Public Opinion Quarterly, 24*, 163–204.

Kunda, Z., & Schwartz, S. (1983). Undermining intrinsic moral motivation: External reward and self-presentation. *Journal of Personality and Social Psychology, 45*, 763–771.

Lasswell, H. D. (1948). The structure and function of communication in society. In L. Bryson (Ed.), *The communication of ideas* (pp. 37–51). New York: Harper & Row.

Lee, L., Piliavin, J. A., & Call, V. (1999). Giving time, money, and blood: Similarities and differences. *Social Psychology Quarterly, 62*, 276–290.

Lepper, M. R., Greene, D., & Nisbett, R. E. (1973). Undermining children's intrinsic interest with extrinsic reward: A test of the "overjustification" hypothesis. *Journal of Personality and Social Psychology, 28*, 129–137.

McClanahan, W. S. (1998). *Relationships in a career mentoring program: Lessons learned from the Hospital Youth Mentoring Program.* Philadelphia: Public/Private Ventures.

McLearn, K. T., Colasanto, D., & Schoen, C. (1998). *Mentoring makes a difference: Findings from the Commonwealth Fund 1998 survey of adults mentoring young people.* Retrieved on June 13, 2003, from http://www.ecs.org/html/Document.asp?chouseid=2843

Miller, L. E., Powell, G. N., & Seltzer, J. (1990). Determinants of turnover among volunteers. *Human Relations, 43*(9), 901–917.

O'Connor, R. (2002). *Mentoring in America 2002: Research sponsored by AOL Time Warner Foundation.* Pathfinder Research & MarketFacts for MENTOR/National Mentoring Partnership. Retrieved on June 13, 2003, from http://mentoring.web.aol.com/common/one_report/national_poll_report_final.pdf

Okun, M. (2002). Application of planned behavior theory to predicting volunteer enrollment by college students in a campus-based program. *Social Behavior and Personality, 30*(3), 243–250.

Okun, M. A., & Schultz, A. (2003). Age and motives for volunteering: Testing hypotheses derived from socioemotional selectivity theory. *Psychology and Aging, 18*, 231–239.

Omoto, A. M., & Snyder, M. (1995). Sustained helping without obligation: Motivation, longevity of service, and perceived attitude change among AIDS volunteers. *Journal of Personality and Social Psychology, 68*(4), 671–686.

Omoto, A. M., & Snyder, M. (2002). Considerations of community: The context and process of volunteerism. *American Behavioral Scientist, 45*(5), 846–867.

Parra, G. R., DuBois, D. L., Neville, H. A., Pugh-Lilly, A. O., & Povinelli, N. (2002). Mentoring relationships for youth: Investigation of a process-oriented model. *Journal of Community Psychology, 30*, 367–388.

Penner, L. A. (2002). Dispositional and organizational influences on sustained volunteerism: An interactionist perspective. *Journal of Social Issues, 58*(3), 447–467.

Penner, L. A., & Finkelstein, M. A. (1998). Dispositional and structural determinants of volunteerism. *Journal of Personality and Social Psychology, 74*(2), 525–537.

Petty, R., & Cacioppo, J. T. (1986). The elaboration likelihood model of persuasion. In L. Berkowitz (Ed.), *Advances in experimental social psychology* (Vol. 19, pp. 123–205). San Diego: Academic Press.

Piliavin, J. A., & Callero, P. L. (1991). *Giving blood: The development of an altruistic identity.* Baltimore: Johns Hopkins University Press.

Putnam, R. D. (2000). *Bowling alone: The collapse and revival of American community.* New York: Simon & Schuster.

Rhodes, J. E. (2002). *Stand by me: The risks and rewards of mentoring today's youth.* Cambridge, MA: Harvard University Press.

Roaf, P. A., Tierney, J. P., & Hunte, D. E. I. (1994). *Big Brothers/Big Sisters of America: A study of volunteer recruitment and screening.* Philadelphia: Public/Private Ventures.

Rubin, A., & Thorelli, I. M. (1984). Egoistic motives and longevity of participation by social service volunteers. *Journal of Applied Behavioral Science, 20,* 223–235.

Ryan, R. M., & Deci, E. L. (2000). Self-determination theory and the facilitation of intrinsic motivation, social development, and well-being. *American Psychologist, 55,* 68–78.

Scales, P. C. (2003). *Other people's kids: Social expectations and American adults' involvement with children and adolescents.* New York: Kluwer Academic/Plenum.

Scales, P. C., & Leffert, N. (1999). *Developmental assets: A synthesis of the scientific research on adolescent development.* Minneapolis, MN: Search Institute.

Sipe, C. L., & Roder, A. E. (1999). *Mentoring school-age children: A classification of programs.* Philadelphia: Public/Private Ventures.

Smith, M. B., Bruner, J. S., & White, R. W. (1956). *Opinions and personality.* New York: Wiley.

Snyder, M. (1993). Basic research and practical problems: The promise of a "functional" personality and social psychology. *Personality and Social Psychology Bulletin, 19,* 251–264.

Snyder, M., & Cantor, N. (1998). Understanding personality and social behavior: A functionalist strategy. In D. Gilbert, S. Fiske, & G. Lindzey (Eds.), *The handbook of social psychology* (4th ed., Vol. 1, pp. 635–679). New York: McGraw-Hill.

Snyder, M., Clary, E. G., & Stukas, A. A. (2000). The functional approach to volunteerism. In G. R. Maio & J. M. Olson (Eds.), *Why we evaluate: Functions of attitudes* (pp. 365–393). Hillsdale, NJ: Erlbaum.

Sobus, M. S. (1995). Mandating community service: Psychological implications of requiring prosocial behavior. *Law and Psychology Review, 19,* 153–182.

Starke, M. L., & DuBois, D. L. (1997). Characteristics of mentors with successful relationships. *MU McNair Journal* (Fall), 9–14.

Stukas, A. A., Clary, E. G., & Snyder, M. (1999). Service learning: Who benefits and why. *Social Policy Report: Society for Research on Child Development, 13,* 1–19.

Stukas, A. A., Snyder, M., & Clary, E. G. (1999). The effects of "mandatory volunteerism" on intentions to volunteer. *Psychological Science, 10*(1), 59–64.

Stukas, A. A., Switzer, G. E., Dew, M. A., Goycoolea, J. M., & Simmons, R. G. (1999). Parental helping models, gender, and service-learning. *Journal of Prevention and Intervention in the Community, 18*(1/2), 5–18.

Stukas, A. A., & Tanti, C. (2005). Recruiting and sustaining volunteer mentors. In D. L. DuBois & M. J. Karcher (Eds.), *Handbook of youth mentoring* (pp. 235–250). Newbury Park, CA: Sage.

Tschirhart, M., Mesch, D. J., Perry, J. L., Miller, T. K., & Lee, G. (2001). Stipended volunteers: Their goals, experiences, satisfaction, and likelihood of future service. *Nonprofit and Voluntary Sector Quarterly, 30*(3), 422–443.

White, M. J. (1984). Social expectations for prosocial behavior and altruism. *Academic Psychology Bulletin, 6,* 71–93.

Wilson, J. (2000). Volunteering. *Annual Review of Sociology, 26,* 215–240.

Yamagishi, T., & Yamagishi, M. (1994). Trust and commitment in the United States and Japan. *Motivation and Emotion, 18,* 129–166.

5 Generativity and Adult Development: Implications for Mobilizing Volunteers in Support of Youth

Andrea S. Taylor

Temple University

In 1950, the psychologist Erik Erikson introduced the concept of generativity as the seventh of eight stages in his theory of human development and the life cycle. Erikson, a Danish art student, came to the United States in the early 1930s after studying with Anna Freud in exploring ways to apply psychoanalytic methods to children. Erikson's affiliation with the Institute for Human Development at the University of California at Berkeley, where he followed the lives of 50 children, in combination with his own cross-cultural studies, provided the data to propose a perspective on human development suggesting that psychological growth occurs throughout the life cycle and is not limited to the early years. In writing *Childhood and Society* (1950), he became the first social scientist to articulate adult development in the context of growth potential rather than diminishing capacity; he described this potential in terms of an adult's "widening social radius" and "generativity" (Vaillant, 2002). Generativity refers to the capacity of adults to care for family, community, and institutions; to preserve and pass on cultural traditions; and to produce products, outcomes, and ideas that will survive the self and become a legacy for future generations. Generativity is the "concern for establishing and guiding the next generation" (Erikson, 1968, p. 138), and, as Erikson and colleagues later described it, generativity is "I am what survives of me" (Erikson, Erikson, & Kivnick, 1986). Although the first edition of *Childhood and Society* devoted only two pages to generativity, Erikson's later work focused much more on generativity, reflecting both a change in our social conscience and Erikson's personal journey as he aged.

Erikson's landmark work identified eight developmental stages of human growth from infancy to old age, and each was described in terms of both syntonic and dystonic elements. The syntonic supports growth, expansion, and goal achievement, while the dystonic implies dissatisfaction, failure, and dysphoria (1950, 1968). Thus, individuals confront issues of basic trust–mistrust, autonomy–shame and doubt, initiative–guilt, industry–inferiority, identity–identity confusion, intimacy–isolation, generativity–stagnation, and integrity–despair. The stages, however, are not completely rigid; tasks, or crises, may not be fully resolved from one to the next, but appear in some form, with the potential for resolution, throughout development (Newman, Ward, Smith, Wilson, & McCrea, 1997).

Erikson associated "generativity vs. stagnation" with the middle adult years. In his view, the tasks of young adults are to establish a sense of identity (Who am I?) in stage five and achieve intimacy through marriage and/or friendship (Who do I love?) in stage six. Successful resolution of these tasks prepares adults, emotionally and socially, to make a commitment to the next generation and, ultimately, the larger society as a whole (McAdams & de St. Aubin, 1998). The tension of the seventh stage pits care against rejectivity; failure to participate "generatively" can result in "stagnation," which manifests as self-absorption, isolation, and disappointing personal relationships and, ultimately, affects the resolution of the eighth stage, in which the task is to develop a sense of integrity and wisdom strong enough to withstand the physical decline and challenges of old age. Research suggests that nurturing, giving to, and serving others contribute to greater ego integrity, personal happiness, and overall well-being (Sheldon & Kasser, 2001). In Vaillant's (2002) longitudinal study of adult development, generativity in midlife contributed significantly to joy and satisfaction of study participants when they reached their 70s and 80s.

Generativity has its expression in procreativity, productivity, and creativity (Erikson et al., 1986). While generativity often begins in the child-rearing years, it is not limited to parenthood but, ideally, leads to the desire and commitment to provide care, nurturing, and guidance outside of the family ("maintenance of the world"). Thus, in addition to parenting, generative activity entails mentoring, teaching, coaching, and volunteering—in the workplace, schools, faith communities, or other community organizations. Generative activity involves voting, citizen advocacy, and political involvement. Some generative individuals may be less inclined to nurture their personal circle but leave a legacy through the arts, scholarship, or the creation of social movements that affect the lives of millions of people and change the course of history. Mohandas Gandhi, the subject of a psychobiographical study by Erikson (1969), was a distant, sometimes even cruel, parent to his own children and the young people around him, but in freeing his country from British rule, he was highly generative in the public arena (Freedman, 1999).

In his later years, Erikson despaired that our society was losing generativity as a cultural value, and he strongly believed it was imperative to restore generative perspective and commitment in order to promote positive values for the next generation (Goleman, 1988), a sentiment echoed by others who have suggested that we are in need of far greater numbers of generative individuals who demonstrate a more caring approach to environmental, family, and societal concerns (Browning, 1975; Snarey, 1993). Robert Bellah and his colleagues (1991) suggested that Americans were more concerned about their accumulated wealth and personal success than about the welfare of future generations, and they called for a "politics of generativity" to help narrow the chasm of inequality that characterizes the United States. The apparent decline of generative activity has also been articulated as the unraveling of the "social compact" (Achenbaum, 1999; Cornman & Kingson, 1999; Reich, 1999). The social compact, essential for human development and progress, is based on the reciprocal ties that hold families, governance, and society together over time. A successful social compact rests on the exchange of knowledge and resources across generations within families and age groups, and across cohorts within societies (Cornman & Kingson, 1999). A strong and pervasive social compact was first described by Alexis de Tocqueville in *Democracy in America* (1835). He noted that Americans, regardless of blood ties, cooperated with one another and helped each other out when necessary. Altruism, according to Tocqueville, was not the motivation. Rather, given the contingencies of life, doing "good" was a wise investment in the future (Achenbaum, 1999). Despite the evidence that society benefits from such an investment, we are, for many reasons, now experiencing a marked decline in civic engagement, which can be defined as the manifestation of generativity outside of one's family. According to sociologist Robert Putnam (2000), post–World War II America has seen a steady decrease in political activity, religious affiliation, volunteering, and membership in a community club or organization. While the 2004 U.S. presidential campaign appears to have stimulated interest in civic participation and even resulted in increased voter registration in some states (Fessenden, 2004), it remains to be seen whether this will have an enduring effect that might begin to reverse the current declines.

As researchers and practitioners, we have a far better understanding of child and adolescent development, which is shorter and more clearly defined and observable, than we do of the long and complex period known as "adulthood" (Snarey & Clark, 1998). Erikson's seventh stage lasts longer than any other, but only in the past two decades have researchers begun to examine the complexity and nuance of generativity, with regard both to individual development and to the implications for society (Kotre, 1984). The United States is currently poised on the edge of an unprecedented demographic shift as the baby boom generation (born 1946–1964) moves into mid- and late life (U.S. Census Bureau, 2000). Consequently, there is a significant population of adults who could be available as resources for youth. Researchers have concluded that the need to be generative is a powerful motivator for people at this stage of life because they are looking for productive roles and want to provide leadership and guidance that will foster the development of the next generation (Freedman, 1988; Henkin and Kingson, 1999a; Newman et al., 1997; Taylor & Bressler, 2000; Taylor, LoSciuto, Fox, & Hilbert, 1999). In light of this assumption, it is the goal of this chapter to explore generativity theory, with its tensions and ambiguities, and provide a better understanding of the social, psychological, and emotional dynamics of midlife and older adults. It is anticipated that a review of this research will both enhance our understanding of generativity in midlife and inform practice in the area of increasing adult participation in youth development activities.

A Generativity Framework

McAdams and his colleagues (1998) have proposed a generativity sequence, incorporating seven elements that provide a useful framework for understanding the principles and progression of generative behavior. In their view, adults are motivated to be generative based on (1) agentic and communal *desire to act* with regard for the future and (2) *cultural demand*, the societal expectation that they will take responsibility for the next generation. Desire and demand combine to promote (3) *concern* for the next generation and (4) a *commitment* to act on the concern. Generative commitment occurs in the context of (5) *belief*, a conviction that human beings are fundamentally worthwhile and, therefore, it is important to protect, nurture, and advance humankind. Erikson (1963) described this as "belief in the species," without which adults may find it impossible to articulate generative goals. Concern and belief lead to (6) *generative action*, which is given meaning by the seventh feature of the model, (7) *narration*. Narration allows adults to describe their lives in a way that provides purpose and identity; narration helps make sense of generative actions by focusing on what has been created (children, products, social movements) that will live on and become a legacy (Charme, 1984; Kotre, 1984; Ricoeur, 1984). Generative individuals tend to articulate their life stories in terms of *redemption*, in which negative experiences are transformed into positive outcomes. In contrast, those who are less generative often tell their stories in terms of *contamination*, in which the negative events supersede all other experiences. Among other things, the importance of the redemption sequence is that it reinforces Erikson's notion of "belief in the species" and allows people to maintain their faith in humankind, affirming hope for the future and the conviction that their own lives have had meaning (McAdams & Logan, 2004).

How Is Generativity Assessed?

Measuring generativity is a complex and challenging task, as is assessment of almost any aspect of an individual's psychosocial makeup. Although the following examples are not exhaustive by any means, they should serve to illustrate the types of assessment strategies that have been used. Two of the most frequently used instruments are the Loyola Generativity Scale (LGS) and the Generative Behavior Checklist (GBC). McAdams and de St. Aubin (1992) constructed and validated the LGS, a 20-item self-report checklist that measures individual differences in generative concern. The LGS focuses on concepts, cited in the literature, such as teaching and passing on knowledge, making positive contributions to society, caring for and taking responsibility for others, being creative and productive, and leaving an enduring legacy. The GBC (McAdams &

de St. Aubin, 1992) assesses what a person actually does, using an act-frequency method asking how many times in the past 2 months a person has engaged in 50 different tasks, 40 of which are indicative of generativity. McAdams, de St. Aubin, and Logan (1993) developed a third tool for assessing generative commitments by collecting *personal strivings*, meaning any goals a person is trying to accomplish in daily life, which are then coded for generative ideas.

Another approach has been proposed by Bradley and Marcia (1998), who have suggested that these scales define the construct along a high–low continuum but may not be useful in considering the ways in which individuals arrive at "particular generativity resolutions" (p. 40) that are not polar opposites. They have developed a model of five generativity statuses based on two criteria, involvement and inclusivity, and the relationship of each to oneself and to others. Involvement reflects the degree of active concern one has for others and the extent to which this manifests in the sharing of skills, knowledge, and prosocial commitment, described by Erikson (1964) as a care that motivates adults to participate in the establishment, guidance, and enrichment of the present generation and the world that will be inherited. Inclusivity relates to who, or what, will be included in the caregiving provided. In Bradley and Marcia's model, combinations of involvement and inclusivity provide the five generativity statuses: generative, agentic, communal, conventional, and stagnant. As an example, highly generative individuals are very involved in both dimensions, which manifests in their involvement in work, in promoting the healthy development of young people, and in the broader community. Conventional individuals, on the other hand, score high on involvement with others but low on inclusivity. So, while they may be involved with young people, they also believe that youth need firm guidance and must follow a clearly defined and narrow path that does not depart from established boundaries. A mentor–protégé relationship in which the mentor has strong conventional characteristics might be described as prescriptive, one in which the goals and agenda are determined by the adult rather than mutually agreed upon (Sipe, 1996). Those who are stagnant are low in both involvement and inclusivity. They have low self-esteem and self-satisfaction, are pessimistic about the future, and are negative toward the potential of the young to engage in productive roles and behavior.

Finally, personal narration is a useful tool for identifying and understanding generative themes in people's lives, particularly important for midlife adults who describe their lives in terms of what they have been given by others and how it is their turn to "give back." Generative ideas are often incorporated into life stories and life review and help people make peace with the inevitable conclusion that "I may die but my legacy—children, ideas, products—will live on." The narratives of highly generative adults are much more likely to focus on redemption sequences, in which a bad experience is made better by what follows. The generative adult is able to take a negative experience and use it to create an example that will help someone else avoid the same experience (an ex-convict who can create a different scenario for a youth at risk, for example). The generative adult also tells stories that remind us that hard work and sacrifice can pay off—that generativity is about progress and improvement.

What Has Been Learned about Generativity?

It has been suggested that human development is more fluid than Erikson's stage model theory might suggest (Bradley & Marcia, 1998; McAdams, Hart, & Shadd, 1998; Stewart & Vandewater, 1998; VanderVen, 1999) and that generative activity changes over time and is a function of psychosocial development, life circumstance, and cultural roles. The body of research provides some valuable insights into understanding the construct of generativity.

Generativity Enhances Psychological Well-Being

It appears that generativity is connected to psychological well-being, self-esteem, and life satisfaction (Bradley & Marcia, 1998; McAdams et al., 1998; Stewart & Vandewater, 1998; Vaillant, 2002). In a longitudinal study of two cohorts of college-educated women, Keyes and Ryff (1998) found that generative behavior, generative norms, and generative self-conceptions were linked to well-being, and they suggest that generativity seems to be central to feeling positively about oneself and assessing one's life as meaningful and worthwhile. Generativity has been linked to extensive social networks and personal satisfaction with one's participation (Hart, McAdams, Hirsch, & Bauer, 2001). During the past decades, as the nation has experienced a steady decline in civic engagement, epidemiologists have also noted trends toward more depression, suicide, and malaise. Putnam (2000) has speculated that a possible explanation is social isolation, which supports the idea that generativity, and the accompanying socialization, contribute to overall well-being.

Generativity Is Motivated by Narcissism and Altruism

It has been suggested that we are motivated to be generative both because we have a desire to create something that will outlive us and because we are concerned with nurturing future generations (Kotre, 1984; McAdams, 1985; McAdams & Logan, 2004). Procreation allows us to live on through our children, but we may also leave a legacy through our professional work, or artistic or scholarly endeavors. Kotre's (1984) typology proposes that generativity is expressed in terms of the (1) biological: giving birth to a child; (2) parental: parenting a child; (3) technical: the transmission of skills and societal symbols; and (4) culture: the creation of new or transmission of existing elements of culture. Described by Bakan (1966) as agency (the tendency toward self-protection and promotion of oneself) and communion (the sharing of oneself with others), agentic and communal generativity challenge us to produce products and offspring, and then care, lovingly, and sometimes selflessly, for what we have produced. Ideally, generative adults are highly agentic and communal at the same time, but there may also be a fundamental tension between the two (Bradley & Marcia,

1998; Miller-McLemore, 2004) such that excessive expression of either may be problematic. Bradley and Marcia (1998), for example, suggest that highly agentic individuals are very involved in their own activities, and they often exclude those who are not involved in a project with them. For these people, work and legacy are paramount, and relationships may be important only within the context of career. The generativity literature has provided us with fascinating portraits of such people, including dancer Martha Graham (Lee, 1998) and architect Frank Lloyd Wright (de St. Aubin, 1998). In contrast, those with a predominantly communal style are extremely involved with other people, often subjugating their own needs and viewing themselves as indispensable to others. Excessive communality can potentially encourage dependent relationships, which can be damaging, for example, to a young person struggling to become autonomous and independent.

Generativity Is a Function of Timing

McAdams and his colleagues (1998) agree with Erikson's notion that generativity is primarily an activity of the middle adult years. In a study of adults ages 22 to 72, generative concern, commitment, and behavior were present for all three cohorts. They found, however, that middle-years adults, ages 37 to 42, demonstrated more generative concern and participated in more generative activities than either younger adults, ages 22 to 27, or older adults, ages 67 to 72. Generative commitment appears to be high for both midlife and older adults. They were unable to say whether these differences were due to developmental or historical effects. Stewart and Vandewater (1998) suggest that generativity desire appears in the mid-20s during young adulthood, the capacity for generativity increases during the mid-30s, but is really only accomplished beginning in the later 40s. Finally, Keyes and Ryff (1998) found that midlife (ages 40–59) and older (ages 60–74) adults were able to give more unpaid assistance and emotional support to more people and felt fewer familial and more civic obligations than younger adults, perhaps reflecting the pressure they experience from career and family. While these studies generally support a generativity "peak" in midlife, they do not take into account the increase in the healthy life span of older adults (65 and up) and the lack of opportunities for them to engage in productive activities in the community (Riley, Kahn, & Foner, 1994). If the talent and energies of older people are not valued or used, their access to generative activities outside of the family will reflect that disparity.

What about those individuals who do not follow the traditional trajectory? Research suggests that generativity is not a discrete stage in human development but follows its own course based on cultural roles and life circumstances. While society's expectations regarding the timing of midlife events still prevail, the reality is that many adults are putting off marriage and childbearing until well into their 40s, if they have children at all, and others are becoming parents while they are still in their teen years. Divorce and nontraditional family constellations are also affecting the sequencing of midlife developmental activities (Cohler, Hostetler, & Boxer, 1998). Being "off time" does not preclude generative action. Some researchers have concluded that men who become parents later have a better sense of "self" and actually feel more comfortable with themselves in the parenting role than those who make the transition "on time" (Daniels & Weingarten, 1982; Nydegger, 1981). In recounting the life stories of gay men, Cohler and his colleagues noted the presence of generative behavior despite the absence of predictable life transitions, such as heterosexual marriage and parenthood, that usually characterize the lives of heterosexuals. This suggests that generativity may be a function of development as much as a consequence of social timing (McAdams, 1996).

Generativity Is Influenced by Culture

Different cultures have different expectations with regard to generative practices but share the generative goal of promoting the physical survival and psychological well-being of their children (Kotre, 2004). Generative adults, there-fore, must operate within the social, political, and economic context of their societies (de St. Aubin, 2004). A study of generativity and culture in Japan and the United States provides an illustrative example. Japan is a society in which women's expressions of generativity focus primarily on the household and raising of children. Child rearing in Japan would seem to us to be exces-sively permissive and encouraging of children's dependence, especially on their mothers, but is in keeping with the cultural value of collectivism that exists in Japanese society. In contrast, American mothers encourage independence and exploration, behavior that is in line with the value of autonomy and individ-ualism that predominates in the United States. In the United States, effective mentoring relationships are characterized by reciprocity, whereas in Japan the knowledge resides with the mentor and must be sought out by the protégé (de St. Aubin, 2004).

While most societies have clear expectations regarding generative activity, the timing can vary from one society to the next. There are societies in which parenting is expected to begin in the teen years, which would be considered "off time" in the United States, where it is generally expected that parenting will be delayed until adults are at least in their 20s. By the time U.S. adults are in their 30s and 40s, however, they are expected to assume generative roles—to become parents, to form careers, to be engaged in the civic life of the community (Cohler et al., 1998; McAdams et al., 1998).

In many societies, historically, generativity means passing along cultural traditions and values that inform the ways in which members engage in the civic and religious life of the community, and, often, the well-being of future generations is tied to an understanding of the past (McAdams et al., 1998). In this current period of rapid social change there is often a tremendous disconnect between tradition and the expectations of modern society, also described as a "generativity mismatch"; elders not only are underappreciated but also are unable to provide the kinds of resources and guidance the young may need in order to address the challenges of 21st-century societies.

Even in the United States, understanding cultural differences with regard to generativity has become even more crucial as the country has become increasingly diverse. For example, are communities motivated by collectivist or individualist values, and how might this affect the ways in which people act, or do not act, on their concern for youth?

Generative Action Differs by Gender

It has been argued that agency and communion may be influenced by conventionally defined gender roles still present in our society (Miller-McLemore, 2004). The paired components of narcissism and altruism have been identified by McAdams (2001) as power and love, agency and communion, self-expression and self-surrender, and public–private expressions. In Miller-McLemore's (2004) view, women have been pushed toward the second component of each pair and bear an inordinate responsibility for nurturing and maintaining the next generation, while men are more able to abdicate their caregiving responsibilities in favor of occupational relationships. In a study of generativity in adult lives, Keyes and Ryff (1998) found that women felt more obligated than men to assist social institutions as well as individuals and to extend their emotional support to more people. In their study, they found comparable levels of generative concern as men and women age, but that did not necessarily translate to generative action. Education was a particular enhancement of women's generative self-conceptions but seemed to have the opposite effect in men. In a study assessing adults' motivation and behavior regarding involvement in the lives of children other than their own, women were more likely than men to consider it important (Scales, 2003). These findings, while not conclusive, suggest that women might be more disposed to participate in activities with nonfamilial youth that involve personal relationship development. Assessments of volunteer recruitment in youth mentoring programs, for example, indicate significantly greater numbers of female mentors (Taylor, LoSciuto, & Porcellini, 2005).

Generative Adults Engage in a Range of Social Involvement

As we have noted, generative adults are engaged in a variety of activities. Parenting within the family is one of the first forms of generative behavior we see, and highly generative adults who are parents appear to be more effective in this role than those who are less generative. The research suggests that generative parents prioritize education and prosocial values, enjoy and value their relationships with their children, and take advantage of parenting to pass on lessons and traditions to the next generation (Hart et al., 2001; Nakagawa, 1991). Effective parenting has also been linked to an authoritative style, parents who strike a healthy balance between encouraging autonomy and enforcing reasonable rules and standards (Baumrind, 1991). Authoritarian parents, on the other hand, appear to impede their child's developing competence by being too strict and viewing their behavior as something negative that must be controlled (Pratt, Danso, Arnold, Norris, & Filyer, 2001). Bradley and Marcia (1998) found that an authoritative style was linked to greater inclusivity in caregiving activities with regard to who or what will be included, consistent with Erikson's view that more mature and generative adults have a "greater tolerance of tension and diversity" (1968, p. 82).

Second, more public expressions of generativity include involvement in religious institutions, volunteering in the community, and participating in the political process (Hart et al., 2001). Snyder and Clary (2004) have pointed out that volunteerism is not always directed at future generations, and some people may be generative in the type of paid work they do, but there appears to be enough of an overlap to suggest that volunteerism is an expression of generativity. Hart and her colleagues found that high levels of generativity were associated with extensive social networks and greater levels of satisfaction with social relationships, both of which occur in the context of participation in religious and civic institutions. Finally, in a nationwide survey of 3,000 adults ages 25 to 74, generativity was the strongest predictor of socially responsible behavior, including volunteerism (Rossi, 2001).

Generative Action Is Moderated by Social Status and Education

Education and income appear to have an effect on generativity action, but not necessarily generative concern or commitment. Studies conducted by McAdams (1996) and his colleagues found that higher levels of generativity were modestly related to income and social class. In a study of African American and White adults ages 35 to 65, Hart and her colleagues (2001) found that there appeared to be no differences between the generativity levels of African Americans and Whites with regard to social supports, involvement in religious activities, political participation, and parents emphasizing prosocial roles and seeing themselves as role models. The Whites in the sample were better educated and had higher incomes; when income and education were employed as covariates, African Americans scored significantly higher than Whites.

More education is often an indicator of higher social status, and Putnam (2000) suggests that education appears to be one of the strongest predictors of altruistic behavior. College graduates are more likely than people with a high school education to volunteer (71% compared to 36%) or to be blood donors (13%–18% compared to 6%–10%). Financial resources, however, are not the most important predictors of altruism—poor people who are active in their churches give approximately the same percentage of their income as those who are wealthy (Schervish & Havens, 1995). Keyes and Ryff (1998) found that women with more education felt they had valuable skills and experience, felt more

committed and obligated to society, and were more likely to engage in generative activities. Finally, in assessing whether adults felt it was important to interact
with young people to enhance developmental assets, Scales (2003) found that
Americans with less education and lower income considered engagement with
young people more important than did better educated and affluent Americans.
When income, education, and race were considered together, race had the most
significant impact on whether adults considered the actions important. None
of these variables, however, had an impact on whether adults were *actually*
engaged.

Erikson described *self-preoccupation* as one of the failings of generativity
(1968), but self-preoccupation is very much reflected in cultural and economic
issues. People who are very poor must focus on survival and do not have the
time or luxury to worry about the next generations. It would seem logical, therefore, that most of the studies of generativity have been conducted with middle-
and lower-middle-class adults (Cohler et al., 1998). It has been suggested, however, that more racially and economically inclusive studies would contribute
to a broader understanding of generativity across social class (Cohler et al.,
1998).

Generativity Varies within and across Birth Cohorts

It has been established that generative adults are civically engaged in their
communities. In this era of declining civic engagement, it is therefore essential
to address the differences in participation in generative activities between and
among birth cohorts. Cohler and his colleagues (1998) have noted the influence of
historical events, especially during adolescence, on generative behavior in later
life. For example, the cohort born between 1925 and 1930 attended grade school
during the Depression and was in high school, or the military, during World
War II, established households during the early 1950s, and did not see their first
television until their late 20s. World War II united the country and produced a
generation whose personal narration resonates with hard work, self-sacrifice,
and hope for the future (Kotre, 2004). Called the "long civic generation," this cohort showed extraordinary interest in the civic life of the community and acted
by voting, joining, reading, and volunteering at twice the rates of postwar birth
cohorts (Putnam, 2000). Baby boomers born just after World War II experienced
adolescence during the 1960s, a time of tremendous social upheaval marked by
a search for identity and personal meaning. They were raised watching television, which has had a significant impact on people's leisure time and has greatly
reduced the informal visiting and conversations of the prewar decades. They
came of age during a period of social unrest marked by the assassinations of
political leaders, Watergate, and Vietnam. Despite unprecedented educational
achievement, they are less knowledgeable about politics than their parents' generation, less involved in the political process, and avoid their civic duties more.
Even when their children were in school, the baby boomers were less likely to
be involved in the generative activities typically associated with the parenting

years, such as affiliations with parent–teacher associations or coaching sports teams. There are also differences between those born in the late 1940s and those born, for example, in the early 1960s. The early boomers came of age in the 1970s, when boundaries and role definitions were being challenged to an even greater extent, and while they demonstrate an increased tolerance toward racial, sexual, and political minorities, they also show less trust and assume less responsibility for community life.

The baby boomers are part of an especially large birth cohort and have, all of their lives, faced enhanced competition for resources, from schools to jobs to marital partners and, ultimately, health care and social services as they move into later life. It has been suggested that this type of lifelong competition takes a toll on morale, as the cohort has endured diminished expectations and economic challenges (Cohler et al., 1998; Putnam, 2000). Putnam (2000) also suggests that as a result of the uniformity of the postwar United States in which the boomers grew up, they were more likely to resist traditional social roles, including community participation. The children of the baby boomers, born between 1965 and 1980, also known as "Generation X," are even more disengaged and frustrated than their parents' generation. While they are experiencing even greater social isolation, they are also trying to enter the job market at a time of economic downturn and declining employment, which, in turn, is leading to further delay of careers to the late 20s and, consequently, postponement of expected role transitions such as marriage and family (Cohler et al., 1998). Described by Cohler and his colleagues (1998) as being "late off time" with regard to societal expectations, this generation is shaped by uncertainty and insecurity, both of which have an effect on their social and civic engagement. While the baby boomers often criticize the "Gen Xers" for their consumerism and individualism, the erosion of the social compact started long before the latter group was born.

It must also be noted that employed Americans are working many more hours than they were 20 years ago (Schor, 1991). Women, who traditionally provided most of the volunteer hours to the community, are in the labor force in far greater numbers than they were in 1960; when child rearing and housework are added to full-time employment, women work, on average, 15 hours more per week than men do (Hochschild, 1989). As Freedman (1999) states, all of this equates to squeezing 13 months of work into 12 months, and workweeks consisting of 80 to 100 hours.

In recent decades we have seen a decline in attendance at religious services and club membership, two traditional avenues for volunteer participation. Despite this, individual volunteerism in the late 1990s showed an increase among adults over 60 and young adults in their 20s, although participation in community projects did not (Putnam, 2000). It has been speculated that the increase in generative action on the part of older adults, still members of that "long civic group," is due to greater leisure time in retirement and better health. It is not totally clear why there has been an increase among the young twentysomethings, although increased public encouragement, such as service requirements for graduation, may be one of the reasons (Putnam, 2000).

Implications for Youth Development: Lessons Learned

The research cited here has created a portrait of a generative adult and provided some lessons to provoke our thinking about what makes an individual, and a society, generative. We know that generativity, in its most optimistic configuration, is motivated by both the desire to believe in a positive, healthy future for succeeding generations and by a quest for immortality. Generativity begins in young adulthood, often but not exclusively with parenthood, and increases with age as people have the time and opportunity to turn their attention to broader community affiliations. Generativity is expressed by helping others, either as a volunteer or through paid employment. Generative individuals participate in the civic life of the community and are more likely to vote, to feel trusting of others, and to have faith in a better future. Generativity is not the province of one racial, ethnic, or cultural group but is influenced by the values of the specific community from which it emanates. Generative actions, though not concern or commitment, are positively influenced by higher levels of education, affiliation with a variety of social and religious institutions, and being female. Generative individuals have broader social networks and may be more likely to attend church and belong to social clubs or civic organizations. Generativity is positively associated with well-being and self-efficacy, and it contributes to more positive attitudes in old age. For better or worse, generativity is influenced by sociohistorical events, which can have a profound impact on an entire birth cohort: "Generativity is not just a phase of adult development. It is an encompassing orientation to life" (Miller-McLemore, 2004, p. 186). If that orientation is deficient, it has a profound impact on the life of the community and the future of its children.

Our society needs a population of generative adults if it is to survive and thrive. We need people to care enough about the decisions that are made in the political arena that they are willing to vote for candidates who will best represent the interests of present and future generations. We need people to care enough about the 13 million children living without much hope for a healthy future that they will act supportively, as mentors, teachers, coaches—or just good neighbors. We need people to care enough about education that they will work to make schools safer and stronger, and advocate for the necessary resources. For these things to occur, we need to proactively engage the existing population of midlife and older adults and to motivate young people to take their place as members of a generative and engaged society. What follows are a few possible strategies.

Aim Volunteer Recruitment Efforts at Midlife and Older Adults

The research demonstrates that generativity action peaks in the middle and later years (Erikson et al., 1986; McAdams et al., 1998; Stewart & Vandewater, 1998). It would make sense, therefore, that recruitment efforts for initiatives supporting youth should target midlife and older adults. Despite the aging of the

U.S. population and the significant numbers of healthy older adults available to volunteer, there remains a good deal of ageism. The biggest inducement to volunteer is being asked by someone with whom there is a relationship. Volunteering is often an extension of work, child rearing, and family and social life. After retirement, as these aspects of adults' lives change, they are less likely to be asked to volunteer and, therefore, are less likely to do so (Prisuta, 2003). Programs seeking volunteers frequently target younger adults, who may not have the time, the inclination, or a sense of their own capacity to teach youth about cultural differences, money management, or values (Scales, 2003). Midlife and older adults may be in an ideal position to help youth make the connection between the past and the future. Vaillant (2002) describes this task as being "the keeper of the meaning," the passing along of family history and cultural achievements and the preservation of past traditions. Preservation of the culture goes beyond one's family and extends to the wider community, something that is often beyond the reach of a 30-year-old, who may not yet have the experience or wisdom.

Develop Volunteer Recruitment Campaigns That Are Culturally Sensitive

As we have noted, generativity is defined by culture (de St. Aubin, 2004). While all generative societies are motivated by the desire to perpetuate and nurture the next generation, how they actualize the desire may be very different. Some cultures emphasize a woman's role in caring for children (de St. Aubin, 2004), and some, as in the case of many Native American tribes, have explicit guidelines for the ways in which youth and elders should interact and relate to one another (Jones-Saumty, 2002). Failure to appreciate these differences could result in the loss of a significant number of potential volunteers.

Capitalize on Mutual Benefits for Participants

Benefits for adults engaged in generative action appear to be psychological, emotional, and even physical (McAdams et al., 1998; Keyes & Ryff, 1998; Putnam, 2000). Conversely, social isolation and shrinking social networks appear to contribute to depression and physical complaints such as headaches, insomnia, and indigestion (Diener, 1984; Putnam, 2000). It has been documented that adults participating in reciprocal and effective mentoring relationships with youth report feelings of satisfaction and excitement at having forged a relationship with a young person from whom they are also learning (Rhodes, 2002). Older adults in the mentoring role report fewer complaints about physical ailments, improved relationships with family members, and an overall enhanced feeling of well-being (Taylor et al., 1999). The essence of generativity is that generative action not only appeals to our sense of altruism but also makes us feel better because we are giving to others. This suggests that recruitment efforts to mobilize adult volunteers in support of youth should focus on the benefits to both.

Emphasize the Unique Contributions of Male Volunteers

The generative concern and commitment of men increase appropriately with age (Vaillant, 1977), especially if they have been active and engaged fathers (Snarey & Clark, 1998). This does not appear, however, necessarily to translate into generative action (Keyes & Ryff, 1998), especially in relationship to activities with nonfamilial youth (Scales, 2003). Gender differences also appear in young children and youth. Scales and his colleagues (2000) found that girls were significantly more likely to feel it was their duty to help others and to be concerned about others' social welfare. On an optimistic note, a recent national survey (Radcliffe Public Policy Center, 2000) found that men and women, parents and nonparents, ages 21 to 39, put family issues ahead of money, power, or prestige; it is still speculation, however, whether these attitudes will promote generative action among men later on. It is well documented that programs are badly in need of strong male role models (Taylor et al., 1999). Recruitment efforts, therefore, need to focus explicitly on the contributions that men can make in support of youth, and appropriate messages and campaigns aimed specifically at men must be developed.

Nurture Generative Concern in the Formative Years

One of the most profound lessons to be learned is that generativity does not just "happen" because we get to midlife. As has been demonstrated in studies of highly generative parents (Pratt et al., 2001), children who are raised in families where generative concern, care, and commitment are valued and acted upon are more likely to feel a sense of responsibility for future generations and have the skills and resources to act. Children who begin volunteering at an early age are more likely to continue this activity as adults (Putnam, 2000). As we have seen, generativity is also shaped by education (Keyes & Ryff, 1998; Putnam, 2000). Keyes and Ryff suggest that the perpetuation of a healthy society depends on access to high-quality educational opportunity; education contributes to one's capacity as a wage earner and taxpayer and enhances one's investment in the future of the community.

Generativity is both a developmental task of midlife and an approach to life—a worldview that guides our actions to promote our long-term survival, described by de St. Aubin and his colleagues (2004) as the "cultural adhesive by which valued traditions and beliefs are created, maintained and revitalized through intergenerational transmission" (p. 266). When we think about acting generatively, we must think in terms of our individual responsibility to future generations: How can we make a difference to others? We must also think globally and support policies that will allow societies to thrive, that will promote access to education, health care, and decent housing, all of which will ultimately contribute to a more generative population of individuals who can act on behalf of the community and begin to reverse the disengagement of recent decades.

References

Achenbaum, A. (1999). The social compact in American history. Keeping the promise: Intergenerational strategies for strengthening the social compact. *Generations, 22*(4), 15–18.

Bakan, D. (1966). *The duality of human existence: Isolation and communion in Western man.* Boston: Beacon Press.

Baumrind, D. (1991). Effective parenting of adolescents. In P. Cowan and M. Hetherington (Eds.), *The effects of transitions on families* (pp. 113–163). Hillsdale, NJ: Erlbaum.

Bellah, R. N., Madsen, R., Sullivan, W. M., Swidler, A., & Tipton, S. M. (1991). *The good society.* New York: Knopf.

Bradley, C. L., & Marcia, J. E. (1998). Generativity-stagnation: A five category model. *Journal of Personality, 66*(1), 39–64.

Browning, D. S. (1975). *Generative man: Psychoanalytic perspectives.* New York: Delta.

Charme, S. T. (1984). *Meaning and myth in the study of lives: A Sartrean perspective.* Philadelphia: University of Pennsylvania Press.

Cohler, B. J., Hostetler, A. J., & Boxer, A. M. (1998). Generativity, social context, and lived experience: Narratives of gay men in middle adulthood. In D. McAdams & E. de St. Aubin (Eds.), *Generativity and adult development: How and why we care for the next generation* (pp. 265–310). Washington, DC: American Psychological Association.

Cornman, J., & Kingson, E. R. (1999). What is a social compact? How would we know when we saw it? Keeping the promise: Intergenerational strategies for strengthening the social compact. *Generations, 22*(4), 10–14.

Daniels, P., & Weingarten, K. (1982). *Sooner or later: The timing of parenthood in adult lives.* New York: Norton.

de St. Aubin, E. (1998). Truth against the world: A psychobiographical exploration of generativity in the life of Frank Lloyd Wright. In D. McAdams & E. de St. Aubin (Eds.), *Generativity and adult development: How and why we care for the next generation* (pp. 391–428). Washington, DC: American Psychological Association.

de St. Aubin, E. (2004). The propagation of genes and memes: Generativity through culture in Japan and the United States. In E. de St. Aubin, D. McAdams, & T.-C. Kim (Eds.), *The generative society: Caring for future generations* (pp 63–82). Washington, DC: American Psychological Association.

de St. Aubin, E., McAdams, D., & Kim, T.-C. (Eds.). (2004). *The generative society: Caring for future generations.* Washington, DC: American Psychological Association.

Diener, E. (1984). Subjective well being. *Psychological Bulletin, 95,* 532–575.

Erikson, E. H. (1950). *Childhood and society.* New York: Norton.

Erikson, E. H. (1963). *Childhood and society* (2nd ed.). New York: Norton.

Erikson, E. H. (1964). *Insight and responsibility.* New York: Norton.

Erikson, E. H. (1968). *Identity: Youth and crisis.* New York: Norton.

Erikson, E. H. (1969). *Gandhi's truth.* New York: Norton.

Erikson, E. H., Erikson, J. M., & Kivnick, H. Q. (1986). *Vital involvement in old age.* New York: Norton.

Fessenden, F. (2004, September 26). A big increase in new voters in swing states. *New York Times,* pp. A1, A12.

Freedman, M. (1988). *Partners in growth: Elder mentors and at-risk youth.* Philadelphia: Public/Private Ventures.

Freedman, M. (1999). *Prime time: How baby boomers will revolutionize retirement and transform America.* New York: Public Affairs.

Goleman, D. (1988, June 14). Erikson in his own old age, expands his view of life. *New York Times.*

Hart, H. M., McAdams, D. P., Hirsch, B. J., & Bauer, J. J. (2001). Generativity and social involvement among African-American and White adults. *Journal of Research in Personality, 35,* 208–230.

Henkin, N., & Kingson, E. (1999a). Introduction. Keeping the promise: Intergenerational strategies for strengthening the social compact. *Generations, 22*(4), 6–9.

Henkin, N., & Kingson, E. (1999b). Advancing an intergenerational agenda for the 21st century. Keeping the promise: Intergenerational strategies for strengthening the social compact. *Generations, 22*(4), 99–105.

Hochschild, A. (1989). *The second shift: Working parents and the revolution at home.* New York: Avon.

Jones-Saumty, D. (2002). From an unpublished review of the Across Ages training manual for the American Indian population. Rockville, MD: Center for Substance Abuse Prevention.

Keyes, C. L. M., & Ryff, C. D. (1998). Generativity in adult lives: Social structural contours and quality of life consequences. In D. McAdams & E. de St. Aubin (Eds.), *Generativity and adult development: How and why we care for the next generation* (pp. 227–264). Washington, DC: American Psychological Association.

Kotre, J. (1984). *Outliving the self: Generativity and the interpretation of lives.* Baltimore: Johns Hopkins University Press.

Kotre, J. (2004). Generativity and culture: What meaning can do. In E. de St. Aubin, D. McAdams, & T.-C. Kim (Eds.), *The generative society: Caring for future generations* (pp. 35–50). Washington, DC: American Psychological Association.

Lee, S. A. (1998). Generativity and the life course of Martha Graham. In D. McAdams & E. de St. Aubin (Eds.), *Generativity and adult development: How and why we care for the next generation* (pp. 429–448). Washington, DC: American Psychological Association.

McAdams, D. P. (1985). *Power, intimacy and the life story: Personological inquiries into identity.* New York: Guilford Press.

McAdams, D. P. (1996). Narrating the self in adulthood. In J. E. Birren, G. M. Kenyon, J.-E. Ruth, J. J. F. Schroots, & T. Svensson (Eds.), *Aging and biography: Explorations in adult development* (pp. 131–148). New York: Springer.

McAdams, D. P. (2001). Generativity in midlife. In M. E. Lachman (Ed.), *Handbook of midlife development* (pp. 395–443). New York: Wiley.

McAdams, D., & de St. Aubin, E. (1992). A theory of generativity and its assessment through self report, behavioral acts and narrative themes in autobiography. *Journal of Personality and Social Psychology, 62*, 1003–1015.

McAdams, D., & de St. Aubin, E. (Eds.). (1998). *Generativity and adult development: How and why we care for the next generation.* Washington, DC: American Psychological Association.

McAdams, D. P., de St. Aubin, E., & Logan, R. L. (1993). Generativity among young, midlife and older adults. *Psychology and Aging, 8*, 221–230.

McAdams, D., Hart, H. M., & Shadd, M. (1998). The anatomy of generativity. In D. McAdams & E. de St. Aubin (Eds.), *Generativity and adult development: How and why we care for the next generation* (pp. 7–44). Washington, DC: American Psychological Association.

McAdams, D., & Logan, R. L. (2004). What is generativity? In E. de St. Aubin, D. McAdams, & T.-C. Kim (Eds.), *The generative society: Caring for future generations* (pp. 35–50). Washington, DC: American Psychological Association.

Miller-McLemore, B. J. (2004). Generativity and gender: The politics of care. In E. de St. Aubin, D. McAdams, & T.-C. Kim (Eds.), *The generative society: Caring for future generations* (pp. 175–194). Washington, DC: American Psychological Association.

Nakagawa, K. (1991). *Explorations of correlates into public school reform and parental involvement.* Unpublished doctoral dissertation, Northwestern University, Evanston, IL.

Newman, S., Ward, C., Smith, T., Wilson, J., & McCrea, J. (1997). *Intergenerational programs: Past, present and future.* Washington, DC: Taylor & Francis.

Nydegger, C. (1981). On being caught up in time. *Human Development, 24*, 1–12.

Pratt, M. W., Danso, H. A., Arnold, M. L., Norris, J. E., & Filyer, R. (2001). Adult generativity and the socialization of adolescents: Relation to mothers' and fathers' parenting beliefs, styles and practices. *Journal of Personality, 69*(1), 89–120.

Prisuta, R. (2003). Enhancing volunteerism among aging baby boomers. In *Reinventing aging: Baby boomers and civic engagement.* Cambridge, MA: Harvard School of Public Health–Met Life Foundation Initiative on Retirement and Civic Engagement.

Putnam, R. D. (2000). *Bowling alone: The collapse and revival of American community.* New York: Simon & Schuster.

Radcliffe Public Policy Center. (2000, May 3). *Study finds new generation of young men focusing on family first.* Cambridge, MA: Author.

Reich, R. M. (1999). Broken faith: Why we need to renew the social compact. Keeping the promise: Intergenerational strategies for strengthening the social compact. *Generations, 22*(4), 119–124.

Rhodes, J. E. (2002). *Stand by me: The risks and rewards of mentoring today's youth.* Cambridge, MA: Harvard University Press.

Ricoeur, P. (1984). *Time and narrative.* Chicago: University of Chicago Press.

Riley, M. W., Kahn, R. L., & Foner, A. (Eds.). (1994). *Age and structural lag: Society's failure to provide meaningful opportunities in work, family, and leisure.* New York: Wiley Interscience.

Rossi, A. S. (Ed.). (2001). *Caring and doing for others: Social responsibility in the domains of family, work and community.* Chicago: University of Chicago Press.

Scales, P. C. (with Benson, P. L., Mannes, M., Hintz, N. R., Roehlkepartain, E. C., & Sullivan, T. K.). (2003). *Other people's kids: Social expectations and American adults' involvement with children and adolescents.* New York: Kluwer Academic/Plenum.

Scales, P. C., Benson, P. L., Leffert, N., & Blyth, D. A. (2000). Contribution of developmental assets to the prediction of thriving among adolescents. *Applied Developmental Science, 4,* 27–46.

Schervish, P. G., & Havens, J. J. (1995). Do the poor pay more? Is the U-shaped curve correct? *Nonprofit and Voluntary Sector Quarterly, 2,* 79–90.

Schor, J. (1991). *The overworked American.* New York: Basic Books.

Sheldon, K. M., & Kasser, T. (2001). Getting older, getting better? Personal strivings and psychological maturity across the lifespan. *Developmental Psychology, 37,* 491–501.

Sipe, C. (1996). *Mentoring: A synthesis of P/PV's research, 1988–1995.* Philadelphia: Public/Private Ventures.

Snarey, J. (1993). *How fathers care for the next generation: A four-decade study.* Cambridge, MA: Harvard University Press.

Snarey, J., & Clark, P. Y. (1998). A generative drama: Scenes from a father-son relationship. In D. McAdams & E. de St. Aubin (Eds.), *Generativity and adult development: How and why we care for the next generation* (pp. 75–100). Washington, DC: American Psychological Association.

Snyder, M., & Clary, E. G. (2004). Volunteerism and the generative society. In E. de St. Aubin, D. McAdams, & T.-C. Kim (Eds.), *The generative society: Caring for future generations* (pp. 221–238). Washington, DC: American Psychological Association.

Stewart, A. J., & Vandewater, E. A. (1998). The course of generativity. In D. McAdams & E. de St. Aubin (Eds.), *Generativity and adult development: How and why we care for the next generation* (pp. 75–100). Washington, DC: American Psychological Association.

Taylor, A. S., LoSciuto, L., & Porcellini, L. (2004). Intergenerational mentoring. In D. L. DuBois and M. Karcher (Eds.), *Handbook of youth mentoring* (pp. 286–299). Thousand Oaks, CA: Sage.

Taylor, A., and Bressler, J. (2000). *Mentoring across generations: Partnerships for positive youth development.* New York: Kluwer Academic/Plenum.

Taylor, A., & Dryfoos, J. (1999). Creating a safe passage: Elder mentors and vulnerable youth. Keeping the promise: Intergenerational strategies for strengthening the social compact. *Generations, 22*(4), 43–48.

Taylor, A., LoSciuto, L., Fox, M., & Hilbert, S. (1999). The mentoring factor: An evaluation of Across Ages. In V. Kuehne (Ed.), *Intergenerational programs: Understanding what we have created* (pp. 77–99). Binghamton, NY: Haworth Press.

Tocqueville, A. de. (1945). *Democracy in America* (P. Bradley, Ed.). 2 vols. New York: Vintage Books. (Original work published 1835, 1840)

U.S. Census Bureau. (2000). *65+ in the United States. Current population reports: Special studies.* Washington, DC: Government Printing Office.

Vaillant, G. E. (1977). *Adaptation to life.* Boston: Little, Brown.

Vaillant, G. E. (2002). *Aging well: Surprising guides to a happier life.* Boston: Little, Brown.

VanderVen, K. (1999). Intergenerational theory: The missing element in today's intergenerational programs. In V. S. Kuehne (Ed.), *Intergenerational programs: Understanding what we have created* (pp. 33–47). Binghamton, NY: Haworth Press.

6 Strategies to Motivate Behavior Change: How Can We Mobilize Adults to Promote Positive Youth Development?

Alexander J. Rothman and
Katherine C. Haydon

University of Minnesota

There is little doubt that the healthy development of young people is an essential feature of a healthy, well-functioning society and that the adult members of society play a critical role in this process (Lerner, Dowling, & Anderson, 2003; Rhodes, Bogat, Roffman, Edelman, & Galasso, 2002). National surveys have consistently shown that adults recognize the importance of devoting both time and effort to activities that contribute to youth development. For example, an overwhelming majority of adults believe it is very important that they encourage children and youth to succeed in school (90%), teach them shared values (80%), and set boundaries for their behavior (84%) (Scales, 2003). However, there is a stark disconnect between people's beliefs about what is important and their own actions. Scales (2003) found that only 69% of adults encouraged success in school, only 45% taught shared values, and only 42% set boundaries for behavior. Given the premise that adult involvement in young people's lives is a critical determinant of healthy development, the observed gap between people's beliefs and their behavior is a clear sign that strategies that can enhance adult involvement in activities that promote the development of young people are needed.

In this chapter, we examine the challenge of designing initiatives that can effectively mobilize adults to act on their beliefs and make an active contribution to the healthy development of young people. This chapter is divided into two sections. First, given the observed dissociation between people's beliefs and their behavior, we consider what aspects of involvement should be targeted in developing initiatives to mobilize adults to contribute to youth development. Second, with our framework in hand, we delineate a set of strategies that could be used to encourage adults to engage in activities that have the greatest chance of promoting optimal development.

Our primary aim is to elucidate principles that can guide the efforts of policy makers and investigators to close the gap between people's beliefs about the importance of involvement with young people and their engagement in those activities, and to elicit adult involvement that has the best chance of being sustained over time. However, we must preface our discussion of this aim with a cautionary note: Simply "closing the gap" and involving greater numbers of adults in the lives of young people may not be the most effective strategy. The observation that the involvement of other, nonparental adults in a child's life promotes beneficial outcomes is predicated on the activities currently undertaken by those adults who have been willing to devote time and effort to enriching the lives of youth. These volunteers do not represent a random sample of the adult population. Although these people are motivated to act for reasons ranging from religious or political principles to the simple pleasure derived from helping, taken together we believe these volunteers overrepresent the portion of adults in society who possess the skills to work with young people effectively. Broad-based efforts to motivate adults to become involved in the lives of youth are likely to increase the participation of adults who possess fewer skills (and less interest) than do those who already contribute to the lives of young adults. We believe that variability in the skills and interests that adults bring to their interactions with young people must be considered, as the quality of the relationships afforded by these activities may play a critical role in determining their impact on youth development. Thus, simply increasing the number of adults who contribute to the lives of young people may not produce a proportional increase in healthy developmental outcomes. In fact, efforts to improve the quality of relationships between adults and young people may have as much impact on critical outcome measures as does mobilizing greater numbers of adults to become involved. Therefore, we begin by examining the impact of quality in a variety of relationships between adults and young people, and how strategically targeting adults who are most likely to promote quality interactions may maximize the benefits of adult involvement in young people's lives.

The Importance of Quality across Relational Contexts

Decades of research on optimal developmental outcomes confirm that the value of young people's relationships with adults is not simply due to the quantity of adults available to the child, or to those adults' ability to meet a checklist of basic needs. Rather, a longstanding body of research indicates that the quality of young people's relationships with adults is one of the most important factors in predicting positive outcomes (e.g., Jimerson, Egeland, Sroufe, & Carlson, 2000; Sroufe, 2002). Longitudinal studies of institutionalized children underscore the influence of relational quality above and beyond the provision of basic needs. Children deprived of the opportunity to form interpersonal attachments with caregivers often display severe cognitive and social deficits, yet show remarkable "catch-up" when they are adopted into homes in which they develop quality relationships with adults (Gunnar, Bruce, & Grotevant, 2000).

Young people who develop in more typical environments have the opportunity to form quality relationships across several relational contexts. Of these, the parent–child relationship is primary, and the quality of caregiver–child relationships exerts a substantial influence on optimal development (e.g., Bowlby, 1969/1982; Sroufe, 2002). Quality relationships with nonparental caregivers also play an important role. A national survey of day care facilities found that process features related to quality (e.g., care providers' ability to maintain a positive emotional climate and provide sensitive care to individual children) underlie the effect that structural features of child care centers (e.g., child–staff ratio) had on positive outcomes (NICHD Early Child Care Research Network, 2002). Quality relationships with teachers also positively influence children's school adjustment (Birch & Ladd, 1997), may serve as a protective factor against aggression (Meehan, Hughes, & Cavell, 2003), and may even compensate for deficits in parent–child relationships (Copeland-Mitchell, Denham, & DeMulder, 1997). Adolescents with histories of quality relationships exhibit greater peer competence and lower internalizing, externalizing, and deviant behaviors (Allen, Moore, Kuperminc, & Bell, 1998). They are also less likely to drop out of high school (Jimerson et al., 2000). The opportunity to cultivate quality relationships appears to have a multiplicative, probabilistic influence on optimal developmental outcomes over time.

What makes for a quality relationship? Developmental theorists typically conceptualize quality as sensitive and responsive care (e.g., Ainsworth, Blehar, Waters, & Wall, 1978; Sroufe & Waters, 1997). Across a broad array of dyads, quality relationships may vary in their manifest content (i.e., the activities, goals, and patterns shared by the dyad) but share relational features such as trust, interdependence, investment, and similarity on one or more dimensions (e.g., Kelley & Thibault, 1983; Mikulincer, 1998; Rhodes, Reddy, Grossman, & Lee, 2002; Rusbult, 1983). For example, parents provide quality care by helping children regulate emotional distress, being available to discuss children's experiences, and supporting children's increasing bids for autonomy as they develop. Teachers, comparatively, are sensitive and responsive by calibrating their instruction to individual children's learning abilities and styles, by promoting children's interactions with peers, and by providing a source of confidence and support in the learning environment. Although the content of parent–child and teacher–student relationships differs, quality is manifest in each case as context-appropriate sensitivity and support.

We expect that quality is equally important in young people's relationships with other adults in the social milieu, such as mentors, coaches, and club leaders. Defining quality (i.e., sensitive and responsive interactions) for these relationships, however, is more difficult because each of these relationships is characterized by different roles, interaction settings, goals, and levels of involvement for both adults and adolescents. The skills needed to be a quality coach may be different from skills needed to be a quality mentor, reading tutor, or youth group leader. For example, a quality coach may be especially skilled at building young people's confidence in their athletic skills and balancing the group's sense of competition with teamwork. A quality mentor, on the other hand, may be best at encouraging individual young people to formulate goals and at strategically providing instrumental support to help them achieve their goals. In each of these examples, the quality of the relationship is, in part, contingent on the skills adults bring to their role. Although the specific skills needed differ across relational contexts, relationship quality appears to regulate the impact that an adult's efforts have on youth. Recent findings support the contribution of relationship quality to the positive outcomes of mentor relationships. DuBois, Neville, Parra, and Pugh-Lilly (2002) reported that mentoring programs had the greatest positive impact on young people's self-esteem, emotional adjustment, and behavioral problems when youth identified mentors as significant adults in their lives. Grossman and Rhodes (2002) found that relational quality partially mediated the connection between a variety of relationship characteristics and length of mentoring involvement, where duration was associated with more positive outcomes.

We believe that initiatives to motivate adults to be more involved in formal and informal relationships with youth need to attend to what quality means in the context of a particular role, with the goal of recruiting adults who are best able to provide quality care within each context. The consideration of relational quality may offer some insights into the observed gap between adults' beliefs in the importance of particular activities and their willingness to engage in those activities. Recognizing that particular activities play a strong role in youth development is not the same thing as possessing the skills needed to perform those activities effectively. Among those people who have yet to act in line with their beliefs, there are likely to be adults who possess the skills that will allow them to make a positive contribution to youth development and also those who do not possess the necessary skills. Moreover, even those adults with particular skills may be waiting for an opportunity that would allow them to take advantage of their abilities. Efforts to promote adults' involvement in youth development may need to attend to these distinctions. It is important to note that we are *not* suggesting that only select, highly skilled adults are capable of positive involvement with young people. Rather, we suggest that adults possess a range of skills, which may or may not promote quality interactions with youth in a given context. Effective strategies to promote optimal youth development should strive to place adults in roles in which their skills and experiences maximize their ability to form quality relationships with young people.

We believe there are at least three important reasons to be mindful of this matching process. First, matching should afford the development of quality relationships between youth and adults, which in turn will promote better outcomes for youth in a wide array of contexts. Second, adults are likely to derive a sense of satisfaction from both the quality relationships they foster with young people and the observation that their efforts are making a meaningful contribution. This may serve to sustain an adult's motivation to stay involved in a program. Third, lower rates of burnout and turnover among adults involved in youth-related activities should reduce the financial and logistical burden of recruiting and training additional adults. In the long run, placing adults in roles that match their skills may allow better quality relationships to form between adults and young people, which, in turn, allow communities to be more successful and more efficient in how they use their resources.

Mobilizing Adults: Who, Why, and How

What can be done to effectively mobilize adults to contribute to the development of youth? Are there strategies that have been developed to promote other patterns of behavior that might generalize to this domain? Over the past few decades investigators have grappled with the challenge of developing initiatives to persuade people to engage in healthy behaviors (Rothman & Salovey, in press; Salovey, Rothman, & Rodin, 1998). As has been observed in the domain of youth development, these efforts often involve persuading people to stop behaviors that are harmful (e.g., smoking) or to start or increase behaviors that are beneficial (e.g., exercise). Traditionally, efforts to promote a desired behavior have relied on a communication strategy, perhaps a message to remind people of the importance of getting regular exercise, which targets all who would benefit from changing their behavior. This approach is predicated on the assumption that everyone who has yet to act would respond favorably to the issue or construct addressed in the message. For example, if the primary aim of an appeal was to remind people to take time to exercise, the underlying assumption would be that the reason people fail to exercise is that they forget to set aside time.

More recently, investigators have challenged this approach and have argued that it is a mistake to assume that everyone who is not currently engaging in a behavior is not only equally ready to take action but also responsive to the same set of concerns (Prochaska, DiClemente, & Norcross, 1992). To be maximally effective, intervention messages may need to address the issues or concerns that keep a given person or group of people from acting (Skinner, Campbell, Rimer, Curry, & Prochaska, 1999). Tailoring messages to the factors that keep people from taking action makes people more likely to see these messages as personally relevant and, consequently, more likely to read them, remember them, and talk about them with others (Brug, Steenhuis, van Assema, & de Vries, 1996; Kreuter, Bull, Clark, & Oswald, 1999; Skinner, Strecher, & Hospers, 1994).

To date, message-tailoring efforts have tended to focus on the specific reasons why a person needs to modify his or her behavior. These often reflect the dangers or costs posed by current behavior. For example, after an initial assessment to determine people's thoughts and feelings about smoking, one smoker might receive a message highlighting the social stigma of smoking, whereas another smoker might receive a message highlighting the effects that smoking has on the health of his or her children. However, message tailoring could also be used to focus on and highlight a person's unique talents and strengths. In this manner, the same procedures that have been used to target people's health concerns could be used to help people recognize the talents they possess and how specific youth development activities would allow them to use their skills.

To the extent that the outcomes that arise out of adult involvement in the lives of young people depend on how the adult performs in his or her role, tailoring messages to a person's talents may prove to be a valuable intervention strategy. In this way, mobilizing adults to be involved in the lives of youth is different from mobilizing people to exercise 30 minutes a day or to make healthy food choices. The health benefits afforded by regular exercise or by eating a diet that is rich in fruits and vegetables are relatively certain. Of course, some vegetables are more nutritious than others and some exercise routines are more effective than others, but the benefits afforded by these behaviors are incremental and predictable. For example, dietary guidelines may advise people to eat three to five servings of vegetables a day, but an individual will gain some benefits even if he or she eats fewer than the recommended number of servings. In contrast, predictions regarding the benefits afforded by adult involvement in the lives of young people are uncertain and critically depend on the quality of the relationship that is formed between the adult and a young person. For example, a person can dedicate time each week to mentor young students in grade school, but the outcomes that arise from those efforts are uncertain and depend on the relationship that forms between the mentor and student.

It is our belief that the best way to maximize the quality of these relationships is to maximize the fit between the skills an adult brings to the interaction and the needs of the young person. The Harvard Mentoring Project has used a similar approach in recent media campaigns that emphasize every adult's potential to make valuable contributions and encourage adults to "share what you know." The campaign directs potential volunteers to a Web site (www.mentoring.org) that outlines important aspects of effective mentoring relationships, features tools to assess one's mentoring skills, and provides guidelines for how to find the best-fitting mentor role in one's community. The Harvard Project and its affiliates illustrate a successful application of matching adults' skills to roles in order to promote the best fit between volunteers and involvement contexts.

Differential Barriers to Involvement

Regardless of whether one uses a message that is broad based or tailored, the effectiveness of the intervention strategy is predicated on accurately assessing the factors that inhibit people from taking action or would encourage people to take action or both (Weinstein, Rothman, & Sutton, 1998). Thus, an intervention effort critically depends on an accurate assessment of why people are not performing the behavior of interest. This means that efforts to develop initiatives to get adults more engaged in the lives of young people require a comprehensive understanding of why people are not currently involved and what skills they possess that would enable them to contribute.

The observation that a substantial number of adults endorse the importance of participating in the lives of young people but fail to act in accord with those beliefs would seem to suggest that there is a single reason or set of reasons that keeps people from taking action (e.g., awareness of opportunities, time conflicts).

Although this may be true, we believe there is likely to be value in distinguishing between at least three groups of adults who are not currently involved.

First, there are people who believe they have the talents needed to contribute to the lives of young people and recognize the importance of these activities, but are not helping because of a structural barrier to action, such as time conflicts or lack of awareness of opportunities in their communities. Efforts to target these people would need to address the primary factors shown to interfere with people's efforts to participate in the lives of young people. For example, people in this group might benefit from initiatives that disseminate information about the range of opportunities available in their community so that they could identify one that matches their skills and interests and fits into their hectic work or family schedule.

A second group of people might also recognize the importance of working with young people, but in their case the decision not to get involved rests on the belief that they don't possess the skills needed to contribute effectively. Although efforts to target these people could attempt to make people aware of activities that do match the skills they possess, they might also focus on the development of new skills and promote people's confidence in the skills they already possess.

Finally, the third group of people might recognize the importance of working with young people but have concluded that this would not be the best use of their talents. Regardless of whether this conclusion is correct, because these people have made a decision not to participate in the lives of young people, any initiative to convince them to take action is likely to be a substantial undertaking as it would require that people reconsider a prior decision (Weinstein, 1988).

Although tailoring messages to an individual's primary needs has considerable promise, it is important to recognize that the advantages may come only at a sizable, and perhaps at times unjustifiable, cost. To tailor messages to either the needs of individuals or the needs of members of a given social group, investigators must be able to assess accurately people's needs prior to the development and dissemination of the message. This necessitates having both a reliable assessment tool and access to the population of people one wants to target. Moreover, investigators need an infrastructure that enables them to deliver specific messages to a particular person or group of people. In many cases, investigators may determine that the costs associated with assessment and message delivery are sufficiently high that they mitigate any benefit that might arise from a message-tailoring approach.

Initiating and Maintaining a New Behavior: Challenges and Pitfalls

To this point, we have focused on the value of differentiating between groups of people who are not currently contributing to the lives of young people. Although we have briefly considered the classes of factors that might distinguish among these groups, we have yet to consider the processes by which people choose to initiate a change in their behavior (i.e., become involved in the lives of young people) and those that underlie the decision to maintain that behavior (i.e., remain involved in the lives of young people). This distinction may be important because initiatives that effectively convince people to get involved in an activity may not be the same as those that will convince them to remain involved. Rothman and colleagues (Rothman, 2000; Rothman, Baldwin, & Hertel, 2004) have argued that the criteria that underlie the decision to initiate a new pattern of behavior are distinct from those that underlie the decision to maintain that pattern of behavior over time. Specifically, the decision to initiate a new pattern of behavior is predicated on people's expectations about the desirability of the outcomes afforded by the behavior and their confidence in their ability to achieve those outcomes, whereas the decision to maintain the behavior is guided by people's sense of satisfaction with the outcomes afforded by the change in their behavior. Those who find their experiences with the new behavior satisfying will strive to continue their efforts, whereas those who are unsatisfied will find it difficult to remain motivated to sustain their behavior. Although investigators have only begun to test the full range of predictions derived from the model, the assumptions regarding the determinants of behavioral initiation are well grounded in the empirical literature (Bandura, 1997; Salovey et al., 1998). Moreover, evidence regarding the differential predictors of behavioral initiation and behavioral maintenance has begun to accumulate (Baldwin et al., in press; Finch et al., 2005; Hertel et al., 2005).

What are the implications of this framework for developing initiatives to promote the participation of adults in activities to enhance youth development? First, let's consider initiatives designed to get people to start contributing to the lives of young adults. According to the framework outlined by Rothman and colleagues, efforts to motivate the initiation of a new behavior should work to strengthen people's confidence that they can perform the relevant behavior (i.e., self-efficacy) and heighten their perception that their efforts will produce desirable outcomes. Although both of these factors are believed to be critical determinants of the decision to take action, it may be useful to distinguish between the functions they serve in persuading someone to initiate a new course of action. The belief that the new behavior will yield outcomes that are significantly better than those afforded by one's current behavior may play a critical role in motivating people to decide whether to adopt a new behavior. For example, the decision to serve as a mentor to students in a public high school is likely to depend on people believing that their efforts will have a meaningful effect on the lives of the students with whom they work.

To date, research regarding how outcome expectations affect people's behavioral decisions has focused almost exclusively on behaviors whose primary purpose is to improve the well-being of the person taking action. Individuals have been shown to vary in the degree to which their efforts are motivated by selfish or selfless concerns (Clary & Snyder, 1999), but there has yet to be a systematic assessment of whether intervention strategies that highlight outcome expectations can be used to motivate a pattern of behavior that primarily benefits another person. Although there are ways in which adults benefit from being involved with young people (e.g., feeling proud after having helped a young adult master a new skill; enjoying the benefits of living in a community with greater social capital), these outcomes are contingent on the experiences of the young people with whom they are working. Moreover, since the outcomes do not depend solely on the actions of the adult, there is less certainty at the outset as to whether participating in a program to help young adults will be productive. Given these conditions, it may be particularly important for intervention initiatives to highlight the broad array of benefits that can come from active involvement in the lives of young people.

Once adults have made the decision to become involved in the lives of young people, their confidence in their own abilities is likely to play a critical role in determining whether they turn their intentions into action. According to Weinstein and colleagues (Weinstein, Lyon, Sandman, & Cuite, 1998), initiatives designed to enhance perceptions of self-efficacy will be particularly effective when they are directed at people who have decided to take action (e.g., have decided to contribute some of their time to youth activities), but have yet to act on their decision. If people have confidence in their abilities to perform a set of behaviors, they are less likely to be thwarted by barriers that may arise and are more likely to seek out opportunities to take action. Bandura (1997) has identified a number of strategies that can be used to enhance people's confidence in their ability to perform a given behavior; two of them involve having other people model the behavior and providing people with clear, supportive messages about how to perform the behavior. Additionally, initiatives that purposefully match people to roles in which they are most likely to perform the expected behavior well (e.g., serve as quality mentors) should increase the likelihood that people will work to overcome any initial barriers to action and increase people's confidence in their ability to perform well once action has begun.

In a similar vein, several investigators have shown that an effective way to increase the likelihood that people will act on their behavioral intention is to have them formulate an action plan that specifies how, when, and where they will perform the behavior (Gollwitzer, 1999; Milne, Orbell, & Sheeran, 2002; Sheeran & Orbell, 2000). According to Gollwitzer, an action plan serves to heighten a person's commitment to a specific course of action. Furthermore, by linking a course of action to a particular context (e.g., agreeing to sign up to coach a soccer team the next time you are at the community recreation center), an action plan can facilitate the creation of cues that automatically remind a person of his or her decision to take action.

Once people have initiated a new course of action (e.g., started serving as coach of the neighborhood soccer team), it is important that they are able to sustain their beliefs about both their abilities and the outcomes that will come from their actions. These beliefs allow people to feel confident that the decision to take on this new responsibility was a wise one and that their efforts will over time be beneficial. To the extent that a new activity involves substantial up-front costs (e.g., the need to reorganize one's schedule), these favorable beliefs about the process and future outcomes serve as an important counterweight. After a period of time, however, people may find that their expectations about future outcomes are no longer sufficient to motivate behavior and that they need some evidence that their efforts have been worthwhile. It is at this point that people start to consider whether to maintain their new behavior. Although the time it takes for people to reach this decision point is likely to depend on both people's personal style (e.g., dispositionally optimistic individuals may be willing to wait longer for evidence of benefits) and the tasks they have undertaken (e.g., coaches may wait for the season to end), it represents a critical juncture in the behavior change process.

Satisfaction and Continued Involvement

According to the framework outlined by Rothman and his colleagues (2004), efforts to promote sustained, long-term patterns of behavior depend on whether people feel satisfied with their experiences with the new behavior. The critical premise is that people choose to continue a course of action because they *want* to perform the behavior and not because they *can* do the behavior. If satisfaction is a critical determinant of people's behavior, attention must be paid to the processes that underlie people's sense of satisfaction. To date, little is known about the factors that maximize the satisfaction people derive from their efforts. However, satisfaction is likely to rest, at least in part, on people recognizing the benefits that have come from their actions. If this is true, it will be critical to determine whether people find it difficult to fully appreciate or even at times to recognize the favorable outcomes that are experienced by the young people they are working with. In a similar manner, unlike behavior change efforts that target an aspect of one's own life (e.g., a weight control program), it may be difficult for people to discern how things would be different if they hadn't become involved in a youth program. Although limitations in the information adults have about the consequences of their action may hinder people's ability to recognize when things are going well, these limitations may also make people less aware of any negative consequences that may arise from their behavior. Over time, this may hamper people's ability to adjust their behavior in ways that can maximize the impact of their efforts.

The point at which people decide whether to move from behavior initiation to behavior maintenance may be particularly problematic for initiatives in the youth-involvement domain. By nature, youth development unfolds slowly and gradually; volunteers are unlikely to witness sudden "tangible" improvements in the youth they support. In fact, benefits of adult involvement may frequently be protective, such that the absence of negative outcomes (e.g., an adolescent has not joined a gang) is the primary indicator of success. Because people have difficulty recognizing the absence of an event, volunteers may remain unaware of the positive outcomes that have come from their efforts. Benefits of adult involvement may also act indirectly to evidence positive change. Positive effects of mentor relationships are often mediated by improvements in the parent–youth relationship, rather than manifesting as direct consequences of mentors' efforts (Rhodes, Grossman, & Resche, 2000). For these reasons, volunteers may be especially likely to fail to recognize that their involvement played a causal role in eliciting positive outcomes. To encourage volunteers to maintain their decisions to help, it is essential that programs devote resources to reminding volunteers of the direct, indirect, and gradual benefits of their continued involvement. Volunteer training may also facilitate this process, as people who are knowledgeable about the area in which they are working may have a better understanding of the types of outcomes that may come from their efforts and thus be better able to detect favorable (and unfavorable) consequences.

To the extent that satisfaction is a critical determinant of sustained participation in youth-related activities, it is important that people can situate themselves in settings that allow them to take advantage of their talents. As we noted earlier, the quality of the interaction between an adult and a youth is an important determinant of whether that relationship will produce favorable outcomes. Initiatives that maximize the likelihood that favorable outcomes will come from the activity are critical not only for the young people involved in the relationship but also for the adult who is committing his or her time and effort to the relationship. Relationships that promote favorable outcomes are likely to be more satisfying for the participants and, thus, are likely to be sustained over time. To the extent that people find themselves participating in activities for which they do not have the requisite skills, the poorer quality of the interaction may not only prove detrimental for the young people participating in the activity but also undermine any interest the adult has in sustaining the relationship over time. Thus, encouraging people to participate in activities that they are not suited for may have the short-term benefit of increasing the percentage of adults who are actively involved in the lives of young people but is likely to have the long-term cost of undermining people's perceptions of the value of these interactions.

The framework outlined in this chapter raises several important issues for how we might design systems to promote greater adult involvement in the lives of young people. The goal of matching people to opportunities in which they can make best use of their skills will require the development of instruments that can reliably assess people's skills and a network able to direct people toward specific volunteer opportunities. Because many programs tend to offer a limited number of roles in which to work with young people, there would need to be consortiums that link programs and provide a way for potential volunteers to be directed to an activity that best matches their skills. These limited observations make it clear that any new efforts to encourage more active involvement of adults in the lives of young people must be made in close cooperation with the organizations that will ultimately be placing new volunteers. Recruiting more volunteers into the system will yield maximum benefits only if the system is structured in a way to fully capitalize on the abilities and commitment of the volunteers.

An Eye toward the Future: Enhancing Quality and Quantity

Initiatives designed to engage adults in youth development efforts are faced with the dual charge of motivating adults to take action to become involved and retaining adults who have already acted. Although the second charge is likely to prove the greater challenge, we believe it may be accomplished by thoughtfully placing mobilized adults in roles that best fit their skills and strengths. Doing so would maximize adults' satisfaction and confidence in their performance and reaffirm their commitment to stay involved. Most important, it would enable adults and young people to form quality relationships that have the greatest chance of promoting young people's optimal development.

Further, involving greater numbers of adults in roles to which they are best suited may increase the normative pressure for involvement in youth activities among adults who have yet to act. Initiatives that simultaneously increase the perceived value of possessing talents that are valuable in interactions with young adults and raise awareness about opportunities for contributing to youth development may be most effective in fostering positive outcomes for youth and adults alike. Finally, increased normative pressure to become involved may lower the demand for the activities to be satisfying. In other words, people's motivation to become involved and stay involved may rest more on their response to normative pressure than on their own level of satisfaction with their involvement. If participating in the lives of young people is perceived to be what one *ought* to do, questions about what one *wants* to do may become less important.

We envision communities in which most adults are qualified and expected to become involved in youth development in the capacity that best suits their talents. Further, we envision communities in which a wide array of opportunities is readily available and targeted at specific subgroups of adults who are likely to provide the highest quality interactions in a given context. In the long run, youth development initiatives may increase the number of involved adults by attending more proximally to the quality of adults' involvement with young people. With these objectives in mind, initiatives may fully realize adults' differential promise to contribute to optimal development of young people in their communities.

Authors' Note

The preparation of this chapter was supported in part by grant NS38441 from the National Institute of Neurological Disorders and Stroke. Correspondence concerning this article should be addressed to Alexander J. Rothman, Department of Psychology, University of Minnesota, 75 East River Road, Minneapolis, MN 55455; e-mail: rothm001@umn.edu.

References

Ainsworth, M. D. S., Blehar, M. C., Waters, E., & Wall, S. (1978). *Patterns of attachment*. Hillsdale, NJ: Erlbaum.

Allen, J. P., Moore, C., Kuperminc, G., & Bell, K. (1998). Attachment and adolescent psychosocial functioning. *Child Development, 69*, 1406–1419.

Baldwin, A. S., Rothman, A. J., Hertel, A.W., Linde, J. A., Jeffery, R. W., Finch, E., et al. (in press). Specifying the determinants of the initiation and maintenance of behavior change: An examination of self-efficacy, satisfaction, and smoking cessation. *Health Psychology*.

Bandura, A. (1997). *Self-efficacy: The exercise of control*. New York: W. H. Freeman.

Birch, S. H., & Ladd, G. W. (1997). The teacher-child relationship and children's early school adjustment. *Journal of School Psychology, 35*, 61–79.

Bowlby, J. (1969/1982). *Attachment and loss: Vol. 1. Attachment*. New York: Basic Books.

Brug, J., Steenhuis, I., van Assema, P., & de Vries, H. (1996). The impact of a computer-tailored nutrition intervention. *Preventative Medicine, 25*, 236–242.

Clary, E. G., & Snyder, M. (1999). The motivations to volunteer: Theoretical and practical considerations. *Current Directions in Psychological Science, 8*, 156–159.

Copeland-Mitchell, J., Denham, S. A., & DeMulder, E. K. (1997). Q-sort assessment of child-teacher attachment relationships and social competence in the preschool. *Early Education & Development, 8*, 27–39.

DuBois, D. L., Neville, H. A., Parra, G. R., & Pugh-Lilly, A. O. (2002). Testing a new model of mentoring. In J. E. Rhodes (Ed.), *A critical view of youth mentoring. New directions for youth development: Theory, practice, research* (pp. 21–57). San Francisco: Jossey-Bass.

Finch, E. A., Linde, J. A., Jeffery, R. W., Rothman, A. J., King, C. M., & Levy, R. L. (2005). The effects of outcome expectations and satisfaction on weight loss and maintenance: Correlational and experimental analyses. *Health Psychology, 24*, 608–616.

Gollwitzer, P. M. (1999). Implementation intentions: Strong effects of simple plans. *American Psychologist, 54*, 493–503.

Grossman, J. B., & Rhodes, J. E. (2002). The test of time: Predictors and effects of duration in youth mentoring relationships. *American Journal of Community Psychology, 30*, 199–219.

Gunnar, M. R., Bruce, J., & Grotevant, H. D. (2000). International adoption of institutionally reared children: Research and policy. *Development and Psychopathology, 12*, 677–693.

Harvard Mentoring Project. (2004, September). Available from http://www.hsph.harvard.edu/chc/wmy2005/index.html http://www.hsph.harvard.edu/chc/mentoring.html

Hertel, A. W., Finch, E. A., Kelly, K. M., King, C., Lando, H., Linde, J. A., et al. (2005). *The impact of outcome expectations and satisfaction on the initiation and maintenance of smoking cessation: An experimental test*. Unpublished manuscript, University of Minnesota, Minneapolis.

Jimerson, S., Egeland, B., Sroufe, L. A., & Carlson, B. (2000). A prospective longitudinal study of high school dropouts: Examining multiple predictors across development. *Journal of School Psychology, 38*, 525–549.

Kelley, H. H., & Thibault, J. W. (1983). *Interpersonal relations: A theory of interdependence*, New York: Wiley.

Kreuter, M. K., Bull, F. C., Clark, E. M., & Oswald, D. L. (1999). Understanding how people process health information: A comparison of tailored and non-tailored weight-loss materials. *Health Psychology, 18*, 487–494.

Lerner, R. M., Dowling, E. M, & Anderson, P. M. (2003). Positive youth development: Thriving as the basis of personhood and civil society. *Applied Developmental Science, 7*, 172–180.

Meehan, B. T., Hughes, J. N., & Cavell, T. A. (2003). Teacher-student relationships as compensatory resources for aggressive children. *Child Development, 74*, 1145–1157.

Mikulincer, M. (1998). Attachment working models and the sense of trust: An exploration of interaction goals and affect regulation. *Journal of Personality & Social Psychology, 74*, 1209–1224.

Milne, S., Orbell, S., & Sheeran, P. (2002). Combining motivational and volitional interventions to promote exercise participation: Protection motivation theory and implementation intentions. *British Journal of Health Psychology, 7*, 163–184.

NICHD Early Child Care Research Network. (2002). Child-care → structure → process outcome: Direct and indirect effects of child-care quality on young children's development. *Psychological Science, 13*, 199–206.

Prochaska, J. O., DiClemente, C. C., & Norcross, J. C. (1992). In search of how people change: Applications to addictive behaviors. *American Psychologist, 47*, 1102–1114.

Rhodes, J. E., Bogat, G. A., Roffman, J., Edelman, P., & Galasso, L. (2002). Youth mentoring in perspective: Introduction to the special issue. *American Journal of Community Psychology, 30*, 149–155.

Rhodes, J. E., Grossman, J. B., & Resche, N. L. (2000). Agents of change: Pathways through which mentoring relationships influence adolescents' academic adjustment. *Child Development, 71,* 1662–1671.

Rhodes, J. E., Reddy, R., Grossman, J. B., & Lee, J. M. (2002). Volunteer mentoring relationships with minority youth: An analysis of same- versus cross-race matches. *Journal of Applied Social Psychology, 32,* 2114–2133.

Rothman, A. J. (2000). Toward a theory-based analysis of behavioral maintenance. *Health Psychology, 19,* 64–69.

Rothman, A. J., & Salovey, P. (in press). The reciprocal relation between principles and practice: Social psychology and health behavior. In A. Kruglanski & E. T. Higgins (Eds.), *Social psychology: Handbook of basic principles* (2nd ed.). New York: Guilford Press.

Rothman, A. J., Baldwin, A. S., & Hertel, A. W. (2004). Self-regulation and behavior change: Disentangling behavioral initiation and behavioral maintenance. In K. Vohs & R. Baumeister (Eds.), *The handbook of self-regulation* (pp. 130–148). New York: Guilford Press.

Rusbult, C. E. (1983). A longitudinal test of the investment model: The development (and deterioration) of satisfaction and commitment in heterosexual involvements. *Journal of Personality & Social Psychology, 45,* 101–117.

Salovey, P., Rothman, A. J., & Rodin, J. (1998). Health behavior. In D. Gilbert, S. Fiske, & G. Lindzey (Eds.), *The handbook of social psychology* (4th ed., Vol. 2, pp. 633–683). New York: McGraw-Hill.

Scales, P. C. (with Benson, P. L., Mannes, M., Hintz, N. R., Roehlkepartain, E. C., & Sullivan, T. K.). (2003). *Other people's kids: Social expectations and American adults' involvement with children and adolescents,* New York: Kluwer Academic/Plenum.

Sheeran, P., & Orbell, S. (2000). Using implementation intentions to increase attendance for cervical cancer screening. *Health Psychology, 19,* 283–289.

Skinner, C. S., Campbell, M. K., Rimer, B. K., Curry, S., & Prochaska, J. O. (1999). How effective is tailored print communication? *Annals of Behavioral Medicine, 21,* 290–298.

Skinner, C. S., Strecher, V. J., & Hospers, H. (1994). Physicians' recommendations for mammography: Do tailored messages make a difference? *American Journal of Public Health, 84,* 43–49.

Sroufe, L. A. (2002). From infant attachment to promotion of adolescent autonomy: Prospective, longitudinal data on the role of parents in development. In J. G. Borkowski, S. L. Ramey, & M. Bristol-Power (Eds.), *Parenting and the child's world: Influences on academic, intellectual, and social-emotional development* (pp. 187–202). Mahwah, NJ: Erlbaum.

Sroufe, L. A., & Waters, E. (1997). On the universality of the link between responsive care and secure base behavior. *International Society for the Study of Behavior and Development Newsletter,* Ser. 31, 3–5.

Weinstein, N. D. (1988). The precaution adoption process. *Health Psychology, 7,* 355–386.

Weinstein, N. D., Lyon, J. E., Sandman, P. M., & Cuite, C. L. (1998). Experimental evidence for stages of health behavior change: The precaution adoption process model applied to home radon testing. *Health Psychology, 17,* 445–453.

Weinstein, N. D., Rothman, A. J., & Sutton, S. R. (1998). Stage theories of health behavior. *Health Psychology, 17,* 290–299.

III Mobilizing Local Groups of Adults

7 Best Practices of Prosocial Organizations in Youth Development

Susan Elaine Murphy

Claremont McKenna College

Ellen A. Ensher

Loyola Marymount University

Today's for-profit organizations are under immense pressure to remain competitive. Global pressure for reduced costs and domestic pressure to provide the latest product or the best service leave many organizations scrambling to work more effectively. Nonetheless, efficiency and competitiveness are not the only means by which organizations become attractive to investors and consumers. Organizations realize the importance of being seen as socially responsible or environmentally sensitive by consumers and investors. To enhance this perception, many companies over the past 20 years have turned to various forms of corporate social responsibility, including forming partnerships with communities in need, making contributions to various charities, and providing their employees with generous leave time for community service.

In this chapter we give an overview of some of the prosocial efforts that for-profit organizations undertake to provide services for youth. Although there are a number of excellent nonprofit organizations serving the needs of youth, this discussion is outside the scope of this chapter, and instead we focus on the considerable and yet often unheralded efforts of for-profit organizations. Recognizing and learning from these efforts are important because effective mobilization of adults for positive youth development is likely to require the contributions of all sectors of society.

We begin by reviewing three main reasons why organizations engage in prosocial activities: societal, economic, and human resource related. We give many examples of the best practices in addressing youth issues from various corporations. We offer an overview of some of the challenges in providing youth programs. Finally, we highlight the need for evaluation research. Surprisingly, although many for-profit organizations describe the services they provide and the amount of money that is spent, there is little in the way of systematic evaluations of the programs they design or efforts they support, representing significant opportunities for researchers to partner with these businesses in the future.

Why Do Some Organizations Adopt a Prosocial Approach?

Societal Reasons

Although the U.S. federal government and a number of nonprofit organizations dedicate many resources to helping youth, there is still a tremendous gap between what is needed and what is provided. Federal and state monies available for youth programs are spread thin. Even in economic boom times the money is limited, but in economic downturns these types of programs suffer greatly. For example, federal spending directed to children under age 18 was about $148 billion in 2000, or about 8.4% of the total federal budget, and that spending is expected to remain fairly constant—between 1.5% and 1.8% of gross domestic product—during the next decade (Congressional Budget Office, 2000). Therefore, rather than depending on tax monies, many organizations find their funding by other means. Prosocial organizations provide programs and resources to help fill that gap by providing such services as mentoring, tutoring, and assisting in school-to-work transitions. In fact, the Web sites of many top companies have a section dedicated to sharing with the public what it is they do for their communities and specifically for youth.

Another societal influence increasing the number of organizations focusing on community involvement is a renewed interest in volunteerism. Rather than relying on government agencies to administer assistance efforts, people in the United States are interested in making a difference on a more personal level. With recent cuts in income taxes, individuals have been encouraged to take the initiative to give back to their communities. Getting involved in one's community is encouraged through many different efforts, and numerous organizations exist to help individuals connect with volunteer agencies, many of which serve youth.

It is not just organizations that have a renewed commitment to philanthropy, it is also wealthy individuals. Wealthy individuals have always donated much, but recent efforts show a changing trend that is likely to affect the way in which for-profit organizations carry out their philanthropic activities. According to a *Business Week* special issue on philanthropy (Byrne, 2002), a number of changes characterize today's philanthropy: New philanthropy is more ambitious—it tackles large issues such as educational reform and finding a cure for cancer. Donors also are more strategic and tend to use systematic approaches similar to those they use in running their businesses. Philanthropy has become more global, with some donors pursuing international agendas. A final difference is that the new philanthropy demands results and requires that milestones must be met or funding could be ended. Each one of these changes affects the way in which organizations will carry out philanthropy in the future.

Increased attention to the importance of volunteerism and the philanthropic efforts of wealthy individuals has increased the salience of community service efforts for large corporations. Whether they give of their employees' time or their organizational resources, organizations adopt a prosocial approach to provide for youth when other funds are not available and when corporate philanthropy fulfills a company's desire to do good (Smith, 2003). An added benefit of prosocial efforts is the opportunity for employees to help youth by volunteering their time or money, which may increase the feeling that they are contributing to society through their paid work.

Economic Reasons

In addition to societal changes, new economic ways of thinking about corporate philanthropy are providing the business case for corporate philanthropy (Smith, 2003). Not so long ago, the award-winning economist Milton Friedman reportedly said that it was immoral to give away the money of corporate shareholders and that nothing that reduced shareholder wealth should be done (Friedman, 1970). Today's organizations, while keeping in mind Friedman's words, look to engage in the type of corporate philanthropy or social responsibility that increases the "reputational" wealth of an organization. Moreover, the need to show themselves as positive contributors to society has never been greater. As Smith (2003) notes, there is pressure on companies to address societal needs because of mistrust of business, backlash against globalization, and economic struggles. Therefore, rather than merely touting the advantages of the marketed product, the organization also enhances its reputation by engaging in and highlighting its charitable activities. McDonald's, for example, is well known for the Ronald McDonald House, an organization that helps terminally ill children and their families. To enhance the company's reputation, it is not enough that McDonald's engages in this and other types of prosocial activities; the company must also advertise its commitment to these causes, and these efforts enhance the firm's reputation. Many firms today do not spend as much money on advertising their good deeds as does McDonald's, but a quick glance at many large companies' Web sites reveals on each a section called "Community." Within that section the organizations describe the varied philanthropic activities in which they engage to better their immediate or larger community. The funding for these efforts does not come exclusively from philanthropic budgets, but from marketing as well as human resource departments (Smith, 1994). This change underscores organizations' understanding of how philanthropy affects their bottom line.

Many organizations now are making concentrated efforts to show that their contributions to society are important to the bottom line. Corporate social responsibility is defined as "the obligation of the firm to use its resources in ways to benefit society, through committed participation as a member of society taking into account the society at large and improving welfare of society at large independent of direct gains of the company" (Kok, Weile, McKenna, & Brown, 2001, p. 288, as cited in Snider, Hill, & Martin, 2003). If, in addition to benefiting society, the organization's efforts increase sales, this should in turn also benefit shareholders. Some corporate philanthropy efforts affect what is known as the triple bottom line, which includes the interrelationship of social, environmental, and financial factors (Aspen Institute, 2003). A recent meta-analysis of 52 studies of 33,878 organizations showed that both social responsibility and, to a lesser extent, environmental responsibility were strongly related to accounting-based measures of corporate financial performance and also, but less so, to market-based indicators (Orlitzky, Schmidt, & Rynes, 2003). Consumers are becoming more cognizant of the triple bottom line and are willing to punish companies that are not socially responsible by switching loyalties to a competitor (Mracek, 2003). In fact, after years of listening to customers, Tom Chappell, CEO of Tom's of Maine (purveyor of natural personal care products), is convinced that there is a vast untapped market across the United States that cares enormously about Tom's values and will buy its products because of their quality and the company's values (Whitford, 2004, p. 30).

Human Resources Reasons

A third compelling reason why organizations adopt a prosocial approach is that it can effectively aid in the management of the organization's human resources. Recruiting and retaining talented people constitute one of the key challenges that organizations face in today's work environment. Several organizations, including top-rated UPS, lead the way in corporate volunteerism by providing managers time off from their regular duties to immerse themselves in a volunteer experience. Managers often return from these experiences changed for the better, according to their subordinates (Whitaker, 2000); the result is higher rates of retention, not only among the managers, but also among their employees. Retention is also facilitated as employees who participate in corporate volunteering projects get to know one another better, which increases their sense of being a team and results in better organizational citizenship behavior (Drury, 2004). Employees at Spectra Contract Flooring who participated in their organization's efforts for Meals on Wheels found that it was an excellent way to do team building without resorting to the much maligned ropes courses and trust falls that characterized many team-building retreats. At the same time that employees got to know each other better, they also gained a more positive sense of the organization that provided them with the time and resources to volunteer, thus enhancing their overall organizational commitment (Drury, 2004).

Illustrative Examples

What socially responsible efforts have organizations developed to focus on youth issues? Among others, prosocial organizations reach out to youth by tutoring, mentoring, and helping them acquire life skills. Some organizations provide comprehensive youth programs that incorporate all three activities. Following an analysis process utilized by Snider et al. (2003), we used the Internet to examine the community-based programs focused on helping youth in a number of organizations to glean the key characteristics of these successful programs. We started with *Fortune* magazine's list of most admired companies, which in addition to ratings of overall admiration provides ratings of companies with respect to how they stack up on the dimension of social responsibility. In 2004, the 10 most admired companies with respect to social responsibility, in descending order, were United Parcel Service, Alcoa, Washington Mutual, BP, McDonald's, Procter & Gamble, Fortune Brands, Altria (Philip Morris), Vulcan Materials, and American Express ("Most Admired Companies," 2004). Through a review of written and electronic literature, we also identified a number of other organizations that were leaders in these arenas, including Ben & Jerry's, Tom's of Maine, Patagonia, REI, and the Body Shop. We visited the Web sites of these companies looking for programs specifically targeted for youth. The lessons provided by these leading-edge companies should be useful to other organizations setting up similar programs.

Comprehensive Programs Can Be Used to Develop Management Talent

United Parcel Service receives the top spot for a number of efforts, but a glance at the company's Web site underscores why it is perceived as the most socially responsible company in the 2004 poll. Its corporate sustainability statement—"At UPS, we believe our business success depends upon balancing economic, social and environmental objectives"—shows a deep commitment to what the organization does. UPS, a company of 340,000 employees, has some of the most comprehensive volunteer programs available. UPS invests approximately $500,000 a year to send managers through its 4-week Community Internship Program, which was created in 1968 during the civil rights movement. Each year about 50 employees participate by working with nonprofit organizations in one of four locations—New York City, Chicago, Chattanooga, Tennessee, and McAllen, Texas—in a range of activities. They may build houses with Habitat for Humanity, mentor, assist adults with physical disabilities, or work with teachers in classrooms. What does UPS expect to get out of its volunteer programs? For one thing, there is the opportunity for managers to learn compassion for those who live in harsh circumstances. Second, this compassion translates directly to managers' ability to listen to and be more understanding of their employees (Whitaker, 2000).

Organizations Leverage Their Technical Strengths

Many companies try to focus on their technical strengths in providing youth programs. The lesson here for organizations thinking about how best to serve their communities is to engage in activities that allow them to use what they know. Specifically, their employees work to share their specialized knowledge. For example, banks tend to provide financial services, whereas technology companies share technology. Washington Mutual provides examples of working with youth in two programs that call on their financial and banking knowledge. The first, a high school internship program called HIP, includes extensive job training and work experience, but also helps Washington Mutual recruit and mentor new talent. In 2003 nearly 800 high school students across the country graduated from the two-year program (Washington Mutual, 2003). To become involved in the program, HIP interns must have at least a 3.0 grade point average and be actively involved at school. Interns also receive career development and life skills training, including how to manage personal finances, write a résumé, and navigate job interviewing processes. After successful completion of the program, interns may apply for open positions at Washington Mutual. Students also are offered counseling for financial assistance for college through the company's education loan program. According to Washington Mutual, approximately 15,000 students received counseling in 2003. The second program that capitalizes on Washington Mutual's technical knowledge is its Financial Education Advisory Team, which recommends curriculum development to improve financial literacy in schools.

The efforts of EDS (Electronic Data Services), an information technology and business process outsourcing company based in the Dallas, Texas, suburb of Plano, take advantage of the firm's excellence in technology. Its 132,000 employees have a chance to spread their talents in a number of ways supported by the organization. For example, they partner with more than 100 schools in 10 countries through an education outreach program. The volunteer opportunities include mentoring, e-mentoring, tutoring, reading, providing technical and consulting assistance, and providing job-shadowing opportunities, as well as involvement in organizations such as Junior Achievement and I Have a Dream. In fact, EDS does this all so well that it received the Points of Light Award for Volunteer Programs in 2001 for the 21,500 employees who volunteered 58,000 hours. EDS ensures effective goodwill to enhance its reputation by using its technology to help others.

Organizational Tactics That Contribute to Positive Youth Development

The previous examples show some of the varied ways in which organizations provide assistance to youth. We suggest the following typology for more systematically examining the youth development efforts of socially responsible organizations. Organizations can provide help by (1) giving employees paid time off to volunteer their time with charities or organizations of employees' choice, such as Tom's of Maine; (2) developing internal programs to aid youth in their development, such as the Los Angeles Times Summer Jobs Training Program; (3) becoming a partner with selected programs by providing ongoing financial resources and employee time and commitment, such as those technology organizations who participate in MentorNet; and (4) raising money for designated organizations and/or donating supplies to schools or youth programs.

Giving Employees Time Off for Volunteer Efforts

Some organizations offer paid time off in the form of sabbaticals or as part of their employee development programs to employees who volunteer to help youth or other needy groups. Tom's of Maine offers several innovative volunteer opportunities to employees who want to help youth ("Tom's of Maine Natural Care Community," 2004). The company's commitment to social responsibility is substantial: 10% of pretax profits goes to charitable organizations, and management provides support for employees to spend 5% of their time volunteering in the community. The commitment to helping youth is extraordinary: The company also offers grants to organizations that help youth.

Tom's of Maine supports—both financially and with employee time and effort—Jane Goodall's Roots and Shoots, an environmental and humanitarian program for youth from preschool through university levels. Roots and Shoots groups are involved in projects as diverse as developing recycling programs, building habitat gardens, and collecting food and clothing for homeless people.

Developing Internal Programs

While some organizations lend out their employees to help youth or other needy groups, other organizations develop their own internal programs to help youth, such as the school-to-work programs offered by Washington Mutual. A national study in 1997 found that 37% of employers provided some school-to-work programs, up from 25% the year before (Hulsey, Van Noy, & Silverberg, 1999). One organization, the Los Angeles Times, designed and implemented a school-to-work program to respond to a particular need in its community. The Summer Jobs Training Program was developed after the Los Angeles riots in 1992 ("Facts about the Los Angeles Times," 2003). The program is intended to provide high-potential, low-opportunity youth not just with a summer internship but also with new skills, connections, and scholarships. It is also an excellent way for the Times to partner with community service agencies and give back to the communities it serves. Typically, the program provides between 50 and 100 young people a year with full-time internships as well as life skills training sessions, personalized career counseling sessions, opportunities to compete for a scholarship, and a one-on-one mentor. The program is evaluated every year and, according to the Times, continues to be effective. As one young participant stated, "The most important thing to me was that the internship at the Times was a real pick me up. It changed my life. I'm more responsible and know how to deal with the corporate world better" (Ensher & Murphy, 1997).

Research shows that school-to-work programs benefit youth. As a result of the School-to-Work Act of 1994, nearly $1.5 billion in grants was available between 1994 and 1998 to develop partnerships involving schools, employers, organized labor, and other entities. Follow-up research on the effectiveness of the programs receiving these grants has yielded somewhat mixed results. A study using the 1997 National Longitudinal Survey of Youth shows that 529 young people who participated in school-to-work programs were more likely than nonparticipants to engage in job-seeking behavior and had stronger positive expectations about the future (Riggio & Riggio, 1999). The participants did not engage in fewer "delinquent" behaviors than the nonparticipants. The variety of school-to-work programs most likely contributed to the mixed results on program effectiveness. These research studies underscore the need for careful program development, keeping in mind appropriate goals and evaluation procedures.

Partnering with Nonprofits

A third way in which organizations help youth is to partner with non-profit organizations by providing ongoing financial support or employee time and commitment. MentorNet is an excellent example of an innovative partnership between a youth-oriented nonprofit organization and for-profit sponsors. The purpose of this electronic mentoring program is to match female science students (science, technology, engineering, and math disciplines) with a professional mentor in a specific field (MentorNet, 2004). Since 1998 MentorNet has matched 20,000 mentors and protégés. MentorNet was initially funded by a grant from the National Science Foundation and founding partners such as AT&T and Intel. It also maintains strong financial partnerships with Alcoa, IBM, Microsoft, and 3M.

MentorNet is a standout, not only in the scope and service it provides, but also in its in-depth approach to program evaluation. In the past several years, protégés have consistently reported increased confidence in their success in science and engineering as well as an increased desire to pursue a career in their field. This is very important as the field of science has difficulty attracting and retaining young women. Mentors report significant rewards as well. Mentors found that they increased their own professional development, increased their commitment to their field and their employers, and found both an opportunity for self-reflection and a sense of satisfaction through being an e-mentor (MentorNet, 2004). In sum, this innovative program offers a valuable and flexible way for working adults to help youth (including both undergraduate and graduate college students) from the convenience of their workstations or laptops, anywhere, anytime.

A wholly different example of for-profit and nonprofit partnering comes from Ben & Jerry's ice cream. Ben & Jerry's has a social and environmental assessment (see "Social and Environmental Assessment," 2002) in which philanthropic and corporate social responsibility aims are made explicit. The company contributed $1,206,412 to the Ben & Jerry's Foundation in 2002 and continues to offer grants to needy organizations. One of its more innovative approaches to helping youth is through its PartnerShop program, which uses Ben & Jerry's scoop shops to provide job and entrepreneurial training to young people who face barriers to employment, such as mental illness, homelessness, or past conviction. Not only can participating nonprofits provide work to their clientele, they can also generate profits to sustain the job training program for the future. Nearly 1,750 youth have been trained through PartnerShops since 1987, and although such stores are not as profitable as the regular scoop shops, Ben & Jerry's has recently taken steps to improve overall profitability for participating shops.

Some organizations work through local school districts to provide opportunities for high school students. A work-based learning program in the Philadelphia school district paired high school students with adult mentors at their work site. Linnehan (2001) found that students who participated in the program for more than half a year had higher grades and improved attendance records. Those who participated for a shorter time did not reflect the same benefits. In a longitudinal study of the same program, Linnehan (2003) compared students who were in informal mentoring relationships at work, those who worked without a mentor, and those who did not work during the academic year. Students who were more satisfied with their mentors were more likely to believe that school was relevant to the workplace in addition to having higher self-esteem at the end of the academic year than students who did not work. These studies showed the tangible benefits of company and school partnerships, as well as proper program evaluation techniques.

Donating Money or Supplies

A fourth way in which organizations help youth is by raising money for designated organizations or by donating supplies. Microsoft, a leader in this area, in 2003 contributed more than $40 million in cash and $224 million in software to nearly 5,000 nonprofit organizations ("Microsoft Citizenship Community Affairs Fact Sheet," 2004). The company's global program, Microsoft Unlimited Potential, focuses on providing technology skills for underserved young people and adults through community-based technology and learning centers. Microsoft has donated $88 million in software and $12 million in cash to Boys and Girls Clubs of America ("Microsoft Community Affairs in the News," 2004). Efforts such as these help bridge the digital divide among youth across society.

Summary

As shown in our many examples, prosocial organizations are helping youth in a wide range of activities through various methods. Companies can either pay individuals or groups to volunteer with agencies that assist youth or they can develop programs alone or by teaming with nonprofits specifically aimed at helping youth. In addition, many organizations choose to donate money or supplies, or have their employees raise funds for youth-related causes. Although all of these efforts provide optional ways for companies to enhance their corporate reputations, fulfill their social responsibilities, and improve their communities, companies can take many more steps to ensure that their efforts are effective. In the next section we turn to ways in which these efforts can be enhanced to assist as many youth as possible to the fullest extent.

Improving Organizations' Efforts in Youth Programs

The efforts of many organizations are to be applauded. The sheer volume of hours, money, and supplies contributed to helping youth in the United States as well as globally is phenomenal. However, these efforts can become all-encompassing and detract from bottom-line profits. Moreover, these efforts are not simple to devise, implement, or evaluate, and are sometimes difficult to explain to shareholders and employees. Employees who may be laid off do not look favorably on corporations giving away money (Smith, 1994). In addition, employees who are asked to increase their workload to meet competitive pressures may not have the time or energy to spend extra hours volunteering. Shareholders may not see the benefits of the efforts. Take the example of Timberland. In 1995, after a number of years of growth, sales began to decline sharply, and the company's community involvement efforts were criticized by shareholders and employees (Austin & Elias, 1996). Communicating to employees the importance of Timberland's service programs as part of its mission helped the company weather the criticism, but it was not an easy time for the organization. Eventually management was able to show a balanced approach that satisfied all stakeholders.

When companies are actively engaged in a wide range of activities that benefit youth, it is exceedingly important for them to conceive, implement, monitor, and evaluate their programs carefully. In other words, it is not enough to offer programs; it is even more important to ensure the quality of the programs. There are a number of ways in which organizations can make sure their efforts to help youth are in fact effective. First and foremost is taking time to understand the specific needs of young people and to recognize the specific challenges one might face in working with youth. Individuals and organizations must understand the issues of working with youth populations. Organizations can help through training and realistic previews of the volunteer efforts to ensure success for the individual. Overcoming barriers one might experience as organizations encourage increasingly more volunteer efforts is also important. Finally, organizations must conduct and publish appropriate program evaluations.

Understanding Special Needs of Youth

> We must recognize the strong need of those just emerging from childhood for supportive adults and settings in which young people can develop a secure identity, explore the world beyond the self, and learn the skills for responsible, productive, and fulfilling adulthood.
>
> —Carnegie Foundation Report on Developing Adolescence, 1995

Adolescence is a special time for youth. Because of developmental processes, the needs of elementary school children differ from those of middle school youth, and both differ from those of high school students. For example, according to Havighurst (1972, as cited in Cobb, 2003), the most important developmental tasks for students in early adolescence involve achieving emotional independence from their parents and establishing a masculine or feminine social role, while for younger children basic school skills and getting along with age mates are very important. By the time a youth reaches high school, another group of issues become salient, especially those surrounding choices about college and vocation. Recent reviews of the concerns facing youth, especially adolescents, show that issues today are very similar to those seen in the past. They include substance use and abuse, failure in school, poverty, delinquency, family problems, and physical and mental health problems (Lerner & Galambos, 1998). Many youth programs are aimed at increasing resiliency factors or building them into the youth's environment. These positive influences include supportive families, caring communities and schools, effective coping strategies, and supportive adult network structures (Cobb, 2003). Exposure to work is an important feature of effective youth programs because work is central to adolescent identity, and programs that give them work experiences help prepare them to enter the labor force (Dryfoos, 1990).

Organizations should hire outside consultants or local school district personnel to become acquainted with the youth population they serve. Although the needs of youth are homogeneous in many respects, there are unique challenges for particular communities. When one of us developed a service-learning mentoring program for our college students, the Kravis Mentoring Program at Claremont McKenna College, we worked closely with the community to determine which children needed what type of assistance. The city's human services department had compiled survey data and demographic data in collaboration with the school district to determine which age students were in particular need of an after-school mentoring program. The mentoring was not generic: A combination of team and one-on-one mentoring was developed to address some of the social issues many of the students were facing as they made the transition from elementary school to a large junior high school. Not only did our background research help in picking the target population and the overall design of the mentoring program, it also gave the mentors a comprehensive background on students, providing them knowledge they needed to make them effective mentors. From our review of many of the company-based youth programs such as those found at EDS, it is clear that these companies have worked closely with the community schools to ensure that the programs that are developed meet the unique needs of the youth population.

Overcoming Challenges in Working with Youth

Regardless of the type of program, working with youth is often challenging; especially youth from backgrounds other than those of adult volunteers. What can organizations do to ensure that employees are prepared to contribute their time in youth programs? For the Los Angeles Times program there was specific training to prepare the supervisors and mentors to help encourage the interns over the course of the summer. The training acquainted the mentors and supervisors with some of the thinking that youth bring to the workplace, as well as reminders that they would be working with very young students and needed to model appropriate behavior. The interns received training in appropriate work behavior. Although some had held jobs previously, this environment was new to them. The Times used role playing and other experiential activities to let interns know what to expect on the job.

In talking with organizations that run youth programs, we discovered that they recognize the importance of having a helpful staff that serves as a supervisory resource. Organizations that have been in their communities for a number of years will have access to other resources to prepare individuals to get involved in their youth programs. It is incumbent on organizations to provide a positive experience for youth and for their employees. The trust that is developed between the community and the organization cannot be jeopardized through shoddy program implementation and follow-through. In this section we describe some of these challenges and what organizations have done or might do to address them.

According to a review, 37% of all students participating in school-to-work partnerships were either African American or Latino (Hulsey et al., 1999, cited in Linnehan, 2001); these programs focused on non-college-bound disadvantaged student populations (Lewis, Stone, Shipley, & Madzar, 1998). Some individuals have a difficult time understanding how different some children's backgrounds might be from their own; there are many things that middle- and upper-middle-class individuals take for granted.

In one of our experiences with a tutoring program, a tutor was attempting to help a child develop better homework habits. He told the child that he would be more successful in completing his homework if he sat at his desk every night in his bedroom from 6:00 to 8:00. The boy gave him a puzzled look. The tutor asked the child, "Don't you have a desk?" Not only did he not have a desk, the boy told him, but he did not have a bedroom. He shared a bedroom with a number of family members and did his homework on the front porch. At that moment, the tutor realized that he would have to listen carefully to the child to understand what types of hints he could offer for improving the child's grades that would be effective given his home situation. The tutoring program later developed a training program for future volunteers based on the lessons the tutors had learned in previous years.

To ensure a positive experience both for volunteers and the young people who receive help, prosocial organizations should prepare employee volunteers for the challenges they may face before they begin their volunteer assignments. Some adults may find it difficult to relate to students of certain ages. Although younger children may be more outgoing and trusting of an unknown adult, they may also be wary of a stranger. The adult may need to win their trust before mentoring, tutoring, helping with homework, or reading can occur. Mentors, tutors, and those helping with other youth tasks need to appreciate the time it may take to get to the real work of the partnership. Numerous online and print resources address some of the challenges and may be useful in helping organizations ensure program success.

Beyond differences that may exist in age and social class, prosocial organizations need to make volunteers aware of the potential challenges ethnic differences can play in a relationship. Training on the Web site of the National Mentoring Partnership (Mentoring.org) might be useful for organizations embarking upon programs in which employees meet one-on-one with youth. In addition, organizations may conduct their own evaluation projects to look at the effects of ethnicity in their volunteer efforts.

In one study, we found that the summer internship program at the Los Angeles Times was cognizant that ethnicity in pairing of interns with mentors might be important. The data revealed that while same-race protégés initially liked their mentors more than those paired with different-race mentors, if, over time, the interns perceived their mentors to hold similar values or goals, then they were just as satisfied with different-race mentors (Ensher & Murphy, 1997). An example of different-race pairing comes from a Vietnamese American colleague of ours who was paired with an African American young man through Big Brothers. When they met, the mentor noticed that the boy looked disappointed. He made a joke, saying that he bet that the last person the boy expected to mentor him would be, as he put it, "an Asian dude." In spite of their different ethnic backgrounds, they quickly bonded over their love of video games and the same type of popular music.

It is also important that in pairings for tutoring, mentoring, and other types of relationships, the parties involved work to build rapport and overcome initial, perhaps stereotypic, beliefs that may impede the relationship. Prosocial organizations can build in exercises that many youth programs use to help the student and the employee get to know one another on a deeper level so that a connection can be made. Previous research shows some benefits to same-race as well as cross-race matching (see, for example, Linnehan, Weer, & Uhl, 2005). However, Rhodes, Reddy, Grossman, and Lee (2002) found that same-race matching was differentially valuable for minority boys and girls involved in the Big Brothers Big Sisters of America program. Therefore, race and gender remain important factors to consider when prosocial organizations design youth programs.

Another way in which prosocial organizations can ensure high-quality programs is to screen employee volunteers who will work with children. Not everyone is equally effective in working with children. Prosocial organizations can help prepare volunteers by having experienced volunteers talk to them about realistic objectives for what they may accomplish in their relationships. As much research has suggested, a bad relationship with an adult volunteer can be exceedingly harmful to a child who may already face a number of life stressors (Murphy, Johnson, Soto, & Gopez, 1997; Rhodes, 2002). Some adults may have a difficult time identifying with youth, especially if they have no children or their own children are of a different age. Music and clothing trends may seem very foreign to them. In addition, those who volunteer often have unrealistic expectations about what they can accomplish with the child they set out to help. Some volunteers think they may be able to somehow "save" the child from whatever problems have led to the child's present situation, or they become disenchanted with their efforts when they see no immediate changes in the child's grades, behavior, or achievement.

Unfortunately, there is a rare possibility that something worse than unmet expectations or misunderstandings due to a so-called generation gap may happen. To prevent child abuse, agencies that have volunteers working with children use many different approaches. The Boy Scouts of America, for example, have developed effective procedures that other organizations could emulate (Potts, 1992). They include preventive leader selection procedures, creating barriers to child abuse, encouraging scouts to report improper behavior, and immediate removal of alleged offenders. Prosocial organizations must develop procedures before a problem arises.

Working with youth is very rewarding for most volunteers, but it takes a degree of preparation that organizations should provide for their employees. Educating employees about the reality of what might happen in relationships with youth and what goals are realistic should go a long way toward enhancing these efforts. Many best-practice prosocial organizations make a considerable effort to provide proper training and guidance to employees, and other organizations considering working with youth should look to them for guidance.

Overcoming Internal and External Organizational Barriers

Corporate volunteerism can boost workers' productivity and morale, and, as we noted earlier, employees who are encouraged to give back to their communities and do something that they might not have done before are more likely to stay with their employer. Moreover, one author notes that employees who volunteer to teach literacy, English as a second language, or time-management skills can help others become more valuable workers and at the same time have an opportunity to demonstrate skills they have not been allowed to exercise in the workplace (Reardon, 2003).

Despite the advantages of volunteering, some employees, managers, and communities resist engaging in these efforts. Management might feel that resources of time and personnel are being diverted while also worrying that the causes they choose may become controversial. A community might worry about becoming dependent on the volunteer efforts of a business that could choose to relocate or to donate its efforts elsewhere (Reardon, 2003).

One way to reduce internal and external organizational barriers is to follow the lead of best-practice organizations and be very up-front in all efforts. For example, McDonald's recently started an annual *Social Responsibility Report* in which the company provides information about the part of the business that is related to the communities it serves, the environment, employees, and relationships with suppliers (www.mcdonalds.com). Another way to reduce organizational barriers is to enlist the support of top management. Of course, no efforts for youth are approved without top management's authorization, but active top management participation in programs is a useful tool for getting employee buy-in for volunteering. According to some reports, a large percentage of executives take time to volunteer, providing invaluable role modeling.

The companies we outline here have done a great job of increasing volunteerism in their organizations. There are, however, many organizations that have to overcome resistance from many different angles. We find that carefully designed programs with specific goals for the company as well as for employees and the youth involved seem to be the most effective in improving general attitudes toward the program. A final tool for overcoming resistance and focusing on effectiveness is discussed in the next section.

Encouraging Evaluation and Sharing Research Results

Many business schools are encouraging research that focuses on both the environmental and the social impact of business decisions. For now, a handful of professors are spearheading that effort. The Beyond Pinstripes study is an ongoing effort to compare the approaches taken by MBA programs and professors to prepare students for a more comprehensive approach to social and environmental stewardship (Aspen Institute, 2003). For example, the study considers the extent to which courses in ethics, corporate social responsibility, sustainability, and business and society are offered, as well as whether those topics are integrated into standard business courses such as accounting and economics. As part of the research effort, "Faculty Pioneers" and M.B.A. programs from many institutions (Michigan, Stanford, Yale, and elsewhere) are selected on the basis of producing cutting-edge research on the environmental and social impact of business decisions (Aspen Institute, 2003).

Although the efforts of socially responsible organizations are laudable, making available comprehensive program evaluations, which might suggest important improvements and be used as a communication tool, would enhance these efforts tremendously. The efforts of many organizations should be compiled in common evaluation practices so that others could learn from lessons about effectiveness and challenges. Evaluation of the effectiveness of youth programs is difficult for a number of reasons: finding a control group, collecting the appropriate outcome data (if collecting data is allowed at all), needing to work closely with a school, understanding when change in outcomes should be assessed, and so on. All of these factors contribute to the reluctance of organizations to evaluate youth programs. The dearth of published research and the challenges in conducting evaluation research provide significant opportunities for researchers to partner with socially responsible organizations to conduct program evaluations.

Summary and Conclusions

The increased emphasis on corporate social responsibility has provided much-needed efforts in helping young people in a wide variety of ways. Societal, economic, and human resources reasons have encouraged more organizations to help youth. In addition, many forward-thinking organizations have done much to volunteer their employees' time, develop programs, and donate resources. There are countless examples of companies that support youth development; however, the results of their programs are not widely disseminated, leaving companies that want to start their own efforts often either duplicating what might already be available or developing a program that will be less than effective. Many of the best-practice companies realize the steps necessary to lead to successful programs and have partnered with existing agencies to serve those who need it most. Their accomplishments are commendable and should be shared with others.

How Adults Can Help

Adults should look inside their companies to see what direct ways are available to help youth in their area. E-mentoring and e-volunteering are the wave of the future for busy professionals (Ensher, Heun, & Blanchard, 2003). Organizations can also engage in indirect methods of helping children, as exemplified by a recent study by the Points of Light Foundation highlighting the concept of "neighboring." Rather than working to help youth directly, volunteers work to help strengthen families in the neighborhood. Many organizations spend time helping in this manner. More assessment of how neighboring efforts affect youth development will encourage more indirect methods of helping youth and may offer opportunities for busy employees to get involved in their communities through their organizations.

Preparing Tomorrow's Workforce

Clearly, corporate America faces a number of challenges for long-term viability, and chief among these challenges is the development of the next generation of employees. Corporate social responsibility enables organizations to invest in future generations by creating an active pipeline of talented workers. Consider the following five major trends facing organizations: (1) greater diversity of the workforce; (2) globalization in terms of increased multinationals and international outsourcing; (3) increased need for better technological skills; (4) increase in service-based economy; and (5) renewed commitment to and interest in corporate ethics. Many of the challenges inherent in these trends can be effectively addressed with proper attention paid to opportunities for corporate social responsibility.

Our workforce continues to grow more diverse, not only in terms of age, race, and gender, but also in terms of sexual orientation, physical ability, and national origin (United States Equal Employment Opportunity Commission, 2002). Preparing people to work collaboratively in spite of their differences led to a number of diversity-related efforts in the early 1990s; these efforts continue today in diversity initiatives, revamped reward systems, and training and development. Organization-sponsored youth programs such as the Los Angeles Times Summer Jobs Training program give both today's workers and their young participants opportunities to enhance their skills in dealing effectively with diversity challenges. Program evaluations conducted by the Times revealed that supervisors, mentors, and the youth all learned valuable lessons about generational differences, leadership, and complementary work styles (Ensher & Murphy, 1997).

One would be hard pressed to read the business section of any newspaper today without finding evidence of increasing globalization for industries and organizations. Youth development programs such as the Tom's of Maine partnership with Jane Goodall's Roots and Shoots program, the Body Shop's Children on the Edge program, and the international burgeoning of MentorNet into 55 countries are all examples of how best-practice organizations act globally. In encouraging employees to get involved on an international and yet very personal level with youth from around the world, these organizations enable employees of today and potential workers of tomorrow to break down traditional barriers of geography and nationality.

One of the greatest tools enhancing globalization is the increased use of technology, and particularly widespread communication via the Internet. At the same time that technology improves so many lives, lack of technology and access to the Internet creates the ever widening gulf between the haves and the have-nots that is known as the digital divide ("Microsoft Citizenship Community Affairs Fact Sheet," 2004). Global programs such as Microsoft's Unlimited Potential are an important first step in bridging this digital divide.

One major aspect of globalization is the trend toward outsourcing, particularly in terms of manufacturing and, more recently, administrative tasks and call service centers as well (Bhagwati, 2004). As the United States continues to move toward a service-based economy, it is more important than ever that employees exhibit skills related to service, such as interpersonal competence and customer service know-how. Therefore, programs such as Ben & Jerry's PartnerShops provide extreme at-risk youth (e.g., homeless, mentally ill) with exactly the skills they will need to survive in this service-based economy and give employers access to a previously underutilized pool of workers.

The trend toward greater accountability and corporate ethics is a final challenge for American business. In recent years we have seen an increasing spate of corporate scandals and high-profile bankruptcies (e.g., Enron and WorldCom). This in turn has led to reforms and new legislation (for example, the Sarbanes-Oxley reporting requirements) and a renewed interest in corporate ethics in colleges and universities (Harris, 2002). The prosocial efforts toward youth development highlighted by best-practice organizations as outlined here all represent important strides toward increased corporate ethics. Corporate America should take note: Social responsibility and youth development have a wide variety of benefits in terms of meeting short-term goals and ensuring long-term sustainability.

References

Aspen Institute and World Resources Institute. (2003). *Beyond grey pinstripes 2003: Preparing M.B.A.s for social and environmental stewardship*. Retrieved May 28, 2004, from www.beyondgreypinstripes.org

Austin, J., & Elias, J. (1996). Timberland and community involvement. *Harvard Business Review Case*. Cambridge, MA: Harvard Business School Publishing.

Bhagwati, J. (2004, March). Why your job isn't moving to Bangalore. *American Enterprise Institute for Public Policy Research*. Retrieved July 1, 2004, from http://www.aworldconnected.com/article.php/609.html

Byrne, J. (2002, December 2). The new face of philanthropy. *Business Week*. Retrieved May 23, 2004, from http://www.businessweek.com/magazine/content/02_48/b3810001.htm

Carnegie Foundation. (1995). *Great transitions: Preparing adolescents for a new century*. New York: Author.

Cobb, N. (2003). *Adolescence: Continuity, change, and diversity* (5th ed.). New York: McGraw-Hill.

Congressional Budget Office. (2000, June). Federal spending on elderly and children. Retrieved May 23, 2004, from http://www.cbo.gov/showdoc.cfm?index=2300 &sequence=0

Drury, T. (2004, May 3). Volunteering, making a difference. *Business First*. Retrieved May 18, 2004, from http://www.bizjournals.com/buffalo/stories/2004/05/03/focus2.html?t =printable

Dryfoos, J. G. (1990). *Adolescents at risk: Prevalence and prevention*. New York: Oxford University Press.

Ensher, E. A., Heun, C., & Blanchard, A. (2003). Online mentoring and computer-mediated communication: New directions in research. *Journal of Vocational Behavior, 63*(2), 264–288.

Ensher, E. A., & Murphy, S. A. (1997). Effects of race, gender, perceived similarity, and contact on mentor relationships. *Journal of Vocational Behavior, 50*, 460–481.

Facts about the Los Angeles Times. Retrieved March 25, 2004, from http://images.latimes.com/media/acrobat/2003-03/7092547.pdf

Friedman, M. (1970, September 13). The social responsibility of business is to increase its profits. *New York Times Magazine*.

Harris, A. (2002, Fall). Corporate governance after Enron. In *CCH: Regulatory Perspective*. Retrieved July 1, 2004, from http://216.239.57.104/search?q=cache:R3jtKhwt9ygJ: www.uhlaw.com/perspectives/publications/pdf-bin/al_harris_rev.pdf+%22impetus+for+Sarbanes+oxley%22&hl=en

Havighurst, R. J. (1972). *Developmental tasks and education*. New York: David McKay.

Hulsey, L., Van Noy, M., & Silverberg, M. (1999). *The 1998 national survey of local school-to-work partnerships: Data summary*. Princeton, NJ: Mathematica Policy Research.

Kok, P., Weile, T. V. D., McKenna, R., & Brown, A. (2001). A corporate social responsibility audit within a quality management framework. *Journal of Business Ethics, 31*(4), 285–297.

Lerner, R. M., & Galambos, N. L. (1998). Adolescent development: Challenges and opportunities for research, programs, and policies. *Annual Review of Psychology, 49*, 413–446.

Lewis, T., Stone, J., Shipley, W., & Madzar, S. (1998). The transition from school to work. *Youth and Society, 29*(3), 259–292.

Linnehan, F. (2001). The relation of a work-based mentoring program to the academic performance and behavior of African-American students. *Journal of Vocational Behavior, 59*, 310–325.

Linnehan, F. (2003). A longitudinal study of work-based, adult-youth mentoring. *Journal of Vocational Behavior, 63*, 40–54.

Linnehan, F., Weer, C., & Uhl, J. (2005). African-American students' early trust beliefs in work-based mentors. *Journal of Vocational Behavior, 66*(3), 501–515.

MentorNet: The E-Mentoring Network for Women in Engineering and Science. Retrieved July 1, 2004, from http://www.mentornet.net/

Microsoft Citizenship Community Affairs Fact Sheet. Retrieved May 18, 2004, from http://www.microsoft.com/presspass/features/2004/Jan04/0123CAFactSheet04.asp

Microsoft Community Affairs in the News. Retrieved May 18, 2004, from http://www.microsoft.com/mscorp/citizenship/giving/news/

Most admired companies. (2004, March 8). Retrieved May, 24, 2004, from http://www.fortune
.com/fortune/mostadmired

Mracek, K. (2003, October 17). Raytheon, Cox among companies honored for community service in
Tucson, Ariz. *Arizona Daily Star*, p. 1.

Murphy, S. E., Johnson, C. S., Soto, D., & Gopez, A. (1997). *Evaluation of mentoring relationship quality
in a team-based youth mentoring program.* Unpublished report prepared for Los Angeles Team
Mentoring, Claremont, CA.

Orlitzky, M., Schmidt, F. L., & Rynes, S. L. (2003). Corporate social and financial performance: A
meta-analysis. *Organization Studies, 24*(3), 403–442.

Potts, L. F. (1992). The Youth Protection Program of the Boy Scouts of America. *Child Abuse & Neglect,
16*(3), 441–445.

Reardon, D. (2003, November 14). Corporate volunteers walk fine line. *Central Penn Business Journal,*
19(48), 3.

Rhodes, J. E. (2002). *Stand by me: The risks and rewards of mentoring today's youth.* Cambridge, MA:
Harvard University Press.

Rhodes, J. E., Reddy, R., Grossman, J. B., & Lee, J. M. (2002). Volunteer mentoring relationships
with minority youth: An analysis of same- versus cross-race matches. *Journal of Applied Social
Psychology, 32*, 2114–2133.

Riggio, R. E., & Riggio, H. R. (1999). *Evaluation of school-to-work programs using the NLSY97 database
report prepared for the Groundhog Job Shadow Day Coalition.* Claremont, CA: Claremont McKenna
College, Kravis Leadership Institute.

Smith, C. (1994, May–June). The new corporate philanthropy. *Harvard Business Review,* 105–116.

Smith, N. C. (2003). Corporate social responsibility: Whether or how? *California Management Review,*
45(4), 52–76

Snider, J., Hill, R. P., & Martin, D. (2003, December). Corporate social responsibility in the
21st century: A view from the world's most successful firms. *Journal of Business Ethics*, 175–
187.

Social and Environmental Assessment. (2002). Retrieved May 18, 2004, from http://www.ben-
jerry.com/our_company/about_us/environment/social_audit/

Tom's of Maine natural care community. Retrieved March 25, 2004, from http://www.
tomsofmaine.com/toms/community/

United States Equal Employment Opportunity Commission. (2002). Annual report on the Federal
Work Force Fiscal Year 2002. In *U.S. Equal Employment Opportunity Commission.* Retrieved July
1, 2004, from http://www.eeoc.gov/federal/fsp2002/index.html

Washington Mutual. *2003 annual report.* Retrieved July 1, 2004, from http://phx.corporate-
ir.net/phoenix.zhtml?c=101159&p=irol-reports#

Whitaker, B. (2000, July 26). Management. *New York Times*. Retrieved May 18, 2003, from
http://query.nytimes.com/gst/abstract.html?res=F50812F8385E0C758EDDAE0894D8404482
&incamp=archive:search

Whitford, D. (2004, June). Go west, old hippie. *Fortune*, 30–32.

8 Mobilizing Communities for Positive Youth Development: Lessons Learned from Neighborhood Groups and Community Coalitions

Pamela S. Imm

University of South Carolina

Renie Kehres

Prevention Partners for Youth Development

Abraham Wandersman

University of South Carolina

Matthew Chinman

RAND Corporation

This chapter highlights the research from neighborhood and community groups (e.g., coalitions) that suggest effective strategies and structures for mobilizing adults to promote positive youth development. The youth development movement contends that neighborhoods and communities should develop ongoing supports, opportunities, and services for youth to promote healthy development and positive behaviors (Pittman, 2000). Simply avoiding risk-taking behaviors and related problems is not sufficient to lead to optimal development and productive young adults. In community settings where formal and informal leaders view youth development as a priority, strategies to ensure the integration of youth development principles and practices into community organizations and coalitions are critical for success. Neighborhoods and communities must provide the conditions for youth to successfully transition into adulthood and attain the larger goal of optimal healthy development.

After research findings in the areas of neighborhood and block organizations, community coalitions, and evaluation strategies are highlighted, this chapter describes the processes and activities of a community coalition, the Onondaga County Prevention Partners for Youth Development (PPYD) in Syracuse, New York. The PPYD coalition exemplifies how a community can mobilize adults, develop infrastructures and processes to engage youth, and implement programs to promote youth development and asset building.

Lessons Learned from Neighborhood and Block Organizations

Research in the area of neighborhood and block organizations can be useful to illustrate the factors that increase (and decrease) the likelihood that residents will participate in a variety of community activities. This research provides a general foundation for understanding why adults become involved in community organizations, community coalitions, and in more specific endeavors, such as involvement in youth development strategies. The general model is that adult participation and community involvement are predicted by qualities of the individual (e.g., level of concern about the issue), the environment (e.g., community setting, resources available), and the interaction of these factors (e.g., sense of community) (Florin & Wandersman, 1990; Kieffer, 1984; McMillan, Florin, Stevenson, Kerman, & Mitchell, 1995; Zimmerman, 2000).

Empirical data indicate that specific variables are important to consider when recruiting adults to participate in any type of community activity ranging from youth development to community organizing and neighborhood participation. An extensive literature review of empirical data (Dalton, Elias, & Wandersman, 2001) indicates that, for participation, the best predictors are as follows:

- Sense of community and civic responsibility;
- Volunteering for other organizations;
- Involvement in community activities;
- Dissatisfaction with neighborhood problems; and
- Satisfaction with quality of life in a neighborhood or other setting.

An additional factor related to recruitment and sustained involvement is the relationship between the costs and benefits of participation (Chinman & Wandersman, 1999). Specifically, people are more likely to become involved and remain involved in community organizations if they perceive that the benefits of doing so outweigh the costs of participation. Typical benefits of community involvement include learning new skills, being involved in exciting issues, making interpersonal contacts, receiving personal recognition, and gaining a sense of improving the community (Dalton et al., 2001). Costs of participation include time, child care and transportation issues, and the experience and anticipation of unpleasant situations (e.g., unproductive meetings, conflicting ideas between members). Efforts at incentive management, or the desire to reduce costs while enhancing the benefits of participation, have been successful in increasing the viability of neighborhood associations (Prestby, Wandersman, Florin, Rich, & Chavis, 1990) and the level of participation in community coalitions (Chinman, Anderson, Imm, Wandersman, & Goodman, 1996).

How Can Communities Organize to Promote Youth Development?

Research indicates that American communities have been negligent in promoting human development infrastructures (Benson, Scales, & Mannes, 2003; Dryfoos, 1994). For example, only about 40% of youth report experiencing developmental assets that are related to support and connection, such as living in a caring neighborhood or community in which adults know and interact with children and adolescents (Benson et al., 2003; Search Institute, 2001). These data, in combination with a lack of other asset-based skills and accessible resources, suggest that a significant proportion of young people experience problems as they transition into adulthood (Dryfoos, 1994) and do not have appropriate environments in which to reach their full potential (Benson et al., 2003; Seligman & Csikszentmihalyi, 2000).

Although a variety of community organizations and programs have been designed to be accessible to youth, formalized youth organizations such as Boy Scouts and Girl Scouts, YMCAs, and other programs (e.g., after-school, faith-based, community-based) have typically targeted lower-risk youth (Bumbarger & Greenberg, 2002). In addition, these programs and organizations frequently require significant expenditures (e.g., uniforms, dues) that make them available only to a subset of youth. Recently, however, communities, nonprofit agencies, and other entities (e.g., towns and municipalities, prevention organizations, schools) have begun to offer programming for youth across all levels of risk. In many settings, community coalitions are formed to plan and/or implement prevention strategies to address particular community needs. A community coalition is defined as "an organization of diverse interest groups that combine their human and material resources to effect a specific change the members are unable to bring about independently" (Brown, 1984, p. 1). Community coalitions are advantageous in that they allow diverse community groups to become involved in new areas, reduce duplication among multiple programs, and show that there is broad community support for efforts to address the problem in question (Butterfoss, Goodman, & Wandersman, 1993).

Developing and sustaining community coalitions present a challenge. They involve a variety of skills related to community mobilization, relationship building, and problem solving. Research indicates that effective community coalitions have similar characteristics, including diverse and broad representation of membership, clarity of mission, organizational structures (e.g., appropriate formal and informal decision-making processes, shared leadership, specific roles and tasks for members), a user-friendly planning framework that includes methods for assessing progress and evaluating outcomes, and diverse funding streams (Backer, 2003; Butterfoss et al., 1993; Community Anti-Drug Coalitions of America, 2002; Livet & Wandersman, 2005). The importance of relationships and relationship building cannot be underestimated when forming coalitions and considering issues of sustainability. This process encompasses the relationships between the coalition members as well as how the members interact with "outside" community members and key stakeholders.

Inevitably, there will be differences of opinions and/or conflict among the membership. Signs of conflict are not always straightforward and may range from arriving late for meetings and leaving meetings early to lack of enthusiasm, unproductive meetings, and noncompliance with assigned tasks. To move the community organization forward in its mission, it is necessary to recognize and deal with any conflict. Well-trained facilitators and evaluators can be helpful in managing conflict by reporting their perceptions and presenting related information in an unbiased, objective manner. Strategies for resolving these conflicts include compromise, developing and adhering to a conflict resolution policy, and obtaining outside consultation and mediation when necessary (Backer & Kunz, 2003).

Community coalitions are increasingly focusing on youth development models such as building developmental assets (Benson, 1997), improving life skills and positive bonding experiences (Botvin, Baker, Dusenbury, Botvin, & Diaz, 1995; Hawkins, Catalano, & Miller, 1992; Thomsen, 2002), and increasing youth competencies for success and thriving (Scales, Benson, Leffert, & Blyth, 2000; Scales & Leffert, 2004; Takanashi, Mortimer, & McGourthy, 1997). Search Institute has identified 40 development assets in eight domains that contribute to optimal youth development. Another example is Karen Pittman's review of the youth development literature, which yielded five outcomes for youth, known as the "five Cs" (Pittman, Irby, & Ferber, 2000). The "five Cs"—competence, confidence, character, connections, and contributions—represent broad domains for positive adolescent development. Educating community groups about the research in youth development is critical to such groups' success in planning, implementing, and evaluating their efforts. Applying models that are straightforward and easily understood, such as the "five Cs," is important in promoting a common language among community members and organizations.

Empirical data indicate that community organizations and programs intent on promoting youth development concepts within their settings need to focus on multiple strategies aimed at various segments of youth (Center for Substance Abuse Prevention, 2002; Nation et al., 2003; National Institute on Drug Abuse, 2003). In addition, structures and processes must be developed to ensure that youth are provided with safe, supportive environments that encourage positive patterns of social interactions and promote meaningful opportunities for youth development (Benson, 1997; Pittman, 2000; Pittman & Wright, 1991; Thomsen, 2002; Wheeler, 2000).

Effective approaches to positive youth development operationalize these themes by fostering connections and supports among youth and others, providing opportunities for meaningful involvement, and ensuring that youth development programs integrate the components related to high-quality interventions.

Community Research Highlighting the Importance of Building Supports
for Youth Development

One critical aspect of youth development is to create structures and processes within communities and organizations that value and work to enhance
the relationships between youth and adults. Building these relationships is particularly relevant given empirical studies indicating that youth feel disconnected
from their community and would like to have more positive interactions with
adults in their neighborhoods and in their communities (Scales, Benson, &
Mannes, 2003; Prevention Partners for Youth Development, 2004). Most of us
can probably recall at least one person (parent or other) who was instrumental
in our development and who offered continued support, encouragement, and
motivation during good times as well as the more difficult times of adolescence.
In fact, it is not uncommon to hear young adults report that certain people (e.g.,
parents, coaches, teachers, neighbors) were critical in making a difference in
their lives. Clearly, many adults recognize the importance of being role models
and informal mentors for youth. Translating this belief into action is critical in
building the support systems necessary to promote healthy development among
all youth.

Supports include the interpersonal relationships and accessibility to information that enable youth to take full advantage of existing opportunities and
services. In addition to families, supports in the community can take many forms,
including the stable adult who is available as a friend to listen and give guidance without judgment, the more proactive adult who might offer information,
mentoring, and resources (e.g., job opportunities), and the adult who provides
ongoing support through meaningful friendship, affirmation, and nurturance.

In 1997, researchers studying the relation of protective factors to adolescent health outcomes related that when demographic characteristics are held
constant, social contexts count. Resnick and colleagues (1997), reporting on the
National Longitudinal Study of Adolescent Health in the *Journal of the American
Medical Association*, indicated that perceived caring and connectedness to others are critical to the health and well-being of youth and that positive support
systems across many settings serve as significant protective factors. Additional
studies have highlighted the need for meaningful support systems in the prevention of substance use (Hawkins et al., 1992), academic achievement (Comer,
1997), and health promotion (Walberg, Reyes, Weissberg, & Kuster, 1997).

Community Research Highlighting the Importance of Promoting
Opportunities for Youth Development

Research has repeatedly shown that meaningful and challenging opportunities for youth are necessary to promote learning experiences (Gambone &
Connell, 2004). Youth need meaningful opportunities to demonstrate their skills
and to interact with adults, peers, and others in order to learn how to behave
in the world around them (Chinman & Linney, 1998; Pittman, 2000; Thomsen,
2002). Opportunities are most powerful when youth perceive them to be relevant

to their lives. The creation and maintenance of opportunities are a critical step in promoting youth development, and a myriad of opportunities in a variety of settings that take into account young people's ecology must be available.

Neighborhoods and community groups may have difficulty recruiting youth if they are not careful in planning how they develop and market opportunities for youth (Young & Sazama, 2001; Zeldin, McDaniel, Topitzes, & Calvert, 2000; Zeldin & Price, 1995). One strategy is to involve youth in deciding what activities and opportunities they would like to have. This could be done by conducting a survey to determine what activities youth would enjoy (e.g., job shadowing, babysitting courses, reading clubs). Involving youth in developing the survey as well as in planning the opportunities that are suggested by the survey results are logical strategies to promote youth development. The most successful community groups provide ways for youth to express their "voices" through participating on community panels, boards, and decision-making and policy-making bodies, and they recognize the importance of providing avenues for recognition and reward that differ according to age, gender, and cultural and ethnic backgrounds (Eccles & Gootman, 2002; Thomsen, 2002; Young & Sazama, 2001).

Community Research Highlighting the Importance of Improving
Youth Development Services

Community-based programs, including after-school and recreational activities, service-learning projects, and involvement in youth-led organizations, provide activities in which youth can thrive and increase their likelihood of successfully transitioning into adulthood. Empirical data now exist highlighting the critical features of services and programs that promote positive youth development (Eccles & Gootman, 2002). These features include:

- Physical and psychological safety;
- Appropriate structure;
- Supportive relationships;
- Opportunities to belong;
- Positive social norms;
- Support for efficacy and mattering;
- Opportunities for skill building; and
- Integration of family, school, and community efforts.

The compilation of "what works best" in youth development programs represents a major milestone for the youth development movement. Practitioners, funders, and community agencies can now articulate how well their program conforms to the standard features of youth development programs. Although the field has moved forward in developing a consensus of critical strategies for youth development programs and standards for program quality (Eccles & Gootman, 2002; Yohalem, 2002), the methods for determining how education and professional training are formalized with standards for practice are less clear. This remains a major challenge for the newly developing area of youth development and is critical as the youth development movement works to become institutionalized and respected as a field of study and practice (Silliman, 2004).

Evaluating Youth Development Interventions

Evaluating the outcomes of youth development interventions is necessary to demonstrate their success. One major challenge is to determine what individual-level outcomes can be expected given the level of intensity of the interventions. This requires conducting both process and outcome evaluations over time. While it is useful to have an outside evaluator provide technical assistance, tools and measures have been developed for communities to provide user-friendly information on evaluation. One self-evaluation model—*Getting to Outcomes 2004: Promoting Accountability Through Methods and Tools for Planning, Implementation and Evaluation* (*GTO*)—is available free of charge at the RAND Web site: http://www.rand.org/publications/TR/TR101/ (Chinman, Imm, & Wandersman, 2004).

The *GTO* process is based on theoretical roots of traditional evaluation (Rossi, Lipsey, & Freeman, 2004), empowerment evaluation (Fetterman, 1996), results-based accountability (Osborne & Gaebler, 1992), and continuous quality improvement (Deming, 1986; Juran, 1989). The *GTO* model was developed to be a user-friendly system that enhances practitioners' prevention skills while empowering them to plan, implement, and evaluate their own programs and community-based strategies (Chinman et al., 2001; Wandersman, Imm, Chinman, & Kaftarian, 2000; Wandersman, Kaftarian, Imm, & Chinman, 1999). The *GTO* model defines accountability as "the systematic inclusion of critical elements of program planning, implementation and evaluation in order to achieve results" (Chinman et al., 2004; Wandersman et al., 1999, 2000). The *GTO* manual and corresponding worksheets are organized to address 10 accountability questions:

1. What are the underlying needs and conditions that must be addressed? (Conditions)
2. What are the goals, target population, and desired outcomes? (Goals)
3. What evidence-based models can be useful in reaching the goals? (Best Practices)
4. How does this intervention fit with other programs already being offered? (Fit)
5. What organizational capacities are needed to implement this intervention? (Capacities)
6. What is the plan for this intervention? (Plan)
7. How will the quality of the implementation be assessed? (Process Evaluation)
8. How well did the intervention work? (Outcome Evaluation)

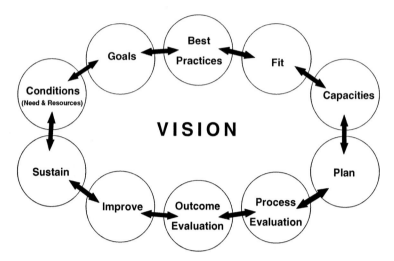

Figure 1. The Getting To Outcomes *Model*

9. How will continuous quality improvement strategies be incorporated? (Improve)
10. If the intervention (or components of the intervention) is successful, how will it be sustained? (Sustain)

The *GTO* process is designed to be prescriptive yet flexible enough to facilitate any evidence-based conversation regarding a prevention or intervention program or initiative. Figure 1 illustrates the circular, ongoing nature of the *GTO* model. The *GTO* process is an example of a model that promotes accountability by addressing the key elements of effective planning, implementation, and evaluation in order to increase the likelihood of positive results.

Bridging the Gap between Research and Practice: A Community Coalition in Action

To illustrate how the *GTO* accountability model can be used to mobilize adults for positive youth development, a case example is presented. This example describes how a youth development coalition, the Onondaga County Prevention Partners for Youth Development (PPYD) in Syracuse, New York, formed to ensure that the conditions are available for youth in their county to have the appropriate supports, opportunities, and services to promote their optimal development.

PPYD is committed to action, which is achieved through strategic planning that includes a focus on accountability. The 10 accountability questions of the *GTO* model are integrated throughout this case example to demonstrate its applicability to a community coalition formed to promote youth development.

PPYD is a community-driven coalition of many Syracuse/Onondaga County organizations, communities, and individuals that work with and on behalf of youth. From the beginning, PPYD sought broad representation in the county by recruiting any group working with youth. PPYD values diversity not only in terms of race, ethnicity, or gender but also by organizational structure and geographic location (urban, suburban, and rural). As a result, the original steering committee consisted of small and large community-based organizations, local and state government, funders, service providers, and schools. Since there were many resources for younger children up to age 12, PPYD focused its work on older youth (ages 12–21).

During the first year (and subsequently revised in the fourth year), the steering committee used a consensual decision-making process to develop a vision that youth-serving community organizations and volunteers endorsed:

> PPYD envisions a community that works together to protect youth and promote their development so they can identify possibilities to achieve their potential.

It is this common vision that brought people from various systems together to work on shared goals. How the community coalition addressed the first two accountability questions is discussed next.

1. *What are the underlying conditions (needs and resources) that must be addressed?*
2. *What are the goals, target population, and desired outcomes?*

PPYD regularly assesses (both quantitatively and qualitatively) the level of needs and protection of youth in the county to identify goals and desired outcomes. The initial assessment process began in 1998 to determine the needs of youth, organizations, and communities as well as to identify resources and set goals. Specific assessment strategies included:

- Administering a risk and protective factor survey in 2000 and publicizing the results to help mobilize the community for change;
- Conducting focus groups with young people and adults to identify priorities among youth and how they relate (or not) to adults' perception of the needs of youth;
- Distributing an annual membership survey to assess coalition functioning and community progress; and
- Developing a Community YouthMapping Initiative in Syracuse with 22 YouthMappers to gather data about needs and resources from a variety of sources, including businesses, citizens, and youth. In addition to the National YouthMapping survey conducted with adults (developed by the Academy for Educational Development), the Syracuse YouthMappers also designed and conducted a Youth Survey for those between the ages of 12 and 18.

On an annual basis, PPYD reviews assessment and resource information to further refine and potentially revise the goals and desired outcomes as suggested

Table 1. *Prevention Partners for Youth Development: Outcomes, Strategies, and Activities, 2003–2004*

Individual Outcomes	Organizational Outcomes	Community Outcomes	PPYD Strategies	PPYD Activities
Young people will: • Be connected to adults who promote their positive development • Develop competencies (civic/social, physical health, emotional health, intellectual/educational, cultural and employability) • Develop confidence (sense of self-worth and mastery, vision for their future) • Build character (responsibility and autonomy, spirituality) • Contribute to and become fully engaged in their families, schools, and communities Pittman et al. (2000)	Organizations will promote youth development by providing: • Supportive relationships • Physical and psychological safety • Positive social norms • Opportunities for skill building • Opportunities for youth to contribute (in decision making, service to others, etc.) • Physical and psychological safety • Appropriate structure • Integration of family, school, and community efforts Community Programs to Promote Youth Development (National Academy of Sciences); Eccles & Gootman (2002)	The Onondaga County Community will support organizations, schools, and communities to embrace youth development principles and implement youth development practices by: • Promoting positive relationships with adults (every young person should have at least one caring adult who is committed to her or his healthy development) • Creating and sustaining safe places for young people • Providing opportunities/possibilities for young people • Having high expectations for young people to succeed (valuing and respecting youth) Bernard (1991); Werner & Smith (1992)	• Training and education on youth development • Community mobilization • Consultation with organizations and communities on implementation and evaluation issues • Advocacy for systems change to create more caring, respectful, and responsive environments for youth • Offering opportunities for networking and collaboration	• YD Training for Supervisors • Organization-specific training • CCB Work Group • Community Youth Mapping • Technical assistance to youth centers and communities • Consultation on integrating YD into various community initiatives • Community YouthMapping • Youth in Decision-Making project • Youth in Philanthropy project • PPYD quarterly Coalition meetings • *StarCatcher* newsletter

by ongoing review of evidence-based strategies and activities. Table 1 lists the desired outcomes for PPYD at the individual, organizational, and community levels. To ensure that PPYD is integrating the latest research into its practice, it conducts ongoing literature reviews about effective practices in youth development. Examples of how PPYD does this are provided by addressing the next two accountability questions:

3. *What evidence-based models (e.g., best practices) can be useful in reaching the goals?*
4. *How does this intervention "fit" with other programs already being offered?*

PPYD emphasizes the integration of research and practice. One of the concerns of the founding PPYD members was whether they would be required to adhere to one specific model of prevention and/or youth development. It was decided that as long as the models and approaches were evidence-based and met the needs identified in the needs assessment, they would be supported by the coalition. This eclectic approach to youth development is one of the key factors that contribute to stakeholders remaining "at the table" (Prevention Partners for Youth Development, 2004).

PPYD uses Pittman and colleagues' (2000) work to create the broader context of youth development and to promote a common language (particularly the "five Cs" of youth outcomes). In addition, PPYD integrates the concept of resiliency, social development theory (risk and protective factors), and Search Institute's framework of developmental assets into various educational and community projects, depending on the context. One role of PPYD is to provide technical assistance to community groups as they determine what best practice processes and interventions are available for their target groups and settings. In addition, PPYD compiles a quarterly synopsis of latest research and resources for distribution to its member agencies and community organizations.

The literature supporting evidence-based strategies is content and process based, both of which are necessary to demonstrate the desired outcomes (Wandersman, 2003). To ensure that the strategies are evidence based and "fit" within the community, PPYD uses various youth development frameworks to organize community youth development efforts. Currently, PPYD is using Search Institute's *Five Action Strategies for Transforming Communities and Society* (2003) to direct the work of the coalition at the community, organizational, and individual levels. The five action strategies as identified by Search Institute are engaging adults, activating sectors, invigorating programs, influencing civic decisions, and mobilizing young people. These action strategies require that certain organizational capacities be in place in order to ensure high-quality implementation. These capacities are addressed by answering the next accountability question:

5. *What organizational capacities are needed to implement this intervention?*

Adequate structures and capacities must be in place to incorporate evidence-based information and implement best practices (Chinman et al., 2004; Wandersman, 2003). PPYD accomplishes its vision and goals through a planning structure that operates on several levels. At the community level, the executive council (which has replaced the steering committee) is composed of community and agency leaders that can create and sustain systems-level change by supporting the strategies to promote youth development. This executive council is charged with activating sectors and engaging adults throughout the community by creating and sustaining a countywide youth development agenda. This effort has the support of the Onondaga County Executive's Office. Creating a countywide youth development agenda is a large task and requires many hands, hearts, and minds. PPYD provides the body (coalition) that coordinates and supports the movement of these various parts by attending to the content (youth development theories and practice) and to the processes (relationship and team building) simultaneously.

The Community Capacity Building Work Group (open to all community members who work with young people) and a training team (composed of citizens with specific training expertise) work to integrate youth development principles into the community by educating groups such as direct service providers, community organizations, and interested stakeholders (e.g., parent groups, teachers). To invigorate programs, engage adults, and activate sectors, PPYD acts at the organizational level as an "intermediary" to provide resources (such as training and ongoing consultation) and to assist organizations and communities in building their capacity to promote positive youth development. PPYD influences civic decisions and mobilizes young people by providing training and promoting opportunities for youth participation and civic engagement.

PPYD believes that for the coalition to be successful, mobilizing youth to be asset builders and agents of change is critical. For the community to view young people as resources and to recognize their strengths, adults need opportunities to interact and work with young people. PPYD creates these opportunities by having young people partner with them in a variety of roles such as decision makers, cotrainers, consultants, and evaluators.

PPYD is staffed with a coordinator and a youth development specialist (both are master's-level positions) and uses a consultant model to involve additional adults and young people, depending on the specific expertise that is needed. PPYD also follows a "Train the Trainers" model so that more people will become equipped to assist their own organizations and communities in understanding and applying youth development principles. In addition, many of PPYD's partners provide staff time as "in-kind" services, which expands the capacities of PPYD and its participating youth-serving organizations. Besides acting as trainers and consultants, coalition members cochair the Community Capacity Building Work Group and Training Team. Building the capacities of youth development experts through training and ongoing technical assistance is critical to achieving the desired outcomes of PPYD.

6. What is the plan for this intervention?

Strategic planning is also necessary to ensure high-quality implementation and fidelity to program goals. PPYD seeks to have an impact on the implementation of evidence-based youth development practices on many levels, including individually (with youth workers and supervisors), organizationally, and systemically (through local and state policy and practice standards). PPYD also plans the implementation of culturally competent, evidence-based practices to promote healthy environments that respect and value youth by using the following five strategies and related activities.

Strategy 1. Building communities' capacity to promote the healthy development of youth:
- Monthly Community Capacity Building Work Group meetings connect community members to plan, implement, and evaluate evidence-based youth development practices in community settings.
- Community YouthMapping Initiative resulted in a report to be used in setting community priorities and planning in Syracuse and Onondaga County.
- Theory is put into practice by assisting a local teen center (e.g., CAN-TEEN) to obtain funding as well as designing, implementing, and evaluating their program (with youth involvement), which now averages approximately 100 youth a day.
- Youth consultants and adult staff from successful local programs transfer their knowledge and practice to other programs.

Strategy 2. Disseminating new knowledge and training concerning evidence-based research and practices:
- Quarterly coalition meetings provide training topics on evidence-based youth development and prevention practices that are prioritized by the coalition members.
- A quarterly newsletter, the *StarCatcher*, reports on current evidence-based practices and showcases effective local youth development efforts.
- With funding from the New York Office of Children and Family Services and the United Way of Central New York, PPYD developed a training curriculum, *Youth Development Training for Supervisors and Administrators*, to help integrate research (e.g., youth development principles) into practice (e.g., youth programming). The training includes follow-up consultation, including monthly group meetings, individualized technical assistance, action planning, and an evaluation component to assist in the transfer of research to practice. Evaluation data have indicated that more intentional, integrated, and institutionalized changes occurred during the more intensive consultation period.

Strategy 3. Consulting with organizations and communities on implementation and evaluation issues:
- Provide technical assistance and consultation (with both adult and youth consultants) on evidence-based practices and assist youth and community centers in translating them into actions and strategies that "fit" their context.

- Share knowledge about youth development with other community initiatives, including the Syracuse Mayor's Office Youth Violence Intervention Task Force and the local Weed and Seed Board.
- Assist community organizations in developing evaluation plans for youth development and prevention practices.

Strategy 4. Offering opportunities for networking and collaboration:

- Quarterly coalition meetings (open to all levels of staff, residents, and youth) offer networking and relationship-building opportunities and the chance to brainstorm and plan regarding the needs of youth, families, and communities in Onondaga County.
- PPYD frequently collaborates with other community partners on grant writing and program development and acts as a conduit for information sharing between programs as well as a connector to bring people with compatible goals together.

Strategy 5. Advocating for systems change to create more caring, respectful, and responsive environments for youth, including involving youth in decision making:

- PPYD collaborated with a local funder, the Central New York Community Foundation, in implementing a community-based model for their Youth in Philanthropy project (which involves youth as decision makers in the grant-making process) with young people from the Spanish Action League and Syracuse's Fowler High School (using data from the Community YouthMapping report to establish funding priorities).
- PPYD collaborated with the New York State Office of Children and Family Services and the Onondaga County Department of Aging and Youth (with funding from the Central New York Community Foundation) to conduct a countywide survey, and develop and disseminate a report on the state of youth involvement in decision making in Syracuse/Onondaga County.
- PPYD collaborated with the Syracuse/Onondaga County Department of Aging and Youth and the County Parks and Recreation Department to involve youth in the planning and administration of a new Skateboarding Park. This joint effort resulted in 120 youth becoming involved in designing the park, and youth participating in Junior Achievement created a business plan for the park. A youth advisory council continues to meet on a regular basis to assist in administering the activities of the park.

To ensure that the strategies and related activities are being implemented well, PPYD tracks implementation variables related to successful coalitions (e.g., satisfaction), strategies and activities (e.g., participation rates), and systems-level changes (e.g., integration of youth development principles into organizations). Specific information about how PPYD assesses implementation is presented next.

7. How will the quality of the implementation be assessed?

Coalition development parallels the adolescent development process as described by Pittman, Irby, Tolman, Yohalem, and Ferber (2003) in that it is ongoing and uneven as it moves toward maturity. As they note, it requires engagement, is fostered through relationships, and influenced by environments. PPYD asserts that the "five Cs" of youth development outcomes identified by Pittman et al. (2000, 2003) can also be applied to further understand and evaluate important processes in community coalitions organized around youth development. Key processes in youth development coalitions are as follows:

- **Connection**—The coalition promotes relationship building (creating safety, trust, membership and belonging) and uses the strength of relationships to create change.
- **Competence**—Applying youth development theory and practice, the coalition fosters the understanding of cultural issues in communities, organizations, and young people, and works collaboratively with others for the larger good.
- **Confidence**—As the coalition evolves and becomes more competent, assurance grows.
- **Character**—The coalition holds itself accountable, being responsible to its members and acting as a positive role model (it "walks the talk").
- **Contributions**—The coalition seeks, creates, and takes advantage of opportunities that move the youth development agenda forward with the goal of providing healthy environments (people, places, and possibilities) for youth; the coalition promotes pathways for youth to fully participate in their communities, schools, families, and organizations.

As the PPYD coalition moves through the stages of development, maintenance, and sustainability (Goodman, Wandersman, Chinman, Imm, & Morrissey, 1996: Snell-Johns, Imm, Wandersman, & Claypoole, 2003), it is critical to regularly assess how the membership perceives its activities, strategies, and effectiveness. To accomplish this, PPYD conducts process evaluations with its coalition members through an annual survey and regular assessments at coalition meetings and training events. On the 2003 annual survey, coalition members were asked to respond to various quantitative and qualitative questions. Of those returning the survey:

- 79% said they had made new connections to other people in youth work;
- 84% said that PPYD had helped them find out about new resources;
- 40% said that they had been able to recruit for their services at PPYD events;
- 76% said that they shared resources as a result of connections through PPYD; and
- 51% said that they had become involved in a collaborative project as a result of PPYD connections.

Survey participants also identified "networking" as one of the biggest benefits of their involvement with PPYD. This is significant in that the factors of connection and contribution are viewed as critical to youth development as well as to the momentum of the coalition. Progress on outcome variables is described in the following sections.

8. How well did the intervention work?

PPYD identifies specific outcomes to measure on an annual basis. Commonly evaluated outcomes include:

- Increases in evidence-based knowledge about youth development and prevention approaches so that adults can work more effectively with youth in their organizations and communities as measured by posttest evaluation;
- Integration and application of youth development principles in coalition members' work in their organizations and communities as measured by pretest/posttest evaluation, an annual survey, focus groups, and individual interviews;
- Organizations reporting that youth involvement in decision making has become the organizational expectation as measured by an annual survey; and
- Youth involvement in advisory and consultation level decision-making opportunities in their organizations and communities as measured by an annual survey and interviews with organizations and communities.

On the PPYD annual survey (2003), 74% of coalition participants reported that PPYD had increased their knowledge of research-based practices in youth development. Training opportunities were the second biggest benefit that people derived from their involvement with PPYD (networking was the first). Eighty-one percent of participants reported integrating and applying youth development principles in their work with youth, staff, and/or organizations by:

- Building supportive relationships;
- Creating a sense of belonging and ownership;
- Building youth competencies and assets; and
- Providing appropriate structure and positive social norms.

Assessing the progress of the desired outcomes as well as obtaining input from the coalition members provides useful data for continuous quality improvement and the potential of ongoing sustainability.

In addition, researchers and community members are beginning to publish case studies and review articles describing the recruitment of youth to assist with evaluation efforts (Checkoway, Dobbie, & Richards-Schuster, 2003; Checkoway & Richards-Schuster, 2003; Goodyear, 2003). Youth participation in evaluation research is a process of involving young people in knowledge development at the community level (Checkoway & Richards-Schuster, 2003). Although such involvement is undeveloped as a field of practice, there are many roles in which youth have been instrumental in the evaluation process. In addition to the traditional role of research subjects, several of these new roles include youth as consultants, partners, and directors (Checkoway & Richards-Schuster,

2003). As communities and professionals work to implement evaluation methods to assess youth development, the inclusion of youth in this process seems quite natural. PPYD has used the expertise of youth in several roles, including survey design, interpretation of results, and suggestions for improvement.

9. *How will continuous quality improvement strategies be incorporated?*
10. *If the intervention (or components of the intervention) is successful, how will it be sustained?*

Data are regularly reviewed to determine the improvements and/or changes that should be made in the coalition. These data are at a variety of levels, including recent research documents, data from coalition members, and information collected during the trainings and other events. Some changes are relatively minor and others have implications for how PPYD does business. For example, since the participants reported that the "networking" benefit was significant during the training of supervisors, subsequent trainings included a networking period whereby individuals could have structured time to network, provide input, and share information.

PPYD carefully plans its approach and operates from a structured plan that includes a variety of outcomes at various levels (e.g., individual, community, systems). Members believe that long-term sustainability will result from a clear mission, strategic activities, inclusivity, and continued evaluation for practice and program improvement. In addition, the ongoing review and integration of evidence-based practice and youth development principles are critical to ongoing success and future sustainability of the PPYD coalition and its partners. Additional steps to promote sustainability include securing additional funding, "spinning off" or institutionalizing youth development strategies in the community, and gaining political support to promote systems-level changes.

Conclusions

The field of youth development continues to grow and emerge as a legitimate area of research and practice. Methods for integrating youth development concepts and principles into community-based structures, such as neighborhood organizations and coalitions, are becoming increasingly common. Communities are implementing interventions and strategies in youth development by applying theories and conceptual models such as the risk and protective model (Hawkins et al., 1992), the assets-based model (Benson, 1997), and the "five Cs" (Pittman et al., 2000). Ensuring accountability in community interventions is a major challenge to community-based organizations that have few resources to spend on outside evaluations and minimal opportunities to work in settings that include evaluation expertise.

The *Getting to Outcomes* model is a user-friendly system for planning and evaluation that was designed for community organizations to help promote accountability in their work (Chinman et al., 2004; Wandersman et al., 1999, 2000).

By using *GTO*, coalitions and other community-based organizations can ensure that they are integrating all aspects of effective planning, high-quality implementation, and evaluation processes necessary to demonstrate accountability. The PPYD coalition highlights the utility of this accountability model as it works to build the capacity of local agencies and organizations to develop the supports, opportunities, and structures necessary to ensure effective youth development initiatives. Additional work is beginning to integrate the *GTO* accountability model into asset-based initiatives to ensure that there are clear evaluation processes for communities that choose to focus on building assets at all levels of a community (Fisher, Imm, Wandersman, & Chinman, in press; Mannes, Imm, Chinman, & Kehres, 2004).

References

Backer, T. E. (2003). *Evaluating community coalitions.* New York: Springer.

Backer, T. E., & Kunz, C. (2003). The human side of evaluating collaborations. In T. E. Backer (Ed.), *Evaluating community coalitions* (pp. 37–55). New York: Springer.

Benson, P. L. (1997). *All kids are our kids. What communities must do to raise caring and responsible children and adolescents.* San Francisco: Jossey-Bass.

Benson, P. L., Scales, P. C., & Mannes, M. (2003). Developmental strengths and their sources. In R. M. Lerner, F. Jacobs, and D. Wertlieb (Eds.), *Handbook of applied developmental science.* (Vol. 1, pp. 370–405). Thousand Oaks, CA: Sage.

Bernard, B. (1991). *Fostering resiliency in kids: Protective factors in the family, school, and community.* San Francisco: Far West Laboratory for Educational Research and Development and the Western Regional Center for Drug-Free Schools and Communities.

Botvin, G., Baker, E., Dusenbury, L., Botvin, E., & Diaz, T. (1995). Long-term follow-up results of a randomized drug abuse prevention trial in a white middle-class population. *Journal of the American Medical Association, 273*(14), 1106–1112.

Brown, C. (1984). *The art of coalition building: A guide for community leaders.* New York: American Jewish Committee.

Bumbarger B., & Greenberg, M. (2002). Next steps in advancing research on positive youth development. *Prevention & Treatment, 5,* Article 16. Retrieved April 12, 2003, from http://journals.apa.org/prevention/volume5/pre0050016c.html

Butterfoss, F., Goodman, R., & Wandersman, A. (1993). Community coalitions for prevention and health promotion. *Health Education Research, 8*(3), 315–330.

Center for Substance Abuse Prevention. (2002). *Science-based prevention programs and principles.* Rockville, MD: Department of Health and Human Services.

Checkoway, B., Dobbie, D., & Richards-Schuster, K. (2003). Involving young people in community evaluation research. *Community Youth Development Journal, 4*(1). Retrieved May 15, 2004, from www.cydjournal.org

Checkoway, B., & Richards-Schuster, K. (2003). Youth participation in community evaluation research. *American Journal of Evaluation, 24*(1), 21–33.

Chinman, M., Anderson, C., Imm, P., Wandersman, A., & Goodman, R. (1996). The perception of costs and benefits of high active versus low active groups in community coalitions at different stages in coalition development. *Journal of Community Psychology, 24*(3), 263–274.

Chinman, M., Imm, P., & Wandersman, A. (2004). *Getting to Outcomes 2004: Promoting accountability through methods and tools for planning, implementation, and evaluation.* Santa Monica, CA: RAND. Available at http://www.rand.org/publications/TR/TR101/

Chinman, M., Imm, P., Wandersman, A., Kaftarian, S., Neal, J., Pendleton, K., et al. (2001). Using the getting to outcomes (GTO) model in a statewide prevention initiative. *Health Promotion Practice, 2,* 302–309.

Chinman, M. J., & Linney, J. (1998). Toward a model of adolescent empowerment: Theoretical and empirical evidence. *Journal of Primary Prevention, 18*(4), 393–413.

Chinman, M., & Wandersman, A. (1999). The benefits and costs of volunteering in community organizations: Review and practical implications. *Nonprofit and Voluntary Sector Quarterly, 28*(1), 46–64.

Comer, J. (1997). *Waiting for a miracle: Why schools can't solve our problems—and how we can.* New York: Dutton.

Community Anti-Drug Coalitions of America. (2002). *Coalition building 104: Collecting data for needs and assets assessment.* Strategizer Technical Assistance Manual 40. Alexandria, VA: Author.

Dalton, J., Elias, M., & Wandersman, A. (2001). *Community psychology: Linking individuals and communities.* Belmont, CA: Wadsworth.

Deming, W. E. (1986). *Out of the crisis.* Cambridge, MA: MIT Press.

Dryfoos, J. (1994). *Full-service schools: A revolution in health and social services for children, youth, and families.* San Francisco: Jossey-Bass.

Eccles, J., & Gootman, J. (Eds.). (2002). Community programs to promote youth development. Washington, DC: National Academy Press.

Fetterman, D. M. (1996). Empowerment evaluation: An introduction to theory and practice. In D. M. Fetterman, S. J. Kaftarian, & A. Wandersman (Eds.), *Empowerment evaluation: Knowledge and tools for self-assessment and accountability* (pp. 3–46). Thousand Oaks, CA: Sage.

Fisher, D., Imm., P. S., Wandersman, A., & Chinman, M. (in press). *Getting to outcomes with developmental assets: Ten steps to measuring success in youth programs and communities.* Minneapolis, MN: Search Institute.

Florin, P., & Wandersman, A. (1990). Citizen participation, voluntary organizations and community development: Insights for empowerment and research. *American Journal of Community Psychology, 18*(1), 41–177.

Gambone, M., & Connell, J. (2004). The community action framework for youth development. *Prevention Researcher, 11*(2), 17–20.

Goodman, R., Wandersman, A., Chinman, M., Imm, P., & Morrissey, E. (1996). An ecological assessment of community-based interventions for prevention and healthy promotion: Approaches to measuring community coalitions. *American Journal of Community Psychology, 41*(1), 33–61,

Goodyear, L. (2003). Engaging young people in evaluation as a strategy for evaluation fieldbuilding and innovation. Retrieved May 15, 2004, from www.cydjournal.org

Hawkins, J., Catalano, R., & Miller, J. (1992). Risk and protective factors for alcohol and other drug problems in adolescence and early adulthood: Implications for substance abuse prevention. *Psychological Bulletin, 112*(1), 64–105.

Juran, J. M. (1989). *Juran on leadership for quality.* New York: Free Press

Kieffer, C. (1984). Citizen empowerment: A development perspective. *Prevention in Human Services, 3, 9*–36. Also published in J. Rappaport, C. Swift, & R. Hess (Eds.). (1984). *Studies in empowerment: Steps toward understanding and action.* New York: Haworth Press.

Livet, M., & Wandersman, A. (2005). Organizational functioning: Facilitating effective interventions and increasing the odds of programming success. In D. Fetterman & A. Wandersman (Eds.), *Empowerment evaluation principles in practice* (pp. 123–154). New York: Guilford Press.

Mannes, M., Imm, P., Chinman, M., & Kehres, R. (2004, November). *Evaluating prevention initiatives: Blending models to provide a comprehensive planning and evaluation system.* Preconference session at Search Institute's Health Communities, Healthy Youth conference. Minneapolis, MN.

McMillan, B., Florin, P., Stevenson, J., Kerman, B., & Mitchell, R. (1995). Empowerment praxis in community coalitions. *American Journal of Community Psychology, 23,* 699–728.

Nation, M., Crusto, C., Wandersman, A., Kumpfer, K., Seybolt, D., Morrissey-Kane, E., et al. (2003). What works in prevention: Principles of effective prevention programs. *American Psychologist, 58*(6/7), 449–456.

National Institute on Drug Abuse. (2003). *Preventing drug use among children and adolescents: A research-based guide for parents, educators, and community leaders* (2nd ed.). Washington, DC: Department of Health and Human Services, National Institutes of Health.

Osborne, D., & Gaebler, T. (1992). *Reinventing government: How the entrepreneurial spirit is transforming the public sector.* Reading, MA: Addison-Wesley.

Pittman, K. (2000). *Supports, opportunities and services.* Washington, DC: Forum for Youth Investment, Impact Strategies.

Pittman, K., Irby, M., & Ferber, T. (2000). Unfinished business: Further reflections on a decade of promoting youth development. *Youth development: Issues, challenges, and directions.* Philadelphia: Public/Private Ventures. Available at http://www.forumfyi.org

Pittman, K., Irby, M., Tolman, J., Yohalem, N., & Ferber, T. (2003). *Preventing problems, promoting development, encouraging engagement: Competing priorities or inseparable goals?* Baltimore: International Youth Foundation. Available online at http://www.forumfyi.org/Files/ppe.pdf

Pittman K., & Wright, M. (1991). *A rationale for enhancing the role of the non-school voluntary sector in youth development* (Rev. ed.). Washington, DC: Carnegie Council on Adolescent Development.

Prestby, J., Wandersman, A., Florin, P., Rich, R., & Chavis, D. (1990). Benefits, costs, incentive management and participation in voluntary organizations: A means to understanding and promoting empowerment. *American Journal of Community Psychology, 18,* 117–150.

Prevention Partners for Youth Development. (2004). What will neighborhoods do? A report on the community YouthMapping project. *StarCatcher, 5*(3), 1–5.

Resnick, M., Bearman, P., Blum, R., Bauman, K., Harris, K., Jones, J., et al. (1997). Protecting adolescents from harm: Findings from the National Longitudinal Study on Adolescent Health. *Journal of the American Medical Association, 278*(10), 823–832.

Rossi, P., Lipsey, M., & Freeman, H. (2004). *Evaluation: A systematic approach* (7th ed.). Thousand Oaks, CA: Sage.

Scales, P., Benson, P., Leffert, N., & Blyth, D. (2000). Contributions of developmental assets to the prediction of thriving among adolescents. *Applied Developmental Science, 4,* 27–46.

Scales, P., Benson, P., & Mannes, M. (2003). *Grading grown-ups 2002: How do American kids and adults relate? A national study.* Minneapolis, MN: Search Institute.

Scales, P., & Leffert, N. (2004). *Developmental assets: A synthesis of the scientific research on adolescent development* (2nd ed.). Minneapolis, MN: Search Institute and Thrivent Financial for Lutherans.

Search Institute. (2001). *Developmental assets: A profile of your youth—Search Institute 1999–2000 aggregate dataset.* Minneapolis, MN: Author.

Search Institute. (2003). *The five action strategies for transforming communities and society: Creating a world where all young people are valued and thrive.* Minneapolis, MN: Author.

Seligman, M., & Csikszentmihalyi, M. (2000). Positive psychology: An introduction. *American Psychologist, 55,* 5–14.

Silliman, B. (2004). Key issues in the practice of youth development. *Family Relations, 53*(1), 12–16.

Snell-Johns, J., Imm, P., Wandersman, A., & Claypoole, J. (2003). Roles assumed by community coalitions when creating environmental and policy-level changes. *Journal of Community Psychology, 31*(6), 661–670.

Takanishi, R., Mortimer, A., & McGourthy, T. (1997). Positive indicators of adolescent development: Redressing the negative image of American adolescents. In R. M. Hauser, B. V. Brown, & W. R. Prosser (Eds.), *Indicators of children's well-being* (pp. 428–441). New York: Russell Sage Foundation.

Thomsen, K. (2002). *Building resilient students: Integrating resiliency into what you already know and do.* Thousand Oaks, CA: Corwin Press.

Walberg, J., Reyes, O., Weissberg, R., & Kuster, C. (1997). Afterword: Strengthening the families, education, and health of urban children and youth. In J. J. Walberg, O. Reyes, & R. Weissbert (Eds.), *Children and youth: Interdisciplinary perspectives* (pp. 363–368). Thousand Oaks, CA: Sage.

Wandersman, A. (2003). Community science. Bridging the gap between science and practice with community-centered models. *American Journal of Community Psychology, 31*(3/4), 227–242.

Wandersman, A., & Florin, P. (2003). Community interventions and effective prevention. *American Psychologist, 58*(6/7), 441–448.

Wandersman, A., Imm, P., Chinman, M., & Kaftarian, S. (2000). Getting to outcomes: A results-based approach to accountability. *Evaluation and Program Planning, 23,* 389–395.

Wandersman, A., Kaftarian, S., Imm, P., & Chinman, M. (1999). *Getting to outcomes: Methods and tools for planning, evaluation, and accountability.* Washington, DC: Center for Substance Abuse Prevention.

Werner, E., & Smith, R. (1992). *Overcoming the odds: High risk children from birth to adulthood.* Ithaca, NY: Cornell University Press.

Wheeler, W. (2000). Emerging organizational theory and the youth development organization. *Applied Developmental Science, 4*(Suppl. 1), 2–10.

Yohalem, N. (2002). *Defining, assessing, and improving youth program quality: Where are we and where do we need to go?* Retrieved May 24, 2003, from http://www.forumfyi.org

Young, K., & Sazama, J. (2001). *Fourteen points: Successfully involving youth in decision making.* Somerville, MA: Youth on Board.

Zeldin, S., McDaniel, A., Topitzes, D., & Calvert, M. (2000). *Youth in decision-making: A study on the impacts of youth on adults and organizations.* Chevy Chase, MD: National 4-H Council.

Zeldin, S., & Price, L. (1995). Creating supportive communities for adolescent development: Challenges to scholars. *Journal of Adolescent Research, 10,* 6–15.

Zimmerman, M. (2000). Empowerment theory: Psychological, organizational and community level of analysis. In J. Rappaport & E. Seidman (Eds.), *Handbook of community psychology* (pp. 43–63). New York: Plenum.

9 Mobilizing Adults for Positive Youth Development: Lessons from Religious Congregations

Kenneth I. Maton and Mariano R. Sto. Domingo

University of Maryland, Baltimore County

Faith-based organizations have a long and rich history contributing to the development of youth in our society. This contribution to positive youth development occurs in part through the substantial volunteering role of congregation members. Adult volunteers participate in a range of congregational activities central to the socialization and development of youth, including Sunday school, youth groups, youth choir, and groups for parents. Adults also volunteer for outreach efforts to aid individuals in need in the larger community, including at-risk youth and families. Such activities include involvement in formal mentoring programs, tutoring in the local schools, and support provided to low-income families. Faith-based efforts to enhance the well-being of at-risk youth, their families, and their communities have become of increased interest in the public policy arena, as evidenced by President Bush's current faith-based social policy initiative. For example, faith-based mentoring programs for youth in need are explicitly listed as one of the possibilities for funding in the federal Mentoring for Success Act (2001).

Congregations are important contexts for efforts to mobilize adult volunteers for positive youth development for five primary reasons. First, given the large number of Americans who belong to churches, synagogues, and mosques, a vast pool of potential adult volunteers, distributed almost equally across all economic and educational levels, exists in the congregational context (cf. Ammerman, 1997). Second, a correspondingly large number of children, youth, and families belong to religious congregations; one primary mission of virtually all congregations is the religious socialization of these children and youth (Roehlkepartain, 2003; Woolever & Bruce, 2004). This mission encompasses positive moral, spiritual, psychological, and social development (Smith, 2003). Third, the spiritual and moral mission of many congregations includes a strong commitment to local communities, including at-risk families and youth (Ammerman, 2002; Chaves, 1999; Cnaan, 2002; Cohen & Jaeger, 1998). Nearly all congregations report some type of human services or educational program, with half of all congregations, for example, conducting educational programs that reach into the surrounding community (Ammerman, 1997).

Fourth, in many minority, immigrant, and inner-city neighborhoods, local congregations have a unique credibility and access to local families and youth that secular organizations appear to lack (Dionne & DiIulio, 2000; Ebaugh & Chafetz, 2000). As a result, adult volunteers mobilized through congregations in urban and minority areas may have the potential to influence children and families that volunteers mobilized through other auspices do not have. Finally, there is special potential for built-in spiritual and religious support for congregational volunteers. This can provide critical "staying power" for faith-based volunteers, which can prove especially important for volunteers working with challenging populations of children, youth, and families (Branch, 2002; Jucovy, 2003).

Besides volunteering activity, there are other important pathways through which congregational adults can contribute directly and indirectly to positive youth development, including social activism for youth causes, financial donations, natural mentoring, and social agenda setting (Ladd, 1999; United Way of Southeastern Pennsylvania, 2004; Wuthnow, 1990; Wuthnow & Evans, 2002). Here we focus primarily on theory, research, and practice related to formal volunteering. We limit our focus in part owing to space limitations and in part to ensure clarity of focus.

Congregational members occupy important roles as volunteers in our society. One study found that churches represent 34% of all volunteer labor in the nonprofit sector (cf. Hall, 1990). Approximately half of church members report volunteering for their congregation (Hoge, Zech, McNamara, & Donahue, 1998); over a two-year period, most regular church attendees report volunteering in church-related activities (75.5%), non-church-related activities (55.9%), or both (82.8%; Park & Smith, 2000). National surveys consistently indicate that Americans volunteer through congregations or other religious groups more than through any other type of organization, with rates of volunteering through religious organizations ranging from 25% to 44% (see Ladd, 1999); the next highest categories (schools, fund-raising for charity, youth development) are 7% to 9% lower. A nationwide study of 5,849 congregations revealed that 74% of all congregations provide volunteers to at least one community-based organization; on average, congregations provided volunteers to 2.8 organizations (Ammerman, 2002).

One limitation of the surveys cited here is that the percentage of congregational volunteer activities that focus on youth, or that indirectly promote youth development through helping families, was not elicited. There is no reason to believe, however, that child- and youth-focused volunteering is not included in these volunteering activities. Indeed, research indicates that individuals who attend services emphasize to a greater extent the importance of becoming involved with children and youth in the community and to contribute (in varied ways) to their development than do those who attend less regularly (Scales, 2003).

Recent national surveys of adult volunteer involvement in youth mentoring provide more direct evidence of volunteering in at least one youth-specific domain. A 1998 survey of 1,504 adults involved in youth mentoring programs found 31% of the mentors taking part in programs sponsored by a local church. This was second only to 33% sponsored by a school, college, or university (McLearn, Colasanto, & Schoen, 1998). Similarly, a 2002 national survey indicated that 24% of the mentors involved in formal mentoring programs mentored in a Sunday school or other religious activity program, second again only to school-based programs (28%) (AOL Time Warner Foundation, 2002). Interestingly, 12% of the U.S. Office of Juvenile Justice and Delinquency Prevention awards for the Juvenile Mentoring Program (JUMP) were to faith-based initiatives (cf. Clarke, Forbush, & Henderson, 2003). Among mainline Protestant congregations, 6% sponsor or participate in a mentoring program (Chaves, Giesel, & Tsitsos, 2002). No data are available concerning the percentage of congregation-sponsored mentoring programs focused on youth in the larger community versus those focused on youth in the sponsoring congregation.

Although survey data suggest a substantial involvement of congregational volunteers in activities directly or indirectly related to youth development, there is scant social science theory or published research focused explicitly on how best to mobilize congregational adults for positive youth development per se. Given this reality, extant theory and research related to religiosity and volunteering more generally constitute the primary focus of the research literature reviewed here. Based on the theory and research reviewed, practical steps congregations can take to support enhanced mobilization of adults for youth development are suggested.

Theory and Research

Social scientists have generated numerous theories and conducted empirical research related to adult volunteering behavior for some time. Here we review some of the key theories, drawing on the conceptual scheme used in a recent review of theories of volunteering by Wilson (2000). For each theoretical approach, we briefly summarize available findings from the empirical literature specifically focused on religiosity and volunteering.

Social Influences on Volunteering

Not surprisingly, social influences are viewed by volunteering theorists and researchers as critical to the mobilization of volunteers. There are multiple interrelated social mechanisms that appear important; four are noted here. Each appears likely to be operative to a substantial extent in the congregational context.

First, social norms related to the importance of volunteering that are present in environments important to and valued by individuals are likely to influence the decision to volunteer (Clary, Snyder, & Stukas, 1996; Jackson, Bachmeier, Wood, & Craft, 1995; Wilson & Janoski, 1995; Wuthnow, 1991, 1999). In the congregational setting, both religious leaders and peers are likely to emphasize the religious and spiritual importance of giving of oneself to help those in need, and the norms of volunteering are likely to be modeled and reinforced on a regular basis (Wilson & Janoski, 1995). Indeed, one study found that volunteers in the religious context are especially likely to report that they volunteer because volunteering is important to the people they respect (Clary et al., 1996).

A second social influence on volunteering is social solidarity, emerging from pursuit of a goal shared with others. This may be especially likely to be experienced among members of an organization with whom one shares deeply held convictions and a common mission, and when one knows in advance who one's fellow volunteers will be, as is the case in congregations (Ammerman, 1997; Becker & Dhingra, 2001; Jackson et al., 1995). Social solidarity helps create and maintain the social norm to volunteer as it reinforces the shared religious beliefs about the importance of volunteerism. Social solidarity also can be expected to influence the quality and quantity of interpersonal appeals.

In addition, organizations with a greater number of volunteering opportunities can be expected to enhance volunteering among their members. Many faith-based organizations have subgroups of individuals, paid staff or volunteers or both, who devote considerable time and effort to develop, facilitate, and coordinate ongoing volunteer opportunities within the congregation and in the larger community (Wilson, 2000; Wuthnow, 1990).

Finally, volunteers are likely to learn about opportunities from interpersonal appeals, rather than the mass media; these appeals are likely to come from one's social network members and organizational peers (Wuthnow, 1991). The faith-based context is a likely source of interpersonal appeals, given the many congregational activities that rely on volunteer labor and the many commitments congregations have related to needs in the larger community. Appeals from individuals one knows and trusts and does not want to let down are prime exemplars of such interpersonal appeals, and are especially likely to be effective (Moscareillo, 2002). When strong social norms to volunteer are present in a given congregation, a greater number of interpersonal appeals may be expected, and their effectiveness is enhanced.

Consistent with contextual theories of volunteering (Wilson, 2000), the social influence factors described here are likely to be influenced by various contextual factors, ultimately influencing levels and types of volunteering. In the faith-based context, contextual features include differences in the theology, mission, structure, organizational capacity, location, social climate, and size of congregations. For example, congregations with strong social justice or social gospel missions may be expected to have high levels of volunteering norms, and those with a theological mission focused on internal community may be expected to have greater social solidarity. Furthermore, greater organizational capacity can be expected to be linked to more volunteering opportunities, and has been hypothesized, along with greater social climate, to be linked to the development of youth mentoring programs (Maton, Sto. Domingo, & King, 2005). Concerning congregational size, on the one hand, very large congregations may be expected to have greater organizational capacity; on the other hand, the presence of more paid staff may reduce the need for and number of opportunities to volunteer within the congregation per se.

There has been little empirical research in the congregational context that directly examines any of the theorized social influences on volunteering outlined here. The most relevant research in the faith-based context looks at the general relationship between religious participation and volunteering. Specifically, consistent with social influence theories, empirical studies generally have found a positive relationship between indices of church participation and levels of volunteering. Participation has been measured in various ways, including church attendance and involvement in church activities. Attendance and involvement generally have been found to be positively related to levels of volunteering in the congregation or sponsored by the congregation (Becker & Dhingra, 2001; Hoge et al., 1998; Wuthnow, 1999) and to volunteering in general (Becker & Dhingra, 2001; Ladd, 1999; Mattis et al., 2000; Musick, Wilson, & Bynum, 2000; Wilson & Musick, 1997). Studies examining the relationship between religious participation and volunteering in the larger community (excluding volunteering within the congregation) have produced a complex set of findings. There is some evidence that high levels of active involvement in congregational activities are related to volunteering in the community (Jackson et al., 1995; Lam, 2002; Park & Smith, 2000), but high levels of attendance are not (Jackson et al., 1995; Lam, 2002; Musick et al., 2000; Park & Smith, 2000; Wilson & Janoski, 1995; Wuthnow, 1999, for evangelicals in particular).

The positive relationship between religious participation and both volunteering for the church and general congregational involvement provides indirect support for social influence theories of volunteering. That is, those who participate more in the congregational context are especially likely to be committed to the mission-oriented goals of the congregation, to be influenced by congregational social norms about volunteering, to be asked to volunteer, to trust and be close to others who do the asking, to hear about volunteer needs, to know others who volunteer, and to desire the social solidarity that can come from volunteer activity. Of course, given the correlational nature of the research to date, alternative interpretations are possible. That is, it is also possible that those who volunteer more are simply the type of people who are active and involved in various settings, including the congregation. Or it may be that involvement in volunteering leads one to become more interested in religious attendance and involvement, rather than vice versa.

The findings in several studies that active involvement in the congregation, beyond attendance per se, may be important to mobilize volunteers for community causes are consistent with social influence theory. That is, stronger mobilization influences may be necessary to influence decisions to volunteer in the community than to influence volunteering in one's congregation. The social influence mechanisms outlined here are likely to be especially salient in the context of personalized, interactive relationships with others, beyond mere attendance at worship services per se.

Differences across Demographic Subgroups

Congregational involvement may be generally more important for some demographic subgroups than others; to the extent this is the case, levels of volunteering may be more strongly influenced by congregational participation for these groups. For example, the church historically has played a central role in the African American community. Relatedly, one study found that church attendance more strongly predicted overall volunteering for African Americans than for Whites (Musick et al., 2000), and a second found participation to be related to environmental volunteering for Blacks but not for Whites (Arp & Boeckelman, 1997). Furthermore, Blacks are more likely than Whites to indicate that their decision to volunteer or to give financially is affected by a church, union, or other organization (Ferree, Barry, & Manno, 1998).

Religion has been found to be especially important for the elderly as well (cf. Fischer & Schaeffer, 1993). Consistent with this reality, survey data indicate that "being active in religion" appears to be the strongest predictor of volunteering among older people (Caro & Bass, 1995; Wilson, 2000, p. 227), a finding that has not consistently been present in studies of other populations.

Volunteer Opportunities

One important social influence on volunteering is the nature of available volunteer opportunities (e.g., Wuthnow, 1990). Not surprisingly, research suggests that different congregations provide different levels and types of opportunities for volunteering. Based on interviews with pastors, for example, Becker and Dhingra (2001) found that Catholic congregations and moderate Protestant congregations are equally likely to foster volunteer opportunities that maintain the congregation (e.g., teaching Sunday school) and those that serve the local community (e.g., working at a food pantry). Evangelical congregations had twice as many opportunities to maintain the congregation as to serve the community, and liberal congregations focused exclusively on maintaining the congregation. Chaves, Giesel, and Tsitsos (2002) found that mainline Protestant congregations had greater community connections than Roman Catholic and other congregations, including sponsoring or participating in nonreligious educational programs (16%, 8%, and 8%, respectively) and youth mentoring programs (6%, 2%, and 2%, respectively). These differential opportunities may partially explain different levels and types of volunteering across different types of congregations (cf. Wuthnow & Evans, 2002; see subsection titled "Contextual Influences," below).

One national development related to types of volunteering opportunities is the sharp rise in the number of immigrants joining existing churches, or establishing their own churches, in recent years. Large churches have allotted spaces for their immigrant congregants to practice their faith and organize services for their own youth (Sullivan, 2000), whereas small immigrant churches frequently establish community centers that provide a variety of social, emotional, and material resources for members and their children (Kurien, 1998; Leon, 1998). A series of case studies on immigrant churches in Houston (see Ebaugh & Chafetz, 2000) found that most organize Sunday schools for their youth, and adult volunteers in about half of the immigrant churches studied provide native language tutorials for the children of their members. This is consistent with their desire to "reproduce ethnicity in the second generation and … to provide a safe, supportive environment for teenagers and young adults, [an environment] in which they can cope with the problems they confront in the broader society and as the children of two cultures" (p. 445). The Vietnamese Buddhist temple, for example, conducts year-round Sunday school in which volunteer adults teach Vietnamese culture, crafts, and language; the Chinese Buddhist temple provides Sunday classes for grade school and high school students in traditional singing and dancing, martial arts, and the Chinese language.

Being Asked to Volunteer

In studies of community samples, being asked to volunteer has consistently predicted levels of volunteering. Musick et al. (2000) found this to be the case in their community sample; furthermore, consistent with social influence theory, they found that those with higher levels of attendance at religious services and religious meetings (and of social interaction in general) reported higher levels of being asked to volunteer. This may help explain the relationship in the research literature between levels of religious participation and volunteering. A descriptive example related to the effectiveness of asking is present in the development of the Amachi Project, a faith-based mentoring program in Philadelphia for children of prisoners. Local church leaders and staff members from participating congregations spent time after worship services talking to congregants to recruit them into the program as volunteers, an effort that produced a substantial number of volunteers (Jucovy, 2003).

Contextual Influences

Only two quantitative studies were located that related features of congregational context to volunteering. Becker and Dhingra (2001) found that members of congregations whose missions were characterized by a greater focus on interaction and intimacy reported higher levels of volunteering for the congregation. Hoge et al. (1998) found that church size was related to volunteering only for Catholics and Lutherans, with members of medium-sized congregations reporting higher levels of volunteering for the congregation. Qualitative studies of congregations (e.g., Ammerman, 1997) further indicate the interplay among congregational context and various facets of member involvement, including volunteering. Additional research on congregational context appears critical to provide practical information useful to the mobilization of volunteers in the faith-based arena.

Individual Differences in Beliefs, Values, and Motivation

In addition to social influences, individual differences in beliefs, values, and motivation are viewed as important contributors to the decision to volunteer. Many studies have examined personality factors and varied motivations to volunteer. Concerning the latter, for example, individuals may volunteer in order to aid those less fortunate than themselves, to improve their communities, or to "give back" for what they have received from others (Wilson, 2000; Wuthnow, 1991). These values and beliefs may be part of an individual's personal life goals; furthermore, they may be deeply embedded in the individual's religious faith and religious meaning system—compassion for others and the principle of helping those most in need are central tenets of most world religions. Religious values may influence volunteer work within the congregation as well as in the larger community.

Interestingly, research to date has provided inconsistent evidence concerning the relationship between religious beliefs and volunteering. Some studies have found various dimensions of religious belief, such as importance of religion (e.g., Becker & Dhingra, 2001; Choi, 2003) and religious experience (e.g., Wuthnow, 1994) to be related to volunteering. Others have not (e.g., Cnann, Kasternakis, & Wineburg, 1993; Lam, 2002; Park & Smith, 2000; Wilson & Janoski, 1995). Additional studies have found religious beliefs linked to volunteering for some groups but not others. Musick et al. (2000), for example, found that strength of religious belief had a positive effect on general volunteering for Whites. For Blacks, however, it had a positive effect for those who attended church regularly, but a negative effect for those who did not attend church regularly.

There are also mixed findings concerning denominational differences in volunteering. Although some studies indicate higher levels of volunteering to support church programs in conservative and evangelical churches and/or higher levels of volunteering in community programs in mainline Protestant churches (cf. Ammerman, 2002; Chaves et al., 2002; Cnann et al., 1993; Gallup Poll, 1994, cited in Hoge et al., 1998; Wuthnow, 1999), other studies only partially support such differences (Wilson & Janoski, 1995) or do not find denominational differences at all for either church-based or community-based volunteering (Clydesdale, 1990; Park & Smith, 2000).

Different demographic and religious groups may differ in their reasons and motivations for volunteering. Parents, for example, may be especially likely to volunteer within the congregational context to support children's activities and youth and family programming. For the elderly, on the other hand, primary volunteering rationales may be to maintain an active, meaningful role in society and to enhance belonging when parenting and work no longer meet these primary needs on a daily basis (Caro & Bass, 1995; Choi, 2003). Minority group members may be especially likely to volunteer as a means of "giving back" to their community, and nonminorities may volunteer primarily to contribute to those who are less fortunate.

Theological differences also can be expected to influence the way volunteering is viewed. For example, research evidence suggests that members of conservative religious denominations view volunteer work in terms of sacrifice and members of evangelical churches in terms of expressing a spiritual value, whereas members of liberal religious denominations view volunteer work in terms of self-improvement or civic duty (Becker & Dhingra, 2001; Wilson, 2000). Generally speaking, mobilization of volunteers in a given congregation is likely to be most effective when it builds upon the specific religious beliefs, values, and motivations of the congregational membership.

Other Theoretical Approaches: Human Capital and Exchange Theory

Two additional theoretical approaches discussed by Wilson (2000) are human capital and exchange theory. Since little relevant research specific to the religious domain has been conducted related to these approaches, only a brief review is presented of each.

Human Capital

The human capital theory of volunteering assumes that individual resources, such as education and socioeconomic status, influence volunteering. Such resources may determine one's ability to volunteer and the capacity to meet the demands of volunteering. Research on community samples indicates that those with higher education levels and occupation status consistently report higher levels of volunteering. Higher levels of education and occupational status may enhance self-confidence, civic skills, and belonging to multiple organizations where one is asked to volunteer; education furthermore may increase empathy and enhance awareness of social and community problems. Other human capital variables, such as income, age, and free time, have not been consistently linked to volunteering (Wilson, 2000).

In studies where educational status and socioeconomic status indicators were included in analyses that focused only on congregational members, the findings confirmed the importance of human capital theory. Hoge et al. (1998), for example, conducted subsample analyses for members of five denominations. In all five cases a positive relationship was found between education and volunteering for the church, and in four of five cases a relationship was found between income and volunteering for the church. Researchers who have limited their sample to congregational attenders also confirm the relationship between these human capital variables and volunteering (Becker & Dhingra, 2001; Park & Smith, 2000). It is less clear, however, whether variation in these human capital variables exists within individual congregations, where variation in human capital will be more limited and where social norms and related attributes of the congregation may possibly override the human capital differences that exist. Without such knowledge, the extent to which extra efforts to recruit volunteers with lower levels of human capital need to occur within congregations is not clear.

Exchange Theory

Exchange theory views the decision to volunteer as the result of an assessment of the relative benefits and costs expected. In the congregational context, one potentially important social benefit is solidarity—the pleasure of socializing and working with fellow congregants and church staff. Another benefit for volunteer work in the congregation is enhanced quality of congregational life and programs. Parents interested in the quality of the experience that accrues to their children can be expected to be influenced by this benefit. Perceived costs of a decision not to volunteer in the congregational context may include an expectation of disapproval from valued others (e.g., clergy, fellow congregants). Research in the congregational context directly linked to exchange theory was not found.

Summary of Theory and Research

Figure 1 depicts the various pathways of influence supported by the theories and empirical research reviewed here. Contextual, social, and individual factors are all viewed as important determinants of volunteering and, in dynamic fashion, as influencing each other. Future empirical research is necessary to examine most of the pathways depicted. Implications of the theory and research reviewed for the mobilization of volunteers are discussed in the following section.

Implications for Mobilization of Adults for Positive Youth Development

Although the theoretical and research literature reviewed generally does not focus explicitly on how best to mobilize adult volunteers for positive youth development in particular, a number of implications for such efforts can nonetheless be drawn. The following seven recommendations, taken together, hold promise to substantially enhance the numbers of adults contributing to positive youth development. Future research, however, is necessary to examine their individual and combined utility in various faith-based mobilization efforts; ideally such research would be collaborative in nature, involving partnerships between researchers and faith-based practitioners.

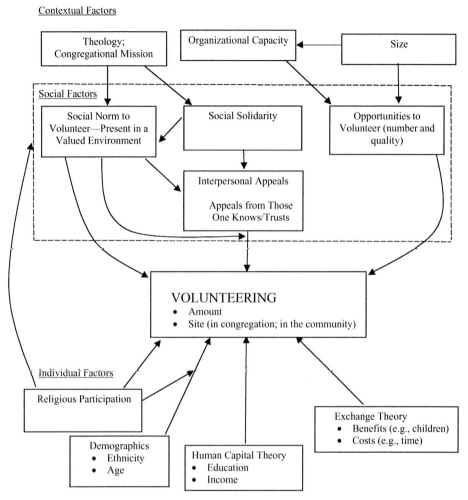

Figure 1. Determinants of Adult Volunteering in Faith-based Context to Help Youth and Families: An Overview

Volunteering Related to Youth as a Normative Congregational Activity

Theory and research suggest that volunteering behavior is influenced to a considerable extent by various social factors, including extant social norms and expectations (e.g., Wilson & Janoski, 1995; Wuthnow, 1991). An overarching strategy, then, for enhancing congregational adult involvement in youth development activities is for such volunteer activity to become a normative (i.e., ongoing, regular) aspect of congregational life. One key component involved in establishing such norms is a consistent emphasis by both the formal and the informal leadership in the congregation on volunteer activity in general and volunteering related to youth development in particular. Such activities ideally would be routinely presented as an integral aspect of religious, spiritual, and congregational mission. Such an emphasis can tap existing religious beliefs about helping young people and supporting families (e.g., Smith, 2003). Communicating the youth- and family-focused mission of the congregation to members, and how this mission can be achieved, in part, through widespread volunteer action, would occur both through formal (sermons, written communications) and informal (conversations with respected members, small-group interactions) channels (e.g., Hudson Institute, 2003). The general principle is to encourage people to see volunteering for youth development as an important application of their religious convictions and faith.

Beyond consistent articulation of the role of volunteering for youth development as part of the larger, faith-based mission, some level of congregational staff and resources should be focused on such efforts. In addition, consistent with social influence theory, volunteers who contribute to youth development should be publicly appreciated and their efforts reinforced by congregational leaders. These steps, along with related activities discussed later, can help to make volunteering related to youth development, both within the congregation and in the wider community, a highly valued social norm within congregational life.

Enhancing the Number of Available Volunteer Opportunities Related to Youth

Consistent with social influence theory, increasing the number of available opportunities for volunteering behavior related to youth should enhance levels of youth-related volunteering. Various volunteer opportunities related to positive youth development (e.g., Sunday school, youth groups) are likely to be present to a considerable extent already in most congregations. These opportunities within the congregation can be broadened by additional, specialized volunteer-driven activities that may be less uniformly present in congregations (academic tutoring, youth mentoring, family support, effective parenting practices, etc.). Youth-related volunteer opportunities in the larger community, whether they are congregation-sponsored or not, are likely to be even less uniformly available.

Mobilization of additional adult volunteers for youth development can be enhanced if these volunteer opportunities represent part of ongoing congregational commitments and sponsored projects. Furthermore, special, high-profile initiatives focused on youth can provide salient new volunteering opportunities to congregational members, whether the initiatives originate in the local congregation, the national denomination, regional faith-based networks, or the local community. As a general rule, providing written descriptions of volunteer opportunities, including important details related to the nature of the volunteering involvement, skills required, and the number of congregational volunteers needed, is recommended for optimal recruitment (Hudson Institute, 2003).

Enhancing the Attractiveness of Volunteering Opportunities Related to Youth

Extant theory and research suggest a number of ways to enhance the appeal of volunteering opportunities to congregational members. As a start, volunteer appeals in the congregational context should be tailored to the belief systems and characteristics of congregational members for optimum recruitment results. For example, consistent with prior research, liberal religious individuals may be attracted to messages about contributing to the community good ("social gospel"), while conservative religious individuals may find messages that appeal to their doctrinal convictions especially important ("personal gospel"). In terms of specific social subgroups, parents may be likely to respond to appeals that relate to the quality of church programs for their children, while elderly members may be motivated to do youth-related volunteering to enhance spiritual and social meaning in their lives, as well as perhaps for the health benefits for elderly volunteers suggested by research (Choi, 2000).

Minority individuals may be especially likely to contribute to volunteering activities that serve youth at risk in their congregation and in their larger community as a means of "giving back" to their community. Relatedly, adult volunteers in immigrant churches may be attracted by activities that contribute to the continuation of cultural traditions and customs at risk of being lost to youth growing up in the United States.

The opportunity for sociability is a potentially strong attraction for volunteers in the congregational context. Volunteer activities in groups, whether within the congregation or in the larger community, will directly build upon this positive feature. Making known which other congregational members are serving or likely to serve in a given volunteer activity is a related feature that can help recruit volunteers.

These and additional considerations congregations should incorporate into their volunteer appeals are aptly summarized by Becker and Dhingra (2001), who suggest that "the message [not only] needs [to] fit their own members' motives for volunteering, but also needs to remind members that the organization is a distinctive place to volunteer and can express needs and preferences that are not expressed through volunteering elsewhere. For congregations to recruit volunteers, they must not only offer unique programs but also make members feel connected, since social bonds encourage stronger connection. Commitments to congregations based on both social bonds and spiritual expression create a confluence of emotional and instrumental motives for volunteering" (p. 333).

The Power of Asking

Consistent with available research, there appears to be no more powerful way of recruiting volunteers than personally and directly asking individuals to get involved and serve (Becker & Dhingra, 2001; Ladd, 1999). Requests can be from clergy or congregational staff asking targeted congregational members to volunteer for a youth-related ministry, or from fellow congregants who ask their friends, family members, or acquaintances to take part. Generally speaking, volunteer recruitment efforts should include face-to-face invitations or personal mailings along with more general use of announcements, bulletin boards, and newsletters.

Volunteer Action Committees

A congregational committee or ministry explicitly focused on volunteers appears to be important, consistent with social influence principles, in contributing to the mobilization of volunteers for youth development. Such groups can centralize information about volunteer activities, seek out new volunteering activities related to youth and families, maintain records of specific volunteer interests and abilities of members in these areas, help match volunteers to available ministries and help train them for their volunteer activities, and periodically organize special initiatives to mobilize new volunteers and sponsor new congregational youth development outreach activities. Although specific domains (e.g., Sunday school, youth groups) may be sufficiently established to mobilize volunteers on their own, new initiatives, and perhaps especially youth development initiatives in the larger community, will be well served by individuals whose primary task is to mobilize and support volunteers. To the extent congregational resources necessary to support such efforts are provided, the odds of successful mobilization of youth development volunteers are likely to be enhanced.

Relatedly, making physical space available for youth-related volunteer activities (e.g., a corner or office for youth ministry, a room for tutoring sessions or youth group meetings) should facilitate volunteer mobilization. Providing physical space helps to underscore the importance the congregation places on youth-related ministries, as well as facilitates meaningful and productive involvement (Ammerman, 1997; Ebaugh & Chafetz, 2000).

Increasing General Congregational Participation

Enhancing the levels of member participation in the congregation is likely to directly increase the pool of potential volunteers. This is consistent with social influence theory and available research, which generally shows a positive relationship between levels of congregational participation and volunteering. As noted earlier, this is likely the case because congregational and volunteer leaders gain direct personal access to larger numbers of potential volunteers, and the congregational members get exposed to information that they may not otherwise be exposed to. Furthermore, through congregational participation, potential volunteers meet people who may be already be involved, who can share with them the needs within the congregation or within the larger community, and who can provide the specifics of what is involved in volunteering and the benefits that accrue. Although there is no simple formula to enhance congregational participation, one of the potential payoffs from sustained, focused efforts to enhance participation is an enlarged pool of active volunteers.

Creating Community-Based and Regional Partnerships and Coalitions

Just as "it takes a village to raise a child," large-scale mobilization of congregational volunteers for youth in need, especially in the larger community, appears most likely to succeed if successful partnerships and coalitions are developed between individual congregations and other groups. For example, strategic partnerships between congregations and individual schools or community agencies can enhance member awareness of youth needs in the community, create an ongoing need for congregational volunteers, and contribute to community "buy-in" for congregational involvement (e.g., Garringer, 2003; Wineburg & Wineburg, 1987). Regional volunteer networks may also be created for congregations to work together to recruit, train, and support volunteers for youth development. Although each congregation can create its own internal volunteer ministry for youth, the regional network can support programs by training coordinators, sharing resources (i.e., information, tools, and ideas), and helping to solve common problems. An exemplar of a regional network is the Philadelphia Church Mentoring Network, which comprises nearly 70 churches and whose mentoring ministries serve more than 700 youth (National Mentoring Partnership, 1999). The potential to make a substantive difference in the lives of children, youth, and families in need in the larger community is likely to be facilitated by such community-based and regional efforts.

References

Ammerman, N. (1997). *Congregation and community*. New Brunswick, NJ: Rutgers University Press.

Ammerman, N. (2002). Connecting mainline Protestant churches with public life. In R. Wuthnow & J. H. Evans (Eds.), *The quiet hand of God: Faith-based activism and the public role of mainline Protestantism* (pp. 129–158). Berkeley and Los Angeles: University of California Press.

AOL Time Warner Foundation. (2002). *Mentoring in America 2002*. New York: Author.

Arp, W., & Boeckelman, K. (1997). Religiosity: A source of Black environmentalism and empowerment? *Journal of Black Studies, 28*, 255–267.

Becker, P. E., & Dhingra, P. (2001). Religious involvement and volunteering: Implications for civil society. *Sociology of Religion, 62*, 315–336.

Branch, A. Y. (2002). *Faith and action: Implementation of the national faith-based initiative for high-risk youth*. Philadelphia: Public/Private Ventures. Retrieved May 30, 2003, from http://www.ppv.org/pdffiles/faithandaction.pdf

Caro, F. G., & Bass, S. A. (1995). Increasing volunteering among older people. In S. Bass (Ed.), *Older and active: How Americans over 55 are contributing to society* (pp. 71–96). New Haven, CT: Yale University Press.

Chaves, M. (1999, Spring). *Religious organizations and welfare reform: Who will take advantage of "charitable choice"?* (Nonprofit Sector Research Fund Working Paper Series). Washington, DC: Aspen Institute.

Chaves, M., Giesel, H., & Tsitsos, W. (2002). Religious variations in public presence: Evidence from the National Congregations Study. In R. Wuthnow & J. H. Evans (Eds.), *The quiet hand of God:*

Faith-based activism and the public role of mainline Protestantism (pp. 108–128). Berkeley and Los Angeles: University of California Press.

Choi, L. H. (2003). Factors affecting volunteerism among older adults. *Journal of Applied Gerontology, 22*, 179–196.

Clarke, S., Forbush, J., & Henderson, J. (2003, April). *Faith-based mentoring: A preventive strategy for at-risk youth.* Paper presented at the 14th National Conference on Child Abuse and Neglect, St. Louis, MO. Retrieved May 30, 2003, from http://itiincorporated.com/Assets/pdf%20files/04-03_FB_Mentoring-StLouis.pdf

Clary, E. G., Snyder, M., & Stukas, A. A. (1996). Volunteers' motivations: Findings from a national survey. *Nonprofit and Voluntary Sector Quarterly, 25*, 485–505.

Clydesdale, T. (1990). Soul-winning and social work: Giving and caring in the evangelical tradition. In R. Wuthnow, V. A. Hodgkinson, & Associates (Eds.), *Faith and philanthropy in America: Exploring the role of religion in America's voluntary sector* (pp. 187–211). San Francisco: Jossey-Bass.

Cnaan, R. (2002, Winter). Religion, congregations and community: The Philadelphia story. *Greater Philadelphia Regional Review*, 28–31.

Cnaan, R. A., Kasternakis, A., & Wineburg, R. J. (1993). Religious people, religious congregations, and volunteerism in human services: Is there a link? *Nonprofit and Voluntary Sector Quarterly, 22*, 33–52.

Cohen, D., & Jaeger, R. A. (1998). *Sacred places at risk: New evidence on how endangered older churches and synagogues serve communities.* Philadelphia: Partners for Sacred Places.

Dionne, E. J., Jr., & DiIulio, J. J., Jr. (Eds.). (2000).*What's God got to do with the American experiment?* Washington, DC: Brookings Institution Press.

Ebaugh, H. R., & Chafetz, J. S. (Eds.). (2000). *Religion and the new immigrants: Continuities and adaptations in immigrant congregations.* Walnut Creek, CA: Altamira Press.

Ferree, G. D., Barry, J., & Manno, B. (1998). *The National Survey of Philanthropy and Civic Renewal.* Washington, DC: National Commission on Philanthropy and Civic Renewal.

Fischer, L. R., & Schaeffer, K. B. (1993). *Older volunteers: A guide to research and practice.* Newbury Park, CA: Sage.

Garringer, M. (2003, Summer). The work of a saint. *National Mentoring Center Bulletin, 12*, 7–12.

Hall, P. D. (1990). The history of religious philanthropy in America. In R. Wuthnow, V. A. Hodgkinson, & Associates (Eds.), *Faith and philanthropy in America: Exploring the role of religion in America's voluntary sector* (pp. 38–62). San Francisco: Jossey-Bass.

Hoge, D. R., Zech, C., McNamara, P., & Donahue, M. J. (1998). The value of volunteers as resources for congregations. *Journal for the Scientific Study of Religion, 37*, 470–480.

Hudson Institute. (2003). *Faith in communities: A Hudson Institute initiative* (pp. 5–6). Retrieved January 20, 2004, from http:www.hudsonfaithincommunities.org/faq.html

Jackson, E. F., Bachmeier, M. D., Wood, J. R., & Craft, E. A. (1995). Volunteering and charitable giving: Do religious and associational ties promote helping behavior? *Nonprofit and Voluntary Sector Quarterly, 24*, 59–78.

Jucovy, L. (2003). *Mentoring children of prisoners in Philadelphia.* Public/Private Ventures. Retrieved May 30, 2003, from http:www.ppv.org/content/reports/amachi.html

Kurien, P. (1998). Becoming American by becoming Hindu: Indian Americans take their place at the multicultural table. In R. S. Warner & J. G. Wittner (Eds.), *Gatherings in diaspora: Religious communities and the new immigration* (pp. 37–70). Philadelphia: Temple University Press.

Ladd, E. C. (1999). *The Ladd report.* New York: Free Press.

Lam, P.-Y. (2002). As the flocks gather: How religion affects voluntary association participation. *Journal for the Scientific Study of Religion, 41*, 405–422.

Leon, L. (1998). Born again in east LA: The congregation as border space. In R. S. Warner & J. G. Wittner (Eds.), *Gatherings in diaspora: Religious communities and the new immigration* (pp. 163–198). Philadelphia: Temple University Press.

Maton, K. I., Sto. Domingo, M. R., & King, J. (2005). Faith-based organizations. In D. DuBois & M. Karcher (Eds.), *Handbook of youth mentoring* (pp. 376–391).Thousand Oaks, CA: Sage.

Mattis, J. S., Jagers, R. J., Hatcher, C. A., Lawhon, G. D., Murphy, E. J., & Murray, Y. F. (2000). Religiosity, volunteerism, and community involvement among African American men: An exploratory analysis. *Journal of Community Psychology, 28*, 391–406.

McLearn, K. T., Colasanto, D., & Schoen, C. (1998). *Mentoring makes a difference: Findings from the Commonwealth Fund 1998 Survey of Adults Mentoring Young People.* New York: Commonwealth Fund.

Mentoring for Success Act, H.R. 1497, 147th Cong. (2001).

Moscareillo, S. (2002). Trust: The unseen component of your volunteer program. Volunteer Services and Community Relations, Baltimore Ronald McDonald House. Retrieved on February 17, 2004, from http://www.charitychannel.com/article_163.shtml

Musick, M., Wilson, J., & Bynum, W. (2000). Race and formal volunteering: The differential effects of class and religion. *Social Forces, 78,* 1539–1571.

National Mentoring Partnership. (1999). *Church mentoring network: A program manual for linking and supporting mentoring ministries.* Philadelphia: Author.

Park, J., & Smith, C. (2000). "To whom has much been given…": Religious capital and community volunteerism among churchgoing Protestants. *Journal for the Scientific Study of Religion, 39,* 272–286.

Roehlkepartain, E. C. (2003). *Building assets, strengthening faith: Results from a field test survey of youth and adults in 15 U.S. congregations.* Minneapolis, MN: Search Institute.

Scales, P. C. (with Benson, P. L., Mannes, M., Hintz, N. R., Roehlkepartain, E. C., & Sullivan, T. K.). (2003). *Other people's kids: Social expectations and American adults' involvement with children and adolescents.* New York: Kluwer.

Smith, C. (2003). Theorizing religious effects among American adolescents. *Journal of the Scientific Study of Religion, 42,* 17–30.

Sullivan, K. (2000). St. Catherine's Catholic Church: One church, parallel congregations. In H. R. Ebaugh & J. S. Chafetz (Eds.), *Religion and the new immigrants: Continuities and adaptation in immigrant congregations* (pp. 255–289). Walnut Creek, CA: Altamira Press.

United Way of Southeastern Pennsylvania. (2004). *The Greater Philadelphia Mentoring Partnership: Programs.* Retrieved on February 29, 2004, from http://secure.uwsepa.org/mentoring/programs.asp

Wilson, J. (2000). Volunteering. *Annual Review of Sociology, 26,* 215–240.

Wilson, J., & Janoski, T. (1995). The contribution of religion to volunteer work. *Sociology of Religion, 56,* 137–152.

Wilson, J., & Musick, M. (1997). Who cares? Toward an integrated theory of volunteer work. *American Sociological Review, 62,* 694–713.

Wineburg, C. R., & Wineburg, R. J. (1987). Local human service development: Institutional utilization of volunteers to solve community problems. *Journal of Volunteer Administration, 4,* 9–14.

Woolever, C., & Bruce, D. (2004). *Beyond the ordinary: 10 strengths of U.S. congregations.* Louisville, KY: Westminster/John Knox Press.

Wuthnow, R. (1990). Religion and the voluntary spirit in the United States: Mapping the terrain. In R. Wuthnow, V. A. Hodgkinson, & Associates (Eds.), *Faith and philanthropy in America: Exploring the role of religion in America's voluntary sector* (pp. 3–21). San Francisco: Jossey-Bass.

Wuthnow, R. (1991). *Acts of compassion: Caring for others and helping ourselves.* Princeton, NJ: Princeton University Press.

Wuthnow, R. (1994). *God and Mammon in America.* New York: Free Press.

Wuthnow, R. (1999). Mobilizing civic engagement: The changing impact of religious involvement. In T. Skocpol & M. P. Fiorina (Eds.), *Civic engagement in American democracy* (pp. 331–366). New York: Russell Sage Foundation.

Wuthnow, R., & Evans, J. H. (Eds.). (2002). *The quiet hand of God: Faith-based activism and the public role of mainline Protestantism.* Berkeley and Los Angeles: University of California Press.

10 Bridging Research and Community Practice in the Field of Youth Development through University Outreach

Linda Camino and Shepherd Zeldin

University of Wisconsin-Madison

This chapter describes our experience and the lessons we have learned in engaging in outreach scholarship to mobilize adults on behalf of youth development. These lessons are grounded in two overarching contemporary trends: the movement to reembrace the civic mission of higher education and the movement to engage adults to contribute to the positive development of youth.

Many analysts have written cogently about the mission drift in higher education that has been occurring since World War II. The argument is that, steadily and incrementally, there has been a shift in emphasis from civic service and development of knowledge to help communities solve problems, to one in which basic research has come to dominate the scholarly agenda. The reasons for the shift are diverse, ranging from the belief that basic research will maintain the economic and military preeminence of the United States (Harkavy, 2003) to the rise and institutionalization of categorical academic disciplines and professional associations (Rice, 1996). The net result is that academic faculty have turned inward toward their disciplines in developing knowledge, and away from the immediate and practical needs of communities (Checkoway, 2001).

The effort to reembrace the civic mission of higher education, and change the direction of the drift, in part, has been stimulated by a seminal report from Ernest Boyer (1990) of the Carnegie Foundation for the Advancement of Teaching. Boyer addressed the narrowing of scholarship and argued for a broader conceptualization. Most certainly, according to Boyer, a strong emphasis on the scholarship of discovery, or basic research, should remain. But other types of scholarship—integration and application—should also be recognized as full academic activity. Specifically, scholars should be encouraged to make sense of, and transform knowledge by, integrating themes across disciplines and placing knowledge in larger contexts. Further, scholars should be encouraged to apply knowledge to human problems. Boyer concludes by addressing the scholarship of teaching. According to Boyer, teaching should go beyond lecturing to fostering learning through a variety of modalities, particularly through cooperative education and service.

Concurrently, outside of the university, complementary community-based efforts have been initiated to strengthen civil society and to change the ways that adults pass on knowledge and experience to the next generation. There has been renewed policy and programmatic interest in engaging community adults on behalf of youth development (Benson, Leffert, Scales, & Blyth, 1998). This interest stems from the fact that youth and nonfamilial adults, as two distinct classes of community residents, remain largely isolated from one another—spatially, socially, and psychologically—in almost all spheres of U.S. society. Several recent social forces serve as barriers to prevent adults from engaging in the lives of youth. These include increased family isolation, civic disengagement, expanding professionalization of care, the marginalization of youth, and a host of assumptions, such as, it is largely parents' responsibility to nurture and guide children and youth (Scales, 2003). The isolation between youth and adults is detrimental and important to address because of both theory and research indicating that caring and supportive relationships with nonfamilial adults contribute to the well-being and healthy development of young people (Bronfenbrenner, 1979; Eccles & Gootman, 2002; Rhodes, 2002).

Outreach Scholarship Related to Families and Youth

Across the country, university departments are beginning to respond to the two trends of reembracing the civic mission of higher education and bridging the community divide between youth and adults. The goal is to support outreach scholarship to mobilize community adults for positive youth development. Many of these efforts are located in land-grant institutions in every state. America's land-grant colleges and universities were established by the Morrill Act of 1862 for the purpose of orienting research, teaching, and service activities to solve practical problems, and to increase the knowledge and skills of citizens. An emphasis of human development and outreach to families and youth has long been expressed in the commitment of land-grant institutions to Extension work, and many colleges and universities that did not originate through land grants orient outreach scholarship toward families and youth (Lerner & Simon, 1998).

In this chapter, we focus on our outreach work in mobilizing adults for youth development through the Department of Human Development and Family Studies, within the School of Human Ecology at the University of Wisconsin-Madison, a land-grant institution. The department is committed to incorporating outreach scholarship, particularly the principles of applied developmental science, into its operations. The department is cross-disciplinary and values applied research interests among its faculty. One of us, Camino, is senior scientist, based in the department; Zeldin is a professor with a joint appointment in the department and Cooperative Extension, 4-H/Youth Development. Our positions require us to work with a host of community adults in various systems and with various levels of authority in Wisconsin and other states throughout the nation. For example, with the Extension system, we work with state-level specialists and county-level agents and educators. These individuals are responsible for engaging adults and youth at state and local levels. Alternatively, we work with members of municipal and county coalitions and commissions. These individuals include government officials, agency executive directors and staff, and volunteers. We also work directly with frontline youth workers and youth in organizations and agencies.

We address here the rationale of adult learning as fundamental to our mobilization efforts and discuss key strategies we use to facilitate adult learning and change. We then provide three case examples of our work to illustrate how we put the key strategies to work, and end with a consideration of new roles for scholars in mobilizing community adults.

Praxis: Facilitating Adults as Learners and Agents for Youth Development

The heart of mobilizing adults for youth development is learning. Practical learning is grounded in the concept of praxis, developed by Paolo Freire (1921–1997), the Brazilian educationalist. According to Freire (1983), praxis consists of a cycle of planning, action, and reflection. Andragogy, or the study of adult learning, emphasizes that praxis may be especially salient to adults because adults learn and make meaning based on the context of their experience, which tends to be broader and lengthier than that of children and youth. Praxis additionally fits with adults' preference for self-direction in learning and desire to apply knowledge to solve practical problems (Knowles, 1980).

Praxis contains two implications for mobilizing adults for youth development. First, adult learning is best fostered by facilitation. Facilitators strive to set up the conditions that will enable adults to be self-directed and experiential learners. Second, there is a need to engage adults in networks of co-learners, who can challenge as well as support one another, and so move the learning process along in a collegial manner.

Through experimentation over the years, we have sought to translate these two implications into practical strategies that foster adult learning and mobilization. There are many reasons to foster adult learning and mobilization. Fundamentally, it is community adults who need to bear a share of responsibility for youth development. Youth-serving programs and organizations cannot take on youth development by themselves, nor can parents, for youth development requires a broad range of strategies and approaches. Second, because youth development necessarily involves integration of efforts on multiple fronts, community adults need to be empowered with the knowledge and skills to act on behalf of youth development. Third, gaining such capacity can help close the demonstrated gap between adults' espoused valuing of youth development principles and lack of active participation in translating the principles to action (Scales, 2003).

In our work we incorporate traditional academic teaching methods, but we have also found it necessary to use a greater variety of learning venues and formats. We have found it necessary to wear a variety of hats, and to change and adapt our roles and responsibilities throughout the learning processes. The four major strategies that have worked consistently are to: (1) ground the work in the philosophy and structure of learning communities, (2) provide and discuss research-based information and action-oriented resources, (3) involve community adults in participatory action research projects, and (4) engage adults in partnerships and shared learning with youth.

Ground the Work in the Philosophy and Structure of Learning Communities

In the past 15 years, several fields have championed the use of what have been called "learning communities" (Senge, 1990), "communities of inquiry" (Friedman, 2000), and "reflective practicums" (Shon, 1987). The unifying concept is the importance of providing opportunities for people to learn and engage in the cycle of praxis. Learning communities provide spaces in which people can build networks, share information, question and challenge one another, problem solve, and attempt to apply new knowledge. Coalitions have similar aims, and there has been an increasing use of coalitions as a community-wide prevention and health-promoting mechanism (Wolff, 2001).

The use of learning communities and coalitions has arisen within larger movements to engage communities for the common good and well-being of residents. Community building, local decision making, and ownership of services are the key approaches (Hyman, 2002; Mattesich & Monsey, 1997). With respect to youth development, learning communities and coalitions have great potential to transform communities by adopting, endorsing, and implementing new ideas, particularly in their ability to build community awareness and capacity for youth development (Benson, 1997).

Given that there are relatively few opportunities for university faculty to come together with community members on a routine basis, we believe that learning communities can be a positive space for faculty, students, and practitioners to link academic theory and research to practitioners' experience, methods, and knowledge. A first task, of course, is to organize learning communities. Whenever possible, we connect to existing networks and coalitions rather than create new groups. We take this approach because practitioners and residents have limited time to devote to such entities, and duplication is counterproductive. However, we also recognize that building broad-based support is critical. We therefore will urge the addition of representatives from agencies, councils, or other organizations when we observe a gap.

The second task is to guide participants toward a common purpose and an agenda devoted to both action and reflection. In accordance with adult learning theory, we rely on methods that foster task-focused and task-related group activities. Task-focused activities are tightly structured and are designed to lead to desired discussion or learning outcomes. For example, a task-focused activity might be asking participants to read an evaluation summary of a youth leadership program, and then to generalize from this information and articulate expected outcomes for their own initiative. Task-related activities, on the other hand, are those that revolve around more unstructured discussions among participants. Although seemingly tangential, such discussions can spark innovation in topic area or direction. In one community-wide meeting, for example, participants deviated to discuss philosophical ideas about youth leadership and assumptions adults make about youth leaders. The discussion led to insights about developing distinct program components relevant to youth of color.

The third task is continuous attention to interpersonal relationships and community building. One does not typically think of relationship building as central to scholarship. However, relationships foster learning, make possible the sharing of information, and smooth the way for collaborations. Building relationships involves attention to community building at three levels: personal, organizational, and professional. All are important, but the personal level typically receives the least amount of attention. Yet, knowing one another personally makes it easier for people to interact professionally. Personal connections help build trust and mutual respect, a fundamental underpinning of networks and social capital (Tschannen-Moran & Hoy, 2000). Accordingly, we try to include time at meetings for participants to form, renew, and deepen their connections in a relaxed atmosphere. Time for breaks, learning formats that include small-group or dyadic dialogue, or even "ice-breaker" exercises contribute to encouraging interaction.

Provide and Discuss Research-Based Information and Action-Oriented Resources

A second major strategy we employ is to provide relevant data and resources to stakeholders. Practitioners, policy makers, and community residents are often bombarded with information, typically focused on the negative, about youth from a myriad of sources—mass media, oral discourse, Web sites, and the like. Stakeholders, we have learned, appreciate research data because they are based on standards of evidence-based and systematic analysis, rather than on what our partners have called "hearsay" or "sensationalization." Stakeholders appreciate knowing the positive, and not just the negative, side of a given issue. They also appreciate research that emphasizes contextual factors as shapers of attitudes and behaviors. Equally important to stakeholders are opportunities to discuss research in a focused way.

Making data truly accessible to community stakeholders is often easier said than done, however. The challenges are many. First, differences exist in writing preferences, types of information, and what constitutes credible sources of data for university-based researchers and faculty on the one hand, and policy makers, community practitioners, and residents on the other hand. Second, consistent with andragogy theory, adults differ in learning style. Some individuals learn best through reading, some through experience, and others through training, lecture, debate, or discussion. Finally, different contexts will present demands for different types of information formats. For example, staff in community-based organizations often have neither the time nor the inclination to read a complete research article, instead preferring summaries or workshop modalities based on research findings.

To accommodate these varying needs and preferences, we draw from our own and others' work. Using the scholarships of integration and application, we create multiple products—literature reviews, research briefs, field reports, and articles—from academic and professional journals, training curricula, selections from tool kits, and assessment instruments, depending on the needs and interests of the group with which we are collaborating. More important, we explain and discuss the products with the stakeholders. While many practitioners and residents can access this information on the Internet, we have found that in terms of actual use of information, there is no substitute for discussing the material and learning different ways of applying it.

Involve Community Adults in Participatory Action Research Projects

The strategy of involving community adults in participatory action research projects synthesizes the scholarship of discovery and application, the aim being that scholars and community participants collaborate to study local issues, disseminate the findings in a timely and easily understood manner, and then use the findings to guide change (Hall, 1993; Lewin, 1946). It is also expected that participants will gain skills and knowledge needed to enhance community programs or influence local policy makers.

For all of its promise, participatory action research can be challenging to carry out. Academics and community staff reside in different cultures and frequently hold conflicting goals. For example, there are differences in temporal orientation and ways of knowing. While university researchers view the research as a cumulative body of knowledge that takes time and patience to build, practitioners often require immediate answers and solutions (Myers-Walls, 2000). Researchers are also socialized to identify empirical support in order to make cautious conclusions; practitioners can rely on tacit knowledge, intuition, and direct experience (Zeldin & Camino, 1999). Finally, university-trained faculty are often intrigued by questions; policy makers and practitioners want answers.

These differences are institutionalized and will not disappear or change shortly. Yet, participatory action research remains fundamental to our work with adults regarding youth development. This is because we have witnessed the powerful ways in which such research can engage adults in learning about youth development, and in sparking adults' actions to improve policies and structures for adolescent well-being. For instance, through engaging in participatory action research, adults in a youth philanthropy program came to fully realize that they needed to set up policies concerning confidentiality and conflict of interest to guide youth reviews of grant applications. The adults had considered such guidelines for a couple of years, but the task had been relegated consistently to the back burner. The action research project provided the motivator to initiate action in this regard, and also led to practical recommendations for the context of the policies and the processes for writing them.

Engage Adults in Partnerships and Shared Learning with Youth

Our fourth strategy to promote adult learning is to help organizations and other entities create youth–adult partnerships and structures for shared learning between adults and youth. A significant barrier to adult engagement with youth is lack of contact with youth (Benson, 1997; Camino & Zeldin, 2002). This divide is a potent risk factor for the positive development of youth and for the health of communities (Zeldin, Camino, & Calvert, 2003). Moreover, it sets up a self-reinforcing cycle: Lack of contact leads to lack of understanding and engagement, which then leads to further avoidance. In contrast, strong relationships between youth and adults serve protective and developmental functions. Strong relationships can help prevent youth from engaging in problem behaviors, while concurrently promoting knowledge, skills, and initiative among youth (Eccles & Gootman, 2002; Scales, 2003). Further, when youth and adults work collaboratively on a common cause, there can be additional positive benefits for organizations and communities, such as greater multicultural understanding and a stronger sense of community connectedness and responsibility (Kirshner, O'Donoghue, & McLaughlin, 2002; Zeldin, Larson, & Camino, 2005).

The challenge is that forming youth–adult partnerships is not easy. The unfortunate fact remains that social structures, institutions, and norms in the United States are not organized to support strong relationships among youth and nonfamilial adults. Moreover, at the interpersonal level, relatively few adults have extensive experience in directly relating to nonfamilial youth. As such, there are relatively few role models for adults, or for that matter youth, who wish to form intergenerational collaborative relationships. Finally, settings such as schools and community organizations can pose the additional complexities of lack of time or meaningful opportunities for adults and youth to get to know each other and form sustained relationships.

Within this context, we view youth–adult partnerships as a potent strategy for engaging adults in their own development and in their own learning about young people. We therefore continuously seek to structure experiences through which adults are given opportunities and the support to collaborate with youth. This works most effectively when youth and adults have opportunities to negotiate the purpose for the partnership, roles and responsibilities, and issues of power (Camino & Zeldin, 2005). In contrast, when youth are either brought into the process late in the game, or not provided time to form relationships with one another and adults, they tend to wind up disengaged. The typical consequence is that negative stereotypes are reinforced.

Table 1. Strategies to Mobilize Adults for the Promotion of Youth Develoment

Key Strategies for University Outreach	Rationale and Key Learnings
Ground the work in the structure and philosophy of learning communities	Adults prefer and benefit from collegial and practical-focused learning. Provides time for focused reflection and collaborative planning. Reflective and collaborative learning leads to shared commitment. Reflective and collaborative learning allows different stakeholders (faculty, students, policy makers, and practitioners) to understand the needs, orientations, and institutional rewards and constraints of one another.
Provide and discuss research-based information and action-oriented resources	Community adults are eager to gain credible and objective information about youth development, including outcomes, effective practices, and theory. Action-oriented resources translate research and theory to practice and effective action, thus providing communities and adults with guidance and support. Data and action-oriented resources allow community adults to shift from risk to asset orientations in youth development.
Involve community adults in participatory action research	Adults gain an increased understanding of the impact of effective and ineffective youth development practices and policies. Involving adults in research and organizational assessment promotes local ownership of the findings. Adults' interpretation of findings provides a foundation for program development and improvement. Dissemination of findings is enhanced.
Engage adults in partnerships and shared learning with youth	Adults can examine stereotypes and assumptions about youth on individual, institutional, cultural, and social levels. Adults experience firsthand the competence of youth. Adults and youth deepen their understanding of the needs and concerns of one another.

Case Examples

We discuss here three examples of how we have attempted to mobilize adults for youth development. The examples illustrate the four key strategies of involving stakeholders in learning communities, providing and discussing research-based information and action-oriented resources, involving community adults in participatory action research, and engaging adults in partnerships and shared learning with youth (Table 1).

University Outreach in Policy-Oriented Participatory Research and Planning

We recently undertook a long-term project to assist the United Way of Greater Milwaukee in developing a policy framework to establish program and funding priorities for youth aged 13 to 18. To help our constituency, a multisectoral community advisory group, establish such priorities, we embarked on a process of participatory action research.

We first consulted with the committee for several months, and together we developed key questions to guide the study. We then mutually negotiated a mixed-method study that included a national scan of recent research and practice from the field of youth development, community surveys, and focus group interviews with Milwaukee stakeholders (adults and youth involved in youth policy and programming). We also engaged youth and adults as partners in designing and implementing role plays to gain perspectives from youth and youth workers on difficult-to-answer questions.

An additional objective was to conduct the project as a learning community. The intention was to establish a group that would continue beyond our participation. We therefore encouraged the committee to include a broad range of organizations, involving those currently funded by the United Way, as well as those not yet funded by the United Way. Overall, we gained the involvement of adults and youth from 41 different youth-oriented foundations, associations, agencies, and organizations. Through several daylong meetings, using the various research methods, we were able to harness diverse perspectives.

We received feedback that the inclusive and participatory policy research process helped the findings of this study become relevant to the expressed needs and experiences of various groups in the community. Moreover, participants appreciated that the meetings also provided them opportunities to discuss issues with their colleagues, and to have their voices explicitly included in the final report. This led to a sense of ownership of the research and widespread commitment to following through on the implications. The United Way used the final report as an initial policy blueprint and has continued to work with local leaders and youth-serving agency personnel in a learning community to flesh out the recommendations and implications.

University-Based Service-Learning to Bridge Theoretical, Practice, and Policy Knowledge

At its best, service-learning in higher education is able to promote student development, while also providing useful assistance to community-based organizations. Within the context of service-learning courses for graduate students, we have incorporated the strategies of adult group learning. For illustration, Zeldin teaches a graduate course titled "Youth Development in Community Context." By and large, the students are young adults, many of whom have had prior experience working in youth-serving organizations. The course is grounded in the experience of these emerging professionals. The classroom portion of the course is therefore conducted as a learning community through which students serve as resources and co-learners for one another. Outside of the classroom, the students are paired with youth organizations, the aim being to bring research-based knowledge and action-oriented resources and tools to the organizations. For example, some students work with youth workers to assess their organizations, based on standards developed from theory and research on youth development. Other students conduct training workshops for staff in the organizations, again based on current knowledge in youth development. Still others prepare newsletters on youth issues, which are then disseminated through community organizations.

Staff profit from these projects. They appreciate being brought up-to-date with current theory and research and being challenged to integrate the knowledge into their own practice. After testing the action-oriented tools and materials, the organizations often find a way to integrate them into their own repertoire of program development resources.

Our aim, however, is to broaden the learning beyond the classroom and particular organizations. Each semester we structure an additional outreach component. The students deliver presentations based on their service to a citywide or countywide governing/funding entity, such as the local Youth Commission or the United Way, both of which are coalitions of agency representatives, local governing officials, and volunteers. Consistent with the learning community strategy, these communications are oriented toward disseminating information on promising practices in youth work. Students engage the governing body in discussion, respond to questions, and follow up with additional information as requested. Frequently, students are requested to give "repeat performances" for other groups.

One of the lessons from these service-learning courses has been that learning communities both within the class of students, and between the class and local organizations and coalitions, take awhile to cohere. Accordingly, the course has been redesigned and will be offered over two semesters, rather than one. It will be team-taught with colleagues to ensure that students are afforded maximum necessary support from the instructors. Finally, to build dissemination into the course, two Extension agents will be invited to take the course, with the explicit expectation that these agents will take their experience and offer workshops to colleagues in the larger state Extension system.

University Outreach to Foster Youth–Adult Partnerships for Assessment and Organizational Change

We are currently directing an initiative, Youth–Adult Partnerships for Assessment and Organizational Change, to help youth-serving organizations and coalitions create the conditions that promote positive youth development. In the initiative, youth and adults partner to assess the program quality of their organization or coalition, and then plan actions to enhance operations.

The initiative has been designed explicitly to integrate the four strategies of promoting adult learning and group mobilization. Fundamentally, the initiative is grounded in research. We have designed assessment instruments based on research and theory about effective practices in youth development. Items include, for instance, supports and opportunities necessary for youth development, youth–adult partnerships, youth outcomes, youth voice, and structures for engaging youth in decision making. This knowledge comes alive, however, through participatory action research and youth–adult partnerships. Youth and adults collect and analyze data to assess how well their organizations are supporting youth development and engagement. Specifically, youth and adults partner in teams to administer the instruments to staff and participants, compile and analyze the data, produce a written report, present findings to interested stakeholders and policy makers, and facilitate an action planning meeting to plan program modifications.

Our role is to provide technical assistance and guidance. Toward that end, we make action-oriented resources available to the youth–adult assessment teams and the organizations. We have developed a resource kit, for example, with input from youth and adult teams (Camino, Zeldin, Mook, & O'Connor, 2004). The kit contains templates for computer data entry and report writing, as well as guidelines for analysis, presentation of results, and action planning. Additionally, we challenge the organizations to constitute themselves as learning communities throughout the assessment and planning process. We emphasize that, consistent with the spirit of learning communities, assessment findings are most significant not in and of themselves, but as a platform from which to launch informed considerations of programmatic modifications or new directions.

We have found that the process promotes learning and skill development among youth and adults. Interestingly, although teams set out to assess aspects of youth engagement and development, the findings often reveal aspects of adult engagement for youth development. Results have revealed, for instance, a need for more adult volunteer training, a desire among youth for more active adult involvement or guidance in partnering with youth, or a desire for adult staff to help formulate more explicit or "affirmative action" policies focusing on youth engagement in decision making. In this manner, the process allows the adults, especially, to reflect critically on their own assumptions about youth and about their own roles in promoting development.

New Roles for Scholars as Bridgers between the University and Community Groups

Two of the four types of scholarship Boyer (1990) describes—discovery (basic research) and teaching—have been understood over the past 60 years as constituting the core of university faculty function. The two others—integration and application—have only recently been reemphasized as vital to the functions of higher education. Integration and application have several facets critical to outreach. These forms of scholarship require the synthesis of research and theory across disciplines and fields. They entail the interpretation and dissemination of research to those outside the professoriate. In brief, the scholarships of integration and application involve putting knowledge to work for individuals, families, and society.

With the broadening of the definition of scholarship, there are necessarily new roles for faculty and staff in higher education to assume. As outreach scholars following the four key strategies we have outlined—grounding the work in the philosophy and structure of learning communities, providing and discussing research-based information and action-oriented resources, involving community adults in participatory action research projects, and engaging adults in partnerships and shared learning with youth—we cast our predominant, overarching role as "bridgers." We regard bridging as a useful metaphor to describe the flow, sharing, and collaboration that must occur among different types of knowledge—theoretical, research, practice, and policy—and among various groups of stakeholders on behalf of youth development. As bridgers, we must be adept in, and employ, a full array of scholarship. In our experience, three roles—facilitator, collaborative researcher, and disseminator—are critical. These roles require the use of all four key strategies in day-to-day outreach practice, albeit in different combinations, depending on the situation. These new roles are described here. While we discuss each as a distinct role, in day-to-day outreach, it is typically necessary to combine them.

Outreach Scholar as Group Facilitator

The role of facilitator is strongly connected to the scholarships of integration and application. The term and concept of facilitator are taken from the fields of training, professional development, and adult learning (Schwartz, 1994). Essentially, to facilitate is to make something possible, to ease a process, or orchestrate or enable a group to be effective. Andragogy stresses that adults learn best when they are not "taught" per se, but when they are provided opportunities to learn, and when their learning can be self-directed and immediately applied (Brookfield, 1986).

As bridgers, we assume the role of facilitator in guiding, and ideally transforming, groups into learning communities. The role involves creating situations in which adults (often with youth) can engage in focused dialogue based on research data as well as their own experience, and come to conclusions on their own. This role is difficult to fulfill, but rewarding when we can. At its core, being a facilitator demands the ability to create a climate of trust, a place where people feel safe to share their successes and mistakes. Many adults, for example, find it difficult to speak candidly in groups about their desire for, but lack of experience with, forging and carrying out partnerships with youth. Facilitation also requires a balancing act, an intuitive understanding of what the group requires of a facilitator, and when. At times, fulfilling this requirement means that we provide short lectures on research and theory. At other times, we facilitate discussions and action planning. Sometimes, groups request that we simply observe and serve as a sounding board.

We do not, however, adhere to the position that group facilitators should be completely neutral in all situations. We recognize that rather than being completely neutral, we are indeed advocates for promoting youth development.

When we "know"—either from our knowledge of theory, research, or practice—that the group appears to be acting on questionable assumptions, for example, we speak up and state a position.

Outreach Scholar as Action and Collaborative Researcher

Bridgers must also be able and willing to engage in research that is action-oriented and collaborative. Research data can be powerful but also threatening. Not surprisingly, we have been in situations in which community members wish to claim all rights to the research, or believe that it is their role to stipulate the research agenda to us. We have also observed, conversely, situations in which university scholars assume that ownership and the right to fashion the agenda should be left entirely to the "experts."

Achieving a balance of interests and power in collaborative research often proves complex. Most basically, we have found it necessary to listen to and respect the needs and concerns of community members, while concurrently honoring and respecting the scholarly expertise and perspective that we bring to the endeavor. The willingness to dialogue with community members is central. For example, in our work with the United Way of Greater Milwaukee, described previously, the committee members initially approached us to study the extent and reasons for high-risk behavior among youth, and what to recommend doing about it. After several meetings with the committee, we heard "between the lines" other dimensions of what stakeholders seemed to want. As we brought these ideas to the surface, articulated them, and helped give them form, a consensus slowly built regarding a set of research and policy questions that reflected the concerns of stakeholders as well as insight gained from previous research and theory. It was this consensus that led the committee (all volunteers) to support the research and dissemination process for an extended period of time.

Outreach Scholar as Disseminator

Dissemination is a key strategy for both individual and organizational change. As with other bridging roles, it is often time-consuming and needs to be done strategically. Foremost, we have learned that when pushing for systemic change, it is necessary to involve individuals at all levels. When disseminating information on youth development, we seek to ensure that the information reaches those at the highest level of the organization, such as a board of directors. The aim is to connect with those who can authorize change efforts. It is equally important to ensure breadth. If a diverse array of stakeholders, including youth, is not included, ownership for the change dissipates and change is unlikely.

Dissemination, and ultimately adoption, of research findings and new ideas is a reciprocal process, involving scholar and organization, of meaning making

(Zeldin, Camino, & Mook, 2005). It is important for us to remember that most organizational stakeholders do not have extensive experience in discussing and interpreting research-based findings. Our experience is that during the interpretation of findings, stakeholders often need to be reminded of the key research questions. Stakeholders can get excited about one or a few pieces of data, and lose sight of the big picture or the purpose of the research. We have found that organizational stakeholders appreciate guidance in the vital task of interpretation, especially when the data are focused on their own programs. They appreciate when we "refocus" them back to their key questions and when we ask probing questions that challenge them to think deeply about the data.

Successfully filling the role of disseminator ultimately revolves around considerations of time and timing. Scholars are under pressure to produce, to get the word out as quickly as possible. When working with community stakeholders and considering change for youth development, however, timing is everything. It makes little sense to present to an executive director, a board of directors, or a group of volunteers, for instance, when an organization is facing a significant programmatic or budget issue or the community is in the midst of its busy season. It is more effective, in terms of long-term utilization, to wait until stakeholders are ready to hear the information. There is, of course, the very real risk that the project will lose momentum while waiting for stakeholders to turn their attention to the research. It has been important—and a challenge—for us to find other ways to engage participants, and to keep the research project visible. In such cases, we try to keep in touch with stakeholders by sending relevant newspaper articles or brief summaries of work or issues related to youth development.

Conclusions

We believe that higher education and outreach scholars have vital contributions to make in mobilizing adults for youth development. Empirical research and scholarly knowledge offer complements to practice-based knowledge. The strategies, approaches, and roles we have described are grounded in our belief, based on the theories of Freire (1983), that learning is a critical component of change and action. In fact, the central tenets of adult learning theory overlap with the core features of community action theory. These shared features include working through the cycle of praxis, learning in collaborative groups, and grounding the work in concrete, local concerns for change (Brookfield, 1986, p. 113).

Applying outreach scholarship to mobilize adults for positive youth development, we have found, is both exciting and challenging. It is exciting to harness the power of scholarship and witness the learning and change that result. It is challenging because university outreach necessitates using a full range of scholarship, and because motivating adults to carry out behaviors consistent with their valuing of youth development principles involves a complex set of interconnected psychological and sociological forces (as volume editors Clary and Rhodes emphasize in their introduction). Further, faculty and students, as well as policy makers, agency staff, and community residents, live in different cultures with different reward systems. Collaboration must truly involve the building of multiple bridges.

In this chapter we have sought to outline the key strategies and roles of outreach to give definition and acknowledgment to the important tasks and roles of being "bridgers." We continue to struggle to learn methods of doing so. Our hope is that the university will increasingly support outreach scholars and their community partners to increase adult involvement—be it through advocacy, policy setting, youth work practice, or volunteering—in the lives of nonfamilial youth.

References

Benson, P. L. (1997). *All kids are our kids: What communities must do to raise caring and responsible children and adolescents.* San Francisco: Jossey-Bass.

Benson, P. L., Leffert, N., Scales, P. C., & Blyth, D. A. (1998). Beyond the "village" rhetoric: Creating healthy communities for children and adolescents. *Applied Developmental Science, 2,* 138–159.

Boyer, E. L. (1990). *Scholarship reconsidered: Priorities of the professoriate.* Princeton, NJ: Princeton University Press.

Bronfenbrenner, U. (1979). *The ecology of human development.* Cambridge, MA: Harvard University Press.

Brookfield, S. D. (1986). *Understanding and facilitating adult learning.* San Francisco: Jossey-Bass.

Camino, L., & Zeldin, S. (2002). From periphery to center: Pathways for youth civic engagement in the day-to-day life of communities. *Applied Developmental Science, 6,* 213–220.

Camino, L., Zeldin, S., Mook, C., & O'Connor, C. (2004). *Youth and adult leaders for program excellence: A practical guide for program assessment and action planning.* Madison: University of Wisconsin-Extension (http://www.actforyouth.net).

Camino, L., & Zeldin, S. (2005). Adults as partners in youth activism. In L. R. Sherrod, C. A. Flanagan, & R. Kassimir (Eds.), *Youth activism: An international encyclopedia.* Greenwich, CT: Greenwood.

Checkoway, B. (2001). Renewing the civic mission of the American research university. *Journal of Higher Education, 72,* 125–146.

Eccles, J., & Gootman, J. A. (Eds.). (2002). *Community programs to promote youth development.* Washington, DC: National Academies Press.

Freire, P. (1983). *Pedagogy of the oppressed* (Myra Bergman Ramos, Trans.). New York: Continuum.

Friedman, V. (2000). Action science: Creating communities of inquiry in communities of practice. In H. Bradbury & P. Reason (Eds.), *The handbook of action research* (pp. 159–170). Thousand Oaks, CA: Sage.

Hall, B. (1993). Introduction. In P. Park, M. Brydon-Miller, B. Hall, & T. Jackson (Eds.), *Voices of change: Participatory research in the United States and Canada* (pp. xii–xxii). Westport, CT: Bergin & Garvey.

Harkavy, I. (2003, November). *Service-learning and the development of democratic universities: Democratic schools and democratic good societies in the 21st century.* Keynote address, Annual International K-H Service-Learning Research Conference, University of Utah, Salt Lake City.

Hyman, J. B. (2002). Exploring social capital and civic engagement to create a framework community building. *Applied Developmental Science, 6,* 196–202.

Kirshner, B., O'Donoghue, J., & McLaughlin, M. W. (Eds.). (2002). *Youth participation: Improving institutions and communities.* San Francisco: Jossey-Bass.

Knowles, M. S. (1980). *The modern practice of adult education: From pedagogy to andragogy* (2nd ed.). Inglewood Cliffs, NJ: Cambridge Adult Education.

Lerner, R. M., & Simon, L. A .K. (Eds.). (1998). *University-community collaborations for the twenty-first century: Outreach scholarship for youth and families.* New York: Garland.

Lewin, K. (1946). Action research and minority problems. *Journal of Social Issues, 2,* 34–36.

Mattesich, P. W., & Monsey, B. R. (1997). *Community building: What makes it work.* St. Paul, MN: Amherst H. Wilder Foundation.

Myers-Walls, J. A. (2000). An odd couple with promise: Researchers and practitioners in evaluation settings. *Journal of Family Relations, 49,* 341–347.

Rhodes, J. E. (2002). *Stand by me: The risks and rewards of mentoring today's youth.* Cambridge, MA: Harvard University Press.

Rice, R. E. (1996). *Making a place for the new American scholar.* Washington, DC: American Association for Higher Education.

Scales, P. C. (with Benson, P. L., Mannes, M., Hintz, N. R., Roehlkepartain, E. C., & Sullivan, T. K.). (2003). *Other people's kids: Social expectations and American adults' involvement with children and adolescents.* New York: Kluwer Academic/Plenum.

Schon, D. (1987). *Educating the reflective practitioner.* San Francisco: Jossey-Bass.

Schwartz, R. M. (1994). *The skilled facilitator: Practical wisdom for developing effective groups.* San Francisco: Jossey-Bass.

Senge, P. M. (1990). *The fifth discipline: The art and practice of the learning organization.* New York: Doubleday.

Tschannen-Moran, M., & Hoy, W. K. (2000). A multidisciplinary analysis of the nature, meaning, and measurement of trust. *Review of Educational Research, 70,* 547–593.

Wolff, T. (2001). Community coalition building: Contemporary practice and research. *American Journal of Community Psychology, 29,* 165–172.

Zeldin, S., & Camino, L. (1999). Youth leadership: Linking research and program theory to exemplary practice. *New Designs for Youth Development, 15,* 10–15.

Zeldin, S., Camino, L., & Calvert, M. (2003). *Toward an understanding of youth in community governance: Policy priorities and research directions.* Ann Arbor: University of Michigan, Society for Research in Child Development.

Zeldin, S., Camino, L., & Mook, C. (2005). The adoption of innovation in youth organizations: Creating the conditions for youth–adult partnerships. *Journal of Community Psychology, 33*(1), 121–135.

Zeldin, S., Larson, R., & Camino, L. (Eds.). (2005). Youth and adult relationships in community programs: Diverse perspectives on best practices [Special issue]. *Journal of Community Psychology, 33*(1).

IV Mobilizing Societies of Adults

11 Public Policy: Encouraging Adult Voluntarism with Young People

Constance A. Flanagan, Nicole S. Webster, and Daniel F. Perkins

Pennsylvania State University

According to national surveys, there is broad consensus among the American public on three points concerning youth in America: (1) that the adolescent years are a difficult time in life; (2) that parents have primary responsibility for their adolescent children; and (3) that there are many other sources of influence on youth besides parents (Ad Council, 2004; Afterschool Alliance, 2003; Scales, Benson, Mannes, Tellett-Royce, & Griffin-Wiesner, 2002). Studies also indicate a willingness on the part of the public to help young people in any way possible. For example, public support for after-school programs for children and youth is high. A 2003 national bipartisan poll of voters found that 94% of those surveyed agreed that there should be organized activities or places every day for children and youth to go and to learn (Afterschool Alliance, 2003). The Ad Council (2004) reported that 97% of American adults surveyed feel that one person can make a difference in the life of a child and the majority (78%) would like to help.

There is less consensus in the public mind, however, about exactly what adults can do in their daily lives to work with youth and foster their development. Stereotypes about "youth" and pessimism about the prognosis for adults' interactions with youth keep many from making overtures toward young people. For example, in a national survey of more than 1,400 adults, Search Institute found that while the vast majority of adults believe it is important to support children and youth, less than one-third feel that adults have meaningful conversations with young people (Scales et al., 2002). How can we, as a society, deal with this apparent gap between the public's goodwill toward younger generations and adults' volunteer engagement with younger generations? We address this question by (1) documenting our historical tradition of voluntarism; (2) providing contemporary examples of voluntarism from different sectors in society; and (3) discussing policies that either impede or facilitate adult–youth interactions.

Our chapter is based on the assumption of goodwill, namely, that adults in the United States are willing and ready. This willingness to reach out and to assist youth is concordant with the American tradition of voluntarism, and we begin with a discussion of the volunteer ethos and government policies that encourage it. Next we discuss the growing phenomenon and practices of corporate responsibility and citizenship with special attention to those practices that encourage adult workers to engage in volunteer work in their communities. Following that, we focus on civil society, the bedrock of volunteer organizations in local communities. Because an exhaustive discussion is beyond the scope of this chapter, we have chosen some prototypical organizations that are venues through which adults can engage with youth. The chapter ends with a brief summary of what youth are looking for and need from relationships with adults, an example of a policy that we believe keeps that from happening, and suggestions for policies that could promote the public's mobilization on behalf of youth development.

We cast a broad net in our discussion of public policy and voluntarism, defining the latter as more than unpaid work in the volunteer sector. Rather, we consider all adult efforts, regardless of the venue and regardless of whether the adult is in a paid professional or volunteer role, to do what they can to facilitate young people's positive development.

Background: Public Policy in the United States

In contrast to many postindustrial nations, social policy in the United States has not been characterized by government intervention from the top. Notable exceptions are periods of social reform such as the Progressive Era at the turn of the last century, the New Deal under President Franklin D. Roosevelt, and President Lyndon B. Johnson's War on Poverty. In part this pattern of nonintervention is due to the importance of local control and states' rights as the tenets on which our nation was founded, and in part it reflects our commitment to individual self-reliance as an organizing principle of social and political relations. During the past decade, the lack of a national youth policy has become even more conspicuous because of the devolution of responsibility for social programs from the federal to the state and local levels and away from government to other sectors such as nongovernment and community-based organizations.

The dearth of government programs in the United States is supposed to be redressed by local community volunteer efforts, and according to recent surveys, the tradition of volunteering is strong. A national survey conducted for the Independent Sector (2001) found that 80 million Americans are engaged in some kind of voluntary activity, that is, approximately 45% of all Americans over the age of 17. "Collectively . . . volunteers donate approximately twenty billion hours of service to their communities each year. These statistics reflect a long tradition of community voluntarism in America."

In the 1830s, the French social philosopher Alexis de Tocqueville toured the United States to learn about the country's mores, practices, and what made Americans tick. He summarized these observations about the national character in a massive work titled *Democracy in America* (1848/1969). Tocqueville observed two prominent aspects of the American character: first, that Americans were rugged individualists who highly valued the opportunity to express their ideas and opinions freely; second, that the United States was a country of joiners. Americans everywhere, Tocqueville observed, were forming associations, volunteering, and addressing their local community's problems together. According to Tocqueville and to many contemporary social scientists (e.g., Putnam, 2002), our inclination to join community-based organizations benefits democracy in America because (a) it acts as a social glue, holding different generations and diverse groups in a community together; (b) it tempers our individualistic tendencies by helping us realize ways that our own self-interests are realized when we invest in a public good that benefit us all; and (c) it builds trust, which acts as a grease for social interactions and cooperation in a community.

Why do adults donate time and money to civic purposes? In their study of the factors that explain Americans' participation in collective action, Verba, Schlozman, and Brady (1995) note that giving time and money challenges the logic of rational choice theories, which hold that citizens will refrain from activity on behalf of a collective good. Because individuals reap the benefits of collective goods, whether or not they participate in the political process, it is smart for citizens to save their resources and take a free ride—that is, to let someone else do the work. "The puzzle of participation, thus, becomes: how are we to explain the fact that millions of citizens, in apparent defiance of this elegant logic, vote or take part in various kinds of voluntary activity on behalf of collective ends?" Verba et al.'s answer is that the benefit of participation includes the satisfaction gained from "doing one's share to make the community, nation, or world a better place" and that "bearing the cost becomes part of the benefit" (pp. 100–103). In other words, people feel that they reap personal benefits from the time and effort they put in. Benefits include a feeling of benevolence in helping, a sense of solidarity with other members of the public, and a sense of accomplishment in preserving public goods and services from which everyone benefits.

Policy Examples from the Public Sector

Throughout our history, local and national leaders have tried to capitalize on this spirit of volunteerism. President John F. Kennedy's was a legendary appeal to Americans that we ask not what our country could do for us but what we could do for our country. More recently, national service programs were written into the 1993 National and Community Service Trust Act, which established the Corporation for National and Community Service (CNCS). The CNCS facilitates the involvement of citizens in local, state, and national service through three programs that target different age groups: Learn and Serve America (students in grades K–12), the National Senior Service Corps (individuals over the age of 55, especially retirees), and AmeriCorps (any adult is eligible, but approximately 60% are between the ages of 16 and 24) (Corporation for National and Community Service, 2004). AmeriCorps refers to a range of local, state, and national nonprofit programs in which individuals work (typically for 1 year) on conservation, literacy, health, public safety, and other public service projects. Annually, approximately 50,000 people enroll. Members are paid a small living allowance and are eligible for an award for postsecondary education (currently set at $4,725), including the payment of education loans.

Senior Corps is a system of programs that recruits retired adults for service in local communities throughout the United States. More than 500,000 seniors lend their time, expertise, and experience in three specific programs: the Retired and Senior Volunteer Program (RSVP), Foster Grandparents, and Senior Companions. Depending on the program, the Senior Corp volunteers may receive reimbursements for meals and transportation or a small monetary stipend ranging from $2.65 to $2.75/hour. Learn and Serve supports service-learning programs in schools and communities across the United States. Service-learning engages students in grades K-12 in projects that assist communities, nonprofit organizations, U.S. territories, and Native American tribes.

Learn and Serve acts as a clearinghouse of financial and technical support and is a national funding source for academic and community-based institutions interested in community service. Eligible organizations include institutions of higher education, K–12 schools, and the nonprofit sector. The purpose of the grants (which are available for 3 years and are renewable) is to engage individuals in their community and strengthen partnerships between institutions. Grants are available for a 3-year term and are renewable, although there are certain stipulations depending on the type of institution. In addition to providing funds to support service-learning programs, Learn and Serve also provides technical support. Teachers and other education professionals, as well as community groups, can access information, such as curricula or assessment tools, to assist in their program development.

Within AmeriCorps, Learn and Serve, and Senior Corps, the CNCS has standard policies regarding volunteers. Although each policy is specific to the organization, they all address proper training, screening, and orientation for volunteers (Corporation for National and Community Service, 2004). The CNCS policy and research division develops training and recruitment pieces. As a result volunteers have a clearer vision of what is expected of them, and the organization is better able to articulate what it needs from the volunteer.

Although service-learning is a relatively new practice in schools, it is a policy that has enjoyed a rapid uptake. In the late 1990s, 64% of all public schools and 83% of public high schools provided some form of community service programs, and nearly a third of all schools had service-learning programs in place (Billig, 2000). Among first-year college students, engaging in some form of volunteer work is considered a norm. Fully 83.1% of a large representative sample of first-year college students reported that they had engaged in volunteer work during their last year of high school (Sax et al., 2003).

The results of a recent survey by the Education Commission of the States indicate the extent to which service-learning has become institutionalized in the policies of various states. Although Maryland is the only state that requires students to complete 40 hours of service-learning before graduating from high school, school systems in many cities also have this requirement. Seven states permit service-learning activities to be applied to graduation requirements (Arkansas, Connecticut, Delaware, Minnesota, Oklahoma, Rhode Island, and Wisconsin). Applying service-learning to graduation requirements can provide students with (1) a link from the curriculum to the community, (2) access to potential employers, (3) networking opportunities, (4) knowledge and skills for potential employment, (5) the ability to use the skills they learn, and (6) the opportunity to make a contribution to the community. In most cases, the service-learning requirement is integrated into a specific course and does not take the place of a class. Often the student is responsible for developing a project and presenting his or her results in a portfolio prior to graduation. Six states have included service-learning in their standards (Idaho, Michigan, Minnesota, New Jersey, New Mexico, and Vermont), and six states have authorized funding appropriations or the creation of service-learning activities and programs (Massachusetts, Minnesota, Mississippi, New Jersey, New Mexico, and Vermont) (Learning in Deed, 2003).

The institutionalization of service-learning in state-level policies reflects a shared belief about the value of connecting K–12 students with their communities. According to a survey of public school administrators conducted by the National Center for Education Statistics (Skinner & Chapman, 1999), connecting students to and helping them become active members of their communities, fostering relationships between the school and community, and increasing students' knowledge and understanding of their communities are the most important reasons that school administrators name for having service-learning programs in public schools.

Language in the states' policies alludes to adult involvement in service-learning programs. In fact, adults from teachers in the schools to professional staff and volunteers in community programs and local government are critical in developing institutional connections, working out logistics, and keeping communication flowing if service-learning projects are going to work. By reflecting together in class, teachers and students make sense of their community work and integrate it with other learning experiences. Adults also provide the mentoring and guidance that enable young people to succeed in service-learning programs. Young people actually report that they are inspired by some of the adults they encounter. When asked what they learned through their community service, youth report that positive views of "others" emerge from these contacts; for example, they realize that "there are a lot of people who care" and "there are a lot of people who are willing to help others" (Flanagan, Gill, & Gallay, 2005). In the body of research on community service, relatively little attention has been given to the fact that the adults who lead voluntary organizations, staff human service agencies, or work in public service are typically people who give of themselves for the benefit of others in their communities. From a developmental point of view, these public servants, these model citizens, could be especially inspiring in the formative years.

Furthermore, the work of adult volunteers—building connections across generations—is the means by which young people develop a sense of membership in the polity and a feeling that they are valued members of their communities. In projects that enable intergenerational community-based work, an ethic of volunteering is built up across generations. Intergenerational programs that link people under the age of 21 and those over the age of 60 through joint projects are growing at a rapid pace (Kaplan & Lawrence-Jacobson, in press). The specifics of individual programs vary widely, but the motivating force behind the intergenerational movement is a concern about age segregation and the belief that connecting across this age divide is good for individuals, groups, and society as a whole. Senior Corps is one example of an intergenerational program that matches youth mentees with senior volunteers. A program such as Senior Corps provides adults with an opportunity to serve as mentors with youth in their local communities in projects such as community gardens or reading circles. Such intergenerational programs play a very important role in maintaining our democratic society because they can be a means by which stereotypes are overcome. Whereas in everyday life, age groups tend to be segregated from one another, intergenerational programs can help reduce the stereotypes adults hold about youth, as well as the stereotypes youth hold about adults.

In research on the developmental benefits of community service, adolescents report that, by engaging in service, they "got to know and to trust the elderly" (Flanagan et al., 2005). Likewise, involving young people on community boards and in intergenerational service projects can be an excellent strategy to help undo adults' negative stereotypes about youth. Adults who see young people acting in these roles report a change in their perceptions; that is, they see young people as competent contributors to the success of the board or project. Perhaps due to youth's vitality or to the fresh viewpoint they bring to the issues, involving young people actually renews and strengthens adults' commitment to the organization and to the issues it is addressing (Wolf, 2002). Similar results are reported by Zeldin, McDaniel, Topitzes, and Calvert (2000), who found an inverse relationship between community volunteering and adults' stereotypes. In other words, when adults volunteer on community projects in which they engage as partners with youth, the negative stereotypes they held about youth (i.e., that they are disrespectful toward society, selfish, and lazy) are put to rest. Furthermore, there are personal benefits of volunteering in community-based organizations: Psychological health, well-being, and a sense of community connectedness are higher among adults who engage in such work (Zeldin et al., 2000). In summary, when adults and youth connect in joint projects, they feel good about being part of a larger community and appreciate one another as people, not as members of stereotyped groups.

Knowing that contact and interactions between generations reduce age group stereotypes is important for several reasons. First, the public's goodwill toward investing in youth is compromised by popular and negative stereotypes of "youth" as a group. These negative stereotypes are strong and resistant to change (Gilliam & Bales, 2001). Second, there are many policy matters that have the potential to pit one generation against another (e.g., Social Security and Medicare; WIC and CHIPS; Pell grants and other student loan programs). Programs that enable large numbers of older and younger generations to get to know each other should help members of each generation see such issues from the perspective of the other and thus minimize political clashes between generations over allocations of public resources.

Despite many examples of policies that enable adults to connect with young people in ways that draw on the assets of both generations, disproportionately our policies focus on young people's deficits rather than their assets and, for the most part, target individual adolescents rather than all youth. In their review of primary prevention programs for children and adolescents, Durlak and Wells (1997) found that of 150 programs, 85% focused on changing individuals and their behaviors rather than trying to change the contexts in which the young people were acting.

But new models of youth development have moved away from concentrating on deficits and focus instead on the assets that young people are to their communities. Thus, it is not surprising that involving youth in community service, community change, and organizational governance projects is becoming more common. Youth report gaining feelings of confidence that they have something of value to contribute and can begin to frame their identities around such assets rather than deficits. One example of these trends is the movement over the past decade to include youth on nonprofit boards and community collaborations. Yet, only Michigan has passed a bill (House Bill 5906, passed in 1998) that gives youth ages 16–17 the ability to be voting members on boards and community collaborations. Thus, youth for the most part are unable to engage as full partners in the decision-making process, thereby perpetuating a barrier to the development of intergenerational partnering.

Policy Examples from Civil Society

Most service-learning projects, whether they involve students in grades K–12 or in college classes, take place in local communities and rely on the institutions of civil society for their infrastructure and their means of connecting to the community. For the purposes of this discussion, civil society includes all of the nonprofits, nongovernment, and faith-based organizations that sustain community life. Typically, these organizations rely so heavily on volunteers that many would fold without them, and thus mobilizing adults to volunteer is a high priority. Because many serve the needs of young people, the safety and well-being of youth are a high priority as well. Although these goals may not seem at odds, to achieve both, the policies of nongovernment organizations have to strike a balance, requiring standards from adult volunteers without being so onerous as to scare off those volunteers.

From libraries to schools to nonprofits, most organizations require background checks of adult volunteers who will be working with youth. Indeed, following the September 11, 2001, terrorist acts and the sex scandals that have rocked the Roman Catholic Church, schools and nonprofits have adopted even tougher security policies for volunteers. For example, in some schools parents willing to volunteer in mentoring programs must provide character references and submit to a criminal background check, fingerprinting, and training (Henderson & Mapp, 2002). While the added protection may be good for the safety of children and youth, the extra effort can pose a barrier to willing adults. Another barrier may be the out-of-pocket expenses to the potential volunteer or to the organization—costs range from $5 to $50 per person (Peña, 2000). To date there is no evidence that extensive screening of volunteers prevents problems. Yet, it is hard to imagine how one would test the efficacy of background checks, since most organizations would be considered remiss in their duties if they abandoned such practices.

But organizations also have to ensure that their policies concerning volunteers do not pose a burden lest they risk losing adult volunteers. Many non-government organizations have created specific policies that address volunteerism. For example, National 4-H Council, the nonprofit partner of 4-H and the Cooperative Extension System, recommends that each state 4-H Youth Development program have a volunteer recruitment and screening process. Although there is no national standard volunteer policy, each state has developed policies regarding volunteers. The lack of a national standard is due in part to individual states' liability coverage as well as a history within 4-H of state autonomy. Common items found within state policies include state background checks (i.e., the person's name and fingerprints are run through the state troopers' database to ensure that the individual has not been convicted of a crime), volunteer orientation, and a signed volunteer commitment form. Volunteer orientation helps to allay concerns adults may have about the work for which they are signing up and creates a sense of community with other adult volunteers. Signing a volunteer commitment form, although not legally binding, can remind adults that they are making a promise to "be there" for the organization and the youth it serves.

Besides protections for young people, adult volunteers and the organizations they serve are protected by Public Law 105-19 from "frivolous, arbitrary, or capricious lawsuits" (Legal Information Institute, 2003). This law protects volunteers serving nonprofit organizations or governmental entities from being sued for harm caused by their acts or omissions if they are acting within the scope of organizational responsibilities. Federal lawmakers felt this was necessary to clarify and limit the liabilities of volunteers and keep them from being subject to unfair or unjust litigations.

Such protections for the adult volunteer and the organizations in which they volunteer are important for recruiting an adult volunteer base. They are likely to be effective if they diminish adults' anxieties about volunteering with a youth-serving organization. Knowing about the immunities guaranteed by this legislation may provide adults with peace of mind about volunteering to work with youth.

Once recruited, how is an organization's adult volunteer base sustained? Studies indicate that volunteering serves different functions for different people and is functional when the opportunity fits the individual's motivation. Whether individuals volunteer for altruistic reasons, as a social outlet, or to get to know their community better, the match between individual motivations and organizational opportunities cannot be overestimated as a factor in retaining adult volunteers in an organization (Clary & Snyder, 1999; see also Stukas, Daly, & Clary, Chapter 4, this volume). A historical look at the 4-H organization and its adult volunteer base provides a useful example of how important it is for organizations to attend to the opinions and recommendations of their volunteers.

In their book, *4-H: An American Idea,* Thomas Wessel and Marilyn Wessel (1982) chart the history of 4-H between 1900 and 1980. In the late 1950s, attrition of volunteer leaders was becoming a serious problem, with many adults dropping out after a year. When they were asked why, it became apparent that, if volunteer leaders were going to continue in their role, they wanted to feel that they were an integral part of the program and that they were not isolated, working alone in their communities. Rather, volunteers wanted to feel that there was a collective purpose to their efforts, that they were part of a larger organization with a mission that the adults believed in, an organization that supported local community efforts. To its credit, the national 4-H organization was responsive. As a result of the input from the adult volunteers, leader forums and volunteer training became part of the program. These meetings provided an opportunity for face-to-face contact in which the volunteers' commitment to the organization was renewed because they could see how the vision they believed in was shared by others.

Unfortunately, volunteer training is not as common in community-based organizations as one would expect. Indeed, most training for adults who want to work with youth has more to do with procedures to follow (e.g., how to conduct a 4-H club; what activities and projects one can do with a little sister or brother in Big Brother Big Sister programs) than with learning strategies to meet the developmental needs of youth. Organizations are trying to address this issue. For example, adult volunteers within 4-H can get comprehensive training about youth development through county and multicounty volunteer training hosted by 4-H youth development educators. In addition, 4-H provides state and multistate leadership training for adult volunteers.

Sports is another venue in which many adults volunteer their time but training for coaches is only a recent phenomenon. Lately, many community-based youth sports organizations host workshops (from 2 hours to a full day) on coaching youth. These workshops focus on increasing knowledge and understanding about the game, the code of ethics, and the rules of the particular community-based organization that is sponsoring the team, but the developmental needs of youth are rarely covered. For example, the well-respected National Youth Sports Coaches Alliance (NYSCA) hosts the most widely used volunteer training program for coaches in the nation. NYSCA has trained more than 1.8 million coaches since 1981 (National Youth Sports Coaches Alliance, 2004), primarily in the code of ethics. The highest level of training, the gold level, does address youth development and appropriate strategies for engaging youth. However, the number of volunteer coaches who actually complete the gold level training is small.

Youth-led organizations imply a new role for adults in community-based youth organizations. Rather than "leading," adults need to be in the background, monitoring, mentoring, and facilitating, but not being in charge. This does not mean that adults are unimportant to the enterprise. In fact, young people want support from adults in the form of dialogue, coaching, and providing connections to sources of institutional, community, and political power (Camino & Zeldin, 2002; Heath, 1999). However, youth envision these roles for adults within a partnering framework in which there is equality and mutual respect between the parties and where adults and youth alike play by the rules (Heath, 1994). The way in which adults interpret their authority and the rules of governance is important to the success of the organization and also helps foster democratic dispositions in the youth with whom they work.

There is consistent evidence from a host of studies about what young people want and need from adults. Contrary to stereotypes of youth who want adults out of their lives, study after study indicates that young people want to connect with adults, but also want those adults to respect them as people with thoughts and opinions of their own (Camino & Zeldin, 2002). Whether with parents, teachers, mentors, or coaches, young people seek a trusting relationship with adults who respect them. In fact, it could be argued that, of all the qualities one would look for in youth–adult relationships, trust and respect are the sine qua nons for success. As simple as this sounds, policies can impede the possibilities of adults realizing these goals. For example, evidence is mounting that zero tolerance policies in our nation's schools undercut trust between students, teachers, and school administrators. In theory, zero tolerance policies were designed as strong measures to ensure the safety of students at school. In practice, the policies are, in many cases, creating a large chasm of mistrust between students and the adults at school in whom they might confide. Why? The answer boils down to whether the policy of a school district allows the responsible adults in a school to give a young person the benefit of the doubt, in other words, to trust him or her.

Zero tolerance policies have evolved from the Federal Gun-Free Schools Act of 1994, which mandates that all states that receive federal education monies require their local education agencies to expel for at least one school year any student who has brought a weapon to school. Although the original law focused on patently dangerous behavior, such as having a gun on school property, many states have extended these laws to include a wide range of items that *could* be considered weapons. So, if a student happens to have a pocketknife in his or her backpack but has no intention of using it on people, this may or may not be considered an infraction, depending on how the state and local school district interpret the law. Furthermore, many states have extended the behaviors deemed punishable to include bringing a toy gun to school, possession of illegal substances, insubordination, and disruptive behavior (Ayers, Dohrn, & Ayers, 2001).

Many elements of the law are subject to interpretation. Whether fact or fiction, what adolescents believe their teachers or counselors will do may impede trust and communication. For example, what should a teenager do if he or she is worried that a friend is abusing illegal substances? Talk to the school counselor?

Confide in a teacher? According to research on the adage, "Friends don't let friends . . . ," adolescents who want to intervene with friends to prevent harm to the friends or to others are often willing to talk to adults but are reticent to confide in adults at school. They are convinced that the costs are too great to the friend and to the self because the adults will turn anyone who is using substances in to a higher authority, most likely the police (Gallay & Flanagan, 2002). As adolescents get older, they are less willing to confide in any adults about their friends' substance use, preferring instead to ignore the behavior or handle concerns on their own (Flanagan, Gallay, & Elek, 2005). But adults are more likely than teenagers to have knowledge about and access to professionals and programs that could help young people in trouble. Thus, policies should be designed to make it easier, not more difficult, for young people to trust and confide in adults.

Policy Examples from the Private Sector

Philanthropy from the private sector has also been a tradition in the United States, and the need for private-sector giving has increased in recent years as social welfare programs from the government have declined. Corporations, like individuals who give some of their income to charity, benefit from tax policies that encourage charitable donations by reducing the tax burden on income. Furthermore, corporate philanthropy tends to be good for the community as well as for business. Not only does it provide services, it provides a good model of how corporations that typically reap benefits from a community (in infrastructure, labor, business, profits) can show that they are reciprocating and are responsible to that community. As Vartan Gregorian (2000, quoted in Sherrod, 2003) wrote, "Businesses are . . . discovering that giving is good for business and public relations as well as for making them part of the community of responsible citizens" (p. 15). In fact, enhancing their public image as responsible citizens is one way in which individual corporations can distance themselves from the socially irresponsible and even criminal activities of some corporations.

In the past few decades, the term *corporate citizenship* has become part of our lexicon to describe the range of ways in which the private sector is acting in a socially responsible manner. Corporate citizenship can be exhibited through providing monies to local communities, goods and services, or time and expertise of company employees. In the report *The State of Corporate Citizenship in the United States* (2003), those companies surveyed felt that businesses need to be part of the solution of social problems and that they should play a very active role in education and economic development in the United States. More than 75% reported that community service and involvement were driven by internal corporate values and customer feedback (Center for Corporate Citizenship, 2003).

Corporate citizenship efforts are mobilized through committed partnerships with local and national nonprofit organizations, as well as with local, state, and federal agencies. Perhaps the most successful component of corporate citizenship has been the establishment of company volunteer programs. For example, in Ypsilanti, Michigan, engineers from Verizon partner with math teachers at the local high school, working with students in designing a computerized robot for competition in an intermural Robotics Olympics. Another example is found within the Citizen Schools in Boston. This nonprofit organization has connected middle school students with lawyers in order to expose youth to the field of law. Youth participants who are considered junior lawyers take part in mock trials that deal with issues relevant to early adolescents (Citizen Schools, 2004). The international chemical company BASF provides life training to youngsters in Brazil. Company employees work with youth ages 14–18 in two main areas, making healthy life choices and having greater exposure to cultural and social activities (BASF, 2003). Such corporate–community connections have multiple benefits. Not only do the young people directly involved benefit from the expertise of practicing professionals, those youth also see concrete connections between the kinds of free-time activities that interest them, the class work they are doing, and career paths in the real world. For the adults there are benefits as well. First of all, as most studies of volunteering find, there is a generally benevolent feeling that derives from such work. Second, the fact that the company posts the opportunity for its employees eases the time burden in finding a project match between an individual's talents and community needs. In some programs employees are compensated by the company for the time they spend on the project, thus facilitating adult volunteer work. As Verba and his colleagues noted (Verba et al., 1995), recruitment into civic work has everything to do with being in the settings where recruitment happens.

An umbrella organization that has enhanced these corporate citizenship efforts is the peer-to-peer, nonpartisan business campaign known as Business Strengthening America (BSA). BSA has helped mobilize more than 700 companies, ranging from small business to Fortune 500 corporations. The goal of the campaign is to stimulate long-lasting cultural change in the workplace that makes service to the community an even more integral part of the American business culture. Company policies and incentives have encouraged greater levels of volunteer involvement. According to the organization's 2003 *Report to the Nation,* the following have been some of the most successful strategies:

- Posting local volunteer opportunities on internal company Web sites;
- Developing or purchasing software to create company volunteer databases;
- Giving paid leave to employees to volunteer in the community;
- Establishing a volunteer policy that addresses leave and pay;
- Formalizing volunteer programs and efforts;
- Partnering with youth organizations such as Junior Achievement;
- Providing formal training to raise awareness about effective community-based partnering and volunteerism;
- Setting up volunteer councils in the company that explore opportunities for community engagement;

- Setting aside time for service events within the company (for example, Duke Energy Corporation in North Carolina dedicates the month of June to global service); and
- Having employee-run volunteer programs.

Company strategies for volunteerism run the gamut from employees' personal motivations to monetary persuasion. Employees have taken the liberty of organizing themselves to address community issues through volunteer councils that facilitate training, placement, and communication between volunteers and program sites. Databases make it possible for volunteers to seek potential sites (i.e., youth centers, schools, or after-school settings) without doing the search on their own. Ultimately, the task of finding a site that caters to youth is facilitated by employee-managed databases and company volunteer centers.

Company policies and methods can be used to entice employees to volunteer for a wide range of community services, including service to youth. Support ranging from training to volunteer centers provides sustainability within the company. In addition, long-term partnerships between companies and youth-serving organizations and schools exact commitments that the company must honor. Individual employees help the company fulfill that obligation; youth benefit from the engagement of adults; and the company's relationship with the public is enhanced.

Whatever the mechanism that employers use, adults are more likely to volunteer if volunteering is a norm in the places where they spend time. According to national studies, civic participation among adults is strongly related to recruitment through one's social networks (Verba et al., 1995). Also, the likelihood of being recruited is much higher if adults are in environments such as workplaces, faith-based settings, or educational institutions where there are norms of volunteering and community participation.

Conclusions

In *Bowling Alone,* Robert Putnam (2000) points to the parallels between the conditions of life in the United States today and those at the turn of the last century. These include disparities in wealth, growing corporate power, waves of immigration, massive changes in the demographics of the population, new forms of technology, commerce, and communication, and a restructured workplace. At the turn of the last century, optimism about the potential for social change was balanced by pessimism about seemingly intractable social ills. The civic culture was revitalized, however, as Americans created and joined an unprecedented number of voluntary associations, not the least of which were new youth organizations. In less than a decade (1901–1910), most of the nationwide youth organizations that were to dominate the 20th century were founded— the Boy and Girl Scouts, Campfire Girls, 4-H, Boys Clubs and Girls Clubs, Big Brothers and Big Sisters, and the American Camping Association (Putnam, 2000, p. 393).

If our goal as a nation is to facilitate adults' engagement with youth, we must look to new signs of civic inventiveness. Intersectoral partnering—partnerships between government, business, and civil society—is one such example and can be a means whereby society makes it both clearer and easier for adults to become engaged with young people. Some of the examples of corporate–school partnerships we discussed under corporate citizenship would fit the definition.

The advantage of intersector partnering is, first of all, the synergy created by connecting the resources and energies from multiple sectors. From a recruitment standpoint alone, this model would benefit from the ecologies of the various settings. Adults can and do play roles in multiple sectors (in the private sector, in faith communities, in families) but still not find smooth ways to parlay their contributions in one sector into another.

Intersectoral partnerships can maximize recruitment opportunities. If a school and corporation form a partnering relationship, the opportunities for adults to connect to youth in their community are expanded. That is, adults who would like to make a difference in the lives of youth, and are willing to do so, are presented with a clear way to act on their motives. Furthermore, they are not acting alone but rather are part of a team effort, part of a company that has made a (collective) commitment. Such team efforts raise the bar on volunteering by making it a norm for other workers in the organization to emulate.

In the end, issues that concern the public, such as how to increase the number of adults volunteering to promote growth and development in the younger generation, will not be solved by policy makers but by the public's will and inventiveness. As Robert Reich (1988), secretary of labor in the Clinton administration, suggests, policy makers need to take advantage of the power of public ideas:

> The core responsibility of those who deal in public policy—elected officials, administrators, policy analysts—is not simply to discover as objectively as possible what people want for themselves and then to determine and implement the best means of satisfying these wants. It is also to provide the public with alternative visions of what is desirable and possible, to stimulate deliberation about them, provoke a reexamination of premises and values, and thus to broaden the range of potential responses and deepen society's understanding of itself. (pp. 3–4)

References

Ad Council. (2004). *Turning point: Engaging the public on behalf of children*. New York: Author. Retrieved June 25, 2004, from http://www.adcouncil.org/pdf/commitment_children_turning_point_report.pdf

Afterschool Alliance. (2003, December). *Across demographic and party lines, American clamor for safe, enriching afterschool programs*. Washington, DC: Author. Retrieved March 23, 2004, from http://www.afterschoolalliance.org/poll_jan_2004.pdf

Ayers, W., Dohrn, B., & Ayers, R. (2001). *Zero tolerance: Resisting the drive for punishment in schools*. New York: Free Press.

BASF. (2003). *Corporate report: Social responsibility*. Retrieved September 25, 2004, from http://berichte.basf.de/en/2003/unternehmensbericht/

Billig, S. H. (2000). Research on K–12 school-based service learning: The evidence builds. *Phi Delta Kappan*, May, 658–664.

Business Strengthening America. (2003). *Report to the nation*. Washington, DC: Author.

Camino, L. A., & Zeldin, S. (2002). Everyday lives in communities: Discovering citizenship through youth-adult partnerships. *Applied Developmental Science, 6*(4), 213–220.

Center for Corporate Citizenship. (2003). *Community involvement index 2003*. Boston: Author. Available online at http://www.bcccc.net

Citizen Schools. (2004, June 23). Boston middle school "apprentice" from Citizen Schools 8th Grade Academy named finalist in contest to gavel in July's Democratic National Convention in Boston. Retrieved September 1, 2004, from http://www.citizenschools.org/aboutcs/DNCGavel. cfm

Clary, E. G., & Snyder, M. (1999). The motivations to volunteer: Theoretical and practical considerations. *Current Directions in Psychological Science, 8*, 156–159.

Corporation for National and Community Service. (2004, June). Fact sheet: Corporation for National and Community Service. Retrieved September 9, 2004, from http://www.nationalservice.org/ news/factsheets/04CNCS.pdf

Durlak, J. A., & Wells, A. M. (1997). Primary prevention programs for children and adolescents: A meta-analytic review. *American Journal of Community Psychology, 25*, 115–152.

Flanagan, C. A., Gallay, L., & Elek, E. (2005). Friends don't let friends . . . or do they? Developmental and gender differences in intervening in friends' ATOD use. *Journal of Drug Education, 34*(4), 351–371.

Flanagan, C. A., Gill, S., & Gallay, L. S. (2005). Social participation and social trust in adolescence: The importance of heterogeneous encounters. In A. Omoto (Ed.), *Processes of community change and social action* (pp. 149–166). Mahwah, NJ: Erlbaum.

Gallay, L. S., & Flanagan, C. A. (2002, April). *Social responsibility and young people: Can peers be allies in prevention?* Poster session presented at the biennial meeting of the Society for Research on Adolescence, New Orleans, LA.

Gilliam, F. D., & Bales, S. N. (2001, July). *Strategic frame analysis: Reframing America's youth. Social Policy Report, 15*(3). A report of the Society for Research in Child Development. Available online at http://www.srcd.org/sprv15n3.pdf

Heath, S. B. (1994). The project of learning from the inner-city youth perspective. *New Directions for Child Development, 63*, 25–34.

Heath, S. B. (1999). Dimensions of language development: Lessons from older children. In A. Masten (Ed.), *Cultural processes in child development: The Minnesota Symposium on Child Psychology* (Vol. 29, pp. 59–75). Mahwah, NJ: Erlbaum.

Henderson, A. T., & Mapp, K. L. (2002). *A new wave of evidence: The impact of school, family, and community connections on student achievement*. Austin, TX: National Center for Family and Community Connections with Schools, Southwest Educational Development Laboratory. Retrieved March 13, 2003, from http://www.sedl.org/connections/resources/ evidence.pdf

Independent Sector. (2001). *Giving and volunteering in the United States: Key Findings*. Retrieved December 1, 2004, from http://www.independentsector.org/PDFs/ GVO1keyfind.pdf

Kaplan, M., & Lawrence-Jacobson, A. (in press). Intergenerational programs and practices. In L. Sherrod, C. A. Flanagan, R. Kassimir, & A. Syvertsen (Eds.), *Youth activism: An international encyclopedia*. Westport, CT: Greenwood.

Learning in Deed. (2003). *The service-learning policy toolkit*. Battle Creek, MI: W. K. Kellogg Foundation.

Legal Information Institute. (2003, July 24). *Title 42—The Public Health and Welfare. Chapter 139: Volunteer protection*. Retrieved September 9, 2004, from http://assembler.law.cornell.edu/ uscode/html/uscode42/usc_sup_01_42.html

National Youth Sports Coaches Alliance. (2004, June). Volunteer coaches training program. Retrieved June 30, 2004, from http://www.nays.org/IntMain.cfm?Page=1&Cat=3

Peña, D. C. (2000). Parent involvement: Influencing factors and implications. *Journal of Educational Research, 94*, 42–54.

Putnam, R. D. (2000). *Bowling alone: The collapse and revival of American community*. New York: Simon & Schuster.

Reich, R. B. (1988). Introduction. In R. B. Reich (Ed.), *The power of public ideas* (pp. 1–12). Cambridge, MA: Harvard University Press.

Sax, L. J., Astin, A. W., Lindhom, J. A., Korn, W. S., Saenz, V. B., & Mahoney, K. M. (2003). *The American freshman: National norms for 2003*. Los Angeles: University of California, Higher Education Research Institute.

Scales, P. C., Benson, P. L., Mannes, M., Tellett-Royce, N., & Griffin-Wiesner, J. (2002). *Grading grownups 2002: How do American kids and adults relate? Key findings from a national study*. Minneapolis, MN: Search Institute. Available online at http://www.search-institute.org/norms/gg2002.pdf

Sherrod, L. S. (2003). Philanthropy, science, and social change: Corporate and operating foundations as engines of applied developmental science. In D. Wertlieb, F. Jacobs, & R. M. Lerner (Eds.), *Handbook of applied developmental science: Vol. 3. Promoting positive child, adolescent, and family development through research, policies, and programs* (pp. 385–402). Thousand Oaks, CA: Sage.

Skinner, R., & Chapman, C. (1999). *Service-learning and community service in K–12 public schools* (NCES Statistical Brief 1999–043).Washington, DC: U.S. Department of Education, National Center for Education Statistics.

Tocqueville, A. C. de (1969). *Democracy in America* (J. P. Mayer, Ed.; G. Lawrence, Trans.). Garden City, NY: Doubleday. (Original work published 1848)

Verba, S., Schlozman, K. L., & Brady, H. E. (1995). *Voice and equality: Civic voluntarism in American politics*. Cambridge, MA: Harvard University Press.

Wessel, T. R., & Wessel, M. (1982). *4-H. An American idea, 1900-1980: A history of 4-H*. Chevy Chase, MD: National 4-H Council.

Wolf, M. (2002, July). *Young people on boards and committees: American and Australian experiences*. Surry Hills, New South Wales: NSW Commission for Children and Young People. Retrieved May 22, 2003, from http://www.kids.nsw.gov.au/files/wolftranscript.pdf

Zeldin, S., McDaniel, A. K., Topitzes, D., & Calvert, M. (2000). *Youth in decision-making: A study on the impacts of youth on adults and organizations*. Takoma Park, MD: The Innovation Center. Retrieved February 22, 2001, from http://www.atthetable.org/handout.asp?id=18

12 Lessons from Research on Social Marketing for Mobilizing Adults for Positive Youth Development

Sameer Deshpande and Michael Basil

University of Lethbridge

There is an urgent need to move from a theoretical understanding of youth development to practical strategies and procedures (Benson, 2003). The present chapter introduces readers to one of the social change tools, social marketing, and attempts to move "the developmental needle" (Benson, 2003, p. 214) of the field in the forward direction. Because of their emphasis on customer orientation, social marketing principles could be applied to understand and satisfy the needs of inactive adults and, by offering them attractive opportunities and lowered barriers, promote their involvement in youth development activities.

This chapter discusses the conceptual foundations of social marketing as well as practical applications that can be used to mobilize adult involvement in youth development initiatives. To illustrate these social marketing concepts, we present a case study of the Kansas Initiative (see the Appendix), two mini-case studies in the text (the Green Ribbon Kid Friendly Award and the Big Brothers Big Sisters and Footstar Athletic Alliance), and numerous other examples. We hope this chapter will serve as an idea-generating device for future social marketing efforts to mobilize adults.

Social Marketing and Youth Development

Social marketing can be defined as "the use of marketing principles and techniques to influence a target audience to voluntarily accept, reject, or abandon a behavior for the benefit of individuals, groups, or society as a whole" (Kotler, Roberto, & Lee, 2002, p. 5). In other words, social marketing attempts to manage behavior by offering benefits and reducing costs in exchange for the desirable behavior (Rothschild, 1999). Social marketing has been used in a variety of contexts such as promoting alternative transportation to reduce driving after drinking, safe sex behaviors, increased fruit and vegetable intake, breast cancer screening, and the use of environmentally friendly products. In social sectors, the term *marketing* is sometimes negatively perceived. This could be caused when questionable applications of marketing become confused with the technique itself. While the technique remains more or less the same, it can be applied in a variety of commercial as well as social contexts. When marketing is applied to a social problem, it provides managers with the tools to persuade individuals to change their behavior, resulting in the achievement of social change goals.

The marketing approach can be contrasted with two other approaches to social change: education and law (Rothschild, 1999). *Education* attempts to elicit behaviors using informational messages. Education informs "but cannot deliver benefits," and thus in order to be effective, "education requires the target to initiate the quest for the benefit and solicit voluntary compliance" (p. 25). *Law* "involves the use of coercion to achieve behavior change in a nonvoluntary manner (e.g., military conscription) or to threaten with punishment for noncompliance or inappropriate behavior (e.g., penalties for littering)" (p. 25). Law can also influence transactions "through free market mechanism ... (by the use of price subsidies or increases via taxes)" (p. 25). The third social change strategy (force of law) is not described further in the chapter because legal strategies do not apply in the present context of adult involvement.

A program manager can decide which strategy is the most appropriate method for achieving social change by examining the target's motivation, opportunity, and ability to enact the behavior (Rothschild, 1999). Based on these criteria, potential target individuals can then be divided into homogeneous segments. This process of segmenting the market is one of the core concepts of social marketing and is described in more detail later in the chapter. If people are motivated, find opportunity in the environment, and are able but lack awareness about the benefits of the behavior, an information-only education campaign is more suitable. However, if people perceive a lack of ability or opportunity, marketing is more suitable. Although we focus on a program manager deciding on a social marketing approach for individuals in that target group, in other cases, a group or coalition of organizations is the focus. To the extent that social marketing involves coordinating the efforts of several organizations, then a similar process is often followed.

In the case of mobilizing adults in youth development, research indicates that women, people over 35, and those affiliated with faith or educational institutions are more likely to volunteer in mentoring programs (Scales, Benson, & Roehlkepartain, 2000). These individuals are already motivated and *prone* to volunteer. If the goal is to maintain the level of participation among individuals from this group who are already performing the behavior, one could use the education approach by sending reminders and/or by appreciating their efforts. The fact that some individuals from this group, although motivated and prone to volunteer, will not be currently active in youth development activities may be due to their lack of awareness. If the goal of the campaign is to attract such individuals, one could take an education approach by sending awareness messages.

Single people and young adult men, however, are less likely to volunteer (Scales et al., 2000). Even though these individuals show positive beliefs, such as "It is important to mentor youth," they report a perceived lack of ability ("I don't have time to help kids") or opportunity to mentor ("Parents may not want me to mentor their kids") (Roehlkepartain, Scales, Roehlkepartain, & Rude, 2002). These costs often prevent them from helping (Scales et al., 2000; Scales, Benson, & Mannes, 2002). When people are unable to behave because of insufficient opportunity for the behavior or inadequate ability to perform the behavior (Tierney, Grossman, & Resch, 1995), a strictly educational effort (just sending messages) would not be effective. In these cases, the application of marketing practices would be necessary. The marketing approach could increase the rate of participation through a variety of means, including offering alternatives, promoting benefits, providing incentives, and lowering costs.

At this point a social marketer would suggest examining the target. If the goal of the campaign is to maintain the number of volunteers at current levels or to attract more of the prone-to-volunteer individuals, an education campaign is suggested. However, if the goal is to increase the variety of volunteers, the marketing approach is in order. The basis of the marketing approach—what it is and why it works—is explained below.

Core Ideas of Social Marketing

Customer Orientation

One of the fundamental concepts of marketing is to take a customer-centric point of view (Kohli & Jaworski, 1990). All activities revolve around target individuals, communities, and organizations. The case study of the Kansas Initiative serves as an example of a program that made use of this customer orientation to enable people to help. Starting with formative research, in which an attempt was made to understand who was inclined to participate and who was not, what barriers they faced, what media messages they would respond to, and, finally, what the outcome of their behaviors would be, the focus on target individuals was central to the campaign.

Social marketing asks that we discover the target costs and benefits to performing a behavior. These may be rooted in the psychological qualities—the motivations, beliefs, and values—of a target individual. By identifying the costs and benefits to the audience, successful marketing then determines and offers the best possible means of satisfying the target's needs or wants. For example, a youngster will be more successful in selling lemonade when people are thirsty. Similarly, a volunteer program will be more successful when it satisfies the need for self-actualization. In other words, social marketing addresses the question, "What's in it for me?"

Research

Although nonprofit agencies almost always face time and money con-straints, it could be penny-wise but pound-foolish to attempt any behavioral initiative without doing sound research. The research need not always be ex-pensive, formal, or even time-consuming, but it is important to gather some background understanding of the behavior itself: who is doing it, what bene-fits they accrue from performing the desired behavior, and who is not doing it. Research ought to be conducted during all three stages: formative, pretest, and outcome evaluation. The Kansas Initiative conducted formative research to understand the costs of keeping adults in Kansas from becoming involved. It also conducted pretest research to assess the attractiveness of messages before releasing them in the mass media.

Segmenting and Targeting the Market

There are often enough similarities in people that they can be segmented into groups. These similarities can be their affiliations, costs, current behaviors, proneness to change behavior, competition, needs, or desired rewards. Segmen-tation helps us identify the most receptive audience and then facilitates interven-tions that address issues common to members within each group. For example, one approach to identifying the most receptive individuals would be to segment members of a market by their motivation, opportunity, and ability. The resulting three segments from this activity were presented earlier in the chapter. To cite an-other example, the Kansas Initiative segmented communities by their readiness to change as assessed by noting already ongoing activities around children's issues in each community.

Once segments are formed, the marketer carries out the targeting exercise. Targeting occurs when the marketer chooses which segment or segments to focus on in order to achieve the marketing objectives. Then, resources and campaigns are allocated to these segments. This enables social marketers to maximize suc-cess with limited resources (Andreasen, 1995). As per the earlier segmentation example, to increase the volunteer pool in the society, social change agents may focus on more willing individuals such as women or people over 35, or on less willing individuals such as young adults or single people.

It is more common to segment and target at the individual level. However, segmenting and targeting can also be accomplished using existing organizations or government agencies. The Kansas Initiative targeted local groups such as churches where adults could engage in positive interactions with youth.

Exchange

Another fundamental marketing concept is that of exchange (Bagozzi, 1975). That is, marketing requires a two-way exchange of something considered valuable to each party (Siegel & Doner, 1998, p. 29). Marketers offer benefits, reduce costs, and satisfy needs. In return, the target individuals undertake the behavior. The more attractive and immediate the benefits and lower the costs, the more likely the behavior. In commercial marketing, the youngster exchanges a glass of lemonade for money. Social marketers should ensure that the benefits are as concrete as lemonade is to a thirsty person. In an adult-mobilizing social marketing campaign, this may require the development of activities that may satisfy personal needs for satisfaction, happiness, and enhanced self-esteem of the participating adults.

Competitor Analysis and Product Positioning

To marketers, competition consists of "forces trying to get the consumer to behave in a different, and often opposite, direction" (Dahl, Gorn, & Weinberg, 1997, p. 174). All possible alternative behaviors compete with the desired one. Understanding which forms of competition the target is facing is critical to achieving success. Competition analysis helps marketers position their product relative to that of competitors and make it attractive in the target's mind. "The aim of positioning is to satisfy the target segment's need...better than others" (Kotler & Roberto, 1989, p. 41).

In the case of adult involvement with youth initiatives, competition can be any alternative activity, such as relaxing, watching television, or spending time with friends (V. Bothner, personal communication, February 2004). In most cases these are likely the bigger threats to involvement. The desirable behavior of mentoring could then be positioned as fun, easy, and popular (Smith, 1999)—feelings normally associated with the competing activities of watching television or spending time with peers, as well as self-actualizing (a benefit not normally associated with the competing behaviors).

The Marketing Mix

The marketing mix or marketing strategy enables the marketer to achieve campaign goals and objectives. This strategy consists of four elements: product, price, place, and promotion. Marketers believe that these "four different sets of factors must be in place before bottom-line behaviors will take place" (Andreasen, 1995, p. 15).

From the target market's perspective, the "four Ps" strategy can be understood in terms of costs versus benefits (Rothschild, 2002). A social marketer offers benefits (product strategy), reduces costs (pricing strategy), ensures convenience (placement strategy), and explains these issues to the audience in a compelling manner (promotion strategy).

Product

Contrary to common perception, the product (not its promotion) is the most important P in the marketing mix. A product is a complex bundle of benefits offered to the market to satisfy some target need (Kotler & Armstrong, 2001,

p. 294). In the present context, *product* represents the benefits of satisfaction, happiness, or enhanced self-esteem that adults may derive by developing assets or by building a safer community (Angus Reid Group, 2000; Tierney et al., 1995). Other benefits include the intrinsic rewards adults may gain by being appreciated by a youth, the youth's family, or the organization. Since the target individual gains benefits in return for desired behavior, the product in social marketing facilitates the exchange mechanism (Rothschild, 2002).

Products or benefits could be offered by promoting either structured or unstructured programs. Organizations such as Big Brothers Big Sisters of America (BBBSA) and the YMCA offer a structured mentoring program with well-defined procedures and steps to interact with youth. By creating such programs, the program manager introduces an alternative in the environment that facilitates the enabling of target behavior. On the other hand, the Kansas Initiative offered benefits by promoting behaviors that were largely unstructured in nature.

Product, or the bundle of benefits, can be offered in the form of any tangible objects or services that support and facilitate the target audience's behavior (Kotler et al., 2002, p. 195). In general, tangible products are easier to promote than intangible ones because "they provide opportunity to brand, and create more attention, appeal and memorability for target audiences" (Kotler & Roberto, 1989, p. 156). Hence it is worthwhile to develop products that are more tangible, even if such a natural alternative is not readily available (Kotler et al., 2002).

Customers also react more positively when products deliver observable benefits over a short duration. For example, organizations targeted by the Colorado Initiative (Colorado Trust, 2002, 2003) that integrated assets in their workplace witnessed enhanced organizational effectiveness. These observable benefits may have contributed to the success of the initiative. However, when such benefits are not associated with the behavior, the social marketer may offer financial or nonfinancial incentives.

In social marketing, *incentives* can enhance product benefits and make the behavior more attractive (Rothschild, 2002). Incentives can take the form of monetary discounts (e.g., a 50% discount on basketball court rentals), free goods (e.g., athletic equipment), or rewards (e.g., the chance of entering a lottery to win a large-screen TV). These incentives can provide extra motivation for the behavior. For the reluctant, a movie ticket or college credit in exchange for spending time with or mentoring youth may provide that extra pull that can spur the desired action. The Coastside Collaborative for Children (see Sidebar 1) in California presents awards (green ribbons) to youth-friendly businesses. In this case, youth seek to offer better behavior in exchange for youth-friendly attitudes and service from businesses.

Price

In the social marketing context, *price* is the cost involved in undertaking the behavior and acquiring the product benefits. Cost to the target could be tangible (monetary) or intangible (time, inconvenience, social risk). Price affects

---

Sidebar 1. The Green Ribbon Kid Friendly Award

(Contributed by and published with permission from Susan Alvaro, executive director, Coastside Collaborative. This example highlights the importance of incentives to motivate target audiences to change their behaviors.)

The Green Ribbon Kid Friendly Award is a program run by the Coastside Collaborative in the Mid-Coast community of San Mateo County in California. During the annual "Coastside Youth Summit" in 1999, high school and middle school participants addressed the issue of youth being treated without respect by local businesses, which would only allow groups of three or fewer teens to enter at a time, required backpacks to be left on the street, and watched all teens carefully. The youth felt it was unfair that all teens were treated like criminals just because they were young. After discussion, it was decided that the approach of presenting a "Kid Friendly Award" to businesses that were nice to teens might yield good results.

With nominations from local adolescents and teens, the Green Ribbon Committee now gives the award to deserving local businesses and services. The recipients are then presented with a green ribbon window decal and a certificate of achievement proclaiming their support and understanding of youth. The "Kid Friendly" decal shows that the business is in fact *Kid Friendly*, and the awardees are mentioned in both the local newspaper and the Chamber of Commerce newsletter. Since 2000, more than 30 businesses and three teachers have received the award. Youth report that, given a choice, they and their parents will support businesses with the "Kid Friendly" decal over ones without, and that they are less inclined to be rowdy or disrespectful in businesses that treat youth right. The business community has shown enthusiasm and desire to win this award as its members see the benefits of increased sales and improved behavior from teenagers.

---

the ability to enact the behavior (e.g., it is difficult to dedicate 4 hours a week for mentoring) (Kotler & Roberto, 1989). Price can also alter the demand for the social product (Ciszewski & Harvey, 1994; Davies & Agha, 1997), since combining a weak product (lower benefits) with a higher price reduces the likelihood of product adoption and the resulting behavior change (Weinreich, 1999).

In addition to offering benefits, successfully identifying and overcoming costs faced by the target audience to enact behavior also enhances the effectiveness of a social marketing campaign. Barriers could be reduced by offering relevant programs, by lowering the monetary price, by reducing inconvenience, and/or by addressing the poor perceptions through promotion messages. An example of reducing cost by developing relevant programs is discussed here. Attempts to reduce inconvenience and address poor perceptions are examined in the discussions of *place* and *promotion*, respectively.

Programs can be developed that reduce costs. For example, to overcome limited time and availability, BBBSA has developed an in-school mentoring program (a 9-month, 1-hour-a-week commitment). This works well with employers, who are more likely to donate employee time if it is limited to 1 hour a week, and with college students because they are normally available only during those months.

Place

Place describes the distribution method by which the social product is made available to the target individuals. The Kansas Initiative considered place as any location or opportunity where adults could interact with youth. These included public parks, churches, and schools. A tangible social product could be made available by using the traditional distribution system of retailers and wholesalers. For an intangible product, however, place is less clear-cut (Weinreich, 1999): another benefit of a tangible over an intangible social product. For example, when benefits for safe sex behavior are offered in tangible form (condoms), the product could be made available through wholesalers and retailers that traditionally sell condoms. The intangible product cannot be similarly distributed.

A good analysis of existing habits and perceptions of target individuals (Weinreich, 1999) helps marketers decide on the most appropriate placement strategies. Having the appropriate placement by being in the right place and at the right time (in terms of hours, flexibility, and facilities) reduces monetary and nonmonetary costs and thus offers the target convenience to undertake the behavior. For example, BBBSA addresses place cost by offering mentoring programs using telephone and Internet technologies. In this case, the place becomes the home or office where adults can contact youth conveniently, without the effort of traveling.

Promotion

According to Kotler and Zaltman (1971), "Promotion is the communication-persuasion strategy and tactics that will make the product familiar, acceptable, and even desirable to the target" (p. 7). Because of its visibility, advertising is often mistakenly perceived as comprising the whole of social marketing. Social marketers do carry out a great deal of promotion. However, the basis of the message is usually promoting the product as well as addressing price and place issues for the target segment. Given this focus, it is critical to assess target needs; develop a product; understand its positioning, price, and place; and only then allow the promotion campaign to evolve.

Among other approaches, a promotion campaign can be employed to focus on a benefit-based approach or a cost reduction approach. The "One Million Matches by 2010" public service announcement (PSA) campaign by BBBSA illustrates the benefit-based approach because it highlights the benefit that mentoring a child can be fun and rewarding for everyone (Ad Council, 2004). An example of a cost reduction campaign is found in the Kansas Initiative campaign.

Formative research conducted by the initiative revealed that individuals reported two important barriers to participating in youth development activities: the belief that it would take too much time and the belief that small amounts of time with children would not make a significant difference in their lives. The communication campaign addressed these barriers by promoting the promise that small acts by adults could make a difference in children's lives. The Kansas Initiative communicated this message with the slogan "Take a second. Make a difference." This simple message resonated with the audience and addressed relevant concerns.

Marketers employ a variety of promotional tools to carry their messages to target individuals. These include both mass media and nonmedia options. Mass media options include paid and unpaid advertising, public relations, and sales promotion. Social marketers use several media to promote their behaviors. Traditionally these media include print (newspapers and magazines), electronic (television, radio, interactive media), and outdoor (billboards, cinema houses) formats. However, social marketers also employ several nonmedia options such as organizing community-based communication campaigns, including interpersonal communication as well as distributing printed materials (brochures) and special promotional items (T-shirts). Social marketers do not necessarily employ mass media options to promote their messages. Whenever appropriate, it is likely more useful to employ nonmedia options. Marketers integrate these promotion tools and media options to achieve efficiency, synergy, and higher effectiveness (Schultz, Tannenbaum, & Lauterborn, 1993).

Marketers usually tailor their messages to specific target groups based on their psychological and sociological makeup. Tailoring is greatly facilitated by media options such as cable TV, specialty magazines, and the interactive media.

Community-Based Approach

As noted earlier, in addition to mass media, social marketers employ a variety of community-based interventions to promote desirable behaviors. Apart from changing individual behaviors, community-based programs also focus on "modifying community structures, processes, and policies" (Baker & Brownson, 1999, pp. 8–9). These community-based strategies allow marketers to tailor an approach that will meet community and individual needs, and to provide opportunities to local communities to influence program development, implementation, and evaluation (Baker & Brownson, 1999, p. 9).

The Colorado Initiative illustrates the example of a community-based campaign (Colorado Trust, 2002, 2003). In addition to media efforts, Assets for Colorado Youth engaged organizations through presentations and training, by providing grants to facilitate the integration of youth initiatives, by culturally adapting asset integration in work processes within Latino and Spanish-language communities, and by strategically targeting policy influencers such as leaders in schools, youth-serving organizations, and government agencies.

Campaign effectiveness can be enhanced by tying community initiatives with mass media campaigns, since both activities complement each other. Media can promote ideas and behaviors to large audiences (breadth of dissemination), while community initiatives can reach specific individuals and communities (depth of dissemination). For example, in the Kansas Initiative, media ads and public relations efforts were employed to (a) increase public awareness about benefits of developmental assets and (b) publicize the community-based initiatives. On the other hand, community efforts helped sustain the effects of media campaigns.

Alliances

It is not unusual for organizations to form strategic partnerships with *publics* that share common goals (Andreasen, 1995). Publics include corporations (BBBSA with Footstar Athletic—see Sidebar 2), ad agencies (BBBSA with the Advertising Council), the media (offering free time or space for PSAs), and other nonprofit organizations. Alliances with commercial outfits offer numerous benefits to nonprofits such as raising funds, reaching otherwise inaccessible sections of society, and implementing the marketing mix more effectively (see Sidebar 2) but can also expose them to various dangers (Deshpande & Hitchon, 2002). Sometimes, partnerships with commercial organizations evoke negative feelings among target individuals, especially among donors. Further, when corporate partners receive negative publicity, target perceptions of nonprofits turn negative as well (Deshpande & Hitchon, 2002).

Summarizing the Discussion

Until now we have discussed ways of understanding the target market, segmenting the target, and determining appropriate social change strategies, followed by discussion of core social marketing concepts that were illustrated with examples. This discussion is summarized in Sidebar 3. Section 1 summarizes the discussion of segmenting the target market as a first step in the process and, based on individuals' motivation, opportunity, and ability, proposes an approach to determine the appropriate social change strategy. For example, to convince segment 3 individuals to increase participation, a marketing strategy is considered appropriate.

In section 2, the core concepts of social marketing, along with examples, are summarized. This summary is presented in the form of a strategic marketing process (as proposed by Andreasen, 1995) that social marketers follow to ensure campaign success. This process places customers at the center of all the steps and is *continuous, iterative, and upward* (Smith, 1993). The process includes (1) conducting extensive background analysis of target individuals, competition, and stakeholders; (2) setting marketing goals and objectives that the campaign is

---

Sidebar 2. The Big Brothers Big Sisters of America (BBBSA) and Footstar Athletic Marketing Alliance

(This case describes the benefits to a nonprofit organization from creating a marketing alliance with a commercial outfit; BBBSA, 2004.)

Since 2000, Footstar Athletic, a footwear retail company, and BBBSA have been running a partnership at national, regional, and local levels in which Footstar and its two concepts, Footaction and Just For Feet, have raised over $1 million for BBBSA through their annual in-store fund-raiser, the Add-A-Buck campaign. During the holidays, Footaction and Just For Feet customers are asked to add a dollar to their purchases to make a *Big Difference* in the life of a child. Footstar donates these proceeds to BBBSA in addition to donating employee time to run the program. Not only has BBBSA gained financially, it has also been able to raise awareness about its traditional and school-based mentoring programs. This effort has helped create awareness about how people can make a difference by getting involved as volunteers.

In May 2003, Footstar Athletic Recruitment Nights were launched in stores. The purpose of the Recruitment Nights was to create a community event within Footaction and Just For Feet stores where associates and the local BBBSA agency recruit volunteers to become "Bigs." After just five market events, more than 600 Bigs have already been recruited. These Recruitment Nights (usually held midweek) also benefit the retail locations through additional sales on normally slow days, thus creating a win-win situation for both partners.

In addition to the Recruitment Nights, Footstar Athletic also rolled out the BBBSA School Based Mentoring program for its more than 800 store managers and field management team members. These associates are given the opportunity to mentor a child at a local school once a week on company time.

In 2004, Footaction and Just For Feet stores also invited local BBBSA agencies and their matches to participate in over seven store-opening celebrations. At these events, the agencies were presented with a $1,000 donation, and the matches who attended were moved to the front of the line to be greeted by the professional athletes and celebrities in attendance.

Adapted with permission.

---

expected to achieve in the forthcoming period and determining marketing strategy (positioning, product, price, place, and promotion) to achieve these goals and objectives; (3) establishing marketing procedures and benchmarks to determine the success of the campaign; (4) testing the effectiveness of key program elements; (5) implementing the strategy in the real world; and (6) monitoring the program progress by conducting outcome evaluation research (Andreasen, 1995, pp. 95–96).

Sidebar 3. Review of Social Marketing Concepts	
Steps	**Brief description or example**
SECTION 1	
<u>Segment</u>: Use formative research to divide the target population into homogeneous groups based on willingness, level of motivation, and perceptions about barriers.	In this case, likely segments include individuals who are: 1. Already involved 2. Prone to volunteer but unaware 3. Unwilling or unable to volunteer
<u>Determine appropriate social change tools</u> Segment 1: Education—reminders Segment 2: Education—awareness Segment 3: Marketing	Employ appropriate social change strategies. <u>Education</u>: Informational messages. <u>Marketing</u>: Offering benefits and reducing costs.
SECTION 2	
<u>Formative research</u>: Research conducted before campaign gets under way. Identify existing needs, wants, benefits, barriers, competition, and stakeholders.	The Kansas Initiative (TKI) conducted focus groups to identify barriers keeping Kansas residents from engaging in youth development activities.
<u>Customer orientation</u>: Focus on target individuals. These include: (1) understanding the needs, wants, benefits, and barriers of the target and (2) providing benefits and reducing barriers by developing the right marketing mix to satisfy target needs and wants.	TKI made use of customer orientation starting with formative research to understand who was inclined to participate and who was not, what barriers they faced, what media messages they would respond to, and what was the outcome of their behaviors; the focus on target individuals was central to the campaign.

Sidebar 3. (*Continued*)	
Exchange: What does the target segment get in return for undertaking the desirable behavior?	The needs of adults to contribute toward a better community and for enhanced self-esteem are satisfied in exchange for participating in youth development activities.
Competition: Forces trying to get the consumer to behave in a different, and often opposite, direction.	Relaxing, watching television, and spending time with friends.
Positioning: Satisfy the target segment's need better than others.	Volunteering is more satisfying than watching TV.
Target behavioral goals	1. Increase adult-child interactions (TKI). 2. Increase mentoring (BBSS).
Product: What is offered to the market?	Benefits: Satisfaction, happiness, or enhanced self-esteem offered by TKI.
Incentives: What is offered to make the product more attractive?	The Green Ribbon Kid Friendly Award.
Price: Consider monetary and nonmonetary costs of the behavior and ways to reduce them.	Convenience: BBBSA offers mentoring using telephone and Internet to reduce travel.
Place: The distribution method of the social product.	All opportunities for interaction (TKI).
Promotion: Communication strategy to make the product familiar and desirable.	Cost focus: "Take a second. Make a difference" by TKI suggests it is easy.
Community-based approach: Modify community structures, processes, and policies.	Community development projects undertaken by TKI and Colorado Initiative.

(*cont.*)

Sidebar 3. (*Continued*)	
Steps	**Brief description or example**
<u>Alliances</u>: Forming strategic partnerships with *publics* who share common goals.	The Big Brothers Big Sisters & Footstar Athletic Alliance.
<u>Pretest research</u>: Asking potential target audience members "Will this campaign work?"	Focus groups to pretest the media campaign (TKI).
<u>Outcome evaluation research</u>: Tracking program progress (including more listening to customers); adjusting strategy and tactics as necessary.	Outcome evaluation based on surveys (TKI).

Analyzing the Case

This chapter discusses several examples of how social marketing can be applied to mobilize adults. Based on our analysis, we conclude that these attempts display several strengths of a social marketing campaign. In an attempt to change behavior, campaign activities seem to revolve around the target, with special focus on the benefits that motivate and costs that prevent individuals and communities from becoming involved in youth development activities. These benefits and costs are then addressed by implementing appropriate marketing strategies. In some cases, attempts are made, first, to offer alternatives (mentoring programs by BBBSA) in an environment that enables the target to become involved in the activities and, second, to offer monetary and nonmonetary incentives to make the exchange offer more attractive. One also observes an increasing trend toward forming alliances with stakeholders such as commercial organizations. Finally, the social change efforts seem to be well supported by research activities at various stages of the campaign.

However, the effectiveness of future social marketing campaigns to mobilize adults could likely be enhanced by conducting a more in-depth analysis of competitive behaviors and by considering the concept of product positioning (i.e., promoting benefits that are superior to the benefits that the target receives from competitive behaviors). In other words, campaign managers would likely achieve higher effectiveness by not just promoting benefits but also positioning them as superior to the existing behaviors. Second, the social change campaigns can be made more effective with the help of a continuous and steady

effort guided by more rigorous research at the formative and outcome evaluation stages (G. Meissen, personal communication, February 2004) and with an
eye to sustainability beyond the project (A. O'Hashi, personal communication,
February 2004).

Concluding Thoughts

While social marketing makes use of advertising and other communication methods, this tool is much more. Through extensive use of research, social
marketing requires the understanding of target individuals and competition. It
then offers attractive products and rewards, and it overcomes barriers, so target
individuals and communities have the opportunity, the ability, and the desire to
perform the new behaviors. Additionally, social marketers do not restrict their
campaigning to mass media vehicles alone, but achieve their objectives by involving the community to bring about societal change at the grassroots level.
Finally, although most of the examples described here are high-budget attempts,
social marketing objectives can be achieved by creatively using limited budgets
or by developing partnerships.

Authors' Note

The authors would like to thank François Lagarde (social marketing and
communications consultant and associate professor in the Faculty of Medicine,
University of Montreal) and Dr. Michael Rothschild (professor emeritus, University of Wisconsin) for their excellent comments on earlier versions of this
chapter.

Appendix

The Kansas Initiative

This case study presents an integrated social marketing effort made by the
Kansas Health Foundation to involve adults in youth development activities
(Kansas Health Foundation, 2001, 2003; University of Kansas, 2000; information
here is adapted by permission).

Background

The Kansas Health Foundation's children's health initiative implemented a
social marketing effort to encourage adults to connect with children. This social
marketing effort was one component of an overall children's health initiative,
the mission of which is to make Kansas the best state in the nation in which to
raise a child. The Kansas Health Foundation believed that the overall level of

adult interactions with children was less than optimal in Kansas; thus, there was a need to increase the rates of interaction.

The first phase of the social marketing effort, which combined mass media and community strategies, was initiated in January 2001 and the second phase began in 2002. The program cost for the two media phases was $3.9 million and $3.25 million, respectively, while the community development effort totaled $2.5 million. Groups involved in the project included Sullivan Higdon & Sink, the Elliott School of Communication at Wichita State University, the Self-Help Network of Wichita State University, and the University of Kansas Work Group on Health Promotion and Community Development.

Formative Research

At the formative research stage, focus groups were conducted with adults who were inclined to connect with children and with adults not inclined to connect, to identify possible barriers preventing people from engaging with children. Individual adults' stories were also collected about how other adults had made a difference in their lives when they were children.

Target Audience(s)

All adults, parents, and nonparents residing in the state of Kansas were targeted by the initiative.

Audience Segmentation

Within the large target audience, specific groups of individuals who were potential influencers were identified during community development initiatives. These influencers, labeled connectors (those who bring others together), mavens (those who share ideas), or salespeople (those who convince others of the efficacy of change), would spread the word and advance the effort the quickest (Gladwell, 2001). The target individuals were also segmented by those who would be early adopters of the initiative's message, people who had experienced the positive adult input during their childhood and would thus immediately recognize that adults make a big difference in children's lives. Communities in Kansas were also segmented by their readiness for change, as assessed by their already ongoing activities around children's issues. Once the segments were identified, the campaign targeted individuals and communities that were either influential or prone to react favorably.

Target Behavior(s)

Creators of this social marketing initiative hoped to increase awareness among adults, to increase adult–child interactions, and to bring about long-term changes in the levels of adult–child interaction. The initiative was designed to convince adults to take advantage of incidental contact with youth and to be deliberately positive, that is, not to ignore a young person they saw at their church or in their neighborhood but to engage in a positive interaction. Individuals deemed high achievers might go so far as to intentionally plan or create new opportunities, such as sending birthday cards to the youth they knew.

Product/Benefits

The campaign promoted the benefit that, in fact, adults can make a difference in a child's life, and that connecting with children is a form of social inoculation. However, the campaign focused more on overcoming barriers than promoting benefits.

Price/Barriers

Although target individuals reported both to themselves and to the youth strong benefits from their interactions, they perceived high costs for enacting the desired behavior, including (1) belief that it took too much time, (2) belief that small amounts of time with children did not make significant differences in their lives, (3) questions about whether getting involved with another person's child might somehow be seen as wrong or questionable, and (4) possibilities of rejection, especially by older youth. The media initiative addressed the first two barriers. The third barrier was addressed by asking local law enforcement to affirm its support for the initiative to decrease adults' concerns. The stranger danger concern was not discussed in the media initiative so as not to project the belief that most adults were a threat to children.

Place

Places where children might be engaged included both geographical location and beyond. Geographically, adult–child engagement occurred everywhere children and youth were and where the adults felt more comfortable exhibiting the behavior (for example, in churches and neighborhoods).

Promotion

The behavior was promoted using both mass media initiatives and community-level efforts. The slogan "Take a second. Make a difference" was chosen as it resonated with the audience, it was simple, and it addressed the concerns about the amount of time it took to make a difference in a child's life. During the formative research stage, it was revealed that the general public audience did not like the use of the term *developmental assets*. They thought it too "professional" and labeled it "jargon." So, while the initiative was based on research focusing on developmental assets, the terms and the information validating it were not used with the general public. Instead, the focus was concentrated on all adults connecting with children and youth. Several ads were produced with varied themes: (1) reinforcing the perception that frequent and varied adult–child interactions were the social norm (a child's voice asked whether the listener was one of the adults who had engaged or ignored it); (2) reinforcing each other for smiling and talking with children; (3) encouraging people to recall their own childhood relationships with adults and reminding them how their lives had been affected by the small kindnesses adults extended to them when they were children (adult narratives were used to increase adult identification); and (4) responding to the "What in the world does waving at a child, smiling at a child, and knowing a child's name have to do with health?" concern.

Strategies demonstrated in the ads included (1) suggesting comfortable, safe places such as churches and neighborhoods to connect with youth; (2) suggesting that connecting with children was a form of social inoculation; and (3) showcasing interactions between business leaders and children. Multiple media were used to increase the message penetration. Television and radio spots, newspapers, the Internet, and public relations efforts were used to convey the message in addition to the one-on-one and small-group efforts in individual communities.

Incentives

Promotional efforts also encouraged individuals to take further actions. For example, those who inquired about the initiative received a packet of inspirational postcards to send to children and youth they knew and to praise or encourage them for something they had done.

Community Initiatives

To maintain the involvement of core members and increase longevity and effectiveness of media messages, the community initiative undertook several activities, which were later publicized in the mass media. These included (1) a series of regional and statewide retreats held for the ready few (Gladwell, 2001) to educate and inspire them to connect with young people and enlist their help to "build the buzz" and effect changes in policies, programs, and practices to create healthier communities; (2) technical assistance to community members and groups (by means of phone calls, presentations, visits to communities, and an interactive Web site) to provide them with ways to access information, ideas, and materials to make a difference in their communities; and (3) the "Good to Great" Award, a mini-grant opportunity for grassroots citizens needing financial support for the material costs of their community change activities. As of fall 2003, the initiative was working in 256 communities and involved 2,080 Kansans.

Table 1. Campaign Impact[a,b]

Behavior Change	Fall 2002	Fall 2003
Took more opportunities to connect with young people in the community	92.3	87.1
"Built the buzz" about the importance of taking a second to make a difference by telling others about the importance of youth and adult interaction	84.6	87.9
Helped effect a change in a program, policy, practice within a group or organization that had a positive impact on youth	65.4	67.9
Shared "Take a second. Make a difference" and/or "Which one were you?" materials	62.8	75.7

Source: Wichita State University, 2003
Notes:
[a]100 community contacts in 2002 and 140 in 2003, representing about 55 different Kansas communities, were asked to respond "yes" or "no" as to whether or not they had done certain activities as a result of the "Take a second. Make a difference" initiative.
[b]Numbers indicate percentage of participants who responded yes to the item.

Pretest and Outcome Evaluation

In addition to the formative research mentioned earlier, several research activities were carried out throughout the initiative. The media initiatives were pretested and revised. Focus groups were used in developing media components for the social marketing effort. People were exposed to various images and messages in order to determine which ones resonated with them. The Kansas Health Foundation made use of feedback to modify its message, hoping to make it more salient and memorable. The community development initiatives were assessed through a random community contact survey (individuals who had contact with the project, attended regional retreats, requested materials, etc.) in fall 2002 and fall 2003. The project staff assessment indicated potential and sustained behavior change in those participating in the initiative (see Table 1).

References

Ad Council. (2004). *The Advertising Council and Big Brothers Big Sisters of America launch new PSAs to attract supporters, volunteers: First round of PSAs reveals success of campaign* [News release]. Retrieved August 17, 2004, from http://www.adcouncil.org/about/news_062904b/

Andreasen, A. (1995). *Marketing social change: Changing behavior to promote health, social development and the environment.* San Francisco: Jossey-Bass.

Angus Reid Group. (2000). *Program effectiveness study: Final report.* Burlington, ON: Big Brothers and Sisters of Canada.

Bagozzi, R. P. (1975). Marketing as exchange. *Journal of Marketing, 39,* 32–39.

Baker, E. A., & Brownson, C. A. (1999). Defining characteristics of community-based health promotion programs. In R. C. Brownson, E. A. Baker, & L. N. Novick (Eds.), *Community-based prevention: Programs that work* (pp. 7–19). Gaithersburg, MD: Aspen.

Benson, P. L. (2003). Toward asset-building communities: How does change occur? In R. M. Lerner & P. L. Benson (Eds.), *Developmental assets and asset-building communities: Implications for research, policy, and practice* (pp. 213–221). New York: Kluwer Academic/Plenum.

Big Brothers Big Sisters of America (BBSSA). (2004). *Corporate case studies: Footstar Athletic puts best foot forward to help Big Brothers/Big Sisters.* Retrieved February 5, 2004, from http://www.bbbsa.org/site/apps/s/content.asp?c=iuJ3JgO2F&b=14852&content_id={9682A31E-FE85-4D5A-A3C3-BA8BE2E9CAE3}

Ciszewski, R. L., & Harvey, P. D. (1994). The effect of price increases on contraceptive sales in Bangladesh. *Journal of Biosocial Science, 26*(1), 25–35.

Colorado Trust. (2002). *Creating social change: The growth of a statewide movement (a summary).* Denver: Author.

Colorado Trust. (2003). *Creating social change: The growth of a statewide movement.* Denver: Author.

Dahl, D. W., Gorn, G. J., & Weinberg, C. B. (1997). Marketing, safer sex, and condom acquisition. In M. E. Goldberg, M. Fishbein, & S. E. Middlestadt (Eds.), *Social marketing: Theoretical and practical perspectives* (pp. 169–185). Mahwah, NJ: Erlbaum.

Davies, J., & Agha, S. (1997). Contraceptive social marketing in Pakistan: A new system for assessing the impact of price increases on condom sales and consumption in a low-resource setting. *1997 Innovation in Social Marketing Conference Proceedings,* 11–15.

Deshpande, S., & Hitchon, J. C. (2002). Cause-related marketing ads in the light of negative news. *Journalism and Mass Communication Quarterly, 79*(4), 905–926.

Gladwell, M. (2001). *The tipping point: How little things can make a big difference.* New York: Little, Brown.

Kansas Health Foundation. (2001). *Foundation asks Kansas, "Take a second. Make a difference" in new campaign.* Retrieved February 5, 2004, from http://www.kansashealth.org/our_news/

Kansas Health Foundation. (2003). *Take a second. Make a difference.* Retrieved February 5, 2004, from http://www.kansashealth.org/our_news/

Kohli, A. K., & Jaworski, B. J. (1990). Market orientation. *Journal of Marketing, 54,* 1–18.

Kotler, P., & Armstrong, G. (2001). *Principles of marketing.* Upper Saddle River, NJ: Prentice-Hall.

Kotler, P., & Roberto, E. L. (1989). *Social marketing: Strategies for changing behavior.* New York: Free Press.

Kotler, P., Roberto, N., & Lee, N. (2002). *Social marketing: Improving the quality of life* (2nd ed.). Thousand Oaks, CA: Sage.

Kotler, P., & Zaltman, G. (1971). Social marketing: An approach to planned social change. *Journal of Marketing, 35,* 3–12.

Roehlkepartain, E. C., Scales, P. C., Roehlkepartain, J. L., & Rude, S. P. (2002). *Building strong families: An in-depth report on a preliminary survey on what parents need to succeed.* Minneapolis, MN: YMCA of the USA and Search Institute.

Rothschild, M. L. (1999). Carrots, sticks, and promises: A conceptual framework for the management of public health and social issue behaviors. *Journal of Marketing, 63,* 24–37.

Rothschild, M. L. (2002, January). *Using social marketing to reduce alcohol impaired driving by 21–34 year olds.* Paper presented at the Changing Options and Outcomes Social Marketing Conference organized by the School of Business, University of Wisconsin-Madison, Wisconsin Department of Transportation, and Sound Partners at University of Wisconsin, Madison.

Scales, P. C., Benson, P. L., & Roehlkepartain, E. C. (2000). *Grading grown-ups: American adults report on their real relationships with kids.* Minneapolis, MN: Lutheran Brotherhood and Search Institute.

Scales, P. C., Benson, P. L., & Mannes, M. (with Tellett-Royce, N., & Griffin-Wiesner, J.). (2002). *Grading grown-ups 2002: How do American kids and adults relate? Key findings from a national study.* Minneapolis, MN: Lutheran Brotherhood and Search Institute.

Schultz, D. E., Tannenbaum, S., & Lauterborn, R. F. (1993). *Integrated marketing communications: Putting it together and making it work.* New York: McGraw-Hill.

Siegel, M., & Doner, L. (1998). *Marketing public health: Strategies to promote social change.* Gaithersburg, MD: Aspen.

Smith, W. A. (1993). *Environmental education and communications.* Washington, DC: Academy for Educational Development.

Smith, W. A. (1999). Social marketing: Marketing with no budget. *Social Marketing Quarterly, 5*(2), 7–8.

Tierney, J., Grossman, J., & Resch, N. (1995). *Making a difference: An impact study of Big Brothers/Big Sisters*. Philadelphia: Public/Private Ventures.

University of Kansas. (2000). *Community tool box: Foundation children's effort as example of social marketing*. Retrieved February 5, 2004, from http://www.kansashealth.org/our_news/

Weinreich, N. K. (1999). *Social marketing library*. Retrieved January 10, 2001, from http://www.social-marketing.com/library.html

Wichita State University. (2003). *Community development for healthy children grant #20003012: Preliminary report on community contact survey 2*. Wichita, KS: Author.

13 Think Globally, Act Locally: A Global Perspective on Mobilizing Adults for Positive Youth Development

Tina M. Durand and M. Brinton Lykes

Boston College

Educators, social scientists, and human service workers have contributed importantly to theorizing youth development and to investigating and defining normal development and its vicissitudes. More recently, those with applied interests have designed and evaluated programs and engaged in more hands-on advocacy with and for youth. Despite this crucial work the editors of this volume, among others, argue that a large percentage of the adult population is not involved with youth, and they urge that we consider new strategies for mobilizing adults for positive youth development. A series of questions emerged for us as we considered this mandate from the perspective of our international fieldwork and years of collaborating with youth and adults in community-based psychosocial and development programs. Specifically, we have been challenged to consider: What do youth today really need? And, what do they want? Who is best positioned to identify, evaluate, prioritize, and address youth's needs and concerns?

It is perhaps a truism among social scientists today that the development and best interests of youth are likely to be defined differently in different social contexts. Based on years of experiences working with young people within and beyond the United States, we argue that this reality also raises a subtler, yet no less profound, set of issues concerning the social scientist's underlying assumptions about children and youth. Indeed, adult ideas regarding the child and childhood (Burman, 1994) and youth (White & Wyn, 2004) are replete with ideological, social, and political meanings, which in turn inform our decisions about the kinds of activities we think children and youth should both engage in and be prohibited from. Such considerations are critical to any exploration of adult engagement in the lives of youth.

We begin our discussion with a brief overview of whom we have in mind when we talk about youth today and, more particularly, youth from a global perspective. We then briefly describe a wide range of programs and projects developed by and/or serving youth around the globe. Some of these projects are designed and funded by adults, whereas others are in the hands of the youth who initiated them, often with the guidance and financial assistance of adults. We will argue that despite these excellent resources youth are still challenged by a range of social, political, and economic problems, many of which continue to marginalize them from opportunities to participate actively in their schools, families, and communities. In hopes of better understanding why, and of improving our responses to these realities, we explore some of the assumptions underlying psychological theories of human development that inform many of these existing youth programs. We discuss problems attendant to the application of these theories to practice and, more specifically, to policy; for example, to international conventions that bear on the rights and responsibilities of adults vis-à-vis youth, such as the Convention on the Rights of the Child (CRC). We briefly discuss the opportunities these challenges afford us, as social scientists and educators, to rethink selected dominant theories about youth.

Drawing on this developing knowledge, we then look to youth worldwide to inform our thinking about how to mobilize other adults for positive youth development. We explore youth activism and organizing using two youth-driven and -directed activities and participatory action research, a dialectically grounded, action-based system of knowledge construction and social change, as resources that challenge conventional wisdom about how youth gather their own stories and "speak truth to power." We suggest a more critical analysis of youth empowerment as we urge a position of *solidarity with* youth rather than one of *empowerment of* youth. We conclude with several suggestions for future action and research with youth wherein and through which we, as adults, "think globally and act locally" with youth.

Thinking Globally about Youth

Who or What Are We Thinking About?

Youth are increasingly integral to the sustenance of future nations as their numbers increase worldwide. In the United States, there were approximately 51,148,000 young people 10–19 years old in 2001 (U.S. Census Bureau, 2002). Worldwide, there are an estimated 1.2 billion young people ages 10–19, which is the largest generation of adolescents in history (UNICEF, 2002). According to the *Statistical Handbook on the World's Children* (Kaul, 2002), children represented 34% of the total population in North America in 2000, but the proportion of children to adults is much higher in some other continents: In 2000, children aged from birth to age 19 represented 53% of the total population in Africa, 40% of the total population in Asia, and 40% of the total population in South America.

Our attempt to "define youth" within a global context contributes to our developing argument about the deeply contextualized understandings of youth required of all youth-based research and action. Most dictionaries or resource books refer you directly to *adolescence*. The word is Latin in origin, derived from the verb *adolescere*, which means "to grow into adulthood." The *Oxford English Dictionary* (Simpson & Weiner, 1989), for example, defines adolescence as "extending from 14 to 25 in males, and from 12 to 21 in females," where the differences for girls and boys are relative to the distribution of gender-based roles and chores. Some observers have commented on this later period of adolescence for boys as related to the time needed to show sufficient responsibility to provide for a wife and child (Rogoff, 2003). The *Gale Encyclopedia of Childhood and Adolescence* (Kagan & Gall, 1998) defines adolescence as the second decade of the life span, roughly from age 10 to 20. Similarly, the Carnegie Council on Adolescent Development (1995) defines adolescence as the period between ages 11 and 18. They refine the construct, however, distinguishing between early adolescence (ages 11–12) and late adolescence (ages 17–18).

On a global level, *youth* is the term more generally used to describe an individual within this age cohort. The United Nations and its agencies (e.g., UNICEF, 2004) identify those between the ages of 14 or 15 and 24 as youth. Despite this, in such documents as *The Official Summary of the State of the World's Children* (UNICEF, 2004), individuals between the ages of 15 and 49 are considered adults. Hence, while the term youth, when considered on a global level, is elastic, most official documents about youth deploy the terms youth and adolescence to capture that transition between childhood and adulthood.

Both the length and timing of this transition are conceptualized differently among industrialized and majority world[1] countries. It is perhaps ironic that while childhood ends and adulthood begins at an earlier age in nonindustrialized nations, owing, at least in part, to the need for youth to contribute to the economic survival of their family, the United Nations extends this period beyond that usually associated with adolescence in Euro-American psychological theories in many of its policies and practices. As we will see in this chapter, the rights and responsibilities attributed to youth in the global community often reflect not only the age ranges presented here but the rights and responsibilities associated with the roles that youth occupy in these societies. Indeed, developmental transitions in roles across the life span are closely aligned with cultural communities' traditions and practices (Rogoff, 2003). Moreover, the very incorporation of the terminology of adolescence and youth into UN discourse may

[1] Rather than the terms *Third World* or *developing world*, each of which implicitly situates the Northern Hemisphere as normative or "superior," we use the term *majority world* to refer to countries outside the U.S. and European orbit. They have a majority of the world's population and occupy a majority of the earth's land surface or geographical space, excluding China.

reflect the impact of Euro-American ideology rather than a realistic assessment of children and youth[2] in context in the majority world.

Youth Projects and Programs

As we suggested earlier, there are a wide variety of programs designed to serve, help, and empower youth, both within the United States and worldwide. A brief look at both the *Encyclopedia of Associations* (Hunt, 2002) and the *Encyclopedia of Associations: International Associations* (Atterbury, 2002), reference listings of nationally and internationally registered youth programs and services, yielded 732 separate organizations in the United States under the keyword "youth" and approximately 300 more organizations under related keywords such as "young adult," "young women," and "young people." Internationally, there were 253 separate organizations under the keyword "youth." Internet-based information is even more striking with regard to the number of programs and organizations that are youth focused. For example, in February 2004, the Freechild Project (http://www.freechild.org), a Web-based nonprofit organization designed to provide informational resources, support, educational programs, and global advocacy for youth, listed 1,091 individual organizations under the keyword "children and youth" in its user-generated database of significant youth-based organizations around the world. It is important to note that these numbers, although drawn from reputable sources, largely underestimate the number of actual youth programs and organizations that exist both in the United States and in the world, since a wide range of local and community-based programs that service and involve youth are not represented.

In addition, the proliferation of modern technologies, including the Internet, has enabled youth to communicate and connect in ways never before possible. One example that illustrates this point is UNICEF's Voices of Youth (VOY) program (http://www.unicef.org/voy/). Since 1995, VOY has focused on exploring the educational and community-building potential of the Internet and facilitating active and substantive discussions by young people of a variety of youth-generated issues, such as substance abuse, access to resources, child rights, and media portrayals of youth. Through Web-based activities (i.e., Web boards, chat rooms), VOY engages more than 20,000 young people from more than 180 countries in communication, debate, and educational exchanges.

---

[2] Our use of the terms *children* and *youth* in this chapter reflects some of this complexity. Some of the programs and projects described include youth of 11–12 years old, frequently thought of as pubescent or preadolescent in the United States and Western Europe, while others are led by youth of 25 years, often described as young adults in the West. Thus, our use of the terms children and youth, similar to the uses found in the diverse literature included in this chapter, is contextual and changing. Despite this elasticity, the analysis of the ideologies of children and youth presented herein apply broadly to adults' underlying assumptions about those between the ages of 11 and 25.

Challenges Facing Youth Today

Despite the many programs and networks that exist for and among youth at local, regional, national, and international levels, problems facing youth are persistent and far-reaching, especially when viewed through a global lens. Specifically, some 4 million adolescents attempt suicide each year, and of these at least 100,000 are successful (UNICEF, 2002). In 2000, an estimated 199,000 youth murders took place globally—equivalent to 565 children and young people aged 10–29 years dying on average each day as a result of interpersonal violence (World Health Organization, 2002). Globally, youth are bearing the brunt of the AIDS epidemic: Of the 4.2 million new HIV infections in 2003, half were among young people 15–24 years old (UNICEF, 2004). Examples from countries of the majority world are even more compelling with regard to HIV/AIDS: In sub-Saharan Africa alone, about 10 million youth and 2 million children under age 15 are living with HIV/AIDS (UNICEF, 2004). These social realities, while a cause for concern relative to each individual youth, also alert us to the enormous impact of youth's health, well-being, and social conditions on society as a whole.

If we, white professional psychologists, educators, and United Statesians,[3] seek to better the lives of children and youth and mobilize other adults toward those goals, we must first engage in reflective praxis that turns a careful and critical eye to the ideologies that inform our current thinking and our actions toward children and youth. A critical perspective informed by global youth also impels us to examine the scientific and cultural sources of these ideologies. In the following section, we discuss how a global perspective, wherein we think globally while acting within our local contexts, contributes to shifting our understanding of youth, youth organizing, and youth development, challenging dominant theories of adult–youth relations. We critically analyze the modern, Euro-American conception of the child and child development, and identify some of the sources of this Western knowledge about children and youth. We then examine the universalist claims of modern conceptions of childhood and youth that cast the child as object rather than agent. We argue that these perspectives, while purporting to serve children's and youth's best interests across all contexts, are inadequate for today's global world because they either ignore or obscure variabilities in the nature, contexts, and trajectories of children and youth worldwide.

Modern Conceptions of Childhood in a Postmodern and Global World

Although a discourse of childhood appears in the writings of such philosophers as John Locke and Jean-Jacques Rousseau, it was not until the second

---

[3] The term is a translation of the Spanish term *estadounidense* (see Gugelberger, 1996, p. 4; also note 4, p. 119). It is used here rather than the more common "American" since this latter term includes reference to all citizens of the Americas, that is, of Canada, Mexico, Central and South America, and the United States of America.

half of the 19th century that "the child" became an object of serious scientific inquiry, most notably within psychology (e.g., Hall, 1883; Preyer, 1882; both as cited in Archard, 1993). Perhaps the most important feature of the way in which the modern age conceives of the child is in the child's meriting "separateness" from the adult (Archard, 1993). As suggested earlier, the youth or adolescent is seen as "in transition" between childhood and adulthood, or as an "adult in the making." In Europe and the United States, children and youth are seen as distinctly different from adults in their nature and behavior, and as meriting a marked division in the roles and responsibilities that are deemed appropriate for each. In modern Western culture, children neither work nor play alongside adults, and they have limited participation in the adult world of law and politics (Archard, 1993). Indeed, it appears that the categories of "childhood" (Burman, 1994) and "youth" (White & Wyn, 2004) exist primarily, if not exclusively, in relation to the category "adult."

Psychological Theories

Although theories of development from a variety of perspectives (e.g., sociological, economic, philosophical) have made significant contributions to our understanding of human behavior, psychological theories have distinguished themselves among the social sciences for their extensive attention to child and youth development. As such, Euro-American conceptions of the sharp distinction between childhood and adulthood have been heavily influenced by psychologists, for example, the cognitive-developmental theory of Jean Piaget, the psychoanalytic theory of Sigmund Freud, and the psychosocial theory of Erik Erikson, wherein childhood and adolescence are seen as distinct *stages* in human development that are fixed upon an ideal, adult "end state." Piaget (1977) is credited with the recognition that children's thinking is qualitatively different from that of adults. Specifically, he argued that the young child's flawed and deficient reasoning progresses teleologically in a universal, stagelike fashion, toward the logical, abstract thinking that is the hallmark of adulthood. Similarly, for Freud (1975), abnormal adult outcomes are the result of failures to surmount particular stage-specific crises, such as the Oedipus complex. Although Eriksonian theory is more culturally adaptive than either of the former theories, Erikson (1964) also posited that the major developmental task of the adolescent period is the successful resolution of an identity *crisis* that results in a *mature* identity, which is a crucial and necessary step toward becoming a productive adult. Thus, for each of these theorists, adulthood is not merely more of what childhood is less of; it is of a different and higher order (Archard, 1993).

Although there has been extensive critique of these theories (see, e.g., Gergen, 2000) and innovative retheorizing of self and subjectivity within psychology (see, e.g., Henriques, Hollway, Urwin, Venn, & Walkerdine, 1998), the work of Piaget and Freud continues to dominate textbooks and journals within the United States and beyond. These accounts of child development are most often structured in a chronological, age-driven format with respect to stage models, and are based mainly on studies carried out by Euro-American developmental psychologists, working within the contexts and experiences of Western children (Woodhead, 1998). Cross-cultural perspectives on the trajectory of development most often appear as optional extras within applications sections of both introductory and advanced texts, in which cultural issues are treated as informing the content of development, rather than challenging the structures proposed by Piaget and Freud (Burman, 1994). Although the sociocultural view of development (in particular, the idea that cognition is mediated by cultural symbol systems) put forth by Vygotsky (1930/1971, 1978), and expanded upon at both the theoretical and empirical level by psychologists such as Cole (1996), Rogoff (1990, 2003), and Bruner (1990), has contributed to shifting the focus of some developmental psychologists, it has only recently achieved significance in the United States, and is still not central to mainstream theory, research, or practice. Indeed, mainstream developmental psychology has been ethnocentric in its desire to establish a universal science of the person (Greenfield & Cocking, 1994; Rogoff, 2003). Thus, the Euro-American understanding of childhood is as an extended period of dependency, wherein selected rights, tasks, and goals are deemed to be universally good for all children (Boyden, Ling, & Myers, 1998). Within this framework, children are granted certain autonomy and protection from selected risks.

Children's Rights

The Euro-American perspective on childhood has unceasing impact on the global community. One clear indicator of the globalizing of the ideas briefly summarized above is apparent in the UN Convention on the Rights of the Child, which consolidates widely dispersed and frequently vague guarantees of children's rights into a single document. As such, it delineates the various rights to which children (defined as 18 years of age or younger) around the world are entitled, regardless of their status, race, or religion. These rights are purported to address the broad range of children's physical, mental, and social developmental needs, such as the right not to be discriminated against (Article 2), the right to life and development (Article 6), the right to express their views in all matters affecting them (Article 12), the right of protection from physical and mental violence (Article 19), and the right to education that develops the child's personality and talents to her or his greatest potential (Articles 28 and 29).

Despite this important international initiative, many have argued that the varied, lived realities of children worldwide cannot, by nature, be reflected in universal standards or ideals (e.g., Boyden et al., 1998; Swift, 1999; Tolfree, 1998). Others have suggested that the protections extended to children are fundamentally concessions by adults that come with a cost, namely, the negation of an active and responsible role for the child in her or his society (e.g., Liebel, 2001). From this perspective, the relationship between children and adults is inherently paternalistic, with children having minimal say in the decisions that affect them. Based in part on these critiques and on our fieldwork experiences, we will suggest that even an instrument as significant as the 1989 Convention falls short of its aspirations, failing to support and facilitate children's agency and engagement in ways that are consonant with their own lived circumstances. Hence, the paternalistic view of children implicit within the Convention raises complex issues as well as contradictions for those adults seeking to work with children and youth. In lieu of recognizing that all children and youth have a voice, the Convention leaves adults questioning whether children should have a voice and, if so, how great a voice. Youth mobilizations, whereby children and youth take the lead in problematizing and acting upon their own realties, frequently disrupt this traditional adult–child/youth dynamic. This chapter critiques and resituates a paternalistic, adult–child dynamic, challenging ourselves and other adults to critically interrogate our responses to children and youth.

We will argue that an examination of youth activism from a global perspective offers one lens through which to explore how youth mobilizing transforms traditional understandings of youth and adult–youth relations. In the following section, we select a complex and controversial issue, youth labor, and present one example of a global youth movement in which youth define and analyze their own lived circumstances, and work together to generate solutions aimed toward bettering their own lives. Through this discussion we seek to illustrate how youth have exhibited agency in a critical area of their lives and how that agency can resituate our adult understanding of them and what they need and desire. We then discuss a specific resource for adults who seek to collaborate in more egalitarian, less hierarchical relations with youth as they articulate their priorities and their struggles to improve their own lives and the lives of their families and communities, participatory action research (PAR). PAR was developed to engage participants historically marginalized from access to power and decision making, regardless of age, in understanding and transforming their own social realities (Rahman, 1991). We present several PAR projects to elucidate the methodology and its potential as a concrete resource for adults seeking to facilitate authentic change both with and among youth.

Youth as Legitimate Organizers

The Working Children's Movement

Movements and organizations of working children began at the end of the 1970s in Latin America, and in the 1990s in Africa and Asia, where an estimated 40 million children are part of the workforce (Bachman, 2000). Although the political and ideological debate that surrounds the issue of child labor is beyond the scope of this chapter, it is important to note its highly controversial status among both progressive and conservative groups in both industrialized and majority world countries. Some argue for laws that exclude children (generally those up to the age of 15) from the labor market, while others seek to achieve a similar end through international, bilateral, or consumer boycotts and sanctions against products made with child labor. In contrast, various nongovernmental organizations recommend that children's economic contributions to society should not be condemned and that we should listen to children and support their efforts for better working conditions (White, 1996). Despite these differences there is widespread agreement that certain child labor conditions (e.g., children in bondage, kidnapped, enslaved in forced labor, prostitution) are abusive, and all concur that children involved in such situations need to be removed (White, 1996). Within this diversity of views, the main objective of the working children's movement is to band together to advocate for livable wages and proper working conditions, and to resist exclusion from the labor market, a state incongruent with daily realities for many children in the world (White, 1996).

In global terms, UNICEF estimates that at least 190 million children aged 10–14 are working, 75% of them the equivalent of six days a week (UNICEF, 1997). Although unions of child workers have routinely been shut out of the international debate over child labor—indeed, the International Labor Organization (ILO) has specifically excluded any child labor unions from its current campaign to eradicate the worst forms of child labor—working children's organizations have begun to be more visible in some international contexts, for example, at the 1997 Amsterdam Child Labor Conference. Additionally, individual movements are gaining momentum, power, and strength through global unification, as exemplified in the recent World Meeting of Working Children, a 14-day gathering of delegates of African, Asian, and Latin American movements held in Germany in April 2004. Yet this involvement is highly controversial; some charge that these children, particularly those involved in the most hazardous and exploitative forms of work, are not representative of child workers, or that they have been manipulated by adults (Swift, 1999).

The right to work and to organize as workers is fully supported by Article 23 of the Universal Declaration of Human Rights (UDHR), which asserts: "Everyone has the right to work. Everyone has the right to equal pay for equal work. Everyone has the right to form and join trade unions for the protection of his interests." Moreover, Article 12 of the Convention on the Rights of the Child (CRC) specifies the right to be heard, and Article 15, the freedom of association. However, the CRC has also been cited by those opposed to child and youth workers. Article 28, for example, assumes a universally positive role for education, advocating that primary education should be compulsory. Article 32 states further that parties recognize the right of the child to be protected from exploitation, and from any work that is likely to "interfere with the child's education" (Boyden et al., 1998). The CRC, ostensibly grounded in a deep concern for all children and youth, has thus become a tool through which adults on both sides of the important issue of children's and youth's work exert *power over* children and youth. We argue here that the deeply contextualized and constrained environments in which majority world children live, work, and organize compel us to rethink child and youth labor. Moreover, the claim that children's and youths' rights as codified in UN documents are universal is thus exposed as situationally embedded and of only relative guidance in thinking through the complex issues surrounding child and youth labor.

The working children's movement is an excellent example of youth demanding and creating a space in which they have framed and defined a critical issue that affects their lives. Further, these movements are founded on the belief that every individual, regardless of age, is of value and has a contribution to make, thereby challenging conventional power relationships between adults and children (Swift, 1999). The working children's movements have thus become a means by which both children and supportive adults can explore and perhaps redefine their respective roles as citizens (Swift, 1999) and, as significantly, traditional hierarchical relationships between adults and youth.

One example of a particularly well organized child and youth labor movement is Bhima Sangha, an independent union of working children aged 6–18 years old in Bangalore and six districts of the state of Karnataka, India (Swift, 1999). The name was chosen by the children, *Bhima* being a character in a sacred Hindu text that has the strength of 10,000 elephants, and *sangha* signifying union. The association was conceptualized by and for working children, who realized that they were not recognized as workers by the state, local trade unions, or legislation. The union was formally launched in 1990, with the support of The Concerned for Working Children (CWC), a nongovernmental organization that assists local governments, communities, and working children themselves, in the implementation of viable, comprehensive, and appropriate solutions that reflect the lived conditions and experience of working children. With a membership of 13,000 working children that is still growing, Bhima Sangha is active in southern India, and children themselves play central roles. While the scope of their activism has included such activities as informing youth workers of their rights, documenting children's hazardous working conditions, and inspiring parents, the media, and policy makers to advocate for human rights issues, perhaps their greatest accomplishment has been in the area of local policy making and planning. Along with CWC, Bhima Sangha has negotiated the setting up of village task forces that enable children to participate in local politics. Additionally, Bhima Sangha has been instrumental in the formation of *makkala panchayats* (children's councils), which parallel the village *panchayats* and offer children a unique forum to discuss issues that directly concern them, such as the construction of a footbridge that would assist children in traveling to school. Representatives of the makkala panchayat bring their concerns to the task force after in-depth discussions. With an electorate that consists of all working children (aged 6–18), the makkala panchayat helps find solutions for all children (not just those who are working) at the local level, by creating a space for the voices of youth, particularly young girls, to raise issues that concern them, and to participate in critical decision-making processes.

Through Bhima Sangha a significant group of Indian working children and youth have organized on their own behalf and on the behalf of the wider community of children and youth in six districts of one Indian state. We know of no research that has evaluated the impact of their organization on the young participants. Although critically important to assess the movement's effects and its value to those involved, this example of a children and youth movement offers more immediate challenges to an adult readership. Specifically, Bhima

Sangha exemplifies how youth workers can voice their concerns and organize on their own behalf. Adult consultation and support have facilitated their participation in wider social movements and has created conditions through which their voices have been more widely heard. This praxis defies conventional adult wisdom about children, youth, and work. Moreover, it widens our lens as U.S. adults for thinking about how best to "protect" children and raise important considerations about the value of children's and youth's work in the family's and the community's survival in the majority world. Thus, the existence and success of Bhima Sangha challenge Euro-American social scientists and educators as well as community and labor activists to reflect upon and critically interrogate our current thinking about and work with children and youth.

Participatory Action Research and Youth

Participatory action research (PAR) offers an additional resource, that is, a set of strategies and reflexive practices, to think critically about ourselves as adults, about youth, and about the work we do with them. As argued above, youth are frequently marginalized from power and decision making (see, e.g., Prilleltensky, Nelson, & Peirson, 2001; Serrano-Garcia & Bond, 1994). Thus the legitimate, insider knowledge of their own experience is ignored by those who seek to "study" or "serve" them. Participatory action research is an optimal resource for adults who wish rather to collaborate with and accompany youth as they mobilize on their own behalf.

While providing a simple definition of PAR is difficult, we agree with those who argue that PAR is a resource through which individuals self-consciously empower themselves to take effective, collective action toward improving conditions in their own lives (Park, 1993; Reason & Bradbury, 2001). An explicit aim of PAR is to liberate the human spirit, especially the spirit of the marginalized and oppressed, in order to bring about a more just and equitable society. Although PAR is often described as a qualitative research method or approach, it is also conceptualized as a paradigmatic worldview or a "philosophy of life" (Rahman & Fals-Borda, 1991, p. 29). What distinguishes PAR methodologically and philosophically from more traditional approaches to research is a resistance to conventional positivist views of science, knowledge, and practice. PARers reject claims that objective reality can be known through experimental methods and posit distinctive and alternative conceptions of knowledge and its relation to power, of the role of the researcher, and of the relationship between research and practice. Consistent with the central tenets of qualitative inquiry, PAR assumes that all knowledge and observation are value and content laden, subject to social verification (Rahman, 1991). Hence, knowledge is neither universal nor objective; it is situated, local, and socially constructed. Further, PAR assumes that knowledge is inextricably linked with power and challenges traditional knowledge mechanisms, such as socialization, education, and the media, that have defined and legitimized both what counts as useful knowledge and whose interest (the educated, white middle class) this knowledge serves (Gaventa & Cornwall, 2001; Rahman, 1991).

In PAR, the traditional, asymmetrical subject–object relationship between the researcher and participant (with the researcher at the top) that characterizes traditional positivist forms of inquiry is transformed into one of subject–subject, in which both parties collaborate in authentic participation (Fals-Borda, 1991). Put another way, PAR is a means of recognizing the research capabilities of marginalized and disenfranchised people and assisting them in acquiring tools with which they can transform their lives for themselves (Park, 1993).

Participatory action research aims to set in motion the process of consciousness-raising, or *conscientization*, by which participants collectively and critically analyze their understandings and practices, in order to confront and overcome injustice, ignorance, and oppression. The researcher thus plays a supportive and facilitative role. The university-based researcher, often an outsider, joins community participants and in social solidarity they come together within local communities to change the structural features of the social milieu in order to realize a fuller life and a more just society. The fruits of PAR are real and material changes in what people do, what they value, how they interact with others, and how they interpret their world (Kemmis & McTaggart, 2000; Park, 1993).

Several examples of participatory action research projects that involve adults and youth in collaborative, change-based projects serve to illustrate these points. As important, they form the basis for critically analyzing dominant discourse of youth development that currently informs much social scientific and educational research and their applications. Although the projects we have chosen to highlight focus on the development and promotion of youth, they differ in the degree to which they are youth or adult initiated and implemented. Those that offer greater decision making to youth are sites in which traditional adult–child power dynamics can be contested and where, in the words of one 16-year-old boy, youth can become contributing members of society, rather than mere onlookers: "I mean the system is not helping any . . . we're [thought of] as dumb and stupid and the system, they don't even let us vote until we're eighteen . . . we don't have no kind of interest in politics, but then we get eighteen, we all of a sudden got to vote and we don't know [what] we're voting about" (Children's Express, 1993, p. 29). We begin with several examples from youth communities of color in the United States and then discuss several participatory projects beyond U.S. borders.

U.S.-Based Participatory Action Research

The Youth Action Research Institute (YARI) of the Institute for Community Research (a nonprofit independent research and training agency based in Hartford, Connecticut) is a center-based, adult-driven, youth participatory program. YARI seeks to facilitate youth-led action research for development, risk prevention, and social change with preadolescents and adolescents (upper elementary through high school) of diverse ethnic backgrounds, as well as sexual minority youth. Youth gain focused and extensive training in participatory methods through the Summer Youth Research Institute (SYRI). Each year 40 urban youth are formally recruited (i.e., they are hired as paid employees) to participate in a 7-week summer program in which they collectively choose a research issue that is meaningful to them (within the realm of drug, violence, or at-risk sexual behavior), learn and apply social science research methods (i.e., ethnographic observation, interviews), and analyze their results. During the subsequent school year, participants have the opportunity to construct action strategies through which they disseminate prevention messages that are linked to their work in the summer.

In one project, for example, youth chose to examine the explicit and implicit media messages about sexual behavior that are targeted at teens. Through critical observation of media imagery (commercials) and focus group discussions, youth identified the media's influence on youth attitudes, emotions, and behavior. To disseminate their results, they created a montage of videos, commercials, and television shows for use in educating other youth in their communities. Ultimately, youth are involved in the generation of new knowledge about both themselves and their communities (M. Berg, personal communication, April 7, 2004; http://www.incommunityresearch.org/research/yari.htm).

In an ambitious project with younger adolescents, Alice McIntyre (2000) collaborated in participatory action research with 12- and 13-year-old middle school youth of color to investigate how they negotiated their daily lives within an urban community. The research focus was identified and concretized through ongoing dialogue, discussion, and creative activities (i.e., skits, collage). The meanings these youth made of the multiple forms of violence in their lives (interpersonal, educational, structural, environmental) emerged as the central research focus of the project. Unlike programs whereby university people enter communities to either study local residents as "objects of inquiry" or to "rescue" community members who have been labeled as "at-risk," this project attempted to create a space where youth could tell their own insider stories, engage in the coconstruction of knowledge regarding both self and community, and generate youth-initiated action and intervention projects that would address identified concerns.

To this end, youth participants engaged in a community photography project in which they took more than 600 photographs of their communities. Although multiple images and perspectives, many of them positive, were shared by the participants as they described and analyzed their photographs, the abundant trash and disrepair evident in their neighborhoods were particularly disturbing to them. As a result, the group developed and implemented a long-term, ongoing community cleanup project, which they named One STEP (Save the Earth Program), the goal of which was both to raise community awareness regarding local environmental issues and to engage school, community, and city officials in "cleaning up" the community (One STEP Group, McIntyre, & McKeirnan, 2000). Youth presented their project and their vision for a cleaner environment to both university and local city council audiences. Although basic systems of power and privilege that affect youth in urban communities were not dismantled through this effort, McIntyre argues that it facilitated a sense of agency in the urban youth of color who participated. McIntyre's social solidarity not only with the youth but also with their teachers, families, and their community created the conditions for them to exercise leadership and make change.

Another example of PAR within and beyond schools is the Opportunity Gap Project (Fine et al., 2004). Youth collaborated with PAR researchers to investigate the processes of institutional racism in racially integrated suburban high schools in New York and New Jersey, as manifested in areas such as differential opportunity and access for students of color and a collective resistance to examine particular school experiences (e.g., "color blindness"). Youth themselves are the central voices in the project; in fact, upon joining the project, youth insisted the title be changed from "the achievement gap" to its current title, in order to reflect the magnitude and range of discrimination that they faced in schools. More than 50 students of diverse ethnic and class backgrounds were brought together to form a "Youth Research Community" and participated in an initial research "methods training" camp. Research questions initially presented by the adult researchers were discussed and reframed by youth, and youth learned about research methods, including survey design and focus groups. Together with adult researchers, youth crafted a survey including questions focusing on distributive justice in both the schools and the nation. The survey was disseminated to 9th and 12th graders in 13 urban and suburban school districts, yielding rich qualitative and quantitative data. Now several years into the project, youth are presenting analyses of these data back to their own schools. Although the impact these youth might have on actual school policy is not yet known, participatory methodology has enabled them to join a growing movement of youth who are asking the United States to make good on the promises of *Brown v. Board of Education*.

Beyond U.S. Borders

Youth-led participatory education and development projects outside of the United States offer a unique lens through which to understand the critical contributions youth make to the livelihood and sustenance of the families and communities in which they live and work. Peace Child International (with headquarters in the United Kingdom) is one of the world's largest youth-led organizations. Its role is to assist youth (ages 12–25) worldwide in community development, change, and empowerment strategies. Together with the United Nations, Peace Child has produced a number of publications on the environment, sustainable development, and human rights (all of which have been written and illustrated by young people) for young people who wish to engage in collaborative projects regarding community development (http://www.peacechild.org).

These projects are largely realized through Peace Child's Be the Change program. Be the Change is a youth-empowerment program that gives young people the chance to make changes in their community. Launched in 1999, Be the Change is a Web-based international development program for youth-generated projects. The program facilitates low-cost, youth-led community projects by assisting youth (ages 12–25) worldwide in identifying needs within their communities, proposing well-formulated plans of action, finding adult mentors, raising funds to complete projects, and evaluating and reporting project results. Be the Change projects have ranged from health awareness/prevention of HIV/AIDS to the rebuilding of devastated environments. The Dalit Empowerment Project in India is one such example. The project focused on the organization of young people in the village of Gudahatti, which is composed mainly of aboriginal Dalits (lowest caste, oppressed people) of India who have been systematically stripped of their land and dignity by members of the upper castes. The goal of this youth-led project was to address problems facing the village (i.e., health and education) and restore pride within the community. Specific youth-driven, adult-assisted project activities included the construction of a more sanitary drainage system and the construction of a new primary school. With additional funding, the youth plan to implement a recycling and composting project, aimed at improving health and hygiene within the community.

All of these projects were designed by youth, accompanied by adults, to identify and redress the wide range of social, economic, cultural, and political inequalities that they face on a daily basis. All used creative resources—including storytelling, dramatization, and, more recently, technologies such as the Internet and video—as means through which youth narrate their own stories, educate themselves and their peers, and reimagine their worlds. Some, like projects based in YARI, focus on problems (e.g., alcoholism, HIV/AIDS) identified by adults who coordinate research institutes or service centers out of which youth organize. Others, such as One STEP or the Opportunity Gap project, were initiated by PAR adult "outsider" researchers, who sought to engage youth "insiders" (Bartunek & Louis, 1996) in solidarity and who risked entering into collaborative relationships, putting traditional adult–youth power dynamics into creative motion. In contrast, Bhima Sangha and Be the Change programs, efforts that emerged and function beyond U.S. borders, are more clearly youth-initiatied and intimately connected to their material well-being and economic development (White & Wyn, 2004). These efforts challenge adults in the United States to acknowledge youth's complex social situatedness and to listen carefully to their words and deeds in order to resituate our understandings of youth and our work with them. Taking the global perspective articulated through these programs beyond our borders, we, as U.S.-based adults, are challenged to act locally, that is, to risk entering into social solidarity with and among youth. This response remobilizes our adult gaze, shifting the ways in which we see and hear the children and youth among us. These shifts demand that we retheorize child and youth development and rethink the claims of universality of dominant developmental theories and of conventions on children's and youth's human rights. As significantly, they challenge us to reconfigure our relations with children and youth.

Situating Youth Empowerment in Systems of Power
and Processes of Liberation

Prilleltensky et al. (2001), among others, have argued that children and youth, as marginalized populations with little political power, come last in the allocation of resources. The current underfunding of the much heralded No Child Left Behind Act of 2002 is only the most recent example confirming Prilleltensky et al.'s contention. We have argued here that our tendency as social scientific researchers, educators, and human service workers to excel at examining and treating the individual, family, or small group focuses our gaze on victims of this underfunding—poor children and youth, and children and youth of color—rather than on children and youth as actors with the potential to resist and/or transform the social inequalities that confront them. A perspective that focuses primarily on individual well-being contributes to the design of positive youth development programs and projects created to, minimally, help youth and, maximally, empower them. Such projects are primarily, if not exclusively, designed to intervene at the level of the individual or small group. Considerably less emphasis is placed on the social and contextual aspects of youth and their developing communities. Moreover, they tend to psychologize children's and youth's problems, ignoring the social and political contexts that constrain or impede their development (Prilleltensky et al., 2001).

Although some youth have clearly benefited from this perspective, the social indicators of youth worldwide presented at the beginning of this chapter suggest that these social interventions fail youth miserably. The focus on youth activism—through social movements and PAR—discussed in this chapter offers a possible alternative for adults who seek to mobilize themselves for positive youth development. Specifically, the adults who accompanied youth activists and collaborated in the PAR projects described above engaged with them as co-collaborators, daring to risk mobilizing their power as adults in new ways, and "hearing into speech" (Morton, 1985) youth's powerful narratives. Despite this, some of them embraced conclusions similar to more individually oriented youth programs, that is, that youth participants were empowered. While celebrating the multiple contributions the youth and adults described herein have made, we conclude this chapter by interrogating this tendency to psychologize youth activism within a discourse of empowerment and argue rather for a discourse of social solidarity and youth-adult activism. While drawing inspiration from these examples of youth organizing and the PAR youth-adult collaborations, we resituate ourselves as United Statesian psychologists within the critical framework suggested by majority world youth organizing projects described above (Bhima Sangha and the Dalit). Thus positioned, we challenge social scientists, educators, and human service workers to rethink the discourse of empowerment in order to stand more fully in solidarity with the youth of the world and, in solidarity, mobilize adults to join youth in their push for more just and positive youth development.

Specifically, within psychology, empowerment is frequently defined as a process of gaining influence over events and outcomes of importance to an individual or group (Fawcett et al., 1994). Others define it as a process of gaining mastery over one's life (Rappaport, 1984), of learning to see a closer correspondence between one's goals and a sense of how to achieve them, that is, where efforts and life outcomes are in greater congruence (Mechanic, 1991). Community psychologists Serrano-Garcia and Bond (1994), drawing on Zimmerman (2000), among others, argue that empowerment exists on multiple levels, that is, the individual, the organizational, and the community. Yet, despite the importance of these levels and the insistence that groups or communities can be empowered, Serrano-Garcia and Bond (1994) suggest that most research on empowerment, and most empowerment activities, have focused on the individual.

Youth engaged in PAR in the projects described understand their social situatedness within multiple and interconnected social systems and institutional and cultural infrastructures (McIntyre, 2000) that are permeated by social inequalities. As researchers, educators, and parents who accompany them, we are challenged to create conditions or spaces within which youth encounter, reflect upon, and engage their own power. The deeper challenge confronting us as adults is, thus, to facilitate processes whereby youth activism toward social change might be realized by youth themselves. Fine, Weis, Centrie, and Roberts (2000) describe this important function of PAR through a discussion of "meaningful spaces." Meaningful spaces are both geographically centralized over time and historically constituted or created. They are places in which people of all ages come together to critique what is, to shelter themselves from what has been, and to image and redesign what might be (Fine et al., 2000). Meaningful spaces, then, have both a recuperative and a transformative power. While the creation of these spaces is not in and of itself a substitute for the legitimate redistribution of material goods or power, these spaces are necessary bridges to possibilities not seen, and to collective action not yet taken. When viewed in the context of adults mobilizing for youth, these meaningful spaces are critically necessary but not sufficient conditions for positive youth development.

McIntyre (2000) argues that PAR also contributes to clarifying what we see as the second challenge facing adults seeking to mobilize toward positive youth development. Specifically, PAR contributes significantly to responding to the question of what we do *after* we have identified and named some of the systemic obstacles that interfere with youth becoming legitimate members of society. Adults are thus challenged to respond to youth's activism through engaging with them in efforts to redistribute material goods and power toward building a more just and equitable society.

From Empowerment to Social Solidarity: How Do We Shift Our Work with and for Youth?

Most programs and policies concerning youth rest on the premise that youth are not knowledgeable, capable, or agential enough in their own right (White & Wyn, 2004). Such a perspective values young people primarily as future adults, that is, for "what they will become" (White & Wyn, 2004, p. 81). This provides a rationale for adults controlling and monitoring the lives and activities of youth, in the interest of protecting their future (White & Wyn, 2004). Thus, youth can be legitimately excluded from truly participating in the programming decisions that might affect them the most.

As we have suggested in this chapter, before we, as adults, can begin to engage in practices that seek solidarity with youth, we must critically examine and challenge our paternalistic and paradoxical conceptions about children and youth and the nature of youth involvement. On the one hand, adults claim that today's youth are unmotivated and uninvolved with social issues that concern them. Yet when youth do mobilize politically (e.g., an antiracist demonstration at a high school or college), their efforts are often discounted as idealistic, insubordinate, or merely reflective of an adult-run organization that possibly is manipulating them.

One key issue underlying adults' hesitancy in reconciling themselves to youth organizing and advocacy is trust. That is, do youth really possess legitimate knowledge that is trustworthy? Or, can we trust youth enough to let them make more of their own decisions? This requires that we suspend our own beliefs about what is in the best interests of youth and believe that youth themselves have something important to share. To do this, in addition to engaging in the reflective praxis we have described earlier, adults must commit to spending time with youth. We have to "hang out" with them in nonthreatening ways in a variety of settings. We must listen to and seek to understand their culturally specific ways of knowing, speaking, and acting, as exemplified in the projects described previously by McIntyre (2000) and Fine et al. (2004). Only then will we adults hear what they have to say and support the multiple and diverse ways in which they respond to challenges in their lives.

We must also consider trust from the perspectives of youth themselves. Youth frequently view adults as "outsiders" who are either unwilling to or incapable of fully understanding their points of view. These realities are further compounded by race, ethnicity, and class. The imposition of teachers, human service workers, and psychologists, the majority of whom are white and middle class, on the lives of poor youth or youth of color may be felt strongly and resisted. Forging relationships and collaborative efforts between adults and youth marginalized from power is difficult for all involved. As adults, by virtue of holding more societal status, controlling more resources, and having more *power over*, we must assume primary responsibility for addressing these inequalities and the challenges inherent in any effort to forge relationships characterized by social solidarity.

Researchers using participatory approaches have reflected on the complex processes and dilemmas inherent in gaining the trust of participants, with regard to power, ethnicity, class, and gender (see LeCompte, 1995; Lykes, 1997; Reinharz, 1997). Although no simple solutions exist, trust is often forged with patience, sensitivity, reflexivity, and a commitment to long-term relationships. Essentially, establishing trust through relationships with individuals (in this case, youth) involves sustained effort over time. To do so, we must avoid the "hello–goodbye" approach (LeCompte, 1995, p. 96) to research, practice, and program development in which there is minimal contact, collaboration, and long-term commitment between participant and researcher.

Once the processes of reflection, trust, and commitment have been initiated, those adults who seek to engage in solidarity with youth through youth development programs will be better positioned to work alongside them in more legitimate ways. In so doing, programs must strive to provide maximal, rather than minimal, youth involvement and engagement, where youth have both authentic and important roles (White & Wyn, 2004). Based on our discussion of youth activism and youth-based participatory projects, we present a selection of strategies through which traditional, adult-driven youth programs might move toward ones that reflect social solidarity, where adults might work *with* rather than *for* youth:

1. Analyzing, modifying, and/or rewriting the goals or mission statement of the organization or project based on the insights and perspectives of youth involved;
2. Asking youth to evaluate the current scope and content of activities and projects within the organization, and allowing them to both redesign and execute activities with adult assistance;
3. Involving youth in training, seminars, and mentorship that might equip them with skills to become teachers and instructors within the program;
4. Engaging youth in program recruitment and dissemination of information regarding the program;
5. Having youth assume responsibility for publicity of the organization at local venues about which they have ample knowledge, such as local hangouts, shopping malls, schools, parks, or youth community centers;
6. Working alongside youth as spokespersons and advocates for the organization and its goals, through public forums and the media and ensuring that youth have significant roles in public debates;
7. Creating a governing board within the organization in which youth, not adults, assume the primary roles;
8. Working alongside youth in developing program evaluation tools, where youth assume responsibility for the implementation and reporting of the evaluation; and,
9. Using our "status" as adults to advocate for the needs of youth with regard to the program (funding, space, materials/supplies).

Although these suggestions are by no means exhaustive, they represent critical places whereby individual programs, projects, or organizations might facilitate change. As such, they represent some of the many ways that youth development programs can become more participatory and collaborative, where youth and adults might work together in social solidarity.

Through resituating youth and the discourse of youth empowerment—both theoretically and in practice—we invite adults to accompany youth through social solidarity. These experiences of accompaniment deeply inform not only our understandings of youth and youth development but also our understandings of what it means to be an adult within a grossly inequitable world at a time when youth are actively organizing and mobilizing on their own behalf. A global lens challenges us to interrogate claims of universality in both our social scientific theories of development and in the applications of these theories in UN conventions, policies, and practices. Youth organizing complexifies adult theorizing about youth, challenging us to rethink basic assumptions and their applications. We are invited to engage in solidarity with youth-organized collectivities and communities. As significantly, mobilizing adults toward positive youth development within a global context means mobilizing adults in solidarity with youth's activism, an activism that seeks to transform material conditions toward building a more just and equitable world.

References

Archard, D. (1993). *Children: Rights and childhood*. London and New York: Routledge.
Atterbury, T. E. (Ed.). (2002). *Encyclopedia of associations: International organizations*. Detroit, MI: Gale Group.
Bachman, S. (2000, November/December). Underage unions: Child laborers speak up. *Mother Jones, 25*.
Bartunek, J. M., & Louis, M. R. (1996). *Qualitative research methods series: Vol. 40. Insider/outsider team research*. Thousand Oaks, CA: Sage.
Be the Change. (n.d). Retrieved April 5, 2004, from http://www.peacechild.org/bethechange/learnmore.asp
Boyden, J., Ling, B., & Myers, W. (1998). *What works for working children*. Stockholm, Sweden: Radda Barnen.
Bruner, J. (1990). *Acts of meaning*. Cambridge, MA: Harvard University Press.
Burman, E. (1994). *Deconstructing developmental psychology*. New York: Routledge.
Carnegie Council on Adolescent Development. (1995). *Great transitions: Preparing adolescents for a new century*. Washington, DC: Author.
Children's Express. (1993). *Voices from the future: Our children tell us about violence in America*. (S. Goodwillie, Ed.). New York: Crown.
Cole, M. (1996). *Cultural psychology: A once and future discipline*. Cambridge, MA: Harvard University Press.
Erikson, E. H. (1964). *Childhood and society* (2nd ed.). New York: Norton.
Fals-Borda, O. (1991). Some basic ingredients. In O. Fals-Borda & M. A. Rahman (Eds.), *Action and knowledge: Breaking the monopoly with participatory action research* (pp. 3–12). New York: Apex Press.
Fawcett, S. B., White, G. W., Balcazar, F. E., Suarez-Balcazar, Y., Mathews, R. M., Paine, A. L., et al. (1994). A contextual-behavioral model of empowerment: Case studies involving people with physical disabilities. *American Journal of Community Psychology, 22*, 471–486.
Fine, M., Weis, L., Centrie, C., & Roberts, R. (2000). Educating beyond the borders of schooling. *Anthropology & Education Quarterly, 31*(2), 131–151.
Fine, M., Roberts, R.A., Torre, M.E., Bloom, J., Burns, A., & Chajet, L., et al. (2004). *Echoes of Brown: Youth documenting and performing the legacy of Brown V. Board of Education*. New York: Teacher's College Press.
Freechild Project. (n.d.). Retrieved April, 2004, from http://www.freechild.org
Freud, S. (1975). *The standard edition of the complete psychological works of Sigmund Freud*. London, UK: Hogarth Press.
Gaventa, J., & Cornwall, A. (2001). Power and knowledge. In P. Reason & H. Bradbury (Eds.), *Handbook of action research: Participative inquiry and practice* (pp. 70–80). Thousand Oaks, CA: Sage.
Gergen, K. J. (2000). *The saturated self: Dilemmas of identity in contemporary life*. New York: Basic Books.

Greenfield, P. M., & Cocking, R. R. (Eds.). (1994). *Cross-cultural roots of minority child development.* Mahwah, NJ: Erlbaum.

Gugelberger, G.M. (Ed.). (1996). *The real thing: Testimonial discourse and Latin America.* Durham, NC: Duke University Press.

Henriques, H., Holloway, W., Urwin, W., Venn, C., & Walkerdine, V. (1998). *Changing the subject: Psychology, social regulation and subjectivity.* London: Routledge.

Hunt, K. (Ed.). (2002). *Encyclopedia of associations* (38th ed.). Detroit, MI: Gale Group.

Kagan, J., & Gall, S. (Eds.). (1998). *The Gale encyclopedia of childhood and adolescence.* Detroit, MI: Gale Group.

Kaul, C. (Ed.). (2002). *Statistical handbook on the world's children.* Westport, CT: Oryx Press.

Kemmis, S., & McTaggart, R. (2000). Participatory action research. In N. K. Denzin & Y. S. Lincoln (Eds.), *Handbook of qualitative research* (2nd ed., pp. 567–605). Thousand Oaks, CA: Sage.

LeCompte, M. D. (1995). Some notes on power, agenda, and voice: A researcher's personal evolution toward critical collaborative research. In P. L. McLaren & J. M. Giarelli (Eds.), *Critical theory and educational research* (pp. 91–112). Albany: State University of New York Press.

Liebel, M. (2001). *Childhood and work.* Frankfurt and London: IKO.

Lykes, M. B. (1997). Activist participatory research among the Maya of Guatemala: Constructing meanings from situated knowledge. *Journal of Social Issues, 53*(4), 725–746.

McIntyre, A. (2000). *Inner-city kids: Adolescents confront life and violence in an urban community.* New York: New York University Press.

Mechanic, D. (1991, February). *Adolescents at risk: New directions.* Paper presented at the Seventh Annual Conference on Health Policy, Weill Medical College of Cornell University, New York, NY.

Morton, N. (1985). *The journey is home.* Boston: Beacon Press.

One STEP Group, McIntyre, A., & McKeirnan, P. (2000). *At a split second: Visual stories of/by young people living in an urban community.* Farfield, CT: Farfield University Press.

Park, P. (1993). What is participatory research? A theoretical and methodological perspective. In P. Park, M. Brydon-Miller, B. Hall, & T. Jackson (Eds.), *Voices of change: Participatory research in the United States and Canada* (pp. 1–19). Toronto: OISE Press.

Peace Child International. (n.d.). Retrieved April 5, 2004, from http://www.peacechild.org/

Piaget, J. (1977). The language and thought of the child. In J. Gruber & J. Voneche (Eds.), *The essential Piaget* (pp. 65–88). New York: Basic Books.

Prilleltensky, I., Nelson, G., & Peirson, L. (2001). The role of power and control in children's lives: An ecological analysis of pathways toward wellness, resilience, and problems. *Journal of Community & Applied Social Psychology, 11,* 143–158.

Rahman, M. A. (1991). The theoretical standpoint of PAR. In O. Fals-Borda & M. A. Rahman (Eds.), *Action and knowledge: Breaking the monopoly with participatory action research* (pp. 13–23). New York: Apex Press.

Rahman, M. A., & Fals-Borda, O. (1991). A self-review of PAR. In O. Fals-Borda & M. A. Rahman (Eds.), *Action and knowledge: Breaking the monopoly with participatory action research* (pp. 24–34). New York: Apex Press.

Rappaport, J. (1984). Studies in empowerment: Introduction to the issue. *Prevention in Human Services, 3*(2/3), 1–7.

Reason, P., & Bradbury, H. (2001). Introduction: Inquiry and participation in search of a world worthy of human aspiration. In P. Reason & H. Bradbury (Eds.), *Handbook of action research: Participative inquiry and practice* (pp. 1–14). Thousand Oaks, CA: Sage.

Reinharz, S. (1997). Who am I? The need for a variety of selves in the field. In R. Hertz (Ed.), *Reflexivity and voice* (pp. 3–20). Thousand Oaks, CA: Sage.

Rogoff, B. (1990). *Apprenticeship in thinking: Cognitive development in social context.* New York: Oxford University Press.

Rogoff, B. (2003). *The cultural nature of human development.* New York: Oxford University Press.

Serrano-Garcia, I., & Bond, M. A. (1994). Empowering the silent ranks: Introduction. *American Journal of Community Psychology, 22*(4), 433–445.

Simpson, J. A., & Weiner, E. S. C. (Eds.). (1989). *The Oxford English dictionary.* New York: Oxford University Press.

Swift, A. (1999). *Working children get organised*. London: Save the Children.

Tolfree, D. (1998). *Old enough to work, old enough to have a say*. Stockholm, Sweden: Radda Barnen.

UNICEF. (1997). *The state of the world's children*. New York: Author.

UNICEF. (2002). *Adolescence: A time that matters*, from http://www.unicef.org/publications/pub_adolescence_en.pdf

UNICEF. (2004). *UNICEF at a glance*, from http://www.unicef.org/publications/UNICEF_Glance_ENG.pdf

U.S. Census Bureau. (2002). *Statistical abstracts of the United States* (123rd ed.). Washington, DC: Author.

Voices of youth. (n.d.). Retrieved April 15, 2004, from http://www.unicef.org/voy/

Vygotsky, L. S. (1930/1971). The development of higher psychological functions. In J. Wertsch (Ed.), *Soviet activity theory*. Armonk, NY: Sharpe.

Vygotsky, L. S. (1978). *Mind in society*. Cambridge, MA.: Harvard University Press.

White, B. (1996). Globalization and the child labour problem. *Journal of International Development, 8*(6), 829–839.

White, R., & Wyn, J. (2004). *Youth and society: Exploring the social dynamics of youth experience*. New York: Oxford University Press.

Woodhead, M. (1998). *Children's perspectives on their working lives*. Stockholm, Sweden: Radda Barnen.

World Health Organization. (2002). *Youth violence*. Retrieved April 15, 2004, from http://www.who.int/violence_injury_prevention/violence/global_campaign/en/youthviolencefacts.pdf

Youth Action Research Institute. (n.d.). Retrieved January 15, 2004, from http://www.incommunityresearch.org/research/yari.htm

Zimmerman, M. (2000). Psychological, organizational, and community levels of analysis. In J. Rappaport & E. Seidman (Eds.), *Handbook of community psychology* (pp. 43–78). New York: Plenum.

V Commentary

14 Promoting Positive Youth Development: Challenges Posed and Opportunities Provided

Mark Snyder

University of Minnesota

It is a well-known, or at least an often repeated, adage that "it takes a village to raise a child." With this familiar expression, the editors of this volume introduce and define the theme for this collection of essays on promoting positive youth development. Approaching this theme from a variety of conceptual perspectives, and drawing on research conducted with diverse investigative strategies, the authors of these essays articulate a series of lessons learned about how to mobilize adults to engage in activities that will encourage young people to engage in socially valued activities. Whether it is research on prosocial action among individuals or within organizations or in neighborhoods and communities, the message seems to be that it is possible to mobilize adults to promote positive youth development.

Just as the editors introduce their volume with a reference to the notion that "It takes a village . . . ," so too does this commentary begin with that expression. For, if there is one theme that runs through the essays in this volume, it is that promoting positive youth development has to involve collective effort, requiring a "village" if not literally at least metaphorically. It is a collective task in at least three senses. First, it is collective in that socialization involves the aggregated actions of individuals, of organizations, of communities, and of society at large; that is, it involves *collective inputs*. Second, it is collective in that the positive youth development that results from these inputs is aggregated across the effects of the socialization provided by individuals, organizations, communities, and societies; that is, it involves *collective outputs*. And, third, it is collective in that a scientific understanding of promoting positive youth development will involve the aggregated contributions of investigators studying diverse phenomena that converge on the mechanisms of socially valued activities; that is, it involves *collective inquiry*.

However, if adults can be mobilized to promote positive youth development, one should probably not be so optimistic as to expect that it can be easily done or automatically accomplished. For another recurring theme to emerge from the contributions to this volume is that the task of mobilizing adults to promote positive youth development comes bundled with both opportunities and constraints. That is, the task is surrounded by forces that support and promote it, but also by forces that inhibit and prevent it. Let us consider, in turn, some of these opportunities and constraints.

In large measure, the opportunities come from the fact that the goals of promoting positive youth development are highly valued ones; after all, those who do not value positive youth development are probably a distinct minority in most societies. So, too, are the activities by which positive youth development can be promoted themselves socially valued, with volunteerism and membership in and support of charitable and philanthropic organizations being widely endorsed; in U.S. society, the value of these activities is one thing on which both liberals and conservatives agree. Clearly, then, there is a supportive climate of values surrounding activities that can and do promote positive youth development.

Nevertheless, so many of the activities by which adults can promote positive youth development are ones that are associated with constraints. It goes almost without saying that when adults take action to socialize socially valued activities, their actions involve expenditures of time and effort. These expenditures constitute "opportunity costs" in that they take away time and effort from other pursuits, whether those other pursuits are related to jobs and careers, to family and friends, or to the pursuit of leisure and recreation. These opportunity costs, even if they are not outright roadblocks that prevent adults from promoting positive youth development, may in effect constitute a "drag" on their performance, reducing and limiting their involvement.

To some extent, this confluence of opportunities and constraints, of facilitators and barriers, is a state of affairs that is characteristic not only of the activities by which adults can promote positive youth development. Rather, it is more generally characteristic of diverse forms of social engagement, activities by which individuals and groups take action on problems of concern to society, whether by serving as volunteers (perhaps tutoring illiterate children), participating in a community organization (such as working a weekly shift at a homeless shelter), joining a social movement (perhaps a human rights organization), or becoming involved in the political process (whether by voting, working on a campaign, or even running for office). In all cases, the activities are socially valued—they are regarded as good and valuable things to do. At the same time, however, they are not socially mandated; that is, there are no laws or even strong norms that compel people to become involved in their communities or be engaged in their society. Accordingly, such activities enjoy the support of attitudes and values that encourage such activities, but not of social structures and supports that make such activities happen. To the contrary, not only are such activities not mandated, they all require overcoming the fact that they are time-consuming, often effortful, and have the opportunity costs of taking people away from other pursuits. And so it is with adults engaged in promoting positive youth development. To do so is surely socially valued, but not socially obligatory. And, it is accompanied by the same web of supportive values and opportunities and constraining inhibitors and barriers that must be overcome before adults can engage in promoting positive youth development.

That there are both opportunities and constraints at play takes on particular significance in the context of considerations of the strategies considered in this volume for mobilizing adults to promote positive youth development. In fact, it is the intertwined pattern of opportunities and constraints that are associated with socially valued but not socially mandated actions that practically calls for the development of systematic efforts and strategies to actively encourage such activities, to mobilize individuals for action. In this regard, almost to a one, the contributors to this volume offer recommendations for designing such strategies, sometimes with an emphasis on those factors that promote involvement and provide opportunities and sometimes with an emphasis on overcoming those barriers and constraints that may inhibit involvement. The shared conviction is that individuals can be encouraged and persuaded to take action for the social good, that neighborhoods and communities can be designed to promote such action, and that societies can be ones in which successive generations show care and concern and are involved and engaged citizens.

In trying to construct the "big picture" that emerges as the pieces of the puzzle of how to mobilize adults to promote positive youth development are put together, it seems clear that attention both to opportunities and constraints, to facilitators and barriers, will be needed for success. So, too, it would seem that there is a need for strategies that operate simultaneously at differing levels of impact, from individual modes of persuasion (whereby individuals, either through the examples that they set by their own involvement in promoting positive youth development, or through their one-on-one attempts to persuade family, friends, neighbors, and coworkers to become involved) through large-scale, media-based campaigns (involving the "social marketing" of socially valued goals and actions, involving the same principles of mass marketing as are typically applied to selling consumer goods or political candidates). As well, it would seem that there is a clear need for strategies for mobilizing adults to promote positive youth development to remember that "mobilizing" doesn't end with getting adults involved in the first place; rather, it also entails attention to how to foster and promote continued involvement and the recognition that the active ingredients in initiating action in the first place may or may not be the same as the active ingredients in sustaining action for the long term.

How, then, are strategies for mobilizing adults to take action to promote positive youth development to be formed and implemented? Who is to take the lead in designing these strategies, in ensuring their implementation, and in monitoring their outcomes? The research reviewed in this volume may provide the "technologies" to be employed in these strategies, and may reveal the "mechanisms" by which these strategies will succeed. But, it remains to be seen just how such strategies can or will be carried out. Continuing with the "it takes a village" metaphor that pervades (and perhaps even inspired) this volume, it is clear that we are talking about a collective task, one involving the concerted and coordinated efforts of many segments of society—government leaders making it a matter of social policy, scientists providing the knowledge of strategies of persuasion and social influence to mobilize the population, and the cooperation of major institutions, including educational and religious ones. Can such a collective effort succeed? The contributors to this volume provide grounds for a cautious optimism.

That it may be possible to design an agenda for mobilizing adults to become actively involved in promoting positive youth development, and to design this agenda on the basis of lessons learned from research on diverse mechanisms of action, testifies to the value of building bridges between basic science and practical application. Although some of the researchers who have contributed to this volume were drawn into this enterprise because of their work on youth development, many of the contributors were recruited on the basis of their expertise in other fields of inquiry, fields as diverse as the study of volunteers, prosocial organizations, communities, education, and social marketing. Yet, all contributors to this volume have been able to use their research to derive and extrapolate principles that can be used in designing strategies for mobilizing adults to promote positive youth development.

The building of such bridges between basic research and the application of research to addressing societal concerns is one of the hallmarks of the "action research" tradition in the social sciences. Of course, in the action research tradition, the bridge is one on which traffic flows in both directions, not only involving research informing application but also involving the lessons learned from applications "feeding back" to inform the further refinement of the theories that guided the application. Whether the application of the principles articulated in this volume will feed back to the further development of the research programs that generated them remains, of course, to be seen. But, clearly, the potential is there to construct a "real-world laboratory" in which science informs systematic attempts to promote positive youth development and in which science is advanced by the lessons learned from those attempts.

Contributors

Amy E. Alberts is a doctoral student in the Eliot-Pearson Department of Child Development at Tufts University. She is currently a doctoral research assistant on the 4-H Study of Positive Youth Development at the Institute for Applied Research in Youth Development, Tufts University. Her research interests include contextual influences on parenting and adolescent t development, outreach scholarship for promoting positive youth development, the family system, and spiritual development.

Michael Basil is a professor of marketing at the University of Lethbridge in Alberta, Canada, and specializes in advertising, research methods, celebrity effects, and social marketing.

Peter L. Benson is president of Search Institute, Minneapolis, Minnesota, which provides leadership, knowledge, and resources to promote healthy children, youth, and communities. He has written extensively on adolescent development, altruism, spiritual development, and thriving in adolescence. He serves as principal investigator for Search Institute's initiative on spiritual development in childhood and adolescence. In 1991, he received the William James Award for career contributions to psychology of religion from the American Psychological Association. He is author or editor of numerous books and articles, including *Developmental Assets and Asset-Building Communities, All Kids Are Our Kids: What Communities Must Do to Raise Caring and Responsible Children and Adolescents*, and *Religion on Capitol Hill: Myths and Realities.* He is general editor for The Search Institute Series on Developmentally Attentive Community and Society, published by Springer. He holds a doctorate in experimental social psychology from the University of Denver.

Linda Camino is senior scientist, Department of Human Development and Family Studies at the University of Wisconsin-Madison, and a research and evaluation consultant for foundations, community coalitions, and youth organizations. Camino has been bridging research, practice, and policy for 17 years to push the youth development field forward. She has worked in community, policy, and academic settings throughout her career, and brings this combination of first-hand understandings to her work. Camino has published numerous articles and has edited special issues of the *Journal of Community Psychology* and *Applied Developmental Science*. She also produces reports, tools, and training curricula for practitioners, policy makers, and community youth and adults.

Matthew Chinman is a licensed clinical psychologist and a behavioral scientist at the RAND Corporation. His recent focus has been to develop and assess strategies to enhance the capacity of community-based prevention practitioners. He is co-developer of the *Getting To Outcomes* (*GTO*) system and the lead author of the RAND Corporation Technical Report, *Getting To Outcomes 2004: Promoting Accountability through Methods and Tools for Planning, Implementation, and Evaluation.* He is currently the principal investigator of a grant from the Centers for Disease Control and Prevention to examine how the *Getting To Outcomes* system helps improve community capacity in substance abuse prevention practitioners.

E. Gil Clary is professor of psychology at the College of St. Catherine in St. Paul, Minnesota. The majority of his research is devoted to prosocial behavior generally and participation in volunteer work more specifically. Much of this work has been conducted in collaboration with Mark Snyder and Arthur Stukas, and one result of this research has been the development of the Volunteer Functions Inventory, a psychometrically sound instrument for assessing the motivations underlying involvement in volunteer work. In addition, Clary has been engaged in research on other questions concerning the voluntary and nonprofit sector, including the consequences of long-term helpers' philosophies of helping, the socialization of prosocial tendencies, and environmental influences on volunteer activity.

Maree Daly is a Ph.D. candidate in the School of Psychological Science at La Trobe University, Melbourne, Australia. In addition to her research on volunteerism, Maree is researching changes that occur to the self-concept across the transition to motherhood and associated changes in well-being.

Sameer Deshpande is an assistant professor and the marketing director of the Centre for Socially Responsible Marketing at the University of Lethbridge in Lethbridge, Alberta, Canada.

Tina M. Durand is an assistant professor of human development at Wheelock College in Boston. Her research interests include ecological approaches to understanding the early adaptation and success of Latino children and families in schools and American society, cultural interpretations of children's cognitive development, and issues of race, class, and gender in child, youth, and family studies.

Ellen A. Ensher is an associate professor of management at Loyola Marymount University in Los Angeles. Her key areas of research include careers, diversity, and mentoring. Ensher has written about mentoring and issues of race, gender and culture, types of mentoring relationships, career outcomes and benefits, leadership, and more recently, e-mentoring. She has published in journals such as *Academy of Management Executive, Human Resource Development Quarterly, Journal of Career Development, Journal of Vocational Behavior,* and *Organizational Dynamics.*

Ensher's most recent publication with Susan Elaine Murphy is *Power Mentoring: How Successful Mentors and Protégés Get the Most out of their Relationships* (2005). She currently serves on the advisory board for MentorNet, a nationally recognized e-mentoring program.

Constance A. Flanagan is a professor in the Department of Agricultural and Extension Education at the Pennsylvania State University.

Katherine C. Haydon is a graduate student at the Institute of Child Development at the University of Minnesota, Minneapolis. Her research interests include attachment relationships, the influence of close relationships on social development, and developmental pathways toward quality romantic partnerships in adulthood.

Pamela S. Imm is affiliated with the University of South Carolina and the Lexington Richland Alcohol and Drug Abuse Agency in Columbia, South Carolina. Dr. Imm is a trained community psychologist and has extensive experience in the areas of program development, program evaluation, and applied research. Dr. Imm has worked with various local, state, and national agencies and is a coauthor of the award-winning empowerment evaluation manual *Getting To Outcomes (GTO): Methods and Tools for Planning, Self-Assessment, and Accountability,* funded as a joint project between the Center for Substance Abuse Prevention and the National Center for the Advancement of Prevention. The updated version, *GTO-2004*, is published by the RAND Corporation.

Helena Jelicic is a Jacobs Foundation Fellow and a doctoral student in the Eliot-Pearson Department of Child Development at Tufts University. She is currently a doctoral research assistant on the 4-H Study of Positive Youth Development at the Institute for Applied Research in Youth Development, Tufts University. Her professional interests are developmental methodology and longitudinal data analysis, child and youth mental health systems, and university-community collaboration, particularly in the Balkan region.

Renie Kehres is the coordinator for the Onondaga County Prevention Partners for Youth Development Coalition. As a psychiatric-mental health clinical nurse specialist, she has worked in a variety of settings with youth and families, including inpatient, outpatient, and day treatment. She is also an adjunct professor at Syracuse University in the Child and Family Studies Program with research interests in youth development, community mobilization, and transferring research to practice.

Richard J. Lerner is the Bergstrom Chair in Applied Developmental Science at Tufts University. He is the author or editor of 63 books and more than 450 scholarly articles and chapters. Lerner is known for his theory of, and research into, relations between life-span human development and contextual or ecological change. He has done foundational studies of the mutually influential relations between adolescents and their peer, family, school, and community contexts, and is a leader in the study of public policies and community-based programs aimed at the promotion of positive youth development.

M. Brinton Lykes is professor of community-cultural psychology at Boston College. Her action research at the interface of indigenous cultural beliefs and practices and Euro-American psychology focuses on the development and evaluation of community-based programs in war and postwar contexts of transition and transformation. Lykes has published extensively in journals and edited volumes, is coeditor of three books, and coauthor, with the Association of Maya Ixil Women—New Dawn, of *Voces e imágenes: Mujeres Mayas Ixiles de Chajul/Voices and images: Maya Ixil women of Chajul* (2000). She is an associate editor of *Action Research, American Journal of Community Psychology,* and *Peace and Conflict: Journal of Peace Psychology.*

Kenneth I. Maton is a community psychologist and director of the Community-Social Program in Human Services Psychology at the University of Maryland, Baltimore County. His research has focused on various aspects of the community psychology of religion. He coauthored, with Kenneth I. Pargament, *The Handbook of Community Psychology* chapter titled "Religion in American Life: A Community Psychology Perspective." Most recently, with Daniel Dodgen, Mariano R. Sto. Domingo, and David B. Larson, Maton coauthored the article "Religion as a Meaning System: Policy Implications for the New Millennium" in the *Journal of Social Issues.*

Susan Elaine Murphy is an associate professor of psychology at Claremont McKenna College and the associate director of the Henry R. Kravis Leadership Institute in Claremont, California. She currently teaches in organizational psychology and organizational development and is also an adjunct professor at Claremont Graduate University, where she teaches courses in industrial psychology and teams and leaders. Murphy's most recent publication with Ellen Ensher is *Power Mentoring: How Successful Mentors and Protégés Get the Most out of their Relationships* (2005). Her other recent works include two edited books, *The Future of Leadership Development* (with Ron Riggio; 2003) and *Work-Family Balance to Work-Family Interaction: Changing the Metaphor* (with Diane Halpern; 2005). Murphy is actively involved in the development, delivery, and evaluation of youth mentoring programs in the Los Angeles area, both through her service-learning college course on mentoring and her evaluation of youth based mentoring programs, including TeamWorks.

Daniel F. Perkins is an associate professor in the Department of Agricultural and Extension Education at the Pennsylvania State University.

Jean E. Rhodes is professor of psychology at the University of Massachusetts in Boston. For more than a decade, she has conducted research on the mentoring of children and adolescents, including an extensive analysis of the Big Brothers Big Sisters national impact study. In addition, she has explored the influence of natural and assigned mentors on adolescent mothers. Rhodes is a Fellow in the American Psychological Association and the Society for Research and Community Action, a member of the MacArthur Foundation Research Network on the Transition to Adulthood, and a research consultant to the National Mentoring Partnership. She has published three books and more than 30 articles and chapters on the topic of youth mentoring.

Alexander J. Rothman is an associate professor in the Department of Psychology at the University of Minnesota, Minneapolis. His primary program of research concerns the application of social psychological theory to illness prevention and health promotion. It synthesizes basic research on how people process and respond to health information with the development and evaluation of theory-based interventions to promote healthy behavior. In his most recent work, he has focused on specifying the different decision processes that guide the initiation and maintenance of behavior change. In recognition of his work, Rothman received the 2002 Distinguished Scientific Award for Early Career Contribution to Psychology in the area of Health Psychology from the American Psychological Association.

Peter C. Scales, senior fellow in the Office of the President at Search Institute, is a developmental psychologist widely recognized as a leading authority on adolescent development, family relationships, effective schools, and healthy communities. In addition to more than 250 scientific articles and chapters, Dr. Scales is author or coauthor of more than a dozen books and monographs, including *Developmental Assets: A Synthesis of the Scientific Research on Adolescent Development* (Search Institute), *Great Places to Lean: How Asset-Building Schools Help Students Succeed* (Search Institute), and *Other People's Kids: Social Expectations and American Adults' Involvement with Children and Adolescents* (Kluwer Academic/Plenum).

Lisa M. Smith is currently the research specialist at the National Center for Family Literacy in Louisville, Kentucky. She has also worked as a research assistant on the 4-H Study of Positive Youth Development at the Institute for Applied Research in Youth Development, Tufts University. Smith's current research interests center on the application of scientifically based best practices in supporting and promoting family literacy.

Mark Snyder is a member of the faculty in psychology at the University of Minnesota, where he holds the McKnight Presidential Chair in Psychology. His research interests include theoretical and empirical issues associated with the motivational foundations of individual and collective behavior, and the applications of basic theory and research in personality and social psychology to addressing practical problems confronting society. He has served as president of the Society for Personality and Social Psychology, as well as on the board of directors of the American Psychological Society and the Council of the Society for the Psychological Study of Social Issues. Snyder is also the author of *Public Appearances/Private Realities: The Psychology of Self-Monitoring* and coeditor of *Cooperation in Modern Society: Promoting the Welfare of Communities, States, and Organizations.*

Mariano R. Sto. Domingo is currently a doctoral candidate in the Human Services Psychology Ph.D. Program in Community Social Psychology at the University of Maryland Baltimore County. He is an adjunct faculty member in the Department of Psychology of McDaniel College in Westminster, Maryland. He has recently coauthored, with Ken Maton, Dan Dodgen, and David Larson, an article on religion and policy (*Journal of Social Issues*) and, with Ken Maton and Jacqueline King, an article on religion and mentoring (*Handbook of Youth Mentoring,* edited by David DuBois and Michael J. Karcher).

Arthur A. Stukas is senior lecturer in social psychology in the School of Psychological Science at La Trobe University, Melbourne, Australia. His research focuses on the role of interpersonal expectations in social interaction, motivations for volunteerism and community involvement, and confronting prejudice and discrimination. With Michelle Dunlap, Stukas recently coedited an issue of the *Journal of Social Issues* titled "Community Involvement: Theoretical Approaches and Educational Initiatives."

Andrea S. Taylor is the director of training at Temple University's Center for Intergenerational Learning in Philadelphia. She is the developer of Across Ages, an intergenerational mentoring program designated as an evidence-based model and listed in the National Registry of Effective Program Practices. Her work in recent years has been supported by the Substance Abuse and Mental Health Services Administration and the U.S. Department of Education and has focused on intergenerational mentoring as an approach to positive youth development and the prevention of school failure, substance abuse, and early or repeat teen pregnancies. Taylor is currently directing a new initiative, supported by the Corporation for National and Community Service and the HRC Foundation, focused on civic engagement of age 50+ adults.

Abraham Wandersman is a professor of psychology at the University of South Carolina in Columbia. He received his Ph.D. from Cornell University in the following areas of specialization: social psychology, environmental psychology, and social organization and change. He is a coauthor of *Getting To Outcomes (GTO): Methods and Tools for Planning, Self-Assessment, and Accountability* and has numerous publications, including *Empowerment Evaluation: Knowledge and Tools for Self Assessment and Accountability* (1996) and the more recent volume, *Empowerment Evaluation Principles in Practice* (2005). In June 2005, he was awarded the Distinquished Theory and Research Contribution award by the APA Division of Community Psychology.

Nicole S. Webster is an assistant professor in the Department of Agricultural and Extension Education at the Pennsylvania State University.

Shepherd Zeldin is an associate professor of human development and family studies at the University of Wisconsin-Madison and a community/youth development specialist for Wisconsin Extension. His research examines the ways in which youth are producers of their own development, as well as contributors to adult development and organizational effectiveness. Zeldin has published numerous articles and has edited special issues of the *Journal of Community Psychology*, *Journal of Adolescent Research*, and *Applied Developmental Science*. He sits on many boards, including the editorial board of the *Journal of Research on Adolescence*. Prior to becoming a professor, Zeldin worked for fifteen years as a policy analyst, trainer, and community organizer.

Index